Bruce and Denise Morcombe ar
abducted and murdered schoolb
and his brothers, Dean and Bradley. This is their story.

Lindsay Simpson is the author and co-author of eight
books, including the groundbreaking *Brothers in Arms*,
with Sandra Harvey, and *To Have and To Hold*, with
Walter Mikac. She worked as an investigative journalist
for the *Sydney Morning Herald* for 12 years and now
writes full-time (www.writinglife.com.au).

The website of the Daniel Morcombe Foundation is
www.danielmorcombe.com.au

Where is Daniel?

The Family's Story

BRUCE *and* DENISE MORCOMBE
with
LINDSAY SIMPSON

MACMILLAN
Pan Macmillan Australia

First published 2014 in Macmillan by Pan Macmillan Australia Pty Ltd
1 Market Street, Sydney, New South Wales, Australia, 2000

Cataloguing-in-Publication entry is available
from the National Library of Australia
http://catalogue.nla.gov.au

Typeset in 12/16 pt Janson by Kirby Jones
Printed by McPherson's Printing Group
Cartographic art by Laurie Whiddon, Map Illustrations

Correspondence from the McCann family reproduced with permission.

The author and the publisher have made every effort to contact copyright holders for material used in this book. Any person or organisation that may have been overlooked should contact the publisher.

Papers used by Pan Macmillan Australia Pty Ltd are natural, recyclable products made from wood grown in sustainable forests. The manufacturing processes conform to the environmental regulations of the country of origin.

A percentage of the proceeds from the sale of this book will go to the Daniel Morcombe Foundation.

The Morcombe family received the gravest news concerning Daniel.

Sadly, many families are still searching for a missing loved one.

This book is dedicated to them.

Our thoughts, prayers and wishes are with you all. Stay Strong.

Contents

A NOTE FROM
BRUCE AND DENISE MORCOMBE

Where is Daniel? is our private story. It exposes the drama behind the very public reports which were made of the events and our experiences in relation to Daniel's disappearance, abduction and murder. Its content is confronting in parts, and we believe that it will challenge perceptions and raise questions about the human spirit – how individuals cope and a family's resilience.

We have chosen to write the book with the very capable assistance of Dr Lindsay Simpson.

As accidental public figures, we wished to place the reader in our shoes, and allow you to view the world as we saw it. This allows you to experience the balance of 'light and dark', as we have done for over ten years.

As a mark of respect to Daniel, we have made the conscious decision not to include images of the primary search areas or of any forensic evidence.

The story of *Where is Daniel?* spans more than a decade and features many people, from the police officers involved in the largest investigation in Queensland history, to the large number of witnesses involved in the investigation and the trial, and the Persons of Interest to the legal representatives throughout the legal proceedings, as well as the Morcombe family and their relatives and friends.

Daniel's family

Bruce Morcombe	Daniel's father
Denise Morcombe	Daniel's mother
Dean Morcombe	Daniel's older brother
Bradley (Brad) Morcombe	Daniel's twin brother
Sienna Keegan	Dean's partner since 2012
Anna Martin	Bradley's fiancée

The Morcombes' extended family

Monique Beavis	Denise's mother
Kevin Beavis	Denise's father
Michael Beavis (snr)	Denise's uncle
Damien Beavis	Denise's older brother
Kerry Beavis	Denise's older brother Damien's wife
Ashlea Beavis	Damien and Kerry Beavis's daughter, Daniel's cousin
Michael Beavis (jnr)	Damien and Kerry Beavis's son, Daniel's cousin
Paul Beavis	Denise's younger brother
Christa Beavis	Denise's younger brother Paul's wife

Edward (Ted) Morcombe	Bruce's father
Wendy Morcombe	Bruce's mother
Perry Morcombe	Bruce's older brother
Joan Morcombe	Bruce's older brother Perry's wife
Lindy Colebrook (neé Morcombe)	Bruce's sister
Andrew Colebrook	Bruce's sister Lindy's husband
Scott Morcombe	Bruce's younger brother
Shelly Morcombe	Bruce's younger brother Scott's wife

Members of the community and friends of the Morcombes

Chris Barnard	Family friend since 1994
Fathern Jan Bialasiewicz	Family's priest
Graeme Hight	Acting Principal, then Principal of Siena Catholic College
Denice Hutchinson	Family friend since 1994
Kelvin Kruger	Neighbour
Debbie Morgan	Family friend since 1994
Keith and Judy Paxton	Neighbours

Friends of Daniel and pallbearers

Scott Balkin
Josh Hannah
Matt Hannah
Tom Palmer

Members of the Daniel Morcombe Foundation

Peter Boyce	Committee member and the Morcombes' pro bono legal representative throughout their ordeal
Tracy McAsey	Committee member
Kay McGrath	Foundation Patron
John Pearce	Committee member
Tim Ryan	Committee member
Robin Sherwell	Committee member
Gina Van Wezel	Committee member
Brett Winkler	Committee member

Key police officers who worked on the case

Police Commissioner Bob Atkinson	Commissioner of the Queensland Police Service at the time Daniel went missing
Detective Sergeant Tracey Barnes	Quality-control officer and one of the 'readers' who checked all incoming information on Daniel's case
Detective Senior Sergeant Steve Blanchfield	Investigator on Daniel's case and one of the officers who arrested Brett Cowan
Senior Constable Paul Campbell	The second police officer Bruce and Denise spoke to about their missing son
Detective Superintendent Maurice Carless	Took over from Inspector Maloney as North Coast Regional Crime Coordinator, heading up the team investigating Daniel's disappearance
Detective Inspector Mike Condon	Operations Manager of the Homicide Investigation Unit, who allocated resources to the case, later became Assistant Police Commissioner
Detective Senior Sergeant Greg Daniels	As a detective with the Sunshine Coast Juvenile Aid Bureau (JAB) and a member of the Parents and Friends Association at Siena Catholic College, he became a liaison between family, school and police
Sergeant Laurie Davison	The first to meet the Morcombes at Palmwoods Police Station, where he officially opened the investigation the day after Daniel's disappearance
Senior Constable Peter Drew	Scenes of Crime officer who first photographed and searched the area where Daniel went missing
Senior Sergeant Julie Elliott	Member of the Queensland Police Media Unit who worked very closely with the Morcombes, also a founding committee member of the Daniel Morcombe Foundation
Senior Sergeant John Garner	Queensland Police COMFIT and witness-identification sketch artist
Detective Senior Sergeant Dave Hickey	Coordinated the homicide detectives posted north from Brisbane

Detective Sergeant Ray Hoelscher	One of the first investigating officers on Daniel's case
Detective Senior Constable Ross Hutton	Involved in the case almost from the outset, and one of the officers who arrested Brett Cowan
Senior Constable Ken King	Worked through the intelligence list of known sex offenders in the area and within a fortnight strongly suspected Brett Cowan as being involved
Detective Senior Constable Emma Macindoe	One of the officers reviewing Daniel's case as part of Operation Golf Avalon
Senior Constable Samantha Knight (née McDowall)	The Morcombes' liaison officer, under senior liaison officer Greg Daniels, also a founding committee member of the Daniel Morcombe Foundation
Detective Senior Constable Grant Linwood	Member of the Homicide Investigation Unit, and reviewed Brett Cowan's case file, also heavily involved in the covert operation
Detective Maclean	Interviewed Tracey Cowan at Alf's Pinch Road
Detective Inspector John Maloney	North Coast Regional Crime Coordinator, who headed the team investigating Daniel's disappearance
Detective Senior Constable Dennis Martyn	Worked through the intelligence list of known sex offenders with Ken King
Sergeant Robbie Munn	The first police officer to whom the Morcombes reported Daniel missing, at Maroochydore Police Station
Detective Senior Sergeant Damien Powell	In charge of the Missing Persons Unit
Detective Sergeant Mick Pownell	Served Cowan with a search warrant in Moranbah for allegedly stealing from his employer and was struck by his resemblance to the police's sketch in Daniel's case
Detective Senior Sergeant Paul Schmidt	In charge of the Sunshine Coast Criminal Investigation Branch (CIB), which took over operational control of the investigation and the major incident room (MIR). The senior investigator on 'Operation Vista'

Assistant Police Commissioner Ian Stewart	Queensland Police Commissioner, replacing Bob Atkinson in 2012
Senior Constable Sharon Tebbutt	Worked with Hoelscher and conducted interviews as part of her role with the Sunshine Coast Juvenile Aid Bureau (JAB)
Inspector Arthur Van Panhuis	Coordinator of Crime Scenes
Detective Sergeant Dave Wilkinson	Homicide detective from Brisbane. In charge of the major incident room (MIR) on Daniel's case for the first 12 months
Detective Sergeant Mark Wright	Interviewed Tracey Cowan with Detective Maclean, interviewed Brett Cowan in 2005 and 2006

Covert police officers

Arnold / Mr Big
Ian
Jeff
Joseph (Joe) Emery
Paul 'Fitzy' Fitzsimmons

Key witnesses

Janice Barringham	Daniel's former Grade 3 teacher, who saw Daniel walking along the Woombye-Palmwoods Road
Katherine Bird	Thirty-year-old who saw a man with his foot up against the wall under the overpass, looking at the boy there rather than the bus
Kenneth Bryant	Seventy-four-year-old who had to brake heavily to avoid a blue, boxy car crossing the road in front of him
Wendy Burnett	Saw a scruffy man standing next to a boy in a brightly coloured T-shirt under the overpass
Jessiah Cocks	Saw a boy in a red T-shirt and shorts and a white four-wheel drive about a hundred metres west of the overpass, opposite Caravan World
Michelle Devlin	Noticed a blue car parked near Caravan World

Chloe Fooks	Saw Daniel on her way to buy petrol at the BP service station on the Bruce Highway
June Gannon	Saw a boy, 'disturbed but not frightened', talking to a man under the overpass
Sarah Gullo	Saw a blue car speeding off the highway near the Christian Outreach Centre
Claude Hamilton	Saw two males and a child standing next to a car under the overpass
Jenny and Peter Harth ('Petrol Pete')	Saw Daniel walking past their petrol station as they were closing up
Andrew Jackson	Gave a description of the 'scruffy man', dressed like someone from a bygone era
Barry Kelsey	Saw a boy standing under the overpass with a rough-looking man walking towards him
Toni Lutherborrow	Had to brake to avoid a white ute coming towards her on Eudlo Road, Palmwoods
Lesley Mahoney	Saw an old-model, pale-blue sedan parked on the side of the road near the overpass
Troy Meiers	Saw a blue car on the Nambour side of the overpass parked in a dangerous spot
Anthony Nash	Saw an old four-door sedan speeding towards him with an out-of-control driver with wispy blonde hair and two others in the car
Abby North	Saw a boy and a man under the overpass and provided police with a COMFIT
Fiona Theuerkauf	Saw Daniel trying to wave down the bus, with a man standing behind him
Terry Theuerkauf	Provided police with a COMFIT of the man standing behind Daniel
Judith Van der Meer	Saw a man with dark, straggly hair walking towards the overpass, then later saw a bluey-grey sedan parked dangerously near the Christian Outreach Centre
Vanessa Weier	Saw Daniel twice on his way to the Hail and Ride stop
Aaron and Amanda Wood	Saw a late-'80s car parked dangerously near the overpass with two or three people in it

Sunbus staff

Ross Edmonds	Driver of the 1A bus that broke down and the replacement bus that did not stop for Daniel
Jeff Norman	Duty Controller for Sunbus on the Sunshine Coast on the day of Daniel's disappearance. He drove a small shuttle bus to pick up Stuart Rose and also any new passengers waiting between Woombye and Maroochydore, but there weren't any
Stuart Rose	Drove his bus to the site of the broken down 1A bus to replace it

Queensland Coroner's Office

State Coroner Michael Barnes	Presided over Daniel's Coronial Inquest
Daniel Grice	Team Leader Coordinator of the State Coroner's investigation team
Peter Johns SC	Senior Counsel assisting the State Coroner

Department of Public Prosecutions legal team

Tony Moynihan QC
Michael Byrne QC
Glen Cash

Defence legal team

Michael Bosscher
Angus Edwards
Tim Meehan

Trial Judge

Justice Roslyn Atkinson

Persons of Interest

POI number	Name or Pseudonym
1	Bill Dooley (pseudonym)
2	Alexander Meyer (pseudonym)
3	Alise Smythe (pseudonym)
5	Douglas Brian Jackway
7	Brett Peter Cowan
32	POI32 (not named)
33	POI33 (not named)

Friends, partners and associates of Persons of Interest

Danielle Richardson (pseudonym)	Douglas Jackway's girlfriend, who he was living with at the time of Daniel's disappearance
Vincent Tournoff	Former de facto partner of Richardson
Stephen Park (pseudonym)	Jackway's 16-year-old friend, whose girlfriend was one of Richardson's daughters
Rose-Marie Scanlan	Stephen Park's mother
Stephen Scanlan	Stephen Park's stepfather
Paul Carrington	Douglas Jackway's friend
Tracey Cowan	Brett Cowan's wife at the time of Daniel's abduction
Hayley McDonald (pseudonym)	Brett Cowan's girlfriend after leaving Tracey Cowan
Keith and Jenny Philbrook	Brett Cowan's aunt and uncle
Frank Davis	Friend from whom Brett Peter Cowan borrowed a mulcher on the day of Daniel's disappearance
Sandy Drummond	Brett Cowan's drug dealer

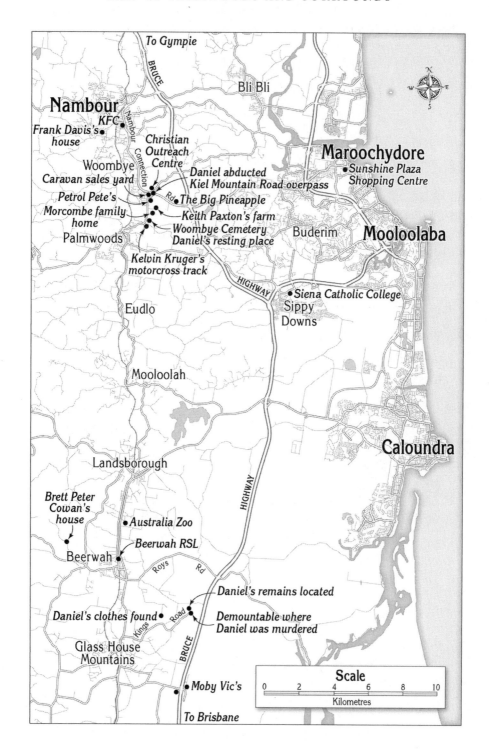

To Gympie

BRUCE

Bli Bli

Nambour

Nambour Connection

KFC

Frank Davis's house

Christian Outreach Centre

Maroochydore

• Sunshine Plaza Shopping Centre

Woombye
Caravan sales yard

Daniel abducted
Kiel Mountain Road overpass

Petrol Pete's

Rd • The Big Pineapple

Morcombe family home

• Keith Paxton's farm

Buderim

Mooloolaba

Palmwoods

Woombye Cemetery
Daniel's resting place

Kelvin Kruger's motorcross track

HIGHWAY

• Siena Catholic College

Eudlo

Sippy Downs

Mooloolah

Landsborough

Caloundra

HIGHWAY

Brett Peter Cowan's house

• Australia Zoo

• Beerwah RSL

Beerwah •

Roys Rd

Daniel's remains located

Daniel's clothes found •

Road

Demountable where
Daniel was murdered

Kings

BRUCE

Glass House
Mountains

• Moby Vic's

To Brisbane

Scale

0   2   4   6   8   10

Kilometres

FOREWORD

by the Honourable Kevin Rudd

There are few people you meet in life who embody human courage, compassion and commitment like the Morcombes. That is why Australians right across the country have developed such a deep bond with this remarkable family. Bruce, Denise and their sons Dean, Bradley and of course little Daniel, have touched us in a way which I believe will be of enduring effect.

The sheer courage of enduring the loss of their little boy – the search; the hopelessness of ever finding him; the arrest, trial and conviction of Daniel's murderer; and then the funeral when they were finally able to lay him lovingly to rest. If it were me, I know I could not have coped. But they did. They are a living testimony to the resilience of a family, leaning on each other all the way through this most painful of journeys. And at journey's end still being together when so many other families would simply have imploded. They are an example for us all.

And then there is the compassion they have had for others who have lost children in horrific circumstances, although few, if any, in circumstances as horrific as for Daniel. Bearing the scars and wounds of Daniel's loss, while still being able to offer a shoulder to cry on, and words of encouragement, for perfect strangers walking up to them in the street to share their own stories of loss and grief. Once again, I know I could not have done that. Yet they have, and they continue to do so. The common refrain from those who have met them is that 'if the Morcombes could come through the tragedy they have been through and still manage to hold it together, then I can come through mine as well.'

As for the commitment to turn their personal grief into a public mission to advance child safety across the country through the Daniel Morcombe Foundation, this too is an example for the nation. Rather than feeling sorry for themselves, while in their case being utterly entitled to do so, they reached out beyond themselves to help others. And in so doing they have been saving the lives of others who would otherwise have found themselves in grave danger.

The Morcombe's wish is to make the Daniel Morcombe Child Safety Curriculum a part of the national curriculum with the support of every government – Commonwealth, state and territory. I fully support them in this initiative. And I call on all governments, whatever their political persuasion, to do the same. There could be no more fitting testament to the life and death of this brave Australian boy.

It has been my privilege to have known the Morcombes for many years now. They are an inspiration to the nation. They are an inspiration to me. And their story is one which now needs to be told through the pages of this book. Which is why I am honoured to have been asked by the family to write this short introduction to Daniel's story.

The Honourable Kevin Rudd
26th Prime Minister of Australia.

PROLOGUE

It was an ordinary Saturday, 13 August 2011. Denise had booked a hair appointment for a cut and colour and she still needed a fancy-dress outfit for her niece, Jessica's, 21st birthday at Scarborough that night. After putting on some washing, Denise grabbed a cup of coffee and walked outside to the back verandah. Looking out at their lush tropical Queensland garden, she noticed a black and white butterfly, about the size of a saucer, on the grass. That was unusual. Usually they were high up on a tree somewhere or on a bush. Perhaps it had broken its wings? She walked across the grass, bent down and picked it up. It didn't fly away. Carefully, she placed it on to Daniel's Hibiscus which was planted about a metre away, near the back door. The hibiscus, a bright luscious red with white swirls, was by now about a metre high. It had been named in her son's memory and had been launched at Australia Zoo.

Later, as Denise pottered in the kitchen, she looked out of the window. The butterfly had gone. Its wings mustn't have been broken after all. Then the phone rang. It was Mike

Condon, the Assistant Commissioner of the Queensland Police Service. He was coming up to the Sunshine Coast and thought he might drop in to say hello. Probably a routine call to update them about the police investigation and the usual progress report: nothing new.

Later that day he rang again. He'd been held up. They'd be leaving at around 6 pm for their niece's party, Denise told him. Condon assured them he'd be there before then. Around 5 pm, Denise tried on the suit she'd picked up at a garage sale that morning for the fancy dress – it looked good. Even if it was a little big, it worked well for the detective theme of the party. She put on black ankle boots and then the hat. The phone rang again, and Bruce picked it up.

It was Channel Nine news reporter Neil Doorley. They were accustomed to these calls. After all, their son's disappearance was the focus of the biggest manhunt the country had ever seen.

'Is it true?' Doorley asked.

'Is what true?' Bruce asked, immediately alert. 'What do you know?'

But Doorley did not say. He had his answer.

No sooner had Bruce ended the conversation with Doorley than the new iPhone they'd bought for the Daniel Morcombe Foundation began to ring. Denise answered. It was Bob Atkinson, the Police Commissioner.

'Is Bruce with you?' he asked.

'Yes,' Denise said. 'Why?'

'Can you put the phone on speaker?'

She fumbled with the new phone trying to put it on speaker.

'I can't work out how to do it, Bob,' Denise said, frustrated. 'I'll relay what you say to Bruce.'

Atkinson paused.

'A man has been arrested for killing Daniel. They'll be charging him soon.'

'Who is it?'

'It's Cowan.'

Denise handed the phone to Bruce, unable to hear more, her mind suddenly blank.

There was a knock at the front door. It was Mike Condon.

Bruce opened the door while still on the phone to the Police Commissioner. Condon, who rarely smiled, was especially grave. They knew now why he was there.

For almost eight years they had been waiting to hear these words.

PART ONE

Daniel Disappears

CHAPTER ONE

A COUNTRY LIFE

The small village of Palmwoods lies 15 kilometres inland from the sprawling Sunshine Coast towns of South East Queensland. Like many towns in the fertile hinterland, Palmwoods grew up around the railway line. But it was pineapples that put Palmwoods on the map. In 1910, six small pineapple canneries were established. Palmwoods even produced a pineapple grower who went on to become a premier of Queensland. Today, heritage buildings – old Queenslanders from white settlement in the early 1890s – serve as craft shops. The original pub underwent a million-dollar overhaul and Palmwoods is the kind of town that attracts the Sunday driver. Once through the main street in the wet season, the cleared pastures of rolling hills are incandescent green, so picturesque that the scene borders on heavenly.

According to the 2011 census, the population of Palmwoods and its nearby hamlets is 5492 – mostly people seeking acreage. Almost half of those living there have bought their own home. More than 60 per cent are Christians. The majority are married. The place is a drawcard for families and hobby farmers alike: 15 minutes from the beach but far enough away from the busy roads and retail warehouses of coastal Maroochydore, Mooloolaba and Caloundra to be called the countryside.

Two main highways intersect the sleepy hollow. To reach the beach, you need to cross the 1700-kilometre Bruce Highway, the major artery along the coast of Queensland, which forms part of the national highway around Australia. The Nambour Connection Road, once the old Bruce Highway, links Maroochydore to Nambour, the administrative inland centre of the Sunshine Coast, intersecting the new Bruce Highway just north of Forest Glen, where a large sign entices travellers to the renowned, 16-metre Big Pineapple. Visitors then turn on to the Nambour Connection Road to the site of the old pineapple farm and one of Queensland's most iconic tourist attractions and landmarks.

In 2000, Denise and Bruce Morcombe owned a four-bedroom, brand-new canal home in Buddina, a beachside suburb east of Palmwoods. They had bought a 26-foot cruiser named *Louise* for fishing at the weekends, which they moored at a pontoon at the bottom of the garden. In designing the home, which they moved into in 1999, Denise was keenly aware of the distance between Australia's northern state and her southern home state of Victoria, where her parents lived, so the Morcombes built a granny flat on the ground floor. There was also a home office for their business, a double garage and a pool. The canal house was, as Denise described, 'a beautiful home'. So, the day they decided to go for a drive to Palmwoods in February 2000, they had no intention of buying another house.

As chance would have it, Camellia Cottage, on Woombye-Palmwoods Road, Palmwoods, on the stretch of country road between the Nambour Connection Road and Palmwoods, was open for inspection. The property was on a battleaxe block, off the busy main road. Tucked away below the road on the ridge, the two-storey wooden home had spacious verandahs, four bedrooms and a sweeping five-acre garden, with a magnificent poinciana tree, hundreds of established camellias and two turpentine mango trees almost one hundred years old.

There was something about the property that caught both of their imaginations: the past grandeur of the place, the potential to restore it to its former glory. For Bruce, a keen gardener and the regional franchisor for Jim's Mowing on the Sunshine Coast, the dilapidated barn and stables spelt an opportunity to shape a garden of his own. The barn was also part of Palmwoods' heritage. It had originally been used for packing pineapples.

But perhaps the most enticing part of all was that this was a place where their three boys, Dean, 12, and twins Bradley and Daniel, 10, could grow up in the country. They could have ponies and motocross bikes and enjoy the kind of environment their parents had relished as children, in a place where time seemed to have stood still. So, in May 2000, having sold the Buddina property for a handsome profit, they moved in.

The Morcombes were unafraid of hard work. Bruce and Denise both came from that kind of stock. Denise Marie Beavis was born in Melbourne in November 1960, a middle child. By the age of 18, she was a shift worker doing data entry and accounts in the data centre for the Bank of New South Wales, before it became Westpac. Bruce David Morcombe was born in Adelaide in 1959, the second youngest of four children. In 1970, Bruce's family moved to Melbourne, and in February 1977 Bruce started work at the Melbourne Metropolitan Board of Works, where he stayed for 15 years. Bruce's father, Ted, taught him never to be a quitter. Sticking to the task at hand is vital in life.

Bruce met Denise on 15 February 1980, when Bruce was 20 and Denise 19, in the seaside town of Lorne on the Great

Ocean Road. Denise had gone away with her girlfriend, Sue, whose brother, Maurice, worked with Bruce at the Board of Works. Bruce was spending the weekend with his mates. Straightaway, they recognised in each other the same kind of work ethic. They fell into easy conversation. And there were other attractions. Denise was taken with Bruce's red Celica, as well as his white peroxide hair, fashionable for the 1980s. Bruce was taken by Denise's friendly nature and the chemistry he felt between them. The following week, they spoke every day on the phone. Their first date, the following Saturday evening, was at the movies to see *Apocalypse Now*. Their relationship developed quickly from there.

It wasn't all smooth sailing, though. One Saturday night, they had gone out with a couple of friends to the Mooney Valley trots. Denise was the designated driver. They had dinner and a punt on the course. Somehow, the night turned sour and they ended up squabbling. Bruce decided to walk out of the relationship that night. He left the trots, caught two trams and then had a long walk back to his car, which was parked outside Denise's house. He reached the car in the small hours to find a note under the windscreen wipers. It was an apology from Denise. The message they both took from that night was to move on and not bear grudges, because nobody is perfect. They were not to know how important this early lesson would be in the years to follow.

A year later, they holidayed in Palm Cove in Northern Queensland, where, after a meal at a local restaurant, Bruce sprang a surprise at the dinner table. He had sold his red Celica to buy an engagement ring.

Sitting with Denise's family on a Sunday evening after returning to Melbourne, Bruce was too nervous to report the news. When Denise's father, Kevin, suddenly said, 'I'm off to bed,' Bruce blurted out, 'We are engaged.' Kevin turned to Denise immediately: 'You're not pregnant, are you?' Relieved to find this was not the case, Kevin cracked open a bottle of sparkling wine and they all toasted the happy event. They were married on 3 September 1983, three and a half years after they met.

Married life began modestly enough in a one-bedroom flat in Glenhuntly in Melbourne's south-east before they bought a four-bedroom house in Forest Hill, further east in the suburbs. After saving for their future, it was time to start a family. Their first child, Dean, was born on 4 October 1987. Over a year later, Denise fell pregnant again: but this time, it was with twins. Sadly, Bruce's dad, Ted, died while Denise was pregnant with the twins. Two years and two months after they had their first son, on 19 December 1989, Denise gave birth to twins, eight weeks prematurely, after being rushed to the Monash Medical Centre. Bradley was 1615 grams, arriving nine minutes before Daniel, who weighed only 1530 grams. Denise called them her 'number 15 and 16 chickens', because of their weights.

When they were born, the babies were so small they could fit into the palm of Denise's hands. The boys spent one week in intensive care. After four weeks in the neonatal ward for premature babies, Bradley came home, while Daniel was transferred to the neonatal ward at Box Hill Hospital the same day. The hospital rang up wanting to know why Bruce and Denise were not with Daniel following the transfer and they had to explain that Bradley had just come home.

Bruce received a small redundancy package from the Board of Works in February 1992 and the couple bought the Jim's Mowing franchise in Boronia, not far from Mount Dandenong in Melbourne's eastern suburbs. As parents of three boys under the age of four, including two-year-old twins, it was a busy life. A year later, an opportunity came up that was hard to resist: to swap the franchise in Victoria for the Queensland regional franchisor territory with the phone prefix '074', an area from Caboolture to Gympie, which essentially encompassed the Sunshine Coast. Much later Denise was to recall that she was reluctant to move to the Sunshine State, but they decided the prospects were too good for their young family.

While waiting for their place in Victoria to sell, they rented a house for three months in the Sunshine Coast town of Maroochydore. As regional franchisor, the Morcombes were able to break up territories within the region to sell to franchisees. At first, though, they had no franchisees, only 23 mowing clients. Bruce spent his time mowing and gardening for these customers, building up their customer base. The first franchisee came on board in August 1993, the same month that the Morcombes moved into their new home in Mountain Creek, just off the Sunshine Motorway, four kilometres west of Mooloolaba. Denise juggled parenthood and dispensing the bookings across the franchisees, which were growing steadily. The boys understood from an early age that, when the phone rang, it was their parents' livelihood.

Mountain Creek State School was only 400 metres from the house, and it was a good fit for the boys. One day, the twins came home from Grade 1 and told their parents they were learning about outer space. Bruce and Denise had just had some flat-pack goods from Freedom Furniture which had arrived in massive cardboard boxes. Bruce used the boxes and designed a space shuttle for Daniel, with shoulder straps attached. Daniel walked along wearing the two-metre shuttle as though he were flying it. 'Now, Bradley,' Bruce pondered, 'how about planet Earth?' He sat on the lounge floor and cut out two huge circles. The plan was for Bradley to wear them on shoulder straps and walk around as Earth. They all painted the blue oceans and continents and islands on the globe. One side was daytime and in sunlight, and the other in semi-darkness for night. Their teacher Jan Bennett liked them so much they ended up being displayed in the school library. And the twins celebrated Easter in similar style. Bruce made rabbit ears out of wire coathangers and cotton wool, and attached them to a couple of broad-brimmed straw hats. The costumes went down a treat with the teachers and other kids at school.

At Mountain Creek, the Morcombe boys became used to a level of independence, riding their bikes to school. When Daniel was six, while playing on his bike with Bradley in front of the house, he rode out from behind a parked car and was hit by a four-wheel drive. Bradley remembers seeing his twin lying on the road and Daniel spending a night in hospital. Luckily, Daniel had been wearing a helmet. The story made the front page of the local newspaper, the *Sunshine Coast Daily*. Nevertheless, this did not faze Daniel. He was strong for his small build, broad-shouldered and plucky.

There was no way the twins could ever be mistaken for being identical. Bradley looked more like Bruce's side of the family while Daniel had inherited Denise's eyes. They were bluey-grey and, like his mother's, a window into his soul. When they moved from Mountain Creek to nearby Buddina in the canal development, the boys continued to ride to school unless their parents drove them. Sometimes, they would ride down to Big W and buy ten Pokémon cards in a foil packet in the hope of expanding their collections. They would trade pocket money for elusive cards, which meant negotiating with friends until they had the whole set.

By 2001, business was booming. The Morcombes owned their Buddina home outright when they sold it and moved to Palmwoods. In 2002, they also bought an investment property in Maroochydore in Amaroo Street right near the Sunshine Plaza. They rented it out and it was showing a good return. Shortly after moving in, they renovated the Palmwoods property. The boys had a bedroom each. Daniel's was at the top southern corner, looking out over the swimming pool. Bradley's was next door. Bruce and Denise's room was on the same side of the house to Daniel's but overlooked the steep driveway. Dean had his own room downstairs, facing out to the sheds, the dam at the bottom of one of the paddocks and the poinciana tree. He also had a separate bathroom in recognition of his big-brother status.

On weekends, Denise and the boys helped Bruce get the garden into shape. The camellias were being strangled by a vigorous creeper, Velcro vine, which tore at your skin, the plant's sap often leading to rashes, and there was plenty of fencing to do. They planted agapanthus down by the dam. Denise's mother, Monique, gave Bruce some money to buy some bamboo in small pots to plant in the paddock near the dam, which was stocked with Australian bass, barramundi and golden perch. The family stripped the land around the dam, planting more than one hundred exotic fruit trees, including citrus, guava, lychee, custard apple, macadamia nut, ice-cream bean and mulberry. With waterlilies often flowering on the water, it was a tropical heaven, and it was not surprising the boys preferred to stay at home rather than look for other distractions after school. One day, Denise was in the kitchen when she heard the boys laughing and saying, 'Don't tell Mum.' Curious, she went outside and saw an enormous carpet python spread across the barbecue area. They had been trying to move it so she wouldn't be scared.

The Morcombes began adding a host of animals to their happy family. Bruce found two ponies at a local nursery in nearby Chevallum, where he used to buy wholesale plants. They were born from the same father a day apart to different mothers. Most weekends, the twins visited them with Bruce and Denise. They would bring carrots and pat them and sometimes have riding lessons. They began the ritual of feeding them peanut-butter sandwiches when visiting them each New Year's Day and on the ponies' birthdays. When the ponies were old enough, they brought them home to Palmwoods. Bruce and Denise bought saddles for them. Daniel loved his brown pony, which he called Bullet because the mark on his crown reminded him of a bullet hole. Brad's pony was already named Sorrento. The twins would walk them around the paddocks like dogs on a leash and, every second day, they would have a half-hour ride. They never tired of playing with them. The Morcombes then bought two more horses, Katie and Shambala.

The twins also occupied themselves with other activities around their home. The Turpentine mango tree was unpredictable in its yield of fruit. At first, there would be nothing, but two years after they moved in there was an abundance. The juicy missiles would drop out of the tree unexpectedly and the boys would bring the delicious treats inside. Everyone's teeth suffered, with stringy mango fruit getting stuck in the gaps. The boys kept the best ones for the family and the rest went to the ponies and the cows. Daniel and Brad would fill a wheelbarrow each with the rejects. Bullet and Sorrento would put them on the ground with their mouths. Then, using their hooves and mouths, they would peel the flesh away from the large seed and eat it. The boys had to limit how many the ponies ate or they would get the runs. Hugo and Millie, the bull and cow, were also eating machines, and the boys would bring them up to a hundred mangos in the wheelbarrow. The boys would hand feed them one at a time, and they would swallow the mangos whole, seed and all, the juice squirting out of their mouths. In the next few days, the cow patties would be littered with mango kernels.

In May 2003, the Morcombes had another addition to their family: a grey and white cat that they called Mittens. Daniel claimed Mittens and took it to his bedroom each night to join the other cat, Gitana, a white, beautiful ragdoll pedigree. They also had a German shepherd called Chief. Chief was Daniel's best buddy, despite the dog being very protective and not particularly friendly with anyone outside the immediate family. On top of this, they also had chickens and ducks on their property.

One day, when everyone arrived back earlier than usual from school, they found some of the animals congregated in the back barbecue area. The chickens were on the outdoor chairs, Gitana was lying on the table and Chief was on an outdoor lounge by the pool. It was Animal Farm. And it was about to get larger. In October 2003, Bruce was heading to the shower one morning and saw, from the window, Katie standing in the paddock looking like she was about to give birth. By the time he got out of the shower, Katie had had her foal. There was much family excitement when they rushed down to the paddock to greet the new arrival, which the boys named Lily. Lily was already standing up next to her mum.

Daniel had a natural way with animals. He wanted to be a vet, had more patience than most kids and was an innate animal whisperer. Shy and quiet by temperament, he would confide in the animals. Daniel and Chief would often sit together, and Daniel would pat him on his head and back. He would also endlessly throw Chief's ball for him in the paddocks.

Up until he was 10 or 11, Daniel had always been frightened of the dark. He would take his parents' bedspread off their bed, put it on the floor next to them and sleep on it. When they lived at Buddina, the night-time visits were a regular occurrence, but, even after moving to Palmwoods, Daniel would appear at night to sleep in his parents' room troubled with nightmares and dark thoughts. Yet, during the day, he was fearless, muscular, into physical exploits and forever demonstrating his strength.

Dean did not share the same love for the ponies as Daniel and Brad. One Saturday, after the ponies had been broken in and the boys had sufficient riding prowess after lessons at Yandina Riding School, Dean decided he would have a go. With helmet on and Bullet saddled up, he only managed a few metres before the pony reared up and he fell backwards onto the cement driveway, injuring his arm. Denise and Bruce drove him to Nambour Hospital, where X-rays revealed a broken bone near his elbow. From then on, he said, he would stick to motocross bikes.

And there were funny times too, such as the day Denise picked up the boys from school and parked the car in the garage near the big shed. They all noticed Millie the cow running around the paddock with her head stuck in the feeding container. The boys, who were splitting their sides laughing, got out of the car and raced into the paddock to help. It took about 15 minutes to calm her down. Daniel and Brad went to fetch a bucket with pellets and molasses to feed Hugo, the bull, and Millie. On another day, it was Hugo's turn. They returned to find him missing from the paddocks. In a panic, they searched everywhere, then found him relaxing under the boys' trampoline. Daniel and Bradley had to coax him back home using a bucket of food.

Every Wednesday after school, after feeding the animals, Daniel and Bradley would head for the kitchen to make 'spaghetti bol'. They would argue over who was cutting the onion and garlic, who would brown the meat, who would add the ingredients. Then, there would be an argument as to which pasta they would use. The kitchen inevitably looked like a bomb had hit it, but the food was good.

Denise's parents, Nana and Pa to the boys, would visit every August and sometimes at Christmas. Bruce's mother, Wendy, would also visit occasionally, coming once for Christmas lunch. One day, Pa, aged 70, was riding the family's orange Vespa scooter around the property when he was forced to brake hard to avoid hitting Chief. He fell off and was covered in bruises – black and blue. Nana was there too. But it was the boys who rang for the ambulance. It was all part of living in the country. Responsibility – one of the Morcombes' core values – had been learnt.

* * *

The Morcombes' business now had 50 franchisees and was going so well that, in 2003, Bruce and Denise put an offer in on a second investment property in Buderim, the ginger town sitting on a 500-metre mountain above the Sunshine Coast and once connected by railway to Palmwoods. They had decided to divide their regional franchisor region into three zones, allowing them more profit on the sales.

Working hard meant making time for holidays, although those holidays, out of necessity, had to be short. Hamilton Island became a favourite destination for the family. They had visited the island four times by the middle of 2003. The boys loved the place, as they would get around using the traditional transport: a golf buggy. Although the regulations meant that you had to be over 18 to drive them, it was not uncommon in the back streets to see a youngster holding the wheel of one of them and a parent beside the driver. On a few occasions, Bruce and Denise would go out to the lookout after dark or get up early and let the boys have a go.

On another vacation, the Morcombes went to the Whitsundays on a sailing trip to Chalky Reef, where they had a snorkel, and then continued to Whitehaven Beach. It had the purest white sand in the country. It was the perfect family holiday. Everyone was happy. The boys enjoyed the marine life on the Great Barrier Reef. On Easter Monday, 21 April 2003, Bruce and the boys did an induction course and then went for their first dive. Denise elected to snorkel. This became the first of many times they dived to explore the reef.

In August 2003, Bruce and Denise decided to celebrate their 20th wedding anniversary by holidaying in Greece for 17 days. They visited Athens, Mykonos, Naxos, Santorini and Paros, while Nana and Pa stayed at Palmwoods to look after the boys. It was Bruce and Denise's first holiday on their own since they'd had children. They returned to Palmwoods late and jetlagged to three eager sons waiting to see what booty they'd got. Denise had bought each of them a gold chain.

The twins were especially excited as, while Bruce and Denise were away, they had come up with the idea to clean out the concrete fishpond in the front garden bed at Camellia Cottage. The pond was full of mud and slushy water. They decided that, once they'd cleaned it, they would put goldfish in there as a birthday present for Bruce. Pa later told Bruce and Denise how hard Daniel had worked on the task, bucketing out the mud and cleaning the pond for days, and how he had dirt all over his clothes. Finally, the pool was filled with water. Pa drove the boys to the pet shop in Nambour and they chose two goldfish and bought food for them, ready to spring the surprise on their dad.

In July, before they went to Greece, Bruce and Denise had sold the remainder of their mowing franchises, having dispensed of a third of them in May 2002. They still ran Jim's Mowing call centre, taking calls from the region from Caboolture to Mackay and covering Jim's Services, which included mowing, trees, computers, bookkeeping and antennas. In October 2003, they sold all regional rights and the call centre, and bought the regional franchisor rights for Jim's Tree Removal and Stump Grinding in Queensland. This allowed the Morcombes to sell franchises for tree surgery for the whole of Queensland, with them retaining responsibility for advertising, training and finding work for the operators.

From 1 October, Denise and Bruce decided to run their operations from home again, so they could spend more time with the boys. After working from home in Mountain Creek and then Buddina, they had leased a commercial office at Emerald Springs Shopping Centre in Mooloolaba. In May, they moved the office to their investment property in Amaroo Street near the Sunshine Plaza. They had no idea that they would have only ten more weeks left together as a family unit. Later, they were glad to have made that decision to work from home. Tucked away in their country paradise, they were convinced they had built a safe and secure haven for their family.

CHAPTER TWO

CHRISTMAS PRESENTS

Keith Paxton is a sandy-haired, no-nonsense farmer accustomed to hard work, with the muscled calves and weathered skin of someone who is continually outdoors. He and his wife, Judy, had been living in their house on Atkinsons Road on the ridge that adjoined the Morcombes' house for around 20 years. The Paxtons own two farms. One, that was next to the Morcombes' property, has 18 acres and two dams. The other includes their house on Atkinsons Road. The Paxtons' passionfruit vines and lychees stretch as far as the eye can see, and some of the vines bordered the Morcombes' house. The Paxton farm also has custard apples, longans and avocados.

Shortly after moving to Palmwoods, when the twins were aged 11 and Dean was 13, the three boys began picking passionfruit to boost their pocket money. They would walk up and down the endless rows of vines, collecting the ripe fruit from the ground earlier than 8 am before the sun got to it. Barefoot and dressed in T-shirts and board shorts, with Daniel in his usual black baseball cap, they would place the fruit in orange buckets at the end of the rows. They would pick up to a thousand passionfruit a day. In a matter of weeks, the boys went from being what Paxton described as 'a bit soft' to becoming his best pickers. He was fond of them and had once taken them fishing, as well as teaching them to drive his quad bike so they could deliver the fruit to his shed at the top of the hill.

The boys gave their passionfruit money to Denise, who banked it in their Commonwealth Bank accounts. The casual work meant they could save up for things they wanted to buy, as well as learn the value of money. Since moving to Palmwoods, Dean and Daniel had developed a love of motorbikes. Using some of their savings from picking passionfruit, they decided to pool their resources to buy a Honda XR100 motocross bike. They learnt to ride it on the property.

When Dean managed to raise enough funds to buy another bike, as the first bike was getting too small for him, he bought a Suzuki RM125 and Daniel inherited the old bike. Weekends were spent working on their bikes. They were either cleaning them after a ride or fixing mechanical problems, learning together as they went. At other times, they would visit motorbike shops and ogle the new bikes for sale.

In November 2003, Bruce gave the boys some money to put into a hobby of their choice. The boys sold their old motorbikes and bought new ones. Daniel got a Honda 2003 CR85 and Dean a yellow Yamaha Yz125. Daniel's passion was obvious from the motocross posters plastered on his walls. Dean had bought Daniel a poster book with pictures of freestyle motocross inside as a gesture of thanks for helping him fix his RM125.

On Friday nights, Daniel and Dean would go motocross riding at a nearby property on Nicklin Road, off the Woombye-Palmwoods Road closer to Palmwoods. Kelvin Kruger was a steel fabricator working from home on a former pineapple farm who also managed a mobile sandblasting business that was based in an industrial shed not far from his property. He owned about ten acres of unused, undulating land, which formed a perfect motocross track for dirt bikes. Each week, he invited friends who had bikes to join him for a couple of hours. The track had jumps and dips and hairpin bends, plus fast, sweeping corners. The riders would have a beer afterwards.

Dean had a desire to join the action; his head would turn that way when the family drove to the Palmwoods shops and, on Saturday afternoons, the boys would hear the bikes going around the track. Finally, Dean plucked up enough courage to ask Kruger whether they could ride there, even though he was 15 and Daniel only 13. So it was that Dean and Daniel joined the other, mostly adult, motocross enthusiasts.

Bradley did not share his brothers' love of motorbikes. He wanted to become a pilot one day, and his bedroom was full of planes. On the weekends, though, they all played computer games: James Bond 007 was a favourite.

* * *

After finishing Grade 7 and primary school at Mountain Creek State School, the twins had followed their brother, Dean, to Siena Catholic College, a coeducational college in Sippy Downs. The college was one of only a few Catholic colleges on the Sunshine Coast, and Denise had worked hard at getting Dean entry there. She had been brought up a Catholic and frequently went to mass, and the family never missed Easter and Christmas services. Bruce was enthusiastic about the choice of school. The college badge stated its ethos was to establish and maintain 'Prayer, Care and Learning'. The morals and values dovetailed with what the Morcombes wanted for their sons.

One day, in Grade 9, Daniel came home from the college with a wooden briefcase he had made in carpentry. He had engraved his name on it. Proudly, he gave it to Denise, who put it on top of their wardrobe. Later, Daniel saw it there. 'Are you going to use that case?' he asked Denise.

Denise smiled at him. 'Yes, I am keeping it to put special things in it,' she said, having little idea how treasured that wooden box was to become.

Daniel had several good schoolfriends. One, named Scott Balkin, had been friends with Daniel since Grade 8 at Siena, when the boys were sent to the same home-room, 'MK'. They studied English, Science and Religion together. Throughout Grade 9, their friendship had grown. Daniel said he would show Scott his pony and motorbike, even promising that he would put Scott's name forward for a job passionfruit picking. Daniel rarely had friends over, preferring to occupy himself with his motocross magazines, playing with his brothers or his animals, watching television or on the computer, where he had his own MSN Hotmail address. Tom Palmer, an old friend of Scott's, also became friendly with Daniel. At morning tea, the boys would wait for each other and walk to class together. Sometimes, Tom and Daniel wouldn't have done their homework, and it would be a scramble for them to complete it before the class started. Often, they would have lunch together.

Daniel excelled at Maths, getting an A+ that year, but Tom and Daniel both hated drama. Daniel was naturally shy. Their favourite sports were wrestling, touch footy, soccer and handball. Then they had school tennis. Once, Daniel had run up to the net to hit the ball back over but, in his haste, had run straight into it. It was what the boys called being 'clotheslined'. Tom and the other boys looked on, concerned, but Daniel stood up quickly: 'Oh, I've fallen over.' They all burst out laughing. Daniel was tough. He was never one to show physical pain, a trait probably inherited from his parents.

And there was a passing interest in girls. That year, Daniel had plucked up enough courage to ask a girl out. One day, he met up with Tom near the admin block and was in tears. She had said no. Tom was surprised, as Daniel had never mentioned this girl. He consoled his friend, just as Daniel was to do for him later over a different girl. They had gone back to their locker to get books for the next class. It was all part of growing up.

English wasn't Daniel's favourite subject, nor was it Tom's. But worse than English was giving speeches. Two minutes felt like 20. Daniel became adept at timetabling his speeches to take place during lunchtime, which meant there were fewer people in the room, to cut down on his anxiety. Two were enough to constitute an audience, according to his teacher. Tom would congratulate him when he got through it, knowing what a challenge it was for him.

Daniel was always loyal. Once, one of his friends hadn't studied for an exam. The essay question in the exam was on a book called *Jim and Me*. Halfway through, his friend signalled to Daniel. He hadn't studied and hadn't even started writing. Risking being caught, Daniel scribbled notes on a piece of paper, tore it off and passed it to his friend. After being caught, Daniel displayed no anger at the consequences.

Even though the boys were growing up fast, Daniel retained a charming innocence. The week before school broke up, Denise took Daniel, Dean and Bradley to Subway for a treat. They ordered their usual foot-long meatball sub and the boys grabbed a table. Denise went over to sit with them.

'No, sit over there, Mum,' Dean and Bradley said.

Denise sighed, used to the antics of teenage boys. She moved away and then was surprised, as Daniel had moved tables too. He patted the chair next to his. 'Come and sit with me,' he said.

Daniel's caring nature extended to his pets. One sad day, Gitana the cat did not return home in the evening. They never saw her again, and concluded that she had probably been taken by a fox. The boys were heartbroken, Daniel especially, who from then on spent more time with Mittens, concerned that she too may get lost in the large acreage of Camellia Cottage.

Occasionally, the boys would go grocery shopping with Denise. Leading up to Christmas that year, Daniel had spied a selection of Christmas pens that had lollies inside in clear casing. He bought one and, when he came home, handed it to Denise. A few days passed. 'Are you going to eat those lollies?' he asked.

'Maybe not,' Denise admitted.

'Well, I will,' he answered, and picked up the pen and demolished them in one hit. He was always the joker in the family.

Denise had a special relationship with Daniel. He would make her laugh. Coming up behind her in the kitchen, he would tap her on the left shoulder so she would look in that direction while he was on her right. When they lived in Mountain Creek, there was a park on the way to school with a bottlebrush flower. Daniel would pick the red flower for her most days on the way home from school. In Palmwoods, he had changed the ritual to a white camellia, when it was in bloom, which he would leave on the kitchen bench. Denise could see the plant near the swimming pool from the kitchen window.

As the 2003 school year drew to a close, the twins were still working hard, picking passionfruit from 6 to 7.30 am, and were looking forward to spending their earnings over the upcoming holiday season.

When the school term ended on Thursday 4 December, the twins had completed Grade 9 and Dean had finished Grade 11. Dean was toying with the idea of not going back to school and pursuing a TAFE course or an apprenticeship instead. All the boys were waiting for their report cards, which were due in a few days.

The holiday season started with rain, which began on the Friday afternoon with a thunderstorm. In spite of the downpour, Bruce drove the boys up to the pet shop in Nambour to buy food for Daniel and Brad's three Mexican fighting fish, which they kept in their bedrooms in separate fish tanks.

Earlier that day, Daniel and Brad also carried on a tradition that had begun at the end of Grade 7 to mark the end of primary school. Back then all of their friends had come around, bringing books and uniforms. Bruce had made scarecrows and dressed them in the boys' uniforms. *Whoof.* Up in smoke they went, as everyone laughed and cheered. This year, Daniel and Bradley carried their schoolbooks to the far side of the dam. In spite of the wet conditions, they managed to set fire to them.

The Morcombes had no particular plans for Christmas 2003. Daniel and Brad had been saving to go down to Melbourne to see Denise's parents in January. Daniel had already compiled a list of Christmas presents for everyone, which he left in his bedroom. He had already secretly opened his present from his Nana and Pa. It was a silver motorbike clock. He sealed the wrapping shut so no one would know, but he told Bradley about it. The twins would be turning 14 six days before Christmas. They had bought each other early birthday presents and had already exchanged gifts. Daniel had bought Brad a model aeroplane, and Brad had paid for an engraving on a silver and gold fob watch on a silver chain that Daniel had bought for himself back in October 2003. Because each letter came at a cost, Brad had chosen a simple inscription: the abbreviation 'Dan'. Daniel put his birthday card for Brad beside his bed, planning to sign it before their birthday.

The December rain developed into floods in South East Queensland. The paddocks near the dam at the Morcombes' house were awash with water, and the run-off was flowing into the dam. Not that this stopped the boys having their fun. Daniel and Brad got boogie boards and careered down the grassy slope in the horse paddocks, using it like a giant water slide. Once at the bottom, they would hike back up the hill to go down again, whooping shouts of glee. They had made plans to go to the movies that Friday afternoon, their first day of school holidays, but the rain changed things. Besides, two of the boys who were to join them at the cinema had gone rollerblading, which ended just 20 minutes before the movie started. Instead, Daniel and Brad played video games and decided to go on Saturday.

The Sunshine Plaza is the largest shopping centre on the Sunshine Coast, with more than 220 speciality stores, larger stores such as Myer and Target, and another major attraction: the Birch, Carroll and Coyle cinema. On Saturday 6 December 2003, *S.W.A.T.*, the action crime thriller based on the television series of the same name, was every boy's dream movie. Helicopters were shot down by high-powered rifles, and a French drug lord killed his father and uncle to take control of the family's criminal empire. Daniel was a loyalty member of the Cinebuzz club from the cinema chain, so his friends Scott, Sean Higgins, Sam Murray and Mitchell Duffy could get cheap tickets.

Denise drove Daniel there shortly before 6 pm and agreed to pick him up at around 9 pm. She parked the car in one of the Plaza's many car parks and followed Daniel inside. He was early. As none of his friends were there, he went to the Virgin record store with his mother to buy a Christmas present for his cousin Ashlea Beavis in Melbourne. Once his first friend arrived – Mitchell Duffy, a tall boy with blondish hair aged about 14 or 15 – Daniel told his mother that she could leave. The boys bought popcorn and frozen raspberry Coke. Scott, Sean and Sam arrived later. While they bought their tickets, Daniel went inside to reserve some seats.

'What are you doing tomorrow?' Scott asked after Daniel came back from the toilet and returned to the cinema.

'I'm going to a work Christmas do with Mum and Dad,' Daniel replied.

After the movie, while waiting for their parents, the boys gave their ratings. Daniel was his usual quiet self, enjoying being in the company of his mates. Later, Scott couldn't remember him saying much. He did tell Scott how much he was looking forward to going to Melbourne in January.

'We should go and see *Lord of the Rings* on Boxing Day,' Sam Murray said.

It was agreed they would go when the movie, the last in the trilogy, was released.

When Denise arrived to pick up Daniel at around 9 pm, she asked him how the movie was. 'Okay,' he responded. They drove home without saying much. After arriving back home, Daniel got out of the car and smiled. 'Thanks, Mum.' He was never big on conversation. Then he headed inside for a drink and went upstairs to bed.

* * *

On Sunday morning, 7 December 2003, Bruce and Denise woke up shortly before 6 am to cloudy skies and threatening rain. It was the day they had selected for the work Christmas party, for the five franchisees of Jim's Trees. With her usual organisational skills, Denise had already shopped the day before. She'd bought bread rolls and other bits and pieces from Coles at the Sunshine Plaza, and cheesecakes from The Cheesecake Shop at Maroochydore. The Morcombes had chosen Broadwater Picnic Ground in the southern suburbs of Brisbane off the M1 Gateway Motorway.

They had already done a reconnoitre of the picnic ground the week before when visiting Bruce's sister Lindy and brother-in-law Andrew Colebrook who were also franchisees and lived nearby. The Morcombes had planned everything, as they always did, down to the last minute. If they left at 8.30 am, they would have time to call into the local IGA at Woombye, for bags of ice and any last-minute items, then head down the Woombye-Palmwoods Road, across the Kiel Mountain Road overpass, south down the Nambour Connection Road and onto the Bruce Highway, then south to Brisbane. The plan was to reach the park by 10 am. That way, they could claim a picnic table before others arrived, in the busy time leading up to Christmas. They had already worked out where the nearest Red Rooster takeaway was and had planned to buy the chicken after arriving at the park. The boys were to begin passionfruit picking at 6 am and would be finished by 7.30 am, leaving plenty of time for them to have a shower, eat breakfast and help pack the car.

But that morning the phone rang at 5.55 am. It was Keith Paxton. 'Look, I think we'll hold off the picking for an hour because of the rain,' he told Bruce. 'It's just a shower and I'm sure it'll pass. Save the boys getting wet.'

Bruce did the sums. It would be too tight a turnaround. There were too many franchisees relying upon them. If the boys didn't start until 7 am, it meant they wouldn't finish until 8.30 am, and that was when he and Denise wanted to leave. In the kitchen, the heart of the house, they had a family meeting.

'Do you want to come with us or not?' Bruce asked. 'The timing is marginal.'

'Look, Dad,' they said almost with one voice, based on previous experience of having attended a few of their parents' work functions. 'We'll do our fruit picking. It's the beginning of the holidays. We'd rather just relax at home.'

Denise remembers Dean had cooked carbonara noodles out of a packet in the microwave. Daniel was eating them out of a bowl. The boys had less than an hour before they started picking. Bruce and Denise started packing the car. The morning was taking shape. A plan had been worked out.

A while later, out at the clothes line, Daniel passed his mother on his way down the driveway to the back shed, where Keith Paxton was to pick them up. It was almost time to start work. 'Has Dad bought you anything for Christmas from that magazine that we bought on Friday?' Daniel asked as she was reaching up to peg one of the boys' shorts on the line.

'What magazine?'

'The one Dad bought.'

'I don't know,' Denise said, returning to the laundry basket.

It was not until much later that Denise remembered that conversation. She found the *Collectormania* magazine on the kitchen bench. This small exchange was the last time she ever spoke to her son.

Bruce doesn't recall any particular conversation, but he clearly remembers seeing the tops of his sons' heads that morning as he packed the car. The passionfruit grew on vines a metre and a half high, and he could see their heads above the countless rows of supporting trellis. He could also hear their voices and laughter as they settled into the familiar routine. The three of them were picking together. There were no other labourers that day.

Keith Paxton was netting the lychees near the Morcombes' house that morning. He took the trailer over to the boys at the appointed time of 7 am. Normally, he would see the boys at the end of the picking, but that day he asked his wife to help. 'Fellas,' he said. 'When you've finished, I'm off netting. Jude'll help you and pay you and take you home.'

Dean ended up finishing early and took himself home, and at 9.50 am Jude delivered Brad and Daniel back to their house on her quad bike. She paid them all what was owed, including the money they had earned that week. The boys always kept the Paxtons on their toes, noting down the dates and hours worked. They were quick to pick up any discrepancies. Before she left, the twins told Judy how much they were looking forward to going to see their grandparents in Melbourne in January.

Back at home, after picking, the boys began to unwind. Weeks of school holidays yawned ahead. As with all school holidays, the first few days were filled with the urgency of having to plan activities to fill the upcoming days. Bradley and Daniel settled in to watch *Franklin and Friends*, a Canadian television series about a curious turtle and his animal friends. While they'd been picking, Daniel had been pestering Dean to go to the Sunshine Plaza, which was open on a Sunday for pre-Christmas shopping. The passionfruit money was burning a hole in his pocket. Daniel had told Dean that he also wanted to get his hair cut. But Dean had made plans to go and visit his friend, Matt Hannah. Daniel had tried Brad, too, explaining that one of their friends from school's mum was working at Just Cuts that morning and that he might get a good deal on his haircut. But neither of his brothers seemed interested. 'No, mate,' Brad said. 'I'd rather go on Monday.'

Later that morning, Dean and Daniel went upstairs to their parents' bedroom. The coast was clear. They had been watching the World Wrestling Federation's *WrestleMania* on the cable television downstairs. Their favourite wrestlers included The Rock, The Undertaker and Stone Cold Steve Austin, and they loved body slams. Their parents' bed served well as a ring. Dean and Daniel began to play-act their best-loved characters on the bed. Wrestling was a cherished pastime. Daniel had the foresight to take off the gold chain that his mum had brought him from Greece, placing it on his father's side of the bed.

Bradley, seeing the activity in the bedroom, raced downstairs to take over the boys' shared computer. Usually, during weeknights, it was strictly rationed to half an hour for each of them. Now, he had it to himself. Bruce and Denise had recently bought speakers and a camera so they could talk to their franchisees, which was an added bonus for the boys. One of the boys' favourite games was Fill It. As Brad settled at the computer, it was marching towards lunchtime. Daniel had run out to the bathroom at one point and Dean was waiting outside to pounce on him when he came out. Then the wrestling had begun in earnest again. After exhausting themselves, Daniel and Dean called the game to an end. Dean remembers the last thing he said to Daniel: 'Truce.' Finally, they could both give up the game safely, as this meant that the other person could not attack.

Dean began cooking their favourite meal – potato gems and gravy – and he brought a plate to Brad, who was still on the computer. Dean and Daniel ate lunch in Daniel's room. The phone rang, and Daniel answered it. It was his Nana, wanting to know whether Denise had a particular Franklin Mint plate with a cat on it, as she knew Denise was a keen collector of them. She had just been out to a garage sale and bought one. They chatted about the upcoming trip to Melbourne. Daniel was clearly excited. Each Sunday at 7 pm, the boys would ring their grandparents and, over the years, they never missed that phone call.

While Dean was stacking the dishwasher, Daniel had a shower. He got dressed in the same clothes he had worn the night before to the movies: his red Billabong T-shirt, long navy-blue shorts, which were fairly new, and pale-coloured Globe skate shoes. Daniel often wore red. Denise's parents, who owned a shoe shop, had given Daniel red boots when he was one year old; his motorbike boots were red; he had red jumpers and red shirts: the colour suited him. He left his two backpacks in his bedroom, one beside the bed and one in his cupboard, and decided to take his newly engraved silver fob watch with him, which he clipped onto his belt. He also took his brown suede wallet. In it was between $50 and $150, a $10 phone card, which he had bought only two weeks before from the newsagency at the Sunshine Plaza, and his school ID. Daniel passed Brad on the computer, who had his earphones on.

'So, do you want to go to the Plaza?'

'What are you gonna do again?' Brad asked.

'Get a haircut, remember? And get some Christmas presents.'

Brad hesitated. He had settled in for a day at home. 'Nah, I'll go tomorrow ...'

After stacking the dishwasher, Dean headed downstairs to the shower on the ground floor. As the water rushed over him, he couldn't help thinking of Daniel's plea and had a sudden change of heart. They were best friends. He would go with his brother to the Plaza instead of visiting his friend in Palmwoods. He wrapped a towel around his waist and headed upstairs to Daniel's bedroom. He passed Brad, who was still on the computer with his earphones on.

'Where's Daniel?'

'He's gone ...' Brad said without looking up.

With his towel still on his waist, Dean rushed to the front door and went outside, peering up the long, steep driveway, which snaked 400 metres up to the main road. Trees obscured his view; he could only see for about 200 metres. Daniel was nowhere in sight.

CHAPTER THREE

THE HIGHWAY

Highways are solitary places. They are a means to an end. On either side of the four-lane Nambour Connection Road, the vegetation is monotonous. Punctuated by occasional billboards and letterboxes from the odd farmhouse, like most highways it was never designed for pedestrians. The roadside has a pervading sense of neglect. Weeds and sometimes discarded rubbish are scattered along the verge. Hoons are known to drive past and honk their horns or yell at pedestrians, taking advantage of the anonymity of the open road.

On Sundays, the bus services are notoriously inadequate in regional Queensland. Services to the Palmwoods area, like many other regional centres, are only offered on the hour. Everyone on 'the Coast', as the Sunshine Coast is known, seems to own a car. The public-transport infrastructure had failed to keep up with a population that had almost doubled in size in the previous decade. In the next two decades, the area was predicted to be home to half a million people. In spite of state government investment, the region was not keeping up with its population growth in regard to public transport infrastructure. The rapid population boom caught the bureaucrats unawares. Instead, areas such as the Gold Coast, or, in the Far North, Cairns, frequently attracted more of the government dollar.

As well as infrequent services, there is a shortage of bus stops along the busy Nambour Connection Road. Heading south from Nambour, the boxy, Dodger-blue 1A Sunbus, with its fiery, bright-yellow smiling-sun logo, crosses the busy Bruce Highway via a roundabout above the highway before travelling east along Maroochydore Road. Some 20 minutes later, it reaches the Sunshine Plaza, at the mouth of the Maroochy River. Sunbus, which plies the metropolitan and major regional routes on the Sunshine Coast, had adopted the policy of its UK parent company, Transit Australia, of providing 'Hail and Ride' stops, rather than official bus stops. This made economic sense and avoided the infrastructure costs of erecting bus stops. Should the driver deem it safe, the bus company's policy allowed the driver to pull over when hailed by passengers. But there were never any guarantees that the bus drivers would stop.

Locals had taken to congregating at particular spots along the highway. In December 2003, the Kiel Mountain Road overpass was one of the unofficial Hail and Ride stops. The overpass carries traffic across the Nambour Connection Road from the Woombye-Palmwoods Road where motorists can join either side of the highway. It is a solid structure, with a five-and-a-half-metre clearance and a roundabout at either end to allow traffic to travel north or south. It straddles the highway on large, cement pylons and is a modern concrete monolith, memorable for its sheer size.

Supporting the overpass on the southbound side is a red-earthed embankment, where a dozen or so pine trees, all less than three metres in height, grow alongside the road, surrounded by long untidy grass. The embankment is otherwise fairly bare. Behind the embankment and across a small side road is a large car park belonging to the Christian Outreach Centre. Practising lively worship, their services include clapping and dancing and invoking the Holy Spirit.

On hot December days, the overpass offered shade for passengers as they waited for the bus. The nature strip there, with long grass that had grown rapidly with the summer rains that year, had ample space to accommodate a bus pulling its left-hand wheels off the highway. The oncoming traffic approaching from Nambour could clearly see the bus should the driver choose to pull over.

Catching a bus independently to the movies or shops or to a friend's house is an initiation into adulthood for young people living in the country, especially over the weekend. Like most teenagers living in the Palmwoods area, by the end of 2003 the Morcombe boys had begun to catch buses on their own. Dean, as the older brother, had started the ritual and the others had followed. Daniel had caught the bus around 15 times, sometimes with Bradley or Dean, sometimes alone.

Once, after the bus didn't stop for them, Daniel, Brad, Dean and a friend walked the one and a half kilometres south down the Nambour Connection Road to the Big Pineapple to buy a drink while they waited for the next one. There was an official bus stop there, and that's where Denise would drop them if she gave them a lift. And there were family rules to catching the bus. The boys had to be on the last one home from the Plaza.

* * *

Daniel had left home at around 1 pm with plenty of time to catch the 1.35 pm bus. Like the other Morcombe boys, he was always punctual. A concrete footpath runs parallel to the Woombye-Palmwoods Road on the opposite side of the road to the Morcombes' letterbox. The pathway follows the

Woombye-Palmwoods Road up to the Nambour Connection Road, exactly one kilometre from the Morcombes' house. In the other direction, the pathway runs as far as Palmwoods, three kilometres away. The path undulates slightly but without any major inclines. Tucked away from the road, it is a pleasant walk, ambling through eucalypt forests and shrubbery, and provides extensive picturesque views of the Blackall Ranges from the cleared land between the houses, which are well spaced. On the other side of the road, there is no pedestrian access. About 300 metres from the Morcombes' house, there is a concrete water tower on the crest of the first hill. Further down is a green traffic sign that shows the Bruce Highway is to the right and Woombye to the left. Then there is the Woombye State School oval and a service station, nicknamed 'Petrol Pete's' by the locals.

About ten minutes after Daniel walked out of his driveway, Peter Harth, the owner of 'Petrol Pete's', was just closing up. He saw Daniel walking past and waved to him: 'G'day.' Daniel waved back. Peter's wife, Jenny, also saw Daniel at about 1.20 pm walking along the Woombye-Palmwoods Road. Shortly after this, Daniel's former Grade 3 teacher, Janice Barringham, had been returning from the Palmwoods pool when she saw Daniel walking south of the council depot holding something in his hand. Vanessa Weier was picking up her son from the Nambour Golf Club and had noticed a boy walking along the road shortly before 1.30 pm, about a hundred metres from the water tower. On the way back, with her son in the car, she saw the same boy under the overpass two to three metres back from the road. She estimated this was just before 2 pm.

* * *

After listening to the boys chattering in the Paxtons' vines and observing them hard at work, Bruce had packed the boot of the 1997 blue Daewoo Leganza with folding chairs, picnic sets and an esky. Denise had chosen a Christmas tablecloth with matching napkins.

As Bruce waited outside the IGA in Woombye for Denise that Sunday morning, he checked his watch and saw that it was 8.48 am. Bruce and Denise had an age-old habit of checking their watches. Reliability was a key factor in their Jim's Mowing and Trees businesses.

It was about 8.52 am when they began heading south to the Bruce Highway. The trip was uneventful. They had an e-TAG on their vehicle back in the days when most people still chose to throw coins into the baskets at the tollbooths, which meant that the toll, when they reached the M1 Gateway Motorway, would be paid automatically. It also meant that their car's journey was documented by the camera on the bridge. Bruce was later to point this out to police, as well as the fact that the e-TAG registered their return. The e-TAG was mainly expedient, representing the fact that they travelled a lot for the business. None of this was important at the time, however. Their mind was on the Christmas party. Over the years, they had already held about ten Christmas parties all over South East Queensland for their Jim's Mowing franchisees. Both of them believed that all three boys were entertaining themselves at home. After all, it was only day three of the school holidays. They deserved to unwind.

* * *

Broadwater Picnic Ground, just off the Gateway Motorway in the Brisbane suburb of Mansfield, is a popular spot, especially leading up to Christmas. It has a significant wildlife corridor running through it, along the course of Bulimba Creek. The location suited most of the franchisees. The creek flowed through Wishart, where Bruce's sister, Lindy, and her husband, Andrew, lived with their two children. Two other franchisees, Ian and Nicole Wilsmith, lived only 50 minutes drive south on the Gold Coast. From the bitumen car park, just inside the gates of the park, it was a short stroll to reach the covered picnic areas with corrugated green roofs and nearby barbecues. Grass stretched out under the shade of the eucalypts and there was a children's playground.

The Morcombes arrived at almost exactly 10 am and chose the two closest picnic tables to the car park that were under cover, in case of rain. Fortunately, the showers held off throughout the day. The gathering had been planned to begin at 11 am. They both started setting up the tablecloths. Denise and Jamie, Bruce's sister's son, later went to the Red Rooster at Wishart, about a kilometre away, to get the chicken and salads. The franchisees arrived on time and the morning unfolded as parties do, with ten adults and eight or so children making plenty of use of the playground and wide open space.

When it was time to pack up, there was even chicken and cheesecake left over to take home for the boys. It was around 2.15 pm when Bruce began loading the chairs and esky into the car in the car park, which, with pre-Christmas festivities, was full. Bruce struck up a conversation with Ian Wilsmith, whose car was right next to their Daewoo, while he was still loading stuff into the boot. They had told the boys they'd be home around 4 pm, so they still had plenty of time.

About 2.30 pm, as planned, the Morcombes turned left out of the car park to head back to the motorway and home. Bruce had plans to watch the cricket on television. At about 2.45 pm, the e-TAG registered again that they were on the M1 motorway. By 3.15 pm, they were well on the way home, their route taking them on the Bruce Highway across Coochin Creek. They had crossed this creek many times before. That day, travelling at the speed limit of 110 kilometres per hour, they had no reason to note this geographical landmark. The significance was to not to hit them until many years later.

* * *

The family's Polish priest, Father Jan, a tall, large-framed man with big hands and soulful eyes, later observed what he described in the secular language as coincidences that day. On a spiritual level, he said evil was stalking Daniel. If the rain had not postponed the passionfruit picking for an hour Daniel would have gone to Brisbane with his parents; if he had left the house minutes later, Dean would have accompanied him. But Daniel's fate was sealed the closer he walked to the Hail and Ride stop under the overpass.

One witness, Delwyn Hallett, who came forward that first week said she was driving north under the overpass at around 1.35 or 1.40 pm when she saw a boy with a red T-shirt trying to cross the highway and she had swerved into the middle lane as she thought he was going to run out. Looking in her rear-view mirror she saw him cross into the median strip before losing sight of him. She had also noticed then the back of an older style car parked under the bridge on the southbound side.

Opposite the Hail and Ride spot, on the northbound side of the highway closer to Nambour, there is Caravan World, a caravan sales yard, one of the oldest caravan dealerships in Queensland. Next door to the caravan sales yard is a truck sales centre and then a sand and gravel supply yard. Further towards Nambour is the Sunshine Coast Motor Lodge. On the southbound side, there are no businesses around the overpass where the Hail and Ride stop was. Past the overpass is a feeder road for vehicles joining the Nambour Connection Road from Palmwoods.

On 7 December 2003, between 1.45 and 2.15 pm, most motorists driving under the overpass were absorbed in weekend tasks. Driving at the legal speed of 90 kilometres per hour, few of them would have captured many details of faces they saw nor be able to be specific about any activity under the overpass. But a surprising number of witnesses were alerted that day by their intuition – something was not quite right in the brief glimpse of the goings on under the Kiel Mountain Road overpass.

The police statements collected over the next few weeks documented typical Sunday journeys. One family was picking up a Christmas tree. Another parent was on an emergency dash to a pharmacy for a toddler with a temperature. Someone from a nearby parish thought he had left his Bible on the roof of his car when he drove out of the church car park after the Sunday service and was returning to the church to see if he could find it. Others were going shopping. The Sunshine Plaza was busy with the pre-Christmas rush.

Despite the confusing kaleidoscope of facts, there *were* consistencies in some of the accounts. Several people gave matching descriptions of vehicles parked on different sides of the overpass. There were specifics about people too: details of tattoos, hair colour and clothing and an unusual stance adopted by a man seen under the overpass. Several people had taken down registration numbers, concerned about the suspicious nature of what they saw. Others gave descriptions of what Daniel was wearing. But none of the versions provided immediate answers. Nor, as the years dragged by, in spite of the 80 or more witnesses, was an arrest made in what was to develop into Australia's biggest manhunt.

* * *

Ross Edmonds was nearing retirement. At 64, he had been driving buses for 40 years.

The 1A service between Nambour and Maroochydore was his second bus route for the day. He had been rostered for duty at 5.55 am.

At about 1.45 pm, only a little over an hour before knock-off time, he began driving the blue Mercedes-Benz Sunbus up the hill near the Woombye bus stop on the Nambour Connection Road heading for Maroochydore. He was about a hundred metres from the turn-off to the Woombye shopping centre, changing down through the gears for the ascent up to the Kiel Mountain Road overpass when he felt something shift – the accelerator cable had snapped. The bus immediately lost acceleration. Edmonds revved the engine a few times. He sighed, knowing right away what the problem was.

'This is as far as we go,' he told the passengers. 'There's a problem with the bus. I'll need to contact Control to bring another one ... Might take about 30 minutes.'

Edmonds checked his watch, wondering if there would even be anyone at Control. It was still before 2 pm, so there should be someone there. Using his mobile phone, he dialled the number. Jeff Norman answered. As the duty controller for Sunbus on the Sunshine Coast that day, his job was to roster and assist drivers, get timetable information and take complaints.

The passengers got off the bus, some muttering about the abrupt change of plan. One had to pick up her kids from some friends. Seventeen-year-old Fiona Theuerkauf was with her 16-year-old brother, Terry, and two other friends, Peter Murchie and Abby North. The Theuerkaufs and their friends were some of the half-dozen adolescents on the bus. Thirteen-year-old Abby and her boyfriend, Peter, had planned to see a movie that started at 2.50 pm at the Plaza. She was worried they might miss it. Fiona and Abby chose to stay on board. Peter and Terry got off to have a cigarette. Most of the passengers congregated on the nature strip on the side of the road.

Jeff Norman, a middle-aged man with white, shaggy hair and a beard, acted straightaway. He rang Stuart Rose, a younger Sunbus driver who had given up driving long-haulage trucks from Brisbane to Melbourne and got back on to driving buses. Rose was on his lunchbreak at the Caltex service station in Bli Bli. He wasn't that far away.

'There's a bus broken down,' Norman told him. 'Can you take your bus up the Woombye turn-off and pick up the stranded passengers?'

Norman then followed in a smaller shuttle bus himself to pick up Rose, once Rose had handed his bus over to Edmonds to complete the route. Norman drove north under the Kiel Mountain Road overpass at about 2.03 pm.

Edmonds had closed the ticket machine on the broken-down bus at 1.49 pm. Sitting by the side of the road, he checked his watch. It was just after 2 pm and the replacement bus still hadn't arrived. Shortly afterwards, though, he saw it coming down the hill towards him on the other side of the road. Stuart Rose parked behind the broken-down bus and the passengers were escorted to the replacement bus. Norman drove further down the hill from the Blackall Street turn-off to Woombye, did a U-turn and then pulled up behind the other two buses. He got out and walked up to Edmonds, who was still loading passengers onto the replacement bus.

'Can you please head straight back to Maroochydore and don't pick up any passengers? I'll take the bus out of service. I'll follow the route and pick up anyone who needs it,' Norman said. 'There's been enough delay already.'

Edmonds nodded.

Given the disruption to the afternoon schedule, Edmonds forgot the common practice for Sunbus drivers to insert their AES card into the reader of any new vehicle, which logged when their shift started, and started the computerised ticketing machine with their PIN and case number, which also recorded the routes they had travelled. It wasn't until he was heading down Maroochydore Road at 2.20 pm that he remembered to do so. Right now, though, he concentrated on the task at hand. Once everyone was seated, he turned the indicator on and pulled out, joining the traffic on the Nambour Connection Road.

Jeff Norman boarded the broken-down bus, pulled the keys out of the ignition and put them on the destination board above the dashboard. He had already ordered a tow truck and told the company where they would find the keys. Two minutes later, he too pulled out into the traffic on the Nambour Connection Road in the smaller shuttle bus, with Stuart Rose sitting one seat behind him on the passenger side.

As the replacement bus continued up the incline, Edmonds began to change down the gears again. He was reaching the brow of the hill when he saw a young boy wearing a red T-shirt standing on the left-hand side of the road. Police later estimated the time was 2.13 pm. Edmonds also saw a man standing four or five metres directly behind the boy beneath the overpass, somewhat obscured by the vegetation. Later, he hazarded a guess that the man would have been in his twenties or thirties. He assumed, at the time, that this was the boy's father. Edmonds knew about the Hail and Ride policy of Sunbus but also decided that the spot under the overpass was not a safe place to stop. Besides, he'd been given orders not to stop. As he got closer to the boy, he slowed down, indicating that there was another bus on the way.

Seventeen-year-old Fiona Theuerkauf was gazing out of the window of the bus when she noticed the boy, who was holding a stick in his right hand and was waving with his left hand.

'That boy's trying to wave down the bus,' she said to her brother, Terry. Fiona considered walking up the aisle to the driver in case he hadn't seen him, and then she saw him motioning to the boy with his thumb pointing backwards towards Nambour. She saw the driver talk on the radio but couldn't hear what he was saying. As the bus drove past, she looked back and saw the boy watching the bus with a 'What do I do?' look on his face.

Fiona Theuerkauf had also seen the man standing behind the boy and later remembered that he might have had a tattoo on his upper left arm. He had been leaning back on the embankment under the overpass with one leg bent and his foot on the wall. Something about the man made her feel uneasy. She, too, thought it might be the boy's dad but then realised he was too young. He looked like 'a farmer gone wrong', she told police later. The last she saw of the boy, he was looking back towards Nambour, having given up on the bus stopping.

Terry Theuerkauf, responding to his sister, had looked out of the back window and had also seen the boy holding a stick in his right hand while watching the bus. The boy was standing on the dirt just beside where the bitumen started. He also saw the man about 10 to 15 metres back from the boy, leaning with his foot up against the wall of the embankment. He also remembered that the man had a goatee beard or a moustache.

The descriptions from the bus's various passengers of both the boy and the man were uncannily similar. Some differences included the man's clothing, tattoo and the length of his hair. Most said he had a goatee and was scruffy. One said he had his arms crossed. Most confirmed that he did not appear to be waiting for the bus. So what was he doing there?

Passing the Woombye Gardens Caravan Park, just a moment later, 500 metres further on from the overpass towards Maroochydore, Ross Edmonds picked up his radio handpiece.

'There's someone at the overpass,' he radioed to Jeff Norman behind him. But the radio did not seem to be working. No one replied. Edmonds replaced the handpiece. He knew there were radio black spots along the Nambour Connection Road.

Jeff Norman *had* heard Ross Edmonds's message about the boy under the overpass. He was only a few minutes behind him, but not close enough to be seen in Edmonds' rear-view mirror. Edmonds's voice had been crackly and had broken up due to bad reception.

'Roger, Ross,' Norman said into the radio in the centre console. The shuttle bus was only about 800 metres away from the overpass and travelling at around 50 to 55 kilometres per hour. Norman picked up speed slightly as he crested the hill, but then slowed down, peering under the overpass. From about 400 metres away, he had a clear view. There was no one there.

He was no more than three minutes behind Edmonds's bus. Clearly, the person had gone.

Between Woombye and Maroochydore, there had been no further passengers waiting for the bus. Norman drove directly to the Sunshine Plaza, getting there at 2.30 pm. Edmonds had taken the replacement bus to Maroochydore and dropped off his passengers. He then drove another shuttle bus back to the depot at Marcoola, ready to knock off. Back at the depot, Jeff Norman arrived. As he was packing up, Edmonds remembered the boy.

'Did you see that young fellow at the Palmwoods turn-off? Did you pick him up?' he asked Norman.

'There was no one there,' Norman replied.

'You'll probably get a phone call from someone for not picking him up,' Edmonds said.

'Well, we'll wait and see what happens,' Norman said.

It was 3.30 pm. Edmonds was half an hour later than usual clocking off. About the same time, the phone rang at the depot. Norman answered. It was a woman. A boy, she said, had been waiting for the bus at the Woombye turn-off on the Nambour Connection Road. He was missing and hadn't been picked up.

Norman immediately rang Edmonds and asked him whether he had picked anyone up at the Woombye turn-off when the bus broke down.

'No, the only boy I know of is the one I saw under the overpass at Palmwoods. The one I radioed you about,' Edmonds said.

The identity of the caller was never discovered, even though a note was made on the police running sheet two days later to follow it up.

The computerised records for Sunbus were not checked until seven years later, after the omission was raised by Bruce and Denise.

* * *

At about 3.40 pm, Bruce turned left off the Woombye-Palmwoods Road into their driveway, parked the car under the carport and carried the esky inside, ready to unload the leftovers.

'Where is everybody?' Bruce asked Brad, noticing that neither of the other boys was home. Brad was on the computer downstairs.

'Daniel's gone to the Plaza and Dean's gone to Matt's place,' Brad said.

'Oh … Why did he go to the Plaza?' Denise asked.

'Aw, for a haircut and to get Christmas presents,' Brad said.

Denise knew her son. Once he came up with a plan, he would have stuck to it. After unpacking the car, Bruce settled downstairs to watch the cricket. It was his favourite way of unwinding. He was looking forward to the game between Pakistan and New Zealand. Kicking off his shoes, he stretched out on the floor, flicking on the television with the remote.

Denise remembered the clothes on the line that she'd pegged out that morning. Armed with the laundry basket, she went outside. It was about 4.20 pm. She was reaching to unpeg one of the boys' T-shirts when she suddenly thought of Daniel. Something wasn't right.

She finished unpegging the clothes and put them in the basket in the laundry. Then she took the car keys and said to Bruce, 'I'll just go and see if Daniel's got the four o'clock bus.' If he happened to be on the earlier one, it would save him the walk home from the bus stop.

Bruce nodded, intent on the television. Yasir Hameed was scoring well.

Denise drove down the Woombye-Palmwoods Road, turned left on the Nambour Connection Road and waited outside the Caravan World sales yard, where the bus normally stopped. She waited a few minutes, but no bus came. Still feeling strangely unsettled, she headed north along the Nambour Connection Road. It was at the Woombye turnoff at Blackall Street that she noticed a broken-down bus on the other side of the highway. It was being loaded onto a tow truck about a hundred metres from the Woombye bus stop. She turned left into Blackall Street and left again into Pine Grove Road, driving past the Woombye State School before returning home, all the way checking the roadside for signs of Daniel. Bruce was still watching the cricket when she pushed open the kitchen door.

'Daniel wasn't on that one,' she said. 'I didn't see the bus. There's a broken-down bus. Maybe the timetable's out.'

'Mmm,' Bruce said, nodding, immersed in the game.

At 5.30 pm, Bruce said he'd go and pick up Daniel. 'He must be on the five o'clock bus.'

Only a matter of ten minutes later, he had returned. 'He wasn't on the bus.'

The implication was obvious to both of them. Something was wrong. The nagging feeling that Denise experienced earlier had seeded and grown.

'What time did he leave the house, Brad?' Bruce asked.

'About one o'clock, I reckon,' Brad answered.

'Could you check the bus timetable on the computer?' Bruce asked. 'Was that definitely the last bus?'

'I think so.'

It was about 5.45 pm when they both jumped in the Daewoo and headed for the Plaza after Brad had confirmed that 5.05 pm was the last bus on the online timetable. Daniel did not have a mobile phone. Denise recalled that, two weeks beforehand, he had shown her a phone card. They both remembered that it had around $10 on it. It was unlikely he had spent that much. But he hadn't rung. Why hadn't he rung?

* * *

The evening had set in, the honeyed yellow twilight of a Queensland summer. After the harsh summer daylight sun, there was a coolness in the lengthening shadows that the eucalypts cast onto the Woombye-Palmwoods Road. There was probably a simple explanation. That much they said to each other as they drove south down the same road they had journeyed on that morning. Daniel had probably dropped his wallet, and that had his phone card in it. He hadn't been able to call. If he'd missed the last bus and lost his wallet, there would have been no way of him getting home. Of two things they were certain: Daniel would not have missed the bus intentionally and, if something were untoward, he would have telephoned if he'd been able to. Besides, the broken-down bus at Woombye could provide an answer: the scheduled service had perhaps changed.

About 20 minutes later, when they arrived at the Plaza, it had emptied of pre-Christmas shoppers. Being a Sunday, the shops had closed at 4 pm. There was a Sunbus waiting to go on another route. Denise jumped on board.

'What time was the last bus back to Nambour?' she asked.

'Five past five,' the driver answered immediately, then confirmed this by reluctantly looking at the timetable.

With no Daniel in sight, they got back into the car and drove home, again looking out for him along the way. After getting in, Denise rang Sunbus and there was no answer. So she rang Translink, another transport company, thinking they might be able to help with Sunbus timetables and asked for their help with establishing the times.

'You'll need to go back on the highway, stop one of the buses and get him to radio the depot,' the voice on the end of the phone told her in a matter-of-fact tone.

The Morcombes got back into the car and drove to Nambour, the other terminus for Sunbus 1A. At the Nambour depot, Denise again jumped on a bus that was waiting there. This time, the bus driver was unhelpful. All he would say was that the depot was closed.

With sinking hearts, and no other immediate plan in mind, they drove back home, but Daniel wasn't there. What could they do now? They both knew something was wrong and were increasingly troubled, yet trying hard to be rational.

Back at home, it was about 7 pm. Dean had returned from his friend Matt's place, getting in before dark. He had got a lift back and put his BMX bike in the back of his friend's car.

'Have you seen Daniel?' Bruce asked both Brad and Dean as soon as they saw them. Their faces said it all. The boys looked blank.

'Let's just check the sheds. He might've come back and started tinkering with his motorbike or something,' Bruce said, sounding brisk. 'And the dam – maybe for some reason he's not come in.'

Everyone left the kitchen and headed down the back of the property. They opened the door to the large old barn that Bruce had renovated. Then they checked the pump shed. No Daniel. They walked up to the letterbox, checking the driveway. At 7.10 pm, Bruce and Denise decided to return to the Sunshine Plaza bus depot, thinking that perhaps Daniel was somehow still waiting for a bus or walking home. They parked in the bus zone at the terminus. At 7.30 pm, the Sunshine Plaza was like a ghost town. They walked about a hundred metres towards the automatic doors to the Plaza, where they knew the Police Beat shopfront was. But the doors to the Plaza were closed and the usual dazzling lights turned off. They even walked past the cinemas in case Daniel had gone in there. Everything was eerily silent. They were at their wit's end and didn't know what to do.

The police will know what to do, Bruce thought. He turned to Denise: 'We're going to report him missing at the police station – at Maroochydore. It's only a hundred metres away.'

Inside the Maroochydore Police Station, all was quiet. As the senior officer on duty on 7 December 2003, Sergeant Robbie Munn was responsible for monitoring the road staff and manning the counter and phones. He was at the other side of the desk when the Morcombes came in.

'How can I help you?'

'We are looking for our son, Daniel. We don't know where he is and we're concerned for his welfare,' said Bruce.

Munn reached for some bits of paper. 'So what was your son wearing?' he asked, pen poised.

Denise and Bruce looked at each other. They didn't know. At least they were able to provide a description of him and gave details of when they had last seen him that morning, which now seemed so long ago. Then they fielded the usual questions. What was his state of mind? Was there trouble at home? Was he argumentative or suffering from depression?

'No, he's well adjusted,' Bruce said. 'He's a happy kid.'

Munn noted down their phone number and made notes from the answers they provided. Then he looked up. He had already decided that it was too early to lodge a Missing Person's Report, as the unit wasn't staffed on Sundays. 'A BOLF – that is "Be on the Lookout For" – report will be broadcast across the Sunshine Coast. If he doesn't return this evening, he will be put into the system in the morning, with official reports taken, which will mean a higher level of police involvement. Go home. If anything changes, please ring me straightaway. My change of shift is at 11 pm. I'll get someone to ring you.' Bruce and Denise distinctly remember Munn telling them to sit tight and not to worry and that Daniel would turn up in a couple of hours.

Sergeant Munn would later say that he provided details to the Sunshine Coast District Communications Centre in the same building to create the BOLF to be added to the Information Management System (IMS). He said this was created at 7.53 pm and broadcast shortly afterwards to all units on the Sunshine Coast. Munn was unable to locate the entries he said he had made on the computerised Occurrence Sheet, neither in electronic nor paper form.

Some 10 to 15 minutes later, Bruce and Denise drove slowly back home again. It was 8.15 pm.

What, they asked both boys, had Daniel been wearing? Neither Brad nor Dean had noticed what Daniel had put on after he got out of the shower. Dean sensed the rising stress levels in his parents. Being a Sunday evening, Denise's parents had rung while Bruce and Denise were at the police station. They were now aware that Daniel was missing.

Denise rang Scott Balkin, Daniel's friend who had gone to the movies with him the night before, and a few other friends. Then they did further searches – around the barn, around the dam and even walking along the Woombye-Palmwoods Road.

They felt they needed to do something. Vital minutes were slipping away. At about 9.40 pm, Bruce grabbed his car keys. 'Let's go down to the bus stop at the overpass. That's where he would've caught the bus,' he said.

Denise diverted the home phone to the mobile, as they were waiting for the phone call from the police. Bruce and Denise parked on the grassed area just near the overpass, then walked the 20 metres down, searching with a torchlight on the southbound side of the highway, towards Maroochydore, and then the northbound heading towards Nambour. Neither of them was quite sure what they were looking for. They might find a discarded bag. Perhaps Daniel had been hit by a car? Maybe he'd fallen down the embankment and broken his leg, and no one had realised? Or perhaps a snake had bitten him?

Ten minutes later, their faces picked up by the lights of the passing traffic, they both looked at each other.

'What the hell are we looking for?' Bruce asked Denise.

She shook her head, her expressive eyes so like Daniel's, worried. She hadn't wanted Bruce to ask that question.

They'd always comforted themselves that they had three boys, not girls, who they thought were more vulnerable. And they were living in the country in a safe haven.

It was just gone 10 pm when they arrived home. After all, the police officer had told them to sit tight. But their unease deepened. He did not know their son. This had never happened before – Daniel was never late.

At about 10.10 pm, the phone finally rang. It was Sergeant Munn from Maroochydore. No, Daniel had not come home, they told him, a little impatiently. Bruce told him of the private searches the family had conducted, the phone calls made to his friends and how they had searched the overpass by torchlight. These activities, Bruce said, would clearly indicate they were concerned for Daniel's welfare and that it was totally out of character for him to disappear like this. Munn told them an officer from Palmwoods would be calling them later that night as he had requested a crew to attend in a police car to get more details from them.

A few minutes before 11 pm, the phone rang again – an alarming, shrill sound that late at night. This time, it was Senior Constable Paul Campbell, an off-duty police officer from Palmwoods Police Station, again reassuring them. The officer also wanted to confirm the descriptions they had given of Daniel.

Bruce and Denise Morcombe

'I'd like you to go down to the police station at Palmwoods at eight in the morning when it opens,' he said. 'Everything will be fine. There's probably a simple explanation.'

This was the third conversation that Bruce and Denise had had with the police about their missing son, and the message was resoundingly the same: wait and see.

The police car never turned up.

CHAPTER FOUR

THE SCRUFFY MAN

As the last minutes ticked by on the worst night of the Morcombes' life, everyone sat in the lounge room looking at each other. The television, uncharacteristically, wasn't on.

'We need to rest,' Bruce said. 'We should go to bed.'

Brad did something that night that he hadn't done for years. He came into his parents' room and snuggled down beside them. It was touchingly similar to what Daniel used to do.

Nobody got any sleep. Denise spent most of the night sitting on the couch and staring out of the lounge-room windows. Several times, she went into Daniel's room but everything was as it had been the evening before. His bedspread, patterned with yachts and seagulls, lay undisturbed, piled high with four pillows. Denise was struck by the fact that, usually, Daniel hastily pulled up the bedspread without making the bed. In typical teenager fashion, it was out of sight, out of mind. But the bed was neatly made and most of his things put away in cupboards, as though he was trying to impress them both. On the end of the bed were his red boxer shorts with Asterix riding a skateboard. His small desk with a hutch for his books and a television on it was next to the window. His school shoes lay on the floor, where he had left them on the last day of school, the right shoe on the left-hand side and the left on the right, discarded in haste to escape into the holidays. Moccasin slippers with bright green and yellow pompoms, another gift from his parents' Greek odyssey, lay next to the shoes. He had left his sunglasses on top of a *Jackass* skateboarding magazine. One of his backpacks lay on the floor.

At 4 am, Denise had a shower. While it was still dark, she got into the Leganza and drove to the Nambour bus depot at the train station and then down to the Plaza and back, covering the same terrain they had covered the day before. There was no sign of Daniel, no more clues as to why he would so abruptly vanish.

At 4.40 am, Bruce was up and about. When Denise returned, he was searching the stables and sheds.

'I can't find him,' she said shaking, tears streaming down her face. 'Something's very wrong.'

Bruce tried his best to comfort her but couldn't think of what to say. 'Let's keep searching. We must find something.'

It was still more than three hours before the police station at Palmwoods would open. Both of them felt powerless against a wall of silence. Best to keep busy.

They walked up the steep driveway to the letterbox, checking the grounds as they went. Reaching the top of the drive, they looked right and left along the Woombye-Palmwoods Road, again having no clear idea what exactly they were looking for. They needed a sign that would help them somehow, but there were no signs there. The road looked the same as it always did. It was 6 am. They returned to the car, checking the grounds again.

About 6.20 am, they drove to the top of the driveway, left the car under the eucalypts on the roadside and began the walk along the edge of the road opposite the concrete footpath that Daniel would have taken to the Nambour Connection Road. Denise had again diverted the home phone to her mobile in case anyone rang. They walked all the way to the Hail and Ride stop at the overpass. There was steep bushland all around. They were still imagining an accident. Perhaps a car had clipped him and he'd fallen down one of the embankments, landed in a ditch and was hurt. Denise's mobile phone rang as they were walking. It was Keith Paxton. One of his workers hadn't turned up. He wanted to know if the boys wanted to pick passionfruit.

'We can't find Daniel. We're out looking for him,' Denise said.

'How long has he been missing?' Paxton asked.

'We've been searching everywhere and we can't seem to find him,' Denise said.

'Let us know when you find him,' Paxton said and hung up.

Paxton was fond of the boys, having known them now for three years. Daniel was always the one who could see a joke if you had a bit of a dig at him. He was more reserved than his twin, Bradley, Keith Paxton had always thought. Judy agreed that Daniel was reserved. It was rare that he would ever start a conversation, and she would usually have to make the effort to engage him in chat.

It was 6.50 am by the time Denise and Bruce got home. Denise knew in her heart things were not looking good. Soon afterwards, Denise walked into their bedroom and saw Bruce crying. Denise had never seen Bruce cry before. Bradley saw his father too. Both of them were shocked. Bruce was the one who always held everything together. His tears were clearly an admission that this might have defeated him. He had been mustering all of their courage. Now, he too was floundering.

Denise rang more of Daniel's friends, but no, none of them had seen or heard from him. She tried Sunbus again to no avail (a man answered but was not helpful), and then she rang the Nambour Hospital, but no boy matching Daniel's description had been brought in. She put the phone down, deeply disheartened. She had rung everyone she could think of.

Dean was getting ready for work, as he was on the second week of his job at the Cedar Hill Plant Nursery in Old Palmwoods Road. Denise and Bruce had both talked about whether Dean should go to work and decided that it was better than him hanging around. They would drive him there. By the time they'd dropped him off, they would finally be able to go to the police station at Palmwoods.

* * *

It was a few minutes before 8 am when the Morcombes pulled up at the Palmwoods Police Station, on Margaret Street – almost 19 hours since Daniel had left home, and 13 hours since Bruce and Denise had reported him missing. On the stroke of 8 am, Sergeant Laurie Davison arrived.

'Are you guys waiting for me?' he asked after getting out of his car.

Laurie looked to be an old-fashioned kind of cop, short and stocky, and well used to routine police work. He unlocked the front door of the station and turned off all the alarms. Then he showed them into a reception room.

'Give us a coupla' minutes,' he said.

He began flicking through the overnight reports. Then he invited them into his office.

Bruce, Denise and Bradley sat opposite him at his desk. They went through what had happened the night before.

Davison suddenly turned to Bradley, pointing at him. 'Where is he, mate?' he asked. 'C'mon. You know where he is. You're his twin. Where is Daniel?'

Bradley, already close to tears, was unprepared for this turn in the questioning. He began to cry.

'Of course you know where he is,' Davison continued unabashed. 'You're his brother. You know where he is.'

Denise and Bruce were alarmed. They knew Bradley knew no such thing and how upset he was. This was the last thing he needed.

'I'm going to make a coupla' calls,' Sergeant Davison said, abruptly giving up on that line of questioning.

Bruce and Denise sat watching him dial some numbers, having no idea who he was talking to. They both watched as his face suddenly drained of colour.

'He saw a boy in a red T-shirt under the overpass, did he?' Davison was asking.

When he replaced the receiver, he didn't illuminate who he had been talking to or what it was about. But it appeared to Bruce that he now had a sense of urgency about him. Gone was the relaxed 'Sit tight' advice that Munn and Campbell had dispensed the night before.

'Go home,' Sergeant Davison told the Morcombes. 'That's the best place to be. Try to determine what Daniel might have been wearing when he disappeared.'

Go home and do what? Denise thought. They needed to find Daniel, but leaving it to the experts seemed like sound advice. At about 8.45 am, Bruce, Denise and Brad left the police station with heavy hearts.

* * *

At 9.19 am, Sergeant Davison wrote on a job log stating that Daniel had not returned home and that the Sunshine Coast Juvenile Aid Bureau (JAB) be engaged. He then continued to make calls. One of his first was to the district officer to request assistance from the JAB, the usual team who worked with juveniles involved in crime and missing children. He spoke to Senior Constable Sharon Tebbutt, who was with the JAB, telling her that Daniel had been reported missing, where he was last seen and that he had been on his way to the Sunshine Plaza to get his hair cut. Possibly, he said, the salon was Just Cuts. Davison also asked Tebbutt to speak to Jeff Norman. Norman provided Ross Edmonds's number. Edmonds later received four phone calls from the police.

Later, Bruce and Denise surmised that Davison had been ringing Sunbus when they were in his office and had spoken to Edmonds, who had told him that there was a scruffy man with Daniel at the bus stop. They believed it was that which had changed his demeanour.

More than 19 hours after Daniel was last seen, at 9.44 am, the police finally realised the urgency of the situation. Davison filed a Missing Person Report via the Queensland Police Service computer. At 11.18 am, Sergeant Davison filed a Significant Event Message. A further BOLF was broadcast at 11.23 am. Daniel's disappearance was finally being broadcast to the outside world.

Davison typed into the job log new information that had come from the morning's calls: a 'scruffy' or 'shadowy' man had been observed standing behind the boy as he waited for the bus.

Tebbutt began chasing other leads and rang Daniel's friends. She rang Scott Balkin's and Tom Palmer's houses but there was no answer. Then she rang Sean Higgins, who had been at the movies on Saturday night with Daniel, and then Sam Murray and Mitchell Duffy. Constable Tebbutt was told that Denise had already contacted them all the night before.

At 10.30 am, Tebbutt and another police officer, Detective Sergeant Ray Hoelscher, visited the Morcombes' house. They were looking for a mobile phone that had once belonged to Denise's father and may have been given to Daniel, as Bruce and Denise had told police that they thought it might be possible Daniel had it with him. Bradley ended up finding the phone still in a box in a cupboard in his room.

Sergeant Davison also dropped in on the Morcombes seeking a recent photograph of Daniel. Denise grabbed a photo of him that was in the kitchen. Daniel's face stared back at her, smiling. He was holding up a glass of orange cordial. Bradley was in the background out of focus. Denise felt a stab of pain looking at her son. Her hand was shaking when she passed the photo to Davison. She was remembering that Daniel had just eaten a bellyful of lasagne, his favourite food, when the photo was taken. He seemed so alive and well.

Davison turned again to Brad. 'You know where he is, don't you? Tell us,' he said aggressively.

Brad, still shaken from what had happened that morning, became upset again. It may have been old-style policing, using confrontation to get answers, but Davison's manner shook the Morcombes to the core. This man didn't know their family. He was making assumptions. From the start, Bruce and Denise had looked to the police for answers. So far, it had been an uphill battle.

The morning was a roller-coaster of emotions. One phone call to the house was to tell them that an investment property they had bought in the nearby suburb of Buderim had settled. It was news they had been waiting for but was now the last thing they wanted to hear about. For days, they did not even bother going to pick up the key. Life on the outside went on as usual. The traffic still hummed along the Woombye-Palmwoods Road as everyone embraced the usual Monday-morning chores. Bruce organised for someone else to instruct prospective franchisees during a three-day training course that had been scheduled that week for Jim's franchisees.

Later that day, Denise found Daniel's gold chain on Bruce's side of the bed. Denise was puzzled. Why had Daniel taken it off? For a fleeting moment, they thought maybe Daniel had run away, but then sense prevailed. He was a happy kid, he was going off to buy Christmas presents for his family. After Bruce and Denise picked Dean up from work that evening, he explained how Daniel had taken it off to wrestle on the bed. Back then, everything had been normal. Now, everything had turned upside down. Their life had stopped. Bruce went outside and began mowing the grass, trying to keep his mind off things. Later, Denise went upstairs to lie on their bed. Bruce appeared with chicken soup he had made, not out of a tin but real soup.

'You'd better have something,' he said. 'It's going to be a long few days.'

* * *

At noon, Laurie Davison drove down to the overpass. He had been assigned to guard the area and to await the attendance of an officer from the JAB. Senior Constable Peter Drew began photographing the area before he commenced a search. He noted no signs of a violent struggle but did find shattered glass and several shoe imprints. Other police officers joined them, including a sergeant in charge of Sunshine Coast crime scenes. The barrier along the pedestrian access across the overpass was tested for fingerprints but nothing was found. Plaster casts were made of the shoe imprints and dispatched for brand identification. One of the prints was subsequently found to be from a Globe Occy Mark 4 shoe. That day Denise handed the police a shoe box from Daniel's bedroom. It was for a pair of Globe Occy Mark 4 shoes.

Tebbutt and Hoelscher contacted the Missing Persons Unit in Brisbane and requested that Daniel's Commonwealth Bank account be checked for any recent transactions. Up to 1.45 pm that day, there had been no transactions on the account. Further checks were organised for two days later. Police were also told that Daniel used a Hotmail account. Constable Tebbutt arranged for colour photocopies to be made of Daniel's photograph, unaware that this particular image of Daniel holding up the orange cordial was to become known across the land.

* * *

At 12.45 pm, Ross Edmonds was interviewed. He told Constable Tebbutt about the bus breaking down and the man he had seen near Daniel. Jeff Norman also confirmed that neither the boy nor the man had been there when he drove past. Other Sunbus drivers were interviewed but they had seen nothing noteworthy. At 1.50 pm, Constable Tebbutt attended the Morcombes' house to update them on the status of the investigation. Another two police officers had visited the hairdressers Just Cuts in the Sunshine Plaza. Later, Daniel's photograph had been shown to one of the hairdressers, who remembered a boy coming in for his haircut the previous afternoon with his mother. But the hairdresser could not commit either way as to whether it was the same boy as in the photo.

At 2 pm, almost 24 hours after Daniel had gone missing, the recent photograph of Daniel, along with a profile and running sheet, was sent to the Missing Persons Unit. The words read:

> Daniel left his home at Palmwoods (approximately 1 km
> from the Kiels Mountain R[oa]d overpass as pictured
> below) to catch a Sunbus to the Sunshine Plaza ...

In a few short paragraphs, Daniel's disappearance was typed up. The report described him as 169 centimetres (a mistake; he was just 150 centimetres), proportionate build, fair complexion, blue eyes and dark-brown hair, and further described him as very pretty. Concerns were had for his safety as he was 'not streetwise'. Further down, police had added:

An older male person was seen at the bus stop whilst Daniel was waiting. A short time later neither persons were at the bus stop. Daniel has not been seen since. The male has been described as of scruffy appearance, brown unkept [*sic*] hair, partial facial growth or goatee. Tanned weather-beaten complexion and appearance. Sunken cheeks. Aged 30s–40s.

As the afternoon wore on, further interviews were conducted. At 2.15 pm, Peter Harth, the owner of Petrol Pete's, was interviewed and identified Daniel from a photograph as the same boy he'd seen the previous day heading towards the Nambour Connection Road. All of Daniel's friends had been tracked down except Tom Palmer, whose phone wasn't answering. They verified that there were no problems at home. Daniel was an ordinary boy. Police officers were dispatched to other hair salons nearby, showing Daniel's photograph to hairdressers. None of them recognised him. Other police officers attended the Plaza to get a photo of the sole of the shoes Daniel was believed to be wearing. Other checks were made. There was no record of Daniel in the Department of Family Services or on the Child Protection Register.

* * *

Pedestrians are easily identifiable on the highway against the neutral hues of the Australian bush and the charcoal grey of the bitumen, especially if they are wearing bright colours. Many people had seen the boy in the red T-shirt that day. Seventeen-year-old Jessiah Cocks was with his mother, Christine, in her white Ford Laser hatch when he saw a person matching Daniel's description at about 1.50 pm that Sunday. He and his mother had pulled into McDonald's for lunch and were travelling north on the Nambour Connection

Road towards Woombye when he saw, on the other side of the road, a boy in a red T-shirt and shorts climbing down the red dirt embankment under the overpass. The boy was on his haunches facing the road towards the bottom part of the embankment.

'What's that boy doing on the side of the road?' Jessiah had asked his mother.

'Where?' his mother asked, but she was concentrating on the traffic and did not see anyone.

Jessiah also noticed a white four-wheel-drive vehicle about a hundred metres on from the overpass, opposite the Caravan World sales yard. It was facing south and had all of its doors shut and there was no one in the vehicle. Later, when questioned further, he said he thought it was an early '90s model four-wheel drive and that it may have had a distinctive white air filter.

Many of the passing motorists, like the bus passengers, also reported seeing a 'scruffy man' standing behind or near the boy under the overpass. Andrew Jackson, a 45-year-old single parent, described the man as having an old-fashioned type of haircut and being dressed like someone from a bygone era, reminiscent of how the *Austin Powers* cast was dressed as though from the '70s.

Wendy Burnett had noticed the man and the boy when driving past in a silver Ford Focus sedan with her husband, Robert Burnett, who was a minister of a nearby church. It was a few minutes either side of 2 pm, Wendy recollected, when her attention had been caught by the child in the brightly coloured T-shirt. But it was not the boy who held her attention; it was the man. His clothes appeared to hang off him. He had the same kind of stance, she thought, as the male actor dressed in a cream suit in the poster for *The Usual Suspects*. His eyes were deep set. He could have been in his 50s, but more than likely, she mused, he was younger and had had a rough life. His clothes were dark coloured and he probably wore a long shirt and long pants with the shirt hanging out. Like many others, she toyed with the idea that they were father and son, but there were too many differences. The man was probably, she later decided, one of those types who lived at the nearby caravan park.

But it was the people on the 1A bus – which, according to the bus driver, slowed momentarily as it passed the young boy in the red T-shirt and navy-blue cargo pants – who had the most time to take in what they saw.

Apart from beginning to talk to witnesses, police also visited businesses on the Nambour Connection Road that day. Caravan World was not open on Sunday, so there was nobody there. Drivers from Coastland Coaches were interviewed. One had seen the boy wearing the red T-shirt at around 2.10 pm. None shed any light on where he might have gone.

* * *

Detective Senior Sergeant Paul Schmidt was in charge of the Sunshine Coast Criminal Investigation Branch (CIB). His role was to look after and coordinate any adult crime investigations in the region, with the exception of offences committed against children. In those cases, the JAB (later to become the Child Protection Investigation Unit), was involved. While Schmidt was aware that there was a 13-year-old child missing, it was not until 2.20 pm that he was asked by District Inspector Limbach to overview the investigation and to provide assistance when necessary. Schmidt was briefed by Tebbutt and Hoelscher. He noted that the Information Management System (IMS) Incident Details had been completed and that JAB had been involved since 9.19 am that morning.

Doorknocks were made at 4.30 pm along Kiel Mountain Road, Woombye-Palmwoods Road and Atkinsons Road, where the Paxtons lived. The Paxtons said they were unaware Daniel had been going anywhere after he'd finished passionfruit picking the previous morning. They confirmed the boys had been paid that Sunday for work that week. One doorknock revealed a break-in on Atkinsons Road, where a number of items, including clothing, had been stolen. Around the same time, Tebbutt and another officer called in on the Christian Outreach Centre and the Big Pineapple armed with Daniel's photograph.

At 5.30 pm, Brad, Dean, Denise and Bruce drove to Maroochydore Police Station to make their official statements. They had been asked to come earlier but they had explained that Dean didn't finish work until 4 pm. While he was at work that morning, Dean had heard his brother being reported missing on a news story on the radio. That was when it suddenly hit him. His brother had made the daily news bulletins. Daniel was gone. His friends heard it too, and they immediately went to the Sunshine Plaza and nearby bushland to search for him. Up until then, Dean wanted to believe that Daniel was somehow staying with friends. Now it was on the radio, it suddenly seemed so much more real. Only the weekend before, Daniel had bought him a Crusty Demons DVD, featuring daredevil jumps and tricks by the group of freestyle motorcyclists. Dean began sending messages out on MySpace. He wanted his friends to look for Daniel.

All four Morcombes were interviewed separately. As they waited to be called for their interviews, Denise's phone started ringing. There had been a piece about Daniel on the television news. Concerned friends wanted to know what was going on.

* * *

Detective Senior Sergeant Greg Daniels was supposed to be on a day off that Monday. Daniels was president of the Parents and Friends Association (P&F) at Siena Catholic College – his children attended the same school as the Morcombe boys.

He also acted as a liaison between the school and the police. Daniels had a background in juvenile crime and was in charge of that unit from 1998 to 2006. He had also done a stint as a police prosecutor in Kingaroy. After his prosecuting years, Daniels had been transferred to Kawana Waters on the Sunshine Coast as a sergeant overseeing a brand-new police station. It was then that he began the liaison role with Siena Catholic College and had been promoted to plain clothes and detective duties with the JAB.

Daniels had heard about a report of a missing person while he was at a family barbecue at home. He had a couple of briefings from staff on the phone. Then the phone rang again. He decided this time that he should call into the station, even though he was meant to be on holiday. The job of a missing boy was usually one for uniform police but Daniels decided he would go in and advise on the situation.

'There's a missing boy,' he told his wife, who was cleaning up after the barbecue. 'I might have to go in.'

One of his children appeared in the kitchen. 'Are you looking for Daniel Morcombe?'

Daniels was surprised how fast the news had travelled.

'Yeah, it's on MySpace,' his son said.

That brought home immediately how close the case was to his own family. Daniels's children were in Grades 8, 9 and 10 at Siena College. As he headed for his car to drive to the Maroochydore Police Station, the years he had spent in the force kicked in. He had honed an ability to push 'stuff into the space it deserved'. Right now, he had to concentrate on finding a missing boy.

He was not prepared, however, for the look on Denise Morcombe's face when he turned up at the police station. The haunted expression, the terror in her eyes as she sat waiting to give her statement, would stay with him for a long time. Senior Constable Tebbutt in plain clothes interviewed Bradley, and Detective Sergeant Ray Hoelscher interviewed

Dean. Tebbutt decided further enquiries needed to be made into the internet chat rooms that Daniel had accessed on the computer at home. It was decided to send the hard drive to Brisbane for analysis.

When it was Bruce's turn to make a statement, he emphasised how much this was out of character for Daniel and that, as a father, he was 'greatly concerned'. He said the family had conducted their own searches and that he and Denise had been to the police on 'multiple occasions'. Deep down he knew the situation was looking grim, and he was extremely worried about the lack of progress.

At 8.45 pm, Denise's interview finished. She had also told police that Daniel's disappearance was 'very out of character'. Bruce and the boys drove home in their car and Denise followed in a police car driven by a female police officer.

'I've never been in a police car before,' Denise remarked.

'You're going to see a lot more police in the days ahead,' the officer answered.

Denise was shocked by the reply. The words confirmed her worst fears. She knew they were facing a terrible outcome.

At 10.15 pm, Constable Henricksen arrived to take possession of the two computers in the house for examination. They were taken back to the Maroochydore Police Station. The Morcombes felt they were under siege. Their house and their possessions were suddenly not their own any more. And worse than anything else, their son was missing.

CHAPTER FIVE

MAKING A PRAYER

Waking from a broken sleep in the early hours of Tuesday 9 December 2003, Bruce and Denise resumed their living nightmare. Daniel had now been missing for almost two days. Their pain was like an arrow lodged in their hearts. There was never a moment when they stopped thinking about Daniel; everything seemed to remind them of him. Suddenly, the home that had been their haven was a living reminder of what had been and what they wanted it to be again. Daniel's bedroom door remained firmly closed, waiting for him to return.

At 6.55 am, a helicopter took to the skies above their house, flying above the Woombye-Palmwoods Road and the Nambour Connection Road. It searched both sides of the road in wide sweeping arcs. A search was also conducted on foot. Water Police were contacted to begin coordinating a search of nearby dams and rivers.

Doorknocks that day flushed out more people who had seen Daniel walking along Woombye-Palmwoods Road near Petrol Pete's on Sunday. Many people had noticed the boy in the red T-shirt. His small stature and clothing stood out like a beacon to Sunday passers-by. Yet more people came forward to say they had seen Daniel under the overpass at around 2 pm, one woman remembering that he had been crouched at the top of the embankment.

Scenarios played through Bruce and Denise's heads like a movie on a constant loop. In the past day and a half, they had sought comfort from each other, trying desperately to make sense of what had happened. They would bolster each other with normal explanations for Daniel's sudden disappearance. But, at the same time, the truth stared down at them. This was wholly uncharacteristic of Daniel. But perhaps he was lying somewhere injured, unable to get help?

The possibility that something sinister had happened now seemed far more likely. The thought was far too hard to contemplate, but they were both now convinced that it might be the only answer. Maybe he had been taken against his will somewhere. What if he wasn't even in the country? What if someone dangerous had offered him a lift? If he had missed the bus, *would* he have got into a car that was passing along the highway?

They both agreed that was not likely. Daniel was their most shy child and not prone to starting conversations with his friends and family, never mind talking to strangers. They could not imagine him getting into a car with a stranger. But what if that person was known to him? What if Daniel had been offered a lift from someone he knew? The thought niggled away at them, and conversations between them changed from finding plausible reasons for his disappearance to making uneasy appraisals of people they knew.

Denise, who had been seeking solace in prayer, was relieved when her friend Debbie Morgan turned up to drive her to St Joseph's Church in Nambour. She stood outside the church, unsure of exactly why she had come but looking for comfort, and asking for guidance.

* * *

Maroochydore Police Headquarters on Cornmeal Parade
is a modern two-storey building, an easy walk from the
Sunshine Plaza. Early on the Tuesday morning, a decision
was made for the CIB to take over operational control of
the investigation. A major incident room (MIR) was to be
set up at Maroochydore. Senior Detective Paul Schmidt
as Officer in Charge was coordinating the investigative
strategies along with senior investigators, and would use this
room to organise operational strategies and intelligence to
concentrate solely on looking for Daniel. Detectives from
the State Crime Operations Homicide Investigation Unit
in Brisbane were sent northwards to assist. One of these was
Detective Sergeant Dave Wilkinson, whose claim to good
detective work involved solving an extortion bid against a
pharmaceutical company. Wilkinson would be put in charge
of the MIR.

Altogether, four officers from the Homicide Investigation
Unit – a detective sergeant and three other senior investigators –
were to remain assigned to the case for a further 18 months.
These four were delegated to the electronic management of
information which included job logs and running sheets. All
information coming into the MIR was placed on a job log
and the job log was then assigned to an officer to investigate.
The officer would electronically record the results from the
investigation and return it to the MIR where it would be
read. One detective sergeant – Tracey Barnes – was appointed
to 'read' all of the information coming in to ensure quality
control. The job of the reader was vital. Even though the cases
were discussed in the MIR room, the reader decided whether
a new job needed to be created, or whether an original job
log needed further investigation. A full-time administrative
person was assigned for clerical duties. There were arrest
teams, investigating teams, exhibit officers, doorknock

coordinators and intelligence officers. Crime scene managers and scientific officers were called upon when needed.

Each day staff would participate in a formal briefing, where information would be shared within the group. A similar briefing would be held at the end of the day. The task force, called Operation Bravo Vista, or Operation Vista for short, was hoping to use a new system called the Investigation Management and Control System (IMAC), recently adopted by the Queensland Police Service to manage major incidents. This system analysed vast datasets, meaning police could drill down to a smaller number of suspects using that data, which was especially useful when dealing with a large amount of information. It also allowed them to send electronic job logs interstate. Early on, police were beginning to realise how much data would have to be sifted through given the public response. However, the IMAC was still quite new. Little did they know then that the investigation they were logging was to become the largest manhunt in Australia.

That morning in Brisbane, Detective Inspector Mike Condon, a sharply dressed, quiet man who carried an air of a person going places, was first briefed by the North Coast Regional Crime Coordinator, Detective Inspector John Maloney, about the investigation. Condon's job, as operations manager of the Homicide Investigation Unit, was to assess command resources for the case. He oversaw around 55 homicide-related offences a year. He arrived at the MIR that morning having no idea that the case of the missing boy in regional Sunshine Coast would play such a major part in his career.

* * *

Detective Senior Sergeant Greg Daniels had a Child Abuse Unit to run. That was his first and foremost duty. It was an extremely busy unit. Quite simply, he didn't want anyone to fall through the cracks. After meeting the Morcombes the previous day, he decided he had to divide his time up between the missing boy, whose case had already been identified as 'a major crime', and his usual role. If things were as dire as police believed, given the boy's continued absence, they could find his body at any moment. Somebody should be with the parents.

Daniels was also in charge of school-based police officers. While he pondered the increased workload, he remembered one such officer called Senior Constable Samantha Knight, who was married to another police officer and whose kids were in the local surf club. A male and female police officer on the Morcombe case would be beneficial in establishing a rapport with the family. Daniels decided that he would take on the senior liaison officer role with the Morcombes and that Knight would report to him as the other liaison officer.

Senior Constable Knight walked into the newly set up MIR of the Maroochydore Police Headquarters that morning in her uniform expecting to go and visit another high school. Sam had pale-blue eyes, short, blonde, layered hair and a kind, open face. She looked more like a country cop, and had a friendly smile. She usually wore navy shorts, owing to the Queensland heat, and was committed to her job.

Instead of a high school visit, she was asked to go to a debriefing with Sergeant Schmidt about a child who had gone missing. A picture of Daniel was up on the wall. There was something about his eyes and his smile that was so innocent it made her stop and look. This could just as easily be her child on a poster. She had a daughter who was the same age. Sam felt an immediate connection – unusual in her job, where she met so many people from all walks of life confronting traumatic situations. How would she feel if her son went missing? Sam heard that Daniel was a twin as she was told all the known details of his disappearance. After the debrief, Greg Daniels and Paul Schmidt told her she had been assigned to looking after the Morcombes as family liaison officer.

So it was that both she and Greg Daniels found themselves out the front of the Morcombes' Palmwoods home on Tuesday morning, shortly before 10 am. Sitting in the car at the top of the Morcombes' driveway, Sergeant Daniels addressed Sam: 'I hope you realise what you're getting yourself into here.' He knew instinctively that he was looking at longevity in this case. There was no point in establishing a relationship with the family and then working elsewhere, he said. This kind of case was for the long haul. He was trusting that she was up to the job. Besides, he knew from years of being involved with child abuse that victims often knew their offenders. Liaising with the family with eyes and ears open was essential. He had to be able to rely on her.

Senior Constable Knight assured him that she was up to the task. She had a calmness about her that was comforting, and empathy as well.

They knocked at the Morcombes' front door and were ushered inside. In the kitchen, sitting at the dining table, Daniels explained to Bruce and Denise that their job was to mediate between the family and police. There were 20 to 30 police officers already assigned to the case, and this would mean Bruce and Denise would not be continually asked to respond to minor questions. 'That can get tiresome, although well meant, so I will be here to help,' Senior Constable Knight reassured them.

Daniels was ever alert to information he might glean from the family that could add to the investigation. He asked a lot of questions. His role at Siena Catholic College gave him plenty to talk about. Although their children were at the same school, he had not met the Morcombes before.

'While, of course, we can't force you to do anything, if you are working with us – talking to the media, for example, that would be extremely helpful,' Daniels said in his forthright way. 'You could use the expertise of the police media as they'd be across certain strategies for the whole investigation and may be able to help give important leads out that police want followed.'

In spite of Sam Knight's friendly demeanour, it took Denise some time before she could bring herself to take her into Daniel's bedroom. Denise felt that Daniel's belongings would be disturbed. What would Knight find in his room? What did the police want? These questions were almost irrelevant. Inside, Senior Constable Knight could sense and smell the teenager, connecting this room to the boy she had seen in the photograph. She took note of everything, using her observational police skills: the yellow walls, the single bed with the yacht bedspread, the pine chest of drawers and bedside table, and the television on top of the chest of drawers. A computer, used for games and not connected to the internet, sat on a desk with a hutch and there was a bedside lamp above his bed. She began searching the room, including magazines, his diary and schoolbooks. It was to be the first encounter of many with some of the facts of the missing boy. She also went through his schoolbag and found some old sandwiches in his lunchbox and a Christmas card. Denise had already found a note in Daniel's handwriting in his bedroom. It was headed 'Coolum Motocross Club' and had the name, phone number and email of the secretary on a piece of paper. The sentence below read, 'Ask if a family membership covers for a senior and a junior.' Denise also found an application form to join the club, where Daniel had clearly wanted to start racing. They hadn't taken him there and it would have been such a simple thing to do. Now it might be too late.

Downstairs, Knight began making phone calls. Then she gathered up the mail that had arrived that Denise and Bruce had not touched. Daniel's report card from school was inside one of the unopened letters. Denise opened it with trembling fingers. The twins had wanted her to drive to Siena Catholic College on the Friday afternoon before Daniel went missing to collect their report cards. But, because there was such a downpour, they had decided not to go to the school. Daniel, she discovered, had got an A for Maths. Not getting this good news sooner was yet another regret to pile upon regret.

That day it became clear that Knight was there to stay, unlike the other police officers, who came and went. She strolled around the garden taking everything in but trying not to be too obtrusive. Bruce found her there one morning under the poinciana tree.

'Why didn't he stop?' Bruce had tears in his eyes.

'Who?'

'The bus driver.'

Knight did her best to reassure Bruce. The bus drivers were being interviewed and they might know more soon.

'We will need to search the dams,' she said, choosing her words carefully. 'I have to ask you – as there will be police divers involved – are there likely to be any chemicals in the dams?'

Bruce looked at her, shocked. The question clearly suggested that Daniel might not be alive. The thought was too hard for either him or Denise to contemplate.

'I mean ... we need to know the quality of the water. How deep it is ... that kind of thing?' Sam Knight prodded gently.

Bruce nodded, appreciating, even in his pain, the need for the questions, but he was deeply upset. Knight knew that Bruce and Denise were slowly confronting the fact that they might not see Daniel again. But she also knew that everything would take time. For now, they had to do everything they could to find him. By the end of the day, she was convinced that she could wholly depend on his parents to help in this task.

* * *

At 11.30 am on Tuesday 9 December, Ross Edmonds – one of the last people to see Daniel alive – was one of the first people to be officially interviewed. He told police he had been ordered not to pick up passengers. Police conducted further searches of Sunbus logs and worked out an estimate of the time he would have seen Daniel after checking the time he had logged on at the Maroochydore Road roundabout and then calculating the distance between the two.

Police also spoke to groups of young people at skate parks and the Sunshine Plaza, but no one recognised the photo of Daniel. Greg Daniels asked Denise about her and Bruce's movements on the Sunday, quizzing her about what time she had rung Sunbus. She confirmed what she had said in her statement – it was that evening at about 6 pm. Daniels had thought it was peculiar that Jeff Norman was adamant that a woman had rung at around 3.30 pm reporting a child missing from the Woombye bus stop the day Daniel disappeared. He made a note that 'verification' was needed on this. Police also attended the Sunbus depot at Marcoola and obtained a list of the 80 people who were employed as Sunbus drivers.

Police also doorknocked the Woombye Gardens Caravan Park which was about 500 metres from the Hail and Ride stop. There were 55 caravan sites and motel rooms at the park and many itinerant residents. Police identified several POIs – police speak for 'persons of interest' to the case. Those who refused to give DNA were noted on a spreadsheet.

Many callers contacted Crime Stoppers or came into the Maroochydore Police Station or their local police station where their reports were then relayed via email to the MIR. Most reports were conflicting. Some had better evidence of the time than others. One of the first witnesses, Chloe Fooks, said she saw Daniel when she was on her way to buy petrol at the BP service station in Forest Glen just off the

Bruce Highway. The receipt showed she had been there at 2.14 pm.

Barry Kelsey was reading the *Sunshine Coast Daily* that Tuesday morning. With a jolt, he recognised the face which featured in a column inside the newspaper about a missing boy. Kelsey had been driving south on the Nambour Connection Road the previous Sunday having left Nambour around 2 pm and had seen the same boy in a red T-shirt and dark, knee-length board shorts standing near the overpass. He had also seen a man about five metres away from the boy, walking slowly towards him. He estimated later that the man was in his early thirties with an average to lean build and shoulder-length hair. He thought he was wearing a checked shirt, similar to a flannelette shirt, and looked 'a bit rough', and he remembered thinking that the two did not appear to be related. He contacted the police immediately to tell them what he had seen. Later, on 11 December, he provided the first of his statements. He had also remembered seeing a car parked outside a nursery just south of the overpass. It was dark blue, but faded, and was a sedan and a late '70s or early '80s model.

* * *

Almost overnight, Bruce and Denise had entered a dark, unknown world they knew nothing about. Anybody could be a suspect. For Daniel's sake, they tried to conserve their strength, but nothing seemed to be working. They were always thinking of anyone or anything that might help. The drive along the Woombye-Palmwoods Road, once a haven of rolling hills and grazing cattle, was now the scene of a nightmare. They were always looking for signs of their missing son.

Driving back along the Nambour Connection Road was worse. Approaching the overpass, they would gaze at the forlorn place under the pylons where Daniel had last been seen, trying to reconstruct snippets of what they had been told by police that other drivers had seen. But much of the progress of the police investigation was kept from them. The breakthrough they were waiting for had not happened. They would jump when the phone rang at the house or rush to answer the door to detectives, hoping against hope that they might have some news. But the words to end their agony never came.

All the while, police officers came and went. It seemed that their main purpose had shifted. What Sergeant Davison had heard on the phone when they were in his office had galvanised the force into action. No longer were they being told to go home and that Daniel would probably turn up. Instead, searches were underway, helicopters were overhead. Officers spoke about running sheets and police logs, and police were being dispatched everywhere to follow up leads. The Morcombes were continually being asked questions. Detective Ray Hoelscher asked Bruce and Denise what plans Daniel had made with his parents if he ever missed the bus on the Nambour Connection Road. They told him that the boys would walk to the Big Pineapple, about one and a half kilometres south along the highway. Bradley told the detective that, five months previously, he and Daniel had flagged the bus but it hadn't stopped, so they had done just this, buying a soft drink before waiting for the next bus.

At 1.20 pm on the Tuesday, Denise's parents, Kevin and Monique Beavis, arrived at Maroochydore Airport. Bruce went to pick them up and drove them sorrowfully home. Denise had opened up the sliding doors early that afternoon. Her parents were standing on the verandah, not with their usual happy smiles but full of concern. Denise felt that she had let her parents down. She hadn't looked after Daniel as a mother should, sensing that something had happened to him. Her guilt was consuming. Denise and Monique spent the afternoon looking at family photo albums, but they only brought tears, not happy memories.

* * *

Daniel's Commonwealth Bank account had still not been accessed since the previous Friday. Senior Constable Sharon Tebbutt contacted Kmart and Target for their security tapes. Satellite maps were obtained from the Maroochy Shire Council. Surrounding properties were superimposed onto the maps. Police also visited the Christian Outreach Centre. The last service had concluded at 12.30 pm on Sunday and the church had been locked somewhere between 1 and 1.15 pm on the day Daniel went missing.

The most obvious line for Operation Vista was to scrutinise known sex offenders in the area, particularly the male sex offenders who had committed offences against male children. Those with links to the Christian Outreach Centre were also interviewed, because of its proximity to the alleged abduction scene. Police searched the car of one known child sex offender who attended the church but found nothing suspicious. It was later confirmed that he had been at the Nambour swimming pool at around the time Daniel went missing.

By 4.10 pm, Senior Constable Knight filed a report for the police log. She had confirmed that the fob watch Daniel had recently bought was missing. The Morcombes gave her the receipt.

* * *

The Stella Maris Catholic Church in Baden Powell Street, Maroochydore, is just north of the Sunshine Plaza. It is the mother church of the Suncoast parish. Greg Daniels had stepped out of his role of police officer into his other role as parishioner of the church.

Devout Catholics, Denise's parents had been asking whether there was somewhere they could say some prayers. Daniels knew they were seeking strength from their Catholic faith and how vital this was, particularly if this journey ended in a worst-case scenario. It was something constructive that he could offer. While he was able to provide policing support, he clearly needed someone else to provide spiritual support at this time of crisis. Besides, the police officer in him knew that the wellbeing of the whole family was essential in helping the police investigation. 'Would you be interested in visiting a priest?' Daniels had asked them.

Daniels and Knight took two cars and drove Denise and Bruce, Dean and Brad, and Kevin and Monique to the Stella Maris Catholic Church.

At around 6 pm that night, parish priest Father Jan Bialasiewicz and the other priests were in the presbytery eating dinner around the table and enjoying a glass of wine. Father Jan heard a knocking at the window. He at first thought that it was probably someone seeking money. But, when he opened the door, he saw Sergeant Greg Daniels.

'There are some people here who are in the parish who would like to see a priest. They have lost their son. We know very little about his whereabouts and they have no one to turn to.'

Behind Daniels, Father Jan could just make out the small group assembled in the falling light. Greg spoke briefly, filling Father Jan in on the events of the past few days.

Father Jan immediately thought of the little chapel that adjoined the church. 'Let's go and make a prayer,' he said, gesturing to the chapel.

As they went next door, he reflected on how he might conduct the gathering. His immediate thoughts were that he did not want to give false hope to the parents and their family, or come up with the kind of meaningless, gratuitous phrases that they had probably already heard from others. People would often react that way when they felt uncomfortable dealing with a catastrophic turn of events. In his native Poland, if there was a heavy storm, they lit candles in the window to drive away evil spirits and to act as a beacon for those who were lost so that they knew there was shelter. The light was to give people direction. Father Jan firmly believed that light was stronger than darkness. A big part of his mission had been to dedicate himself to steering his parish towards the light.

He turned the key in the chapel door, breathed deeply and led the family inside. He would put his trust in God. 'Let us pray,' he said.

Bruce was immediately drawn to the priest's honesty and compassion. As quiet descended, everyone was left to their own thoughts.

Bruce Morcombe was a man who always kept his promises. It was a mark of pride for him. That night, he pledged a promise to Daniel. Whoever had taken their son had picked on the wrong family, and he would never give up the search to find him and to bring that person or persons to justice. It was a sentiment that he was to echo through the ensuing years. The serenity of the chapel helped him to formulate this stance. Nothing would stop his resolve – ever – to find out who had been responsible for taking his son, and that night he decided that would be so.

For Denise, the chapel provided solace. Even though none of the pain shifted, she felt some peace. With strongly Catholic parents, she had grown up being taught to turn to God for help when needed. For the extended family that night, the chapel was a place to face their fear and grief, if only momentarily. Almost an hour after they arrived, the Morcombes shook hands with Father Jan and thanked him. Greg and Sam drove them all home. Day three had drawn to a close.

CHAPTER SIX

'WE WANT DANIEL BACK'

When the Morcombes greeted Wednesday, nothing had changed. Nana and Pa, who would usually be spending holidays with the boys, were sleeping in Dean's room, and Dean was on the couch. Normal life had been turned upside down. It was a waiting game for everyone. Every lead seemed to be a dead end. Daniel's room remained untouched and the door shut, apart from Sam Knight's visits.

That morning, Sergeant Julie Elliott had been planning a trip north from the Brisbane Media Unit to conduct a media-training session for the local Sunshine Coast police. Now, instead of going to a training session, she was heading up the same highway to meet the missing boy's parents. She knew that this would not be an easy job. From the first time she'd seen the boy's piercing bluey-grey eyes in the photograph that accompanied the Significant Event Message that Monday morning, she had felt it in her bones. He wasn't your usual runaway who'd shot through with his friends for the night. Something had happened to this boy.

As she settled into the monotonous flow of traffic heading north, she knew she was a natural choice for the job. When she was 34 and a recruit in the Queensland Police Academy, she had been nicknamed 'Mum' by the other cadets, and she had always been considered empathetic in her policing. She had two sons. Two years ago, she had entered the world of news headlines, quotes, 'grabs', media releases and daily deadlines when the new Police Commissioner, Bob Atkinson, insisted that police be appointed to the Media Unit rather than journalists. Back then, she had had to learn on the job. Almost 50 now, she had 15 years of policing behind her.

In the hour's drive north, she had to work out not only what the media wanted but also how the parents were going to react to the inevitable media attention. She had already been briefed that they were in shock, as expected, and she had typed up a bullet-point list to give to them about what to cover in their first interview. After all, she reasoned, this was the first time they had ever faced the media. Remembering her early days in the Media Unit, she knew they had a lot to learn. She kept the suggested script brief:

- We are appealing to anyone who may have any information about our son Daniel to please contact the police. Daniel has not been seen by any member of the family since Sunday 7 December, when he left our home at one o'clock to catch a bus to the Maroochydore Plaza Shopping Centre.
- We are desperate for information about Daniel. It doesn't matter if you think you saw something insignificant, we plead with you to come forward.
- Daniel's not returning home on Sunday is totally out of character and there is no reason for Daniel not to come home.
- Daniel is a much-loved son, brother and grandson, and we are desperate for any information about him.

- We are appealing to anybody who may have seen Daniel or have any information that might help to please come forward and contact police or Crime Stoppers.

That part had been straightforward: typing the words into a computer and pressing print. But what did you say to a couple who had lost a son in these circumstances? She knew it was her job to coax the parents to put their pain on public display. The tactic, she knew, was tried and true. Media coverage flushed out more information, encouraged more people to come forward. This, of course, is what the parents wanted. Everyone needed to keep the last sighting of Daniel fresh. She knew the drill. But they didn't. They were an ordinary family getting on with their lives and raising their three boys. All they wanted was for their son to walk through the door.

Sergeant Elliott had something on her side: a knack for telling it like it is. Although she did not know it as she turned her car off the Bruce Highway to head towards the coastal town of Maroochydore, it was this trait more than anything that would endear her to the Morcombe family.

Born into a blue-collar family, Julie Elliott was hard-nosed and fiercely independent. Her father had worked at the BHP steelworks in Newcastle. Her mother was working behind a bar before she walked out the door and abandoned the family. From an early age, Elliott had experienced the pain of loss. As a working police officer, she'd found her husband dead behind closed garage doors after he committed suicide, and was forced to confront a personal tragedy that she commonly encountered in her job. In spite of, or perhaps because of, all these adversities, her approach was always to get the job done. It was this that the Morcombes were later to appreciate. No fuss. Just get on with it.

Parking her car in Cornmeal Parade, she walked up the pathway to the police station. With this job, you never knew what would happen from one day to the next. The moment she had been dreading was here. As she put her hand on the door handle to Greg Daniels's office, she rehearsed the first words that she was going to say to the family. But, as the door opened, Elliott caught the full blast of expectancy from both of the parents. Who was this? Was it news?

'This is Sergeant Julie Elliott,' Senior Sergeant Greg Daniels said.

Elliott breathed deeply. They shook hands. Bruce looked at her closely with his characteristically baleful stare. Bruce had a way of engaging people with a look that seemed to appraise everything about them. Elliott felt exposed under his searching gaze. Denise was less confronting but the haunted look in her eyes pierced Elliott. Kevin and Monique, Denise's parents, were also in the room, as was Brad. There were further introductions. Brad was asked to go to the Children's Witness room.

Elliott handed Bruce the dot points. The words on the page filled an awkward silence as they began reading.

'This is a great opportunity for the news about Daniel's disappearance to get out to the general public,' Elliott began.

Denise, sitting next to Bruce, said nothing. Her eyes were pools of water.

Bruce's eyes drilled into Elliott. 'I'm like one of those Easter Island statues,' he said. 'You won't get me to cry, if that's what they want.'

'I'm not asking for that,' Elliott said with equanimity, staring straight back. 'I'm just wanting to use this opportunity to our advantage.'

Elliott was past the first hurdle. She had stood her ground. Bruce nodded. They spent some time discussing tactics. Elliott then handed over her phone numbers, including her mobile number. The Morcombes passed her theirs.

In spite of the preparation, Bruce and Denise had never encountered anything like the bevy of cameras, microphones and leads, and 30 expectant faces pushing towards them in the officers' tearoom, now an impromptu press room, of the Maroochydore Police Station. At most, Bruce had done a couple of editorials with the local newspaper to promote their Jim's Mowing and Jim's Trees businesses, but he had never conducted an interview face to face with a journalist. He recognised it might be a significant opportunity to find Daniel. They both wanted to do their best, even though Denise was terrified. Neither of them had ever witnessed the inner sanctum of a police station. Now they were sitting on a formal panel with Kevin and Monique, flanked by police on their side of the table.

They had seen such scenes unfold on the television news. Now they *were* those people. People who had struck tragedy; people who you only see on the news, and hope you never have to go through what they're experiencing. They tried to focus on the job at hand. They had a message. They were searching for Daniel. They were facing an audience around Australia. There was a highly charged atmosphere of anticipation in the station that day that went far beyond what Bruce and Denise had envisaged as the media waited to hear what they had to say.

Julie Elliott watched the assembled media, telling herself that it was hardly surprising they had responded to her media alert. It had all the elements of a big news story: a local family, a young teenager who was a twin missing in broad daylight on a Sunday afternoon. But now it was up to the Morcombes. Bruce did most of the talking, gazing straight at the camera, unblinking. He held it together. Denise sat by his side, but she was there, at least, and had trouble answering the questions, choked with emotion. Elliott breathed a sigh of relief when it was done.

* * *

The MIR opposite Greg Daniels's office was a small room with computers and a whiteboard. After that first media appearance, the stream of phone calls turned into a torrent. Daniel's photograph and his innocent face had beamed across a nation. The same connection that had touched Julie Elliott and Sam Knight affected everyone, as the news rolled out in newspapers and radios and on televisions across the country.

During the first week, the calls to Maroochydore Police Station jammed the switchboard. But instead of helping, their sheer volume was threatening to stymie the investigation. The director of media rang Police Commissioner Atkinson. A decision was made right away. Elliott's role would be to respond to all of the media requests and to liaise with the family to lighten their burden. As it happened, Elliott and Senior Constable Sam Knight were friends. Sam's then husband, Steve Knight, had taken over Elliott's job when she left Caboolture station. The two women had also worked on 'Bluey Day' together, a fundraiser for the Royal Children's Hospital. Shortly after that, Knight herself had entered the police academy as a new recruit.

'I'm glad we're together on this,' Elliott said to Knight when they had a few moments alone.

Knight nodded.

In spite of this, Elliott still felt apprehension about the enormity of the task ahead. As a victim herself of tragedy, she knew she was vulnerable, even then, to soaking up the Morcombes' pain. When she visited their Palmwoods home for the first time, and drove down the long gravel driveway to the house, she felt a knot of inadequacy in her stomach. She could not give them the answer they wanted. In spite of her cool demeanour, she felt keenly, even in those early days, that she had nothing new to tell them. Instead, she worked hard at trying to reinforce the importance of sending the right message to the media.

On this first visit, it was handshakes and cups of tea. Elliott circled around their hunger for information. She was aware that so much of the conversation was inconsequential, but at the same time she was trying to establish a rapport, forever dancing around the fact that, for everyone else, including her, life was going on as normal. For Bruce and Denise, it was a continuing world of suffering. Months down the track as Elliott got to know Denise, they would recognise a mutual determination of character, a combined resilience and ability to confront the worst head on. Handshakes graduated to pecks on the cheek. One woman to another woman. Much later, there were hugs. Julie Elliott slowly became part of the family.

* * *

Behind the scenes, discoveries were made that were kept from the Morcombes. That Wednesday, 10 December, a cleaner from the Sunshine Coast Motor Lodge, less than half a kilometre from the overpass heading towards Nambour, contacted police to say she had found blood on the sheets in Room 11. That room had been connected with the occupants of Room 16, but both rooms had since been reoccupied and the sheets washed. Photographs were taken of the rooms. Exhibits were collected, including a plastic bag containing a mattress protector and a white sheet that had been washed, as well as fabric from the mattress at the head end of the bed that had tested positive for blood. However, DNA was unable to be developed from the mattress. Fingerprints – on a balcony handrail from one of the units – turned out to belong to one of the police officers. After being put through the National Automated Fingerprint Identification System (NAFIS), the rest of the fingerprints remained unidentified. Police obtained a spreadsheet of everyone who had occupied rooms in the motel between December 4 and 9 and it was discovered that known drug offenders had occupied the two rooms identified by the cleaner. Another dead end.

Police were scrambling for answers. With the list of known paedophiles in the Sunshine Coast, the JAB also provided investigating officers with leads. And there were modus operandi (MO) to consider. To begin with, Daniel's case involved abduction. Paedophiles who abducted their victims were opportunistic and usually in a category of their own, known as 'abductor paedophiles'. This narrowed the field somewhat, as investigators searched for previous criminal history that fitted this MO.

Then there were the conflicting witness reports that flooded into the MIR. Many people had seen the scruffy man talking to the boy who police were now certain was Daniel. Dozens had seen two men at various locations, and there had now been several reported sightings of a blue car. Others reported seeing a mix of other cars, including a white four-wheel drive or van. The accounts of the cars' colour, age and even boxy shape were similar, but there were varying reports of what type of cars they were. The timing differed of when witnesses remembered seeing these people and vehicles.

After the initial media reports, more people came forward with sightings, either to Crime Stoppers by phone or by attending the Maroochydore Police Station. Kim Jennings, who lived in the Woombye Gardens Caravan Park, called into the Maroochydore Police Station on 13 December to say she had been at home gardening at around 1.30 to 1.45 pm when she heard a male child screaming for about five minutes and it stopped after she heard the roar of a car accelerating away. She recalled it was a definite distress scream.

Amanda Wood was certain that she was at the overpass between 2.45 and 2.50 pm as she and her family had left home at 1.25 pm in their Nissan Navara ute towing a green trailer to go to the dump. She had a receipt to verify the time. After

15 minutes of unloading the rubbish, they had driven to a friend's place to pick up some palms, and that had taken 15 minutes. They left their friend's house at about 2.35 pm, as Amanda remembered asking what the time was. After heading south down the Nambour Connection Road, she and her husband saw a car parked under the overpass as they went to turn left on to the feeder road to Palmwoods. Amanda was sure it was a late-'80s model and had noticed it because it was parked half on the road and half off in the turning lane about three metres south of the overpass. Another odd thing was that the car doors had been open on both sides of the car and there were at least two people standing next to it.

Her husband, Aaron, remembered the car too as he was behind the wheel of their ute and what he described as the 'silvery/blue' coloured car had partially blocked him from getting into the turning lane. He remembered having to drive around the open door of the car in order not to hit it, and he remembered both the rear and front passenger doors were open. Three people were on the passenger side. One was standing up and the other two were sitting down on the bank beside the car. One of those sitting down was smaller than the other one, but he could not remember whether this person was a child or not.

'It's a stupid place for someone to park,' Aaron had said to his wife, at the same time noting that the bonnet of the car wasn't up, so it didn't look as though the car had broken down. The Woods had then called into the Palmwoods takeaway near the newsagency and bought four Billabong ice creams. Aaron had bought some cigarettes. The receipt he received, after paying with his Visa card, was another way of verifying the time.

Some had seen a blue car earlier than others. Lesley Mahoney had collected her husband, John, a spray-painter, from his job at a body works near Nambour at 1 pm and put petrol in the car. She estimated that they approached the overpass heading south at around 1.30 pm, when she noticed an old-model, pale-blue sedan parked on the side of the road. Shortly after that, she turned left off the highway to go to Palmwoods, driving over the overpass and was travelling past the council depot on the Woombye-Palmwoods Road near the water tower when she saw the boy in the bright-red T-shirt. Lesley had glanced at him to see if she knew who he was. She had wondered why he was walking by himself along the side of the road.

Others, such as Michelle Devlin, had noticed the blue car with the faded paintwork even earlier, parked near the Caravan World sales yard as she headed north back to Nambour on the Nambour Connection Road after the service finished at the Christian Outreach Centre at 11.18 am. Troy Meiers had seen a blue car on the Nambour-bound side of the overpass and he, too, had thought it was parked in a dangerous spot. He said a man had been standing next to the back of the car on the driver's side with his arms folded and was facing the traffic. He had a long-shaped face and pronounced cheekbones with gaunt cheeks and acne scarring. He also had a goatee beard and unkempt hair, and he was 'druggy looking' and 'feral'. Several other people had seen a blue car speeding on various roads on and near the Nambour Connection Road.

There had also been seven sightings of a white van parked on the opposite side of the road to where Daniel had been standing. Some had seen it on top of the overpass, at the entrance to Shires Road, and others had seen it near the overpass. The sheer volume of witness accounts led to inevitable contradictions and presented the police with the challenge of having to decide which ones to pay attention to and which to discard.

Forensic examination concentrated on the shoe impressions, tyre marks and tinted, shattered glass, as well as the tyre prints from under the overpass, which police claimed were later compared with the cars owned by ten previous paedophiles of interest. However, the other side of the road was not searched, in spite of various witnesses reporting seeing a blue car opposite the Hail and Ride spot. The wall where the scruffy man had reportedly rested his foot was fingerprint tested. The first of a number of water searches also took place, beginning in the dam at the Morcombes' property. Several other dams were searched nearby. Police made a decision that Wednesday to release details about Daniel's fob watch the following day. Second-hand dealers and pawnbrokers began to be contacted from Bundaberg to Caboolture in the hope that someone had seen a fob watch with the inscription 'DAN' engraved on it. There were 61 pawnbrokers and dealers listed in the Sunshine Coast district alone.

* * *

With Christmas approaching, Father Jan was visited by several people, including his parishioners, suggesting that there should be a service for Daniel. School had broken up for the year, and many people were heading away for holidays. Siena Catholic College's assistant principal of Religious Education, Carmel Hewlett, had also contacted him suggesting a service would be appropriate for Daniel. Each day, there had been no breakthrough. Prayers for Daniel would help people, but these requests troubled Father Jan. He was unsure of how to format the service. But people wanted to be together. To be united. To gather strength and feel that they were not alone. It was clear that people wanted direction. He prayed to God to give him answers.

* * *

On Friday 12 December, Denise heard the throbbing of the chopper blades slicing the air above the house. This one was close. For days, she and Bruce had watched them making wide, sweeping arcs across the rugged terrain and countryside as they searched dams and lakes. The search was sometimes across to the Big Pineapple, west of the abduction site and then down to their home in Palmwoods, as police worked around the clock trying to pinpoint their missing son. That morning, a large helicopter had landed in the front paddock. It was news. They had found Daniel. Why else would they land in their yard? Denise's breathing was fast and excited as she rushed and opened the front door to run onto the verandah. But there was no joy in the eyes of the helicopter pilot climbing out of the cockpit of the blue and white Energex Rescue chopper. Watching his silent demeanour, Denise's hopes evaporated. The pilot had just wanted to speak to one of the other police officers. Within minutes he was back in the air again. Denise walked slowly back to the house, wondering why she had been excited. What answer did she expect, what answer could she want?

Late that morning, recent video footage arrived at the police station. Senior Constable Sam Knight had organised it through Denise's brother, Paul Beavis. It was footage of Daniel from Paul's wedding in January 2003. Daniel was smartly dressed in a black shirt, black tie and black pants, smiling his infectious smile at the camera, the picture of innocence.

* * *

Siena Catholic College in Sippy Downs was named after Catherine of Siena, an Italian nun who helped the poor. Cypress and olive trees reminiscent of Catherine's homeland had been planted. They flanked the border between the school and the busy Sippy Downs Drive, which led to the Bruce Highway. During school afternoons, the road was clogged with parents and schoolchildren edging closer to the motorway and home.

Graeme Hight, acting principal of the college, had been winding down for the Christmas holidays at his home in Gympie, a small town north of the Sunshine Coast, preparing for his usual camping trip north of Rainbow Beach with the family. The principal, Bryan Baker, was being treated for cancer, and Hight had devoted all his energies to the role. His well-earned break was about to be interrupted.

He received a call from Greg Daniels giving him 'heads-up' that the Morcombes were in need of whatever support they could get, and expressing his concerns for the family. At this point, Hight had already been fielding phone calls from parents who were expressing helplessness and concern. What could they do?

He rang around some of the staff. It was not the first time sudden action had been required. There had been deaths at the school before – one student through suicide, another through illness, although these had happened during school time. Daniel had gone missing after the holidays had started.

Once the details for an impromptu mass or prayer service were put in place, the word had spread quickly. Children began contacting each other on MySpace. Parents too. Hight started a phone tree among staff, asking certain people to ring other people. Parents met each other in supermarkets. Everyone had heard about Daniel. Several people volunteered to bring morning tea. No one had wanted to head off on holidays as it seemed a churlish thing to do considering a child had been snatched from their midst.

On the Friday morning, chairs were pulled out of classrooms into the multi-purpose all-weather assembly area named Casuarina. Open to the elements on all sides, the hall with a corrugated iron roof was large enough to be used for sporting and academic purposes, and it had also served well as the school's makeshift chapel.

Father Jan had agreed to preside over the service, but he still felt concerned about how to frame it. Was Daniel alive? That was the question on everyone's lips. He was a missing person but what had happened to him? Father Jan could not speak as he might at a funeral. Again, he was plagued by the same thoughts he had when Greg Daniels brought the Morcombes to the presbytery. Giving people false hope, especially the parents, was not a good idea, nor was allowing people to think that prayers would bring Daniel home.

That morning, however, as he entered Casuarina Hall, he was astonished. In this airy space of worship, more than a thousand people sat waiting for him to speak. These people were united against evil, showing their collective strength as a community. 'God,' he said to himself, as he faced the swelling crowd before him, 'you have told me what to do, through the people: get your word out to your flock, take leadership and do what has to be done.'

Father Jan stood on the small makeshift altar at one end of the hall, above which was emblazoned the school motto, 'Prayer, Care, Learning'. Each person was given a prayer card, a ribbon and candle and was asked to light it at home at 6 pm each night to show solidarity with the Morcombe family. Father Jan had chosen green ribbon for the candles to symbolise hope for the Sunshine Coast community. Candles to bring light to give everyone strength. People came up to collect their candles and ribbons. 'Daniel is not with us,' Father Jan said. 'We don't know what happened, but we are here together.'

Bruce and Denise had asked that their family be allowed to sit a couple of rows back, rather than at the front. Bruce wore dark glasses, staring ahead. Tears would roll down his cheeks from under the glasses, but he refused to wipe them away. Denise frequently wiped tears from her eyes, tears that never seemed to stop falling. Brad sat next to Bruce, stoic. Dean sat next to Denise. They were a family thrust into tragedy, the focus of this gathering. Bruce's sister, Lindy, her husband Andrew, and her family sat close by, along with Bruce's older brother, Perry, his wife Joan and their family, Bruce's younger brother, Scott, and his wife Shelly and their family, and Denise's parents, Kevin and Monique.

There were a large number of children there, wiping away tears as well. A soprano from the college sang hymns. Looking out at the bowed heads seated in rows across the large makeshift chapel, Father Jan marvelled at the scene before him. Emotions were raw but the powerful message of unity prevailed. People trying to come to terms with what had happened. In this togetherness, he felt strongly, they would move towards God.

* * *

But no one had prepared Bruce and Denise for the shock they were about to encounter as they drove home from the service and rounded a bend a few hundred metres from their home opposite the Woombye State School.

There was a macabre figure standing at the Pine Grove Road intersection near the school: it was a mannequin of Daniel dressed in a red Billabong T-shirt and blue, knee-length, cargo-style shorts and Globe shoes. It had been placed close to a police van and was designed to trigger passers-by into remembering something.

Bruce had two thoughts. The first was that his family didn't need to see this, especially on this emotionally charged day, and the second was what a terribly cheap, disproportioned representation it was of their son. The mannequin was inadequately sized and looked more like a scarecrow. It was upsetting – was this the best representation the police could come up with? Surely, in this day and age of computer modelling, a three-dimensional likeness could have been captured, he thought. Much later, Bruce was to use the idea of a three-dimensional model for their own investigation. This was the seed of that thought process.

Julie Elliott was not happy with the mannequin either. 'Bloody awful,' she said when they showed it to her. The wig was too long. Its arms hung stiffly forward. The clothes were far too big and it looked more like it belonged in a department-store window. Elliott would have to find a better one.

Earlier that same day, 50 SES volunteers, wearing their orange uniforms in the stifling heat of an early summer, scoured the rugged bushland near Woombye. They were desperately looking for clues. One of them was medically treated after picking up a syringe. After a tip-off from a motorist, the SES also searched bushland near Caloundra, south of Maroochydore.

Detective Inspector John Maloney steadfastly told the media that he would not be releasing COMFITs or artist's sketches of any of the persons described by witnesses at this time. COMFITs are portraits created by witnesses from a catalogue of different facial features – mouths, eyebrows and noses, lips and hairstyles. A face is then compiled from the separate parts and the witness is asked to verify that the composite picture resembles their recollections.

By Friday, the police had three artistic impressions of the man seen under the overpass by some of the people on the bus: one from 16-year-old Terry Theuerkauf, who'd been on the 1A Sunbus with his sister, Fiona, who had also produced a sketch and the other from their friend, 13-year-old Abby North. Fiona had recalled, the man had a goatee and possibly sunglasses. Abby's boyfriend, Peter Murchie, had told police that the man had a beard and was wearing 'dirty old clothes', and he thought he had a suitcase next to him.

'We don't want the media focusing on anyone at this stage,' Maloney told the public, adding that police had not ruled out that Daniel may have known the person who was feared to have abducted him. Maloney added that everyone was hopeful that Daniel would be reunited with his family, while admitting there were no concrete leads.

Maloney was not the only one to publicly refer to 'an abduction' that day. The *Sunshine Coast Daily* printed the word for the first time in one of its headlines. Although everyone was hoping for a fast and happy resolution, the message was slowly filtering through the community that Daniel was not immediately coming home. Letters published in the same newspaper summed up the community feeling. 'I know I am not alone,' stated one. 'Everyone I talk to has been shaken up by this horrible incident. It has hit many residents, including myself, with the harsh reality of life.' Another, from a retiree, said, 'They're our people … good, honest, God-fearing people', adding that he wished to remain anonymous. Yet another letter detailed how many times a woman's teenage children had caught the bus on the same Nambour Connection Road to the Plaza, unaware that 'this adolescent pastime' would put them so much at risk. The family were heartened by the community response.

* * *

Witnesses continued to come forward and many were taken to the abduction scene under the overpass where they pointed out what they had seen to police. Five days after Daniel disappeared, 30-year-old Katherine Mary Louise Bird, a passenger on the bus that failed to pick up Daniel, who was pregnant, told police she had heard the bus driver use the radio as they approached the overpass. She said she saw a man with his foot up against the wall behind him and that he had not even looked at the bus as it went past. Rather, he was looking at a boy standing in front of him. Bird was so distressed after seeing the disappointment in the boy's face when the bus didn't stop that she said she demanded to know why the bus driver had not acted more responsibly. The following Tuesday, she was so concerned that she had rung Crime Stoppers, but it was not until the Friday that she had been invited into Maroochydore Police Station to provide a statement.

In the upcoming weeks, more witnesses came forward to report seeing a car under the overpass. June Gannon had turned onto the Nambour Connection Road at around 2.15 pm on the Sunday, and was heading north. Gannon was a nurse at the Nambour Nursing Home and had been rostered for work from 2.30 to 10.30 pm. She remembered leaving home at 2.10 pm, which was not far from the intersection of the Nambour Connection Road. As she waited to merge with the traffic on the highway, she had looked across the road and had seen a young boy, who she thought looked 'disturbed but not frightened'. The boy had been talking to a man. They were a metre apart. Later, she recalled, it was as though 'they were in some sort of confrontation'. The man had messy, mousey-blond hair down his neck and she thought he was in his late thirties. She had also noticed a car about ten metres from the two people facing south towards Maroochydore, but because of the concrete divider in the middle of the road between her and the car, she could not describe it. As she merged into the traffic on the Nambour Connection Road, she saw the boy and the man walking slowly.

Random incidents hampered what was already a very complex and confusing investigation. On 12 December, a 17-year-old girl from Maroochydore reported that she had been abducted but refused to make a statement. Her mental state was questioned. On the same day there were further doorknocks on residents and businesses on the Nambour Connection Road. A mustard-coloured Corolla was reported abandoned in the nearby suburb of Forest Glen, and a cream-coloured Toyota sedan was found, but the owner of the car was located and he told police that he had broken down.

Later that morning, patrons of the Woombye Bowls Club and staff from the Woombye Hotel were interviewed about their movements that Sunday and asked whether they had seen any strange or suspicious activity in the area. Police also conducted patrols of the Nambour area, focusing on local parks and interrogating vagrants. Aerial photographs were taken of the Christian Outreach Centre, and were enlarged and placed in the MIR. Aerial photos were also taken of the Bruce Highway and the Nambour Connection Road. Two discarded boots were found near the Ilkley overpass that had paint marks on the soles. They were lodged as an exhibit. Daniel's bank account was checked again. There were still no withdrawals or deposits. Police were compiling a list of POIs which was growing, as police methodically worked through the list of known paedophiles in the area.

Later, police began making enquiries at the government-owned forestry offices about vehicles entering the forestry or being abandoned there after two witnesses came forward to say they had seen a blue car and a white van or four-wheel drive enter the forest to the east of the Bruce Highway at Beerwah the afternoon Daniel went missing. However, none of the satellites were operating in that area on that afternoon.

* * *

Exactly a week later, on 14 December, the Sunday after Daniel went missing, police staged a re-enactment under the overpass, standing the same mannequin they'd used near the Woombye State School by the roadway. The re-enactment was accompanied by a media conference intended to keep the case in the public eye, and to bring forward more potential witnesses. Julie Elliott was desperately hoping that Denise would have the courage to face what she knew would be a bevy of cameras assembled under the overpass. Other than some small comments in some interviews, Denise had found it difficult to deal with the media attention. But Elliott knew how important it was for the television journalists to hear from Daniel's mother. She'd already raised this with Bruce and Denise and Elliott knew it wouldn't be an easy task. Bruce was understandably protective.

'I can't do it,' Denise had said when Elliott first raised it.

'You have to. You just have to,' Elliott countered. 'Just say, "I want my Danny back". That'll do.'

One lane of the four-lane highway was especially closed for the interview. The television crews gathered under the overpass, not in their usual jostling fashion but strangely silent. Most had children that were Daniel's age or younger.

Her heart in her mouth, Elliott watched. The cameras began rolling, beginning with Inspector Maloney asking anyone who had seen cars collecting or dropping off passengers near or at the overpass to come forward. Then it was Denise's turn. Somehow she managed to do it, even though to this present day she has no recollection of how she did it. She did it because she had to get Daniel home. Her eyes filled with tears as she looked straight at the camera. 'I just want him to come home,' she cried. 'We want Daniel back.'

Elliott felt torn between feeling for Denise's pain and feeling pleased that the media would run some of the footage, knowing that it would help the cause. More than 30 motorists stopped to talk to the police, some explaining how they had seen a small, blue sedan parked in front of Daniel and an unidentified man.

'I hope we can confidently release a description that we're happy with, but I don't know yet,' Maloney said.

Denise's heartfelt plea reached thousands of ordinary families around Australia, who were preparing dinner, and who were undoubtedly shocked by the notion that such a thing could happen in a country that was supposed to be safe, where the Aussie way was for people to look out for each other.

Detective Sergeant Peter Brewer addressed the congregation of the Christian Outreach Centre that same day. He made a plea for information from anyone who saw anything suspicious happening the previous Sunday.

With the help of Julie Elliott, the family agreed to a series of media interviews. *The Sunday Mail* printed one of the first in-depth stories, running a portrait of the family inside its front page. In it, Bruce talked about the importance of the police checking Daniel's computer to see whether it provided clues. Police were also seeking further information on a group of motorcycle riders seen by some of the witnesses on the bus, who were thought to be members of the Ulysses Club for older bike riders. Denise had one message. 'It could be the tiniest snippet of news that makes the world of difference to the police and to us,' she said. 'Please don't hesitate to come forward.' Photographs that accompanied the story showed Daniel's bedroom as he'd left it and a picture of the Kiel Mountain Road overpass. It finished with an appeal for people to contact Crime Stoppers.

But in spite of the public appeals for help, at the end of the first week, no one had come forward with any evidence of what had happened to Daniel.

It was not until the second week that *The Courier-Mail* also used 'abduction' in one of its headlines, specifically 'Abduction Fears'. The idea that Daniel had just had an accident and was lying somewhere unable to get help was evaporating. People seemed to understand that they had to band together to unite against the unknown. The community galvanised into action. A boy had been seized while on his way to get Christmas presents on a Sunday afternoon – this would not be tolerated. A Nambour retired businessman pledged a $5000 independent reward for anyone who came forward with information to help the police.

On the morning of Monday 15 December, Bruce, Denise and Bradley drove to Maroochydore Police Station to provide samples of their DNA. That same day, shortly after 4 pm, Bruce and Denise, Kevin and Monique, and Brad went to the Palmwoods Hotel to have a quiet drink. They had to get out of the house. A few days later, Sam Knight brought the outing up with Bruce. Police had received a report that someone had seen the Morcombes laughing at the pub. Their life could never be normal again.

Bruce's anger against whoever had taken his son simmered as each helpless day dragged by. Inside the barn, he had painted a message on a large galvanised iron sheet. The sign read: 'Swing you Bastard. Justice will be done. Your days are numbered.' Next to the words was a painted image of a long rope with a noose at one end. He desperately wanted to put it under the overpass to seek vengeance against the unspeakable human being who had taken Daniel. But his better sense of judgement prevailed. As he came and went from the barn, though, it was there for him to see.

CHAPTER SEVEN

DOUGLAS BRIAN JACKWAY

Douglas Brian 'Jacko' Jackway had spent a significant portion of his 26 years behind bars. Straight after he got out of jail on 7 November 2003, following an eight and a half year sentence for the savage rape of a nine-year-old boy in Tannum Sands near Gladstone in 1995, he bought a blue Holden Commodore sedan with black louvres on the back window and the registration number 996 HKL. He had traded his mother's purple Hyundai, given to him as a gift, in for it. Jackway was an intimidating, short muscly man with a small mouth and darting, restless eyes. He rarely engaged in eye contact. He also sported several tattoos, including one each on his left and right upper arms.

Following Jackway's sentence for the rape of the boy in 1995, Dr Christopher Alroe, psychiatrist, ventured an opinion that Jackway was a 'biological psychopath'. 'The picture regarding Mr Jackway is bleak indeed, both for him and society,' Alroe said. Another consultant psychiatrist, Dr Ian Atkinson, declared that Jackway was 'quite unsuitable' for any form of community-based supervision. He said he doubted whether Jackway's release date would 'give him sufficient time to even start to "mellow"'. It was Atkinson's opinion that the sentence Jackway had been given for raping the boy in Gladstone did not fit 'the history of this very serious personality disorder'. Jackway also had a history while incarcerated of wilful damage to property, including assaulting a fellow inmate who refused to fight him. Within weeks of getting out of jail, one of the first things Jackway did was dye his hair blond. Within 12 days of being released, he had committed a minor traffic offence. Shortly after that, on 22 November 2003, he was arrested and charged with dangerous driving after a high-speed car chase on the Sunshine Coast motorway near Noosa, where he clocked up speeds of 170 kilometres per hour in the blue Commodore, which was then impounded. When Daniel went missing, Jackway's profile matched what the police were searching for. There was an even more sinister link: Jackway's early-model blue sedan matched the vehicle that had been described by many of the witnesses at the overpass and, further, Jackway was due to appear in court in Noosa, about 40 kilometres from the abduction site, on dangerous driving charges on 8 December 2003, the day after Daniel disappeared. Jackway knew the Sunshine Coast well, having lived and attended school there for a number of years. His older sister lived in Tewantin, a suburb of Noosa, north of Maroochydore.

Jackway was one of the first people to be interviewed. Police first spoke to him on Wednesday, three days after Daniel went missing, at his address in Bertha Street, Goodna, in Brisbane's south-west, where he had lived with his de facto, Danielle Richardson (pseudonym), after he got out of jail. It was the first of several interviews. Each time his story would change, even when he began making formal statements.

* * *

Jackway's house at Bertha Street, Goodna, was a hop, skip and a jump from the Ipswich Motorway. A fibro structure with aluminium windows facing one of the motorway's busy, featureless connecting roads, it had a small balcony and stairs visible from the street. It resembled a kit home that someone with a limited budget would put together for a quick rental. The address was known to police as a regular callout for domestic violence. The unfenced backyard, also visible from the street, sprawled out behind it. For Douglas Jackway, less than two months out of jail, the position of the house was a bonus. Driving north or south was as simple as pulling out from Bertha Street onto the feeding road and then onto the highway.

On Tuesday 16 December, just over a week after Daniel disappeared, Jackway attended Goodna Police Station, where he provided his first record of interview. Several people had nominated him as being responsible for Daniel's abduction. He had already been questioned three times, on 10, 11 and 12 December, by detectives from the Sexual Crimes Investigation Unit. On the first occasion, he had been casually questioned about his movements on 7 December in front of the people who were to later become crucial alibis and key to establishing whether he had been to the Sunshine Coast on the day Daniel disappeared or not.

He told police that, in the early hours of the day that Daniel went missing, he had been asleep when his girlfriend, Danielle Richardson, came home. The two of them had begun an argument that lasted until the next day. He told police he had only been absent from the house in Bertha Street for a short while that Sunday when he called in on the mother of his 15-year-old friend Stephen Park (pseudonym), in Goodna to get power-steering fluid for his early-model blue sedan. Later, he said he had also visited his older friend Paul Carrington at about 5 or 5.30 pm, returning at 7.30 pm. Carrington, a short man with a long grey ponytail who often wore a baseball cap, was a convicted paedophile whom Jackway had met in jail. Jackway claimed he had not headed up to the Sunshine Coast until the Monday morning, the day after Daniel disappeared, 8 December. He said that he had left home at 5 am to drive to Noosa, where he was facing the court charge for dangerous driving.

Jackway told police that he had made several calls from the landline at Bertha Street on the day Daniel went missing – to his sister and mother, and to Paul Carrington – which established he had been in Goodna. Police interviewed Danielle Richardson that same day. She confirmed that she had been going out with Jackway and that he had been living at her house in Bertha Street since he got out of jail. She also confirmed Jackway's story – that he had visited Park's mother's residence the day Daniel went missing and had gone to Paul Carrington's house somewhere between 4 and 5 pm that afternoon. Park's mother and stepfather, although initially contacted by police, were not interviewed until later in December.

The next day, Wednesday 17 December, several computer-generated images of a dark-blue, early-'80s-model car were released by police to the media. The statement that accompanied the images was that Daniel may have accepted a lift from an unidentified man seen standing near him just before he disappeared. Some witnesses had said the rear door was open.

Inspector John Maloney told the media that police were 'anxious' to speak to the man under the overpass but did not reveal the witness descriptions. 'There's potentially quite a lot of witnesses there that could have seen the man who was with Daniel at the time that haven't come forward,' he told the media. However, no sketches or COMFITs were released of anyone seen near the overpass. Many newspaper articles confused the scruffy man described by witnesses on the Sunbus with the man who had reportedly been seen near the blue car, although it was clear from the witnesses on the Sunbus that the scruffy man had been on his own with Daniel. No car had been seen nearby when passengers had passed under the overpass on the bus around 2.13 pm. As it transpired, sketches from any of the witness descriptions were not released until almost 12 months later.

* * *

For the Morcombes, the days passed achingly slowly. Dean went to work each day. Sometimes, Kevin or Bruce would pick him up. Brad went back to work at the Paxtons' farm. Greg Daniels came up with the idea of tracking the clothes Brad was wearing each day to eliminate the possibility of a report from a member of the public of a sighting of Daniel when in fact it was Bradley. Police needed to confirm or discount quickly all information as it came to hand. This continued for around three weeks. It gave Denise something to contribute to the investigation as she jotted down in a diary where Brad went and what he wore.

Bruce and Denise were continually looking for distractions for Brad. He went to the movies at the Sunshine Plaza with a couple of friends one day to see *Scary Movie 3*. Another day, he had lunch at McDonald's. Everyone went through the motions of what they would usually do in the holidays but no one could enjoy the usual end-of-school freedom.

On Wednesday 17 December, the Forensic Services Branch, led by Sergeant Williams from the Fingerprints Bureau, appeared at the Palmwoods house to collect fingerprints from Daniel's bedroom. They removed all of his posters from the walls and collected anything they could find that he had written on. It was a further intrusion for Denise. Although all of the items, she was told, would be returned, there would be chemicals used to detect fingerprints on them and they would never look the same. They also took Bruce, Denise, Brad and Dean's fingerprints for elimination purposes.

On Thursday 18 December, Greg Daniels contacted Graeme Hight again, asking him to talk to Channel Seven's *Sunrise* program. Hight agreed but told the producer that he would not speculate about why Daniel was missing. The program was on delay. Daylight saving was in effect across the nation but not in Queensland.

'So, do you think Daniel's run away?' David Koch, the presenter, began.

'Not at all. I know this child. I've actually taught him at school. I know his mum and dad,' he answered with conviction.

Hight went around to another teacher's place for breakfast and told him how upset he had been by the question Koch had asked. The other teacher told him it was clever journalism. Koch had only asked the question everyone else had wanted to ask. Hight had informed the general public that indeed there *was* cause for concern.

Judith Van der Meer worked at the Christian Outreach Centre as a teacher's aide. She would travel down the Nambour Connection Road up to six times a day. That Thursday she gave a statement to police. The day Daniel disappeared, she said, she had not attended her regular church service at the Christian Outreach Centre but had dropped her eldest son there instead. Van der Meer ended up giving three statements to police: the first two in the weeks after Daniel disappeared and the last not until August 2004.

In the first two statements, she told police that she was travelling south on the Nambour Connection Road between 11.40 and 11.50 am in her red Toyota Camry when she saw a man walking south along the road towards the overpass. The man had dark, straggly hair. She said she returned home via the same route after dropping off her son. She then returned to the church to pick up her daughter, who had been dropped there for a children's activity and who had rung her between 1.30 and 1.45 pm.

Again in the left-hand lane, coming off the Nambour Connection Road to turn into the church to pick up her daughter, she noticed an '80s-model bluey-grey sedan. It had stopped in the left-hand turning lane on the southern side of the overpass and she had to veer around it as it was parked in a dangerous place. A man was standing near the front of the car, and the back driver's side passenger door was open. She remembers hearing a man shouting and thought she saw three people in the car. She kept driving to the church. In her third statement, much later, she said she had seen Daniel facing the wall at the overpass and at the same time the man she had seen earlier with the straggly hair was taking 'big strides' towards him. She had heard a man yelling as she turned into the side road leading to the roundabout and the church and a child's voice crying 'No'. Then she had heard other men's voices yelling.

* * *

The 19th of December was the day everyone had been dreading. It was the twins' birthday. Sam Knight had already been asking Denise, 'What will you be doing on the twins' birthday?' Every day, the thought had plagued Denise and Bruce. It was Brad's birthday too. There was only one thing he was wishing for: that Daniel would come home.

Father Joe Duffy, who worked in the same parish as Father Jan, had also been thinking about the boys' birthday. He came up with the idea of lighting a candle for each of the three boys who had all been baptised. This would celebrate the occasion of the twins' birthday but would also provide an opportunity to mourn the boy who had disappeared.

At 11 am, the Morcombes set up a table in the garden at Palmwoods, helped by Kevin and Monique. Both Father Jan and Father Joe were invited, as well as some friends. Denise's friend Debbie agreed to do a reading; neither Denise nor

112

Bruce felt up to it. Julie Elliott, Sam Knight and Greg Daniels were there also. Elliott allowed one news camera to be present, but only to film before the service began. She had invited a couple of journalists, including the experienced Steve Marshall and Kim Skubris. Bruce and Denise did not want a public display, but they knew it was important to get Daniel's name and his photo out there. Someone could still come forward with new information. After the media left, everyone sat down around the table. Brad lit the candles. There was no wind. Father Jan gave a blessing and read from the Gospel of Luke.

'Whatever is hidden away will be brought out into the open and whatever is covered up will be found and brought to light. May your servants Daniel and Bradley, who are celebrating their 14th birthday, be abundantly blessed as we thank you for another year of life. We ask you for their protection and guidance,' he prayed.

Sam Knight already had a bad feeling. Her stomach churned. Almost as soon as they were lit, one of the candles flickered and went out. Bruce stared at it, choked with too much emotion to speak. The other two candles kept burning brightly.

After the service, Monique sobbed to Denise, 'My Danny's gone ...' Denise's mother was speaking for all of them.

Denise, too, began to cry, as convinced as her mother that Daniel had indeed left them, but she said nothing, not wanting to admit the worst possible thing she could admit – that her little boy wasn't coming home. To keep going from one day to the next, she needed to believe that he was. Was this a sign from God?

What made matters worse that day was that all of the kitchen chairs had been taken outside from around the dining table. No one had sat in Daniel's chair since he left. Now, Denise did not know which chair was Daniel's. With his chair being removed and his belongings being taken, Denise's little boy was vanishing before her eyes.

Brad struggled through the day, the look on his face was heart-breaking.

Later, Bruce and Denise discovered that Brad had emailed Daniel that day, with the simple, heart-wrenching message: 'Come home.'

That afternoon, Bruce, Denise, Nana and Pa drove Brad to Underwater World for his birthday present: to dive with sharks. While they had been thinking about what kind of present Brad might like, Bruce and Denise knew it had to be something special, something that would take him out of himself for a little while.

At 3 pm, Denise drove to Woombye to collect the birthday cake, which had 'Happy Birthday' iced on top of it. They had left the cake without names as they could not bring themselves to acknowledge Bradley without Daniel. Then Bruce took Brad to the Chinese restaurant at Nambour Junction. They had made it to the end of the day and achieved their mission – to make new memories for Bradley. The second week following Daniel's disappearance was drawing to a close.

PART TWO

The First Year

CHAPTER EIGHT

BRETT PETER COWAN

Senior Constable Ken King was the third generation of his family to work for the Queensland Police Service. He had also spent seven years with the Victoria Police Service. Newly appointed in plain clothes to Task Force Argos, which dealt with child sex exploitation, he had been sent to the Sunshine Coast to assist with Operation Vista. He and his colleague, Detective Dennis Martyn, had been charged with working through the intelligence list of known sex offenders in the area. King considered his offsider to be 'very competent'. The list covered the full spectrum, from convicted paedophiles and child abusers to those who informants had suggested might be connected to the case. It was the kind of police work that was laborious but necessary. King and Martyn had not yet finished their detective training and were only newly appointed to plain clothes, but their training had been much better than that of the average police constable.

Each morning, they were allocated jobs from the MIR. On Sunday 21 December 2003, they were assigned to a POI named Brett Peter Cowan. Martyn and King were told that

Cowan was known to have a history of serious sexual assaults. Like all investigating police officers, King and Martyn were provided with a summary of the case and a form on which to record the result of their investigations. The information provided by all detectives would go back to the MIR for discussion. From that, new jobs arose. One of the main objectives for investigating police officers was to check the POIs' stories. In police parlance, this was called 'running out their alibis': checking what the POIs said, testing the validity of what police had been told. But it was not just a matter of alibis. They would also record the demeanour of the POI, and observe the reaction when the POI answered the unannounced rapid knock at the door. Surprise was an important element of police work. King and Martyn had been asked to see whether they could obtain DNA and a photograph with Cowan's consent, which was common practice. Lastly, they were told to identify any cars linked to the POI.

Cowan's house, in Alf's Pinch Road, Beerwah, was set back from the street up a long dirt driveway behind some macadamia trees. Alf's Pinch Road had neat brick houses with sprawling acreage, some with palm trees facing the road. Cowan's house, a humble, single-storey dwelling, was small in comparison with many of the larger houses, with their well-kept lawns and gardens. King and Martyn drove up the dirt driveway and parked near the carport out the front. When the door opened, King immediately sensed the nerves from the man who stood inside the doorway. He had a smile on his face but King could read the quiet agitation beneath it.

Cowan had been expecting them. A mate from jail whom Cowan had met while working in the kitchen had tipped him off. The mate had rung Cowan to see if he'd already been questioned as word had got out about the list the police were targeting.

King's sharp eyes took it all in. Cowan easily resembled the 'scruffy man'. His eyes were shifty. He had the unkempt look of someone who got out of bed in the morning and never cared or thought about his personal appearance. His hair was shorter than the witness descriptions of the scruffy man and he was mostly clean-shaven, with dark stubble along his moustache line and the extremities of his chin only. Almost two weeks had passed since Daniel had disappeared. It was easily enough time to have gotten a haircut and have a shave. The place was untidy, King saw, as the door opened further and the two police officers entered the house. That, in itself, was not particularly out of the ordinary; King and Martyn were used to untidiness. This was not a home, though; it was more of a place in which to base yourself.

Cowan's wife, Tracey, plump with her dark hair tied in a bun, seemed a timid person. She let Cowan do the talking. They had a four-month-old baby boy, King noted. Constable King had already begun the preamble at the door, explaining what they were there for, producing police badges, establishing credentials. Now that was over, it was time to conduct a further chat, not a formal record of interview. There were some surprises. Questioned about his movements on 7 December, Cowan immediately volunteered that he had driven his white 1990 Mitsubishi Pajero four-wheel drive along the Nambour Connection Road around the time Daniel went missing to visit someone in Perwillowen Road, Nambour. He had gone there to collect a mulcher, he said, for some tree cuttings on his property. He had driven under the Kiel Mountain Road overpass, returning the same way after he had picked up the mulcher. Cowan had noticed nothing in particular except, he remembered, a broken-down bus parked at the Woombye turn-off.

King stared at the man in front of him. Cowan had put himself at the scene of the alleged crime twice as he drove to and from Nambour at around the time Daniel went missing. Yes, he would supply DNA voluntarily, Cowan said. He even allowed the police officers to photograph him. King noted he had a skull tattooed on his left upper arm and a skull and scroll tattoo on his right upper arm. A large, vertical scar was obvious on his chest from open-heart surgery. There were no other tattoos. Cowan told them he had a job at Clayton's Towing Service in Nambour. Tracey, he said, nodding in her direction, was a regular attendee of the Christian Outreach Centre – the same church adjacent to the last place Daniel had been seen.

King was also struck by a number of Cowan's mannerisms. Later, he described the encounter as 'chilling', but not for the usual reasons that he experienced when encountering criminals. There was nothing aggressive in the way Cowan presented. If anything, there was an over-politeness, an obsequiousness that bordered on repulsive. King noted down that Cowan was eager to please. Conversing with a smile that continually played across his mouth, he was quietly spoken and servile, a role King sensed he habitually assumed to get himself out of trouble. Tracey Cowan answered a few questions. She told them she thought her husband had returned from getting the mulcher at around 3 pm but it could have been half an hour either side of that time.

Back in the car, King spoke as soon as he and Martyn buckled up. 'If he's not f—ing right for this, then he's right for something.'

Martyn nodded in agreement. Cowan was a strong suspect. At dinner a few nights afterwards, both constables announced to their wives that someone they had interviewed should be a major suspect, or at least there needed to be further investigation into his movements. They did not provide the POI's name to their wives, but it was a mark of how sure they were of the possibility that they had a chief suspect. The obvious next step, King believed, was to get a search warrant to tip Cowan's place upside down. Police powers in Queensland were strong, he knew, coming from a family with a history of serving the state. It was time to make use of them.

King had already decided he would put his name on a search warrant if asked. Any evidence uncovered in preliminary searches of Cowan's home would have high probative value so would likely be admissible in court. In other words, the court would be on his side. It was standard police procedure that, if you put pressure on the accused person early, they often buckled, wanting to get things off their chest. There was the potential to get the evidence early when the crime was fresh. Meanwhile, it was time to find out more details about Cowan's previous 'form'.

* * *

As the search for Daniel entered its third week, there was a second re-enactment under the Kiel Mountain Road overpass. This flushed out more phone calls from the public. Eight people offered information inside a special booth set up to urge motorists to stop. By this point, a thousand calls had been made to Crime Stoppers, representing the most calls they had ever had for a job in Queensland. In one 24-hour period, there were 210 calls. Among them were many psychics. Detective Senior Sergeant Michael Volk told the media that these calls were not being discarded.

'We send everything. We don't say that because it is from psychics we're not going to send it. We have had circumstances in the past where people have called up presenting themselves as psychics, but they were actually connected to the crime. They couldn't find a way of saying, "I know about this because of my brother or next-door neighbour,"' he said.

Keeping Daniel's image alive to the public was having an effect. Senior Sergeant Julie Elliott commended the input from the community. 'There has been a great response and police will now sift through the new information they've gathered. Unfortunately, though, we still don't have that one vital piece of information that will lead us to Daniel, so if anyone knows something and hasn't come forward, please do so,' she said. She added, 'I feel so sad walking through the shops, watching everyone getting so caught up in the Christmas season and all the fun it brings, and knowing the Morcombes are going through what is certainly the most horrible time of their lives.'

By Monday 22 December, police had interviewed 300 witnesses and recorded 1500 job logs relating to Daniel's disappearance. Meanwhile, they were following the other major line of enquiry: the scruffy man who was seen by various witnesses under the Kiel Mountain Road overpass talking to Daniel. Inside the MIR, descriptions were piling in. Some said he had a goatee. Others said he was clean-shaven. Only one characteristic was consistent: he was unkempt.

* * *

Brett Peter Cowan's white Mitsubishi Pajero four-wheel drive had a distinctive short air filter attached to the driver's side of the vehicle. When he was visiting the house at Alf's Pinch Road, Ken King had snuck under Cowan's vehicle to take photos of the tyre treads. Jessiah Cocks, the 17-year-old boy who had been driving to Nambour with his mother after having lunch at McDonald's, had noticed a white four-wheel drive about 50 to 100 metres north of the overpass. He had said it was locked with no one inside and it was on the same side of the road that Daniel had been waiting for the bus. He had said he thought it might have had an air snorkel.

King and Martyn had filed their job logs. They had also given a verbal briefing to investigating police officers inside the MIR, as was common practice. The investigation, however, was focusing on the blue sedan, especially after the computer-generated images of blue cars had flooded media outlets across the country. There had still been no

COMFITs released of any persons seen under the overpass by witnesses. Inspector Maloney told the media, 'Our primary focus at the moment is to identify this car, that will take us to the person who was with [Daniel].' At the same time, he urged the driver of a commercial, cream-coloured van that was seen nearby to come forward so the driver could be eliminated from the enquiry.

King thought that the investigation had too narrow a focus. With a hundred police officers working around the clock, why wasn't Cowan put under more scrutiny? King and Martyn may well have been constables, but King believed there were ample reasons to focus on Cowan as a major suspect, and the fact he didn't drive a blue car should not have been enough to discount him. Certainly, there was justification for a search warrant. The only person, so far, who corroborated the times Cowan had told the police was Tracey Cowan, his wife.

On 22 December, the day after they first visited Cowan, the constables interviewed the father of Cowan's boss, Frank Davis, in Nambour. Davis, who lived in Perwillowen Road, one of the higher streets above Nambour, confirmed that Cowan had come to pick up a mulcher that Sunday at about 1.30 pm. Martyn and King then went back to interview Cowan and found Tracey there on her own. She told them that Cowan had left to pick up the mulcher at around 12.45 pm and he had been gone for about an hour and a half. They had both had lunch after she returned from church that morning and he had left to get the mulcher shortly after that.

She revealed that her husband had recently shaved his goatee beard because he had just started working at Clayton's Towing Service. She gave them a detailed description of what he might have been wearing the day Daniel disappeared: dark-coloured singlet, dark-coloured board shorts and thongs. The two constables drove the 41 kilometres from Brett Peter Cowan's house at Alf's Pinch Road to Perwillowen Road in Nambour, along the Nambour Connection Road and under the Kiel Mountain Road overpass, carefully timing Cowan's assertions of how long he would have taken to get the mulcher that morning.

After travelling 34 kilometres at the speed limit, King and Martyn reached the overpass in 23 minutes. They then drove to Perwillowen Road in Nambour, noting that the total time for the journey was 34 minutes. If Cowan had picked up the mulcher at around 1.30 pm and stopped to chat to Davis and load the device into his car, they estimated he would have driven back under the overpass at around 2 pm. This was the same time that other witnesses had seen Daniel on the Nambour Connection Road, yet Cowan had denied seeing him while either going or coming from Nambour.

But it was Cowan's criminal record that made King's blood run cold. The files arrived that same day. Cowan's previous opportunistic crimes, and his targets, fitted exactly the type of criminal who might have taken Daniel Morcombe. First, in 1987, he had been charged with minor property offences. That same year, while working as a labourer doing community service work near a childcare centre, he had taken a seven-year-old into a toilet block and sexually assaulted him. He was to serve 14 months of a two-year jail term for that crime. In 1994 he was sentenced to seven years for three charges, including causing grievous bodily harm to a six-year-old boy after he sexually assaulted him at a caravan park in Darwin in the Northern Territory in 1993. The boy, who lived in the same caravan park as Cowan, had been looking for his sister when Cowan had enticed him away from the park on the pretext of finding her. After the assault, the boy had been left for dead in a burnt-out car shell, but managed to escape. At first it was thought that the boy had been run over by a car. There was medical evidence that he had been suffocated after being sodomised and sexually assaulted, and he had severe cuts and abrasions to his body and was haemorrhaging from his eyes. The boy survived, like the previous boy, to tell his story. Although sentenced to seven years for the three charges Cowan only served three years and six months in jail for the offences and his non-parole period was backdated to the date he was first incarcerated.

* * *

Meanwhile, the computer images of the blue car had generated a flood of information and stretched resources. Doing the number-crunching, a total of 426,730 cars were to be identified that might or might not be associated with the case. Police began intercepting and searching blue sedans. People were coming forward with rewards, but police were unable to accept money. Everyone wanted to help to bring Daniel back. Denise's words and her heartfelt plea on television two weeks before had stayed with people long after the words were spoken – they all felt the need to bring him home.

* * *

The following day, 23 December, acting on King and Martyn's information, two detectives, Maclean and Wright, turned up at Alf's Pinch Road. Tracey Cowan was questioned further. She said she thought that Brett might have returned at 3 pm, as that was the time that the sun hit the back of the room and the room heated up, particularly in summer, but she couldn't be sure of the time. She stressed that it could have been up to 30 minutes either side. Working backwards from a 3.30 pm return, King and Martyn had previously estimated that there was a period of 45 minutes during which Tracey's husband was unaccounted for by his alibi. Remarkably, Tracey Cowan was not asked to give a formal police statement.

Brett Cowan was also asked further questions. He told the police he had phoned Frank Davis about 20 minutes before leaving his house and that he would have been at Davis's house for about 15 minutes, as he had to pull the fairing off his Pajero so he could fit the mulcher in. He said he had driven straight home. His neighbour, John Fragos, had then come over to help him with the mulching. Police interviewed John Fragos's son, Eric, who said that Cowan had been working in the yard for most of the day and had continued until dusk. Fragos said he had gone over for a chat with him, possibly at around 2 pm, but he also could not be sure of the time.

The next day was Christmas Eve. Wright and Maclean obtained Cowan's consent to examine the white Pajero. The car was taken to Nambour Police Station, where the Scientific and Fingerprint sections conducted an examination. At the time, the two detectives relayed that Cowan was 'extremely cooperative and understanding of the investigation'. 'Negative results' were noted in a later report. Numerous samples were taken but it was not until more than a decade later that it was revealed that only a routine preliminary search was conducted and that the DNA testing was never carried out.

* * *

As the days passed, King and Martyn were surprised at how few re-enquiries were made to them. It was standard police technique to go back to the original investigative police to check facts. Martyn personally approached senior officers within the Homicide Investigation Unit for updates but was not told anything. King believed in the Victoria Police ethos: a failure to search is a failure to find. They wrote up a major report on the POI. They included Jessiah Cocks who had seen the white four-wheel drive near the overpass and the photograph they had taken of Cowan so it could be used for comparisons with witness descriptions.

Ken King had been convinced that the police had got their man. Here was someone who had a history of multiple opportunistic sexual offences against children involving violence, who also resembled witness descriptions and who had recently shaved off the goatee beard that had been identified in several witness accounts. He had even admitted to police that he had twice driven past the site where Daniel was abducted at around the time he had disappeared. The next step, in King's mind, would be to release Cowan's photo and seek search warrants, which would have included seizing Cowan's computers without warning and checking his phone records.

This would not be done until years later. King and Martyn were told that the Homicide Investigation Unit was running the case. Their investigative role suddenly ended. Perhaps, King thought, when he first questioned Cowan he should have leant on him more, but what if Daniel Morcombe was still alive? There was always that danger, particularly given Cowan's track record. His previous victims' evidence had led to jail sentences. This time, he could kill.

In all, Martyn and King had spent two weeks up on the Sunshine Coast. King admired Martyn for his tenacity: if they could create ten more police officers like Martyn, they could do a lot to lower the Queensland crime rate. But, in spite of their shared expertise, they felt they had achieved nothing. As for the sightings of the blue car, Martyn and King had discussed that there could be multiple offenders who had abducted Daniel. Or perhaps one offender had used more than one vehicle? Cowan's associates should be checked in case they were involved or could give police more information. People might know things but were reluctant to come forward because their lives might be threatened, or maybe they did not understand the importance of what they had seen. Either way, there was no reason that King could see to write off any witness sighting of the white four-wheel drive on the Nambour Connection Road. Failing to find satellite imagery, the accounts from the two witnesses who claimed to have seen a blue car and a white van or four-wheel drive disappear into the Beerwah forest the afternoon Daniel vanished were logged along with all the other accounts.

* * *

Christmas Day 2003 dawned: another day that the Morcombes had been dreading. The family and grandparents arose at 5.30 am, obeying the age-old call of presents to be unwrapped. On top of the Christmas tree was a baby-blue Christmas bauble that had been given to Bruce and Denise to mark Daniel's December birth. Underneath it was a matching trinket for Bradley. Parcels were passed around. The whole process was over in two minutes. There were no presents from Daniel as he had been on his way to the Plaza that day to buy them. Sam Knight had found a Christmas card from Daniel to the family in his schoolbag, which was in pride of place.

Everyone's presents for Daniel remained wrapped under the tree. Brad confessed to the family that Daniel had already opened Nana and Pa's present and that Daniel's response had been, 'That's cool.' Everyone managed a smile at this unexpected news, and Monique wiped away tears. Denise and Bruce had bought Daniel a Fox motocross shirt, a red mag light and some other bits and pieces.

At around 7.30 am, the Morcombe family, and Kevin and Monique, called in to the overpass. They brought some flowers with a card that read, 'Dearest Daniel, we will never forget you. Love you always. Mum, Dad, Dean, Bradley, Nana and Pa'. Their flowers were placed next to a bunch from an unknown wellwisher. They were incredulous at the growing number of gifts under the overpass from complete strangers. They thought of the compassionate strength of the SES volunteers and the support from police who had stayed by their side, united in trying to get an answer. One of the signs read, 'Blessed thoughts are with you, Daniel and family'.

The past 18 days seemed so unreal. One day, they had been an average Australian family. Their young sons were growing into men. They had set up a business to be proud of. Finally, after years of hard work, they had been rewarded. They'd had their first overseas holiday for their 20th wedding anniversary and could afford vacations with the boys. Their children were in a good school and their futures looked rosy. Then the unspeakable had happened. Would they ever know the answer? Would they ever stop talking about whys and what ifs?

At 8 am, the Morcombes, and Kevin and Monique, went to Father Joe's mass. He made a special effort to acknowledge their presence. It was a beautiful gesture, even if all they wanted was to fade into the background. Afterwards, they began the drive south to Brisbane to the house of Bruce's older brother Perry and his wife Joan in Fig Tree Pocket, a Brisbane suburb. Brad went with Bruce, and Denise drove Dean and her parents. The air-conditioner in Denise's car was broken. The heat of a Queensland summer poured in through the open windows. Everyone was listless and melancholy. No one had really wanted to leave the house. Watching everyone else go through Christmas cheer at the family gathering made feeling Daniel's absence more acute. The Morcombes escaped as soon as they could. This outing confirmed something they could no longer deny: their family was permanently scarred.

Julie Elliott made a statement to the media that the search for Daniel would not stop for the holiday. 'Just because it's Christmas Day doesn't lessen the need for the investigation to continue. The team will continue working and everyone else will be on call and ready to come in if anything of significance comes up,' she said.

More than half a dozen churches broke from the traditional message for their Christmas Day church services to pray for Daniel's safe return. Father Joe Duffy told his congregation at the Stella Maris Catholic Church, which had standing room only for the Christmas Mass: 'Children should feel safe using transport, and the simple fact that they aren't is the biggest challenge for the community in 2004. One of the things I encourage the congregation to do is become more observant of children and regard themselves as having stewardship over their safety.'

Two days after Christmas, Denise and Bruce decided to write an open letter to the *Sunshine Coast Daily*. It seemed the best way to express their pain. 'Grave fears are held for Daniel's safety', they wrote. At the bottom of the letter, they urged anyone to contact Crime Stoppers even if their information appeared minor and remote. There had already been 2600 calls made. Whether it was one or more men who had abducted Daniel had not been resolved. On 29 December, a headline in *The Australian* read, 'Police Fear Boy Abducted'. The article stated that Detective Inspector John Maloney believed that Daniel had been abducted 'by at least two men'. The rest of the media followed the new lead. As the newspapers published daily updates, Inspector Maloney continued to state he was 'quite convinced' that the blue sedan was involved in Daniel's disappearance. 'There's no time limits,' he said. 'We'll just keep working on it.'

CHAPTER NINE

RED RIBBONS

Stephen Park had exhibited anti-social behaviour as he went through adolescence, including drinking and smoking. His stepfather, Stephen Scanlan, had been patient with his wayward stepson but, what made matters worse was the fact that Park was associating with unsavoury types. His mate 'Jacko' was only recently out of jail. The two of them had gone fishing on a few occasions. Park was going out with a daughter of Jackway's de facto, Danielle Richardson, and Stephen was spending more and more time with Jacko, whom he seemed to idolise. And now Rose Scanlan, Stephen's mother, was being visited by police for a second time.

Police had already turned up on her doorstep on 12 December. On 30 December 2003, detectives turned up again, this time to conduct an official interview. Shortly after Jackway had been released from jail, Park had moved out of home and into Danielle Richardson's house at Bertha Street, Goodna, where Jackway also lived. Park had first met Jackway in jail while visiting with his girlfriend and her mother. Scanlan told police that, the day before Daniel disappeared, she recalled giving Park and Jacko $50. On the day Daniel vanished, she said that they had turned up at about 10 am and had 'bummed a further $10' from her. Stephen had told her that he and Jacko were going up the coast that day to stay with Jacko's sister in Tewantin, near Noosa, before Jackway had to appear in court on the Monday morning, 8 December.

She had not seen either of them again until Monday afternoon. Then, they had both appeared very tired. She had noticed that Jackway had a bandaid over his left knuckles. They had broken down on the way home, her son told her. The following day, Tuesday, they had returned to pick up Stephen's bedside tables and queen-sized bed, which they had placed on the roof of Jackway's blue Commodore.

Around the same time as the police had first contacted her, her son had rung her to see if she'd heard from them. When she said she had, he asked her to tell the police that he and Jacko had come to pick up his bed on the Sunday Daniel went missing. No, his mother had told him, that was not true. Stephen had hung up on her. Five minutes later, he had turned up at her house with Jackway. Both of them urged her to change her story. Jackway, she recalled, looked very agitated. She also remembered that around 9 December, Jackway had dyed his hair blond.

Steve Scanlan, Stephen Park's stepfather, was also formally interviewed by police on 30 December. Scanlan remembered that both Jackway and his stepson, Stephen, had turned up at 10 am at their Goodna home on 7 December, the day Daniel went missing. They had stayed around half an hour. Scanlan had checked the oil in Jackway's Commodore and added some power-steering fluid. While standing near the car, Jackway had told him, 'I am going up the coast to stay at my sister's place for the hearing at court tomorrow.' He said he had understood that they were heading up the coast that same morning. Jackway, he recalled, was wearing denim shorts and sandshoes. He said he had also seen his stepson the following day, on the Monday, but could not recall whether Jackway was with him. He *did* remember that they had both turned up on the Tuesday to pick up Park's bed and that he had lent them rope to tie the bed onto the roof of the Commodore. On Boxing Day, he had then helped Stephen Park move out of the house at Bertha Street into Paul Carrington's flat in Ipswich.

* * *

Christmas had passed and it was fast approaching a month since Daniel went missing. The Morcombes were not privy to the intricacies of the police investigation. All they knew was that there was no news. Every day they had been waiting for the call saying they had found Daniel. At the three-week mark, they were already worried that Daniel's disappearance could become a cold case. On New Year's Eve, as Brad headed off to bed, he passed Daniel's door.

'Happy New Year, Daniel.'

The comment cut Denise to the core.

Brad's cousin Ashlea in Melbourne tried to cheer him up by saying that Daniel might unexpectedly turn up in Melbourne when Brad visited to see his grandparents, as that's what Brad and Daniel had planned. But Brad boarded the plane alone on 6 January and there was no Daniel at the other end. Kevin and Monique had returned home on New Year's Day and were awaiting his arrival. They had not wanted to leave without answers but Bruce and Denise felt it was important that Brad and Dean got back into a routine.

Early in the New Year, Denise voiced her fears to the media. The public interest in the case had begun to wane. Post-Christmas, the waiting seemed even more unbearable, with nothing to hope for. The regular searches were called off. Although fresh flowers still appeared under the Kiel

Mountain Road overpass, along with crystals and silver angel figurines, even the media coverage had abated. Sometimes, neither Bruce nor Denise could face driving there, and they would take detours to avoid the location that had so radically changed their lives.

Although they attempted to make calls for their Jim's Trees business, they kept their home phone diverted to their mobile in case the call they were waiting for rang in. But news from the police consisted of generalities, sympathy and assurances. The next hurdle coming up at the end of the month would be Bradley's return to school without Daniel. In the meantime, every night at 6 pm, without fail, they continued to light a candle for their missing son.

* * *

On Monday 5 January 2004 – week five of the investigation – police obtained a statement from Jackway's older sister. Jackway had contacted her on the day Daniel disappeared at around 8 am to say he'd been fighting with his de facto and was staying at his mate's house. He asked to come and stay with her. She had been hesitant because of his past. If you come and stay, she had told him, you have to sleep in the car in front of the house. She said that she had been expecting him to arrive around dinnertime but when he had still not turned up at around 7.30 or 8 pm that night, she had checked her answering machine. She found a message that he would no longer be coming and that he had made up with his de facto.

Police examined phone records for the house at Bertha Street and Carrington's house in Ipswich. A call had been made from Bertha Street to Carrington's house at around 11.52 am the day Daniel disappeared and again at 1.03 pm. There was also a call from Carrington's house to Bertha Street at around 12.29 pm for seven and a half minutes. Just over half an hour later, another call was received from

Carrington's house to Bertha Street, which lasted more than eight minutes. Two further calls were made from Carrington's house to Bertha Street at around 3.30 pm, one quite brief and the other lasting eleven minutes, and there was a record that two calls had been made to Jackway's sister's house at 7.15 pm, one only a few seconds long, the other 30 seconds in duration. Carrington had confirmed the times for his calls to the house in Bertha Street in his initial statement. Jackway's bank records showed no withdrawals had been made the day Daniel disappeared, but they did show that his account had been accessed for a balance enquiry at 5 am the next day from the BP service station at Goodna, followed by a $10 withdrawal. Jackway and Park also showed up on footage from the CCTV cameras at the BP service station that day. The footage revealed that they were driving the blue Holden Commodore.

On 9 January, four days after Jackway's sister was interviewed, police carried out a search warrant on Bertha Street, Goodna. Jackway and Danielle Richardson were present, as well as two of Richardson's daughters. Police seized Jackway's Holden Commodore sedan, which was taken to Mount Gravatt Police Station for scientific examination.

Following this, Jackway was taken to Goodna Police Station to provide a record of interview with Detective Ross Hutton and Detective Ward. He told police that, after Park left the house in Bertha Street in Goodna and moved in with Carrington on Boxing Day, he had little to do with him. He added some more details to firm up his alibis. He said Richardson had returned to the house at Bertha Street at about 5.30 am on 7 December and they had argued until 11 am. He had then gone around to Stephen Park's parents' house that same morning and then returned to Bertha Street, leaving again in the evening to go to Carrington's house. He also told police that his car had broken down when he was on his way to court at Noosa.

Danielle Richardson was also officially interviewed for the second time, making a formal statement at Goodna Police Station, which was recorded. She said that Jackway might have been away from Bertha Street for an hour and a half at most the day Daniel disappeared. Police noted in the report, 'There was no indication Richardson was protecting Jackway.'

Carrington's flat in Ipswich was searched and he was also interviewed. Carrington said that, after meeting Jackway in jail in 1997, he'd had no contact with him until 2 December 2003. He said that, shortly after reconnecting with Jackway, Danielle Richardson had phoned him on 5 December to 'bitch' about her de facto. That night, Jackway and Park had turned up for drinks and had stayed until about 11 pm. The following day, they had turned up with clothes to store under his house because Jackway said he had had a fight with Richardson. Carrington said Jackway had then rung him in the early hours of 7 December asking if he could move in because he'd had another fight with Richardson. Later, he had been woken up by another phone call from Jackway, who told him he was going up the coast. He received yet another call from him asking for money for fuel. Carrington rang the house at Bertha Street around lunchtime on the day Daniel disappeared but was told by Richardson that Jackway had left. He claimed that Jackway then rang at about 3 pm and came around and collected $30 off him. He had noticed that there were fishing rods in the car. Carrington had later spoken to both Park and Jackway asking whether they were involved in the Daniel Morcombe case. Both had denied it.

Park was also interviewed on 9 January, in the presence of a justice of the peace, because he was a juvenile. He described how he and Jackway would 'drink together, work on cars and go lapping'. He told police he had borrowed $10 off his mother on 7 December, confirming her story, and that he and Jackway had then returned to Bertha Street. He said he had gone upstairs to watch movies and was under the impression that Jackway was working on his car. At some stage, Jackway had come up to tell him that he was no longer going up the coast that day. Jackway had told him that Danielle Richardson had suggested they leave the following day instead. Park also confirmed that they had stopped at the BP service station in Goodna the following morning. Park appeared to police to be evasive when asked questions, but, later in the interview, he admitted that he and Jackway had stolen a car at Goodna Railway Station on 5 December to go and pick up Jackway's car, which had been impounded after the police chase, and police believed this provided a reason for him to be uncomfortable.

Two days later, on 11 January 2004, police tracked down Vincent Tournoff. Tournoff had been living with another of Danielle Richardson's daughters and her children. Tournoff said Richardson's daughter had asked him to go around and talk to Jackway the day Daniel disappeared as her mother had rung to say she was upset because Jackway would not let her go out. Tournoff said he had turned up at Bertha Street and spent an hour and a half talking to Jackway somewhere around 12 and 1 pm.

* * *

By early January, Bruce was not sure who or what to believe. He had heard stories about a paedophile ring involving police and the judiciary. He refused to take it seriously without concrete proof such as names and places to go on. He had also heard about a gay meeting place in the public toilets at a small park near the turnoff to Woombye on the Nambour Connection Road not far from the abduction site. On two or three occasions, he drove into the carpark, determined to stake it out. Once, he saw a car parked there. He went inside the public toilets and there was a man with his back to the urinal looking at him. Bruce said nothing. Instead, he turned and headed to the cubicles. He got the fright of his life. There was another man standing there facing out with the door open. He quickly turned and walked away. It was a wake-up call. He had walked in on a seedy scene he had not witnessed first-hand before.

Around this time, Denise asked the Catholic community to help police find what everyone now believed were two men who might know Daniel's whereabouts. 'People talk in the pub or at the shops. They may overhear someone else talking. They may remember seeing something, and, if they do, please, please make the call. It will only take one little piece of information to help,' she pleaded.

'It doesn't feel real at the moment,' she told the *Sunshine Coast Daily*. 'If it had been a car accident or he had been sick, at least we'd know what happened, but he just vanished.'

When a loved one goes missing, it is its own special form of hell, and the family were now living it.

The mind plays tricks on you, Bruce thought. Logic tells you it's not good news, but still you hope. Denise was always hoping Daniel would appear at the door, even though she knew in her heart that he wouldn't. And then there was always the worst to imagine. Was Daniel being held somewhere? The thought tortured them – how scared would he be, how much was he suffering? It was unendurable.

Something had to be done. Prior to their son vanishing, Bruce and Denise believed that the media covered stories by researching information and then writing it up and editing it for publication. They quickly realised that story ideas were worked out even before an interview took place, particularly with broadcast news, which relied on sound or vision clips. The journalists, it seemed to them, simply wanted quotes to fill out the story. Gradually, their knowledge grew about what the media expected. It was all part of the strange world they now inhabited. Before Daniel disappeared, actors or sports personalities made the news, not ordinary people like them. Elliott had even warned them to expect the media to invade their privacy, perhaps by filming them over the fence in their dressing gowns, but this hadn't happened. They both largely felt supported by the media and were gaining an inside understanding of how they all operated.

Julie Elliott's expertise had helped them to gain exposure in the all-important task of keeping Daniel's story alive. Her natural maternal instincts meant that she felt hugely protective of Denise. Sometimes, she would remind investigating police, 'These people have lost their son. It's not just as clinical as following up a lead.' But then she would see the officers working through weekends and holidays, all in pursuit of the same aim, to find Daniel, and she would see the energy and dedication they were all putting into the task.

Bruce and Denise often discussed the impact their appearance would have on their story. As they saw it, Joanne Lees, whose boyfriend Peter Falconio disappeared in the Australian outback, and Lindy Chamberlain, who was charged with murdering her infant daughter, later found to have been killed by a dingo, had been innocent people crucified by the media for not acting in the conventional role of the victim. Without any advice, these women had been denigrated for the way they responded to media questions and the public's expectations about the way they grieved. It was not always easy. But there was also a fine line between the Morcombes biting their tongues and delivering a censored message. They had to tread carefully to keep the police onside and not hamper the investigation. It was always a compromise. The Morcombes were determined to get it right, to do anything that might unearth the truth about their son.

* * *

Bruce had been in the barn one day when he'd first noticed a door from one of the many renovations they had made to

Camellia Cottage. It was white with a steel door handle and a lock. He was struck by the fact that it symbolised what he and Denise and the rest of the family wanted: to find the key and open the door, and to solve the puzzle of Daniel's disappearance. He decided then and there to talk to the media directly.

On 16 January 2004, the first of what was to become several doors materialised under the Kiel Mountain Road overpass, bearing the message, 'Where is Daniel? Who took him? Help find the key to unlock this "Horror" of a crime. We will never give up.' It was signed 'The Morcombe Family'.

Julie Elliott had reluctantly given her approval for the door idea. The raw, handwritten words scrawled across it were in stark contrast to the carefully managed media messages appealing to people who might have been involved to come forward to help police.

Afterwards, Bruce and Denise decided to launch a red-ribbon campaign from Daniel's abduction site. The door had sparked media interest and it was to be the first of many occasions where they began to appreciate how to directly engage media attention. To launch the appeal, Bruce attached ribbons to the door, red to symbolise the colour of the T-shirt Daniel was wearing when he disappeared. It provided a photo opportunity as well as vision for the television cameras.

'We'd just like to think that the general public out there will display red ribbons around their letterboxes to symbolise to others that Daniel is not forgotten and we still hope he will be returned,' Bruce said. 'This not only helps us but there are a lot of people who knew Daniel or were touched by his loss and this is some symbolism that he's not forgotten. It would be lovely to see others do it to show they support us and are thinking of Daniel, and hopefully it will jar somebody's conscience to dob in the person that's done this.'

Neither of them wanted to return to the site but they braved the occasion by lighting a candle at a small shrine surrounded by the flowers and tributes to Daniel. This lonely stretch of highway, straddled by the concrete overpass, was the only place to come and visit their son. This time, their plea had changed its emphasis. 'We're really desperate to find the person or persons who did this,' Bruce said.

Launching their own website was also important to them. They wanted to use it as a conduit between them and the public to release information from the police, to thank the community and to appeal for information. They contacted a computer company in Melbourne. Initially, the idea was resisted by the police officers at MIR, but Bruce and Denise insisted, and after consultation with Police Commissioner Bob Atkinson and Greg Daniels, it was agreed that the only contact point for anyone with information about Daniel would still be through Crime Stoppers which ensured that police had control over any leads, and so www. danielmorcombe.com.au was born. It was the first such website, Bruce and Denise believed, that had been produced by family members on an ongoing missing persons case.

Following the Morcombes' campaign launch, Inspector Maloney gave his own media conference, urging anyone who had seen Daniel's brown Billabong sports wallet or silver fob watch to come forward. Maloney was photographed holding up a replica of the one Daniel owned.

The red ribbons on the white door under the overpass sowed a seed that spread like wildflowers. The colour red sprouted everywhere – along streets and shopping malls, in bus stops and schools. It was a public statement. People could join the campaign. Red ribbons were appearing everywhere, on letterboxes from Palmwoods and Woombye to Buderim and Mooloolaba. In the days following Daniel's disappearance, the whole of the Palmwoods community had been buzzing with anxiety. The thumping sound of the choppers' blades overhead reminded them that there was a predator in their midst. People would examine the side of the road looking for a red T-shirt or a shoe Daniel may have discarded, leaving a clue as to where he was. But now there was a communal cause to join.

Speedway fans donated $2000 collected in 30 minutes by passing racing helmets around a 3000-strong crowd at a weekend's Machinery Wars event, and organisers said that further fundraising was planned.

In the midst of the community uniting, however, Daniel's case attracted the first of what were to be several bizarre red herrings. Alex Milat, brother of the serial backpacker murderer Ivan Milat, grabbing his share of the headlines, told police that he had seen Daniel being abducted. An anonymous letter was also sent to *The Courier-Mail* alleging the same thing. Milat, who lived in Palmwoods, claimed to have seen a man on the Nambour Connection Road who was six feet four inches tall with Daniel at 2.12 pm on Sunday 14 December, a week after he went missing. Milat said he 'vaguely' remembered that the boy was wearing a red T-shirt. It was agreed that Milat had in fact observed the police re-enactment, and not the unfolding events a week prior.

Also in January, Operation Vista received information via Crime Stoppers from people about the 1997 abduction and murder of 11-year-old Gerard Ross. Ross, who was with his older brother Malcolm, had been abducted in broad daylight on 14 October while holidaying in the Western Australian town of Rockingham, 50 kilometres south of Perth. His body was found in a nearby pine plantation two weeks after he went missing. There had been no inquest. Operation Shoalwater was set up and, in spite of several POIs, the Director of Public Prosecutions said there was insufficient proof to proceed with charges. One newspaper report later pointed to one person who had been overlooked who knew the Ross family and who had allegedly lied to police about where he was the day Ross disappeared. The man had later moved overseas and then apparently to Queensland. Operation Vista investigators established contact with Western Australian police who forwarded a list of 470 POIs from Operation Shoalwater.

* * *

As the weeks continued to drag on with no breakthroughs, the tide was starting to turn against the Sunshine Coast bus service Sunbus. An industrial dispute loomed between the drivers and their employer, with the Transport Workers Union state organiser saying drivers were being subjected to snide remarks over Daniel's disappearance, while also admitting that the threatened strike was about breakdowns, wages and outdated timetables. One Sunbus driver, however, spoke out to *The Courier-Mail* claiming that, although what had happened to Daniel was 'horrible', 'it was not our fault'. But even Father Joe Duffy, who had been saying communal prayers for Daniel at the Stella Maris Catholic Church, questioned the bus company's policies. Handing out 2000 ribbons at his mass on Sunday 25 January, he told the *Sunshine Coast Daily* that the radios used by bus drivers to communicate that a passenger was stranded could easily be intercepted by scanners.

On 26 January, Australia Day, red ribbons were used for Buderim's celebrations. The following day, another milestone was reached. Denise, in particular, had been dreading it. Bradley had to go back to school, now as the boy with the missing brother whose face had appeared across the nation. Brad had wanted to catch the bus on his own, insisting to his parents that he wanted to go back to the routine of his normal life. But, on the first day, Bruce and Denise drove him to school.

A group of his friends was there to meet him at the school gate, which Graeme Hight had organised, and they took him straight to home-room. Brad noticed the red ribbons on the lockers. Every time he walked past Daniel's locker, he would look at it, a ritual to be repeated many times as he finished his years at school. Classmates had placed drawings of motorbikes inside Daniel's locker for him. As much as Bradley wanted everything to feel normal, a photo of his first day back appeared in the *Nambour & District Community News* and *The Courier-Mail*.

The principal, Bryan Baker, and deputy principal, Graeme Hight, had been discussing how to handle the tragic circumstances of Daniel's disappearance when the children returned to school. Siena Catholic College practised a staggered start for its students. The Grade 8 and Grade 12s returned first, as they were respectively starting and finishing school that year, then Grades 9, 10 and 11 followed a few days later. Bradley was now in Grade 10. It was decided that the whole school would be addressed about Daniel's disappearance once everyone had returned and the first full assembly was held.

Before the liturgy, the prayers that morning were for Daniel. The first newsletter of the year read, 'Evil Persons are Still at Large'. Bruce had to face the task of cancelling Daniel's schoolbook order, which had been placed at the same time as Bradley's. Each day, he and Denise had hoped they wouldn't have to keep making these final decisions. Each was an admission that Daniel was not coming back soon.

Dean had decided in January that he was definitely not going back to school, but would go to TAFE. He started studying a film course on Fridays, and was also still working at the nursery nearby. Dean kept a photo of Daniel next to his bed. Life was moving on, even though everyone wanted to turn the clock back.

After dropping Brad at school that first day, Denise and Bruce visited the shrine beneath the overpass, which included the white-painted door with the steel handle and their handwritten appeal. They placed a vase of fresh roses and red ribbons there.

Two months after he disappeared, Daniel's bedroom still remained untouched, apart from where police had taken Daniel's posters, his school Bible and school cap, his motorbike manual and schoolbooks in the hope they might be able to get some fingerprints. His pyjamas lay folded on his bed and his schoolbag was on a chair where Sam Knight had returned it.

Bullet and Sorrento nonchalantly grazed grass in the paddock near the lily-covered dam. Daniel's motorbike was still in the barn. Everyone was waiting for him to come home. Brad took Daniel's Japanese fighting fish to his own room so he could feed it.

The Morcombes were still enduring all sorts of probing questions from police. Sam Knight had been relaying questions from detectives in the MIR. They knew it was to eliminate them as suspects, but to be quizzed about potential skeletons in the closet, their relationship with Daniel, the health of their marriage, whether they'd had an affair or were concealing other family secrets was all part of their now nightmarish existence. Bruce had even been asked once why he didn't wear a wedding ring. He had immediately gone upstairs and dug it out from a box of trinkets. 'I don't wear it because it doesn't fit me,' he said, balancing the ring on the tip of his wedding finger.

On 2 February, Siena Catholic College held a Red Ribbon Day. Channel Seven came to film the event. As the cameras began to roll, the schoolchildren came over the hill on the school walkway waving red flags, contrasting brightly with their grey school uniforms. The image would always stay in Graeme Hight's mind. He saw them as the cavalry approaching, a sea of brave red surging forward. It was a strong public gesture of support from the school, just like the impromptu mass held in December. Brad walked behind his mum and dad. Principal Bryan Baker, who only had six more weeks to live, and the newly elected school captains, Daniel Craig and Meg De Groot, were on either side of the parade. Bruce and Denise had not been expecting to be filmed by the media as they symbolically walked with the students prior to a prearranged media conference, but some of the cameramen saw the opportunity and captured the footage. The school captains addressed the crowd on behalf of the college, urging witnesses to come forward to help the two-month-old police investigation. Denise and Bruce made the news public that they were starting up a website for Daniel. A special Crime Stoppers bank account had been set up in recognition of the many offers of financial support.

Brad came home that day wearing a red bracelet around his wrist, a gift from his classmates. During one of the media interviews with Steve Marshall for Channel Nine, Brad had been given a remote-control helicopter and had been filmed playing with it in the Morcombes' barn. He was also filmed going for his first helicopter ride. He confided to the reporter from the *Sunshine Coast Daily* that his dream was to become a commercial pilot. When he was only four, he had told his mother that he wanted to be a captain in the Flying Doctor Service.

* * *

Greg Daniels, in his role as a police officer, had organised various police charity golf-club days. These events helped to bring local communities together. Daniels was not much of a golfer, but the idea stuck with him. Around the pine table in the Morcombes' dining room, they discussed ideas of fundraising. Everywhere they went, people were asking how they could donate money.

But it was Peter Owen, editor of the *Sunshine Coast Daily*, who really embraced the idea of a golf day. Owen knew Greg

Bruce and Denise's wedding day on 3 September 1983.

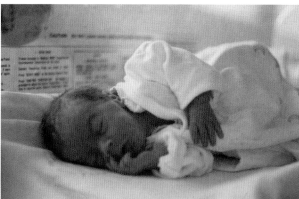

Daniel James Morcombe, a few days old, in a humidity crib at Monash Medical Centre, Victoria.

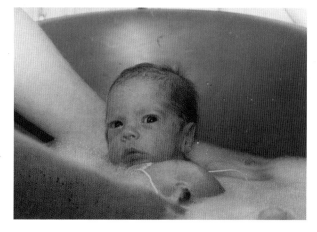

Daniel having a bath at Monash Medical Centre, Victoria.

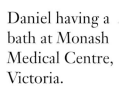

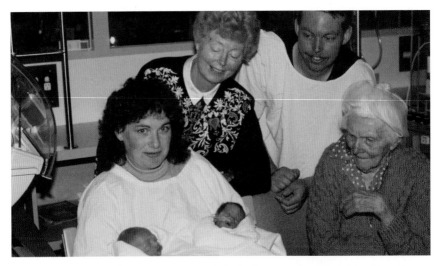

Daniel and Bradley, two days old. *Left to right*: Denise, Bradley (with blond hair), Daniel (with dark hair), Wendy Morcombe (Bruce's mother), Bruce, and Ruby Morcombe (Bruce's grandmother).

Daniel wearing his first pair of red boots after his first birthday.

Denise, Bruce, Daniel, Bradley and Dean. Family photo for Bruce's sister, Lindy's, wedding to Andrew Colebrook, 1992.

Daniel, Dean and Bradley. Queensland, 1993.

Bradley and Daniel. Mountain Creek, Queensland, 1996.

Front: Daniel, Dean and Bradley. *Back*: Monique Beavis (Denise's mum) and Denise in Melbourne, December 1997.

Right: Daniel,
aged eight, and
Chief, 1997.

Below: Daniel
and Bradley's
tenth birthday, 19
December 1999.

Left: Daniel with Gitana at Buddina house, Queensland, 1999.

Below: Bradley, Dean and Daniel's first Communion at Stella Maris Catholic Church, Queensland. This photo was taken in the chapel.

Below: Bradley sitting on a fence behind Sorrento and Daniel saddled up on Bullet.

Above: Daniel (in red) and Bradley's 12th birthday at the end of primary school. Burning uniforms and school books was a group tradition.

Above: Daniel's Grade 7 school camp at Mountain Creek.

Left: Daniel on his 13th birthday.

Right: Bradley and Daniel's first day at secondary school, Grade 8 at Siena Catholic College.

Left: Family photo at Warburton, Victoria: Monique, Bradley, Kevin (Denise's father), Dean and Daniel, January 2003.

Right: Daniel, Dean, Bradley, Denise and Bruce on holiday at Hamilton Island, Easter 2003.

Left: Denise and Bruce in Santorini, Greece, celebrating their 20th wedding anniversary in August 2003.

Right: Daniel and Dean on motorbikes in 2003. Daniel is in the blue T-shirt.

Below: This photo of Daniel was given to the Morcombe family after he was recovered and is Denise's favourite.

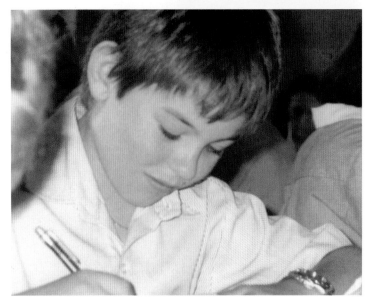

Daniels from primary school, and his son had been in Daniel Morcombe's class at Siena Catholic College. An avid golfer, Owen believed a charity golf day was the perfect opportunity to raise funds for the cause.

Tim Ryan was a charismatic local businessman described by Daniels as 'a genuine human being'. His son, Ben, had ridden motorbikes with Daniel at Kelvin Kruger's property on Nicklin Road. Through his company, Yambah Constructions, he had already distributed signs all over Brisbane, the Gold Coast and the Sunshine Coast asking 'Where is Daniel?'. They were accompanied by a photograph of Daniel with his characteristic smile. Now, he volunteered to donate prizes for the golf day.

The event was to be named 'A Day for Daniel', and the date was set for 6 February. It was organised by the Siena Catholic College P&F and the North Coast branch of Crime Stoppers. Daniels also spoke to the president of Crime Stoppers, Mick Hourigan, who owned a local whitegoods store. Hourigan happened to be president of the Horton Park Golf Club. The club lay behind the Sunshine Plaza, not far from the ocean and the mouth of the Maroochy River. Advertisements were placed in the *Sunshine Coast Daily*. More than $4000 in prizes were up for grabs, the advertisement said, and there would also be a free sausage sizzle. Peter Owen's personal mobile number was given to the public. The $500 'sponsorship positions' were selling like hot cakes. An editorial appeared in the newspaper urging the community to support the day, and an anonymous donation of $5000 had already been received.

More than 280 people teed off that day. It was the largest charity golf day in the Sunshine Coast's history. A number of high-ranking police officers turned up, all sporting red ribbons, including Assistant Commissioner Ian Stewart, and they were joined by prominent local businessmen. Denise's parents, Kevin and Monique, were surprise visitors, flown up for the day. Denise greeted her mother tearfully, and Kevin hugged Dean and Brad close. They were meeting again after only a month. Everyone had hoped that their next meeting would have been because Daniel was found.

Dean was the first to tee off, at 7 am. Brad played with Sergeant Shane Panoho and Bruce played with Greg Daniels, teeing off at 12.30 pm as part of the afternoon group. Denise helped cook the sausages for the free lunch. That night, an auction of electrical goods, holiday packages, business signage and sporting memorabilia, including an autographed rugby league jersey and signed photograph of cricketer Allan Border, raised $75,000. Local artist Kendall Perkins-Brakels, one of the Siena Catholic College parents, had been asked by the P&F to do a painting that included a red ribbon to be auctioned at the event. Her response was a large canvas in greens and red entitled *Forget-Me-Nots*, depicting a field of flowers with a red ribbon flowing through them and a sunset in the background. Tim Ryan and his business partner Darren Newell bought the painting for $2500 and donated it to the Morcombes.

The crowd at the golf day was told that Daniel's case had prompted the greatest amount of public information in the police service's 140-year history. There was good media coverage of the event. Bruce said that the money raised was to continue the campaign to get Daniel's story out there, to pay for television advertisements, posters and billboards, including corflute signs to be displayed on Jim's Mowing trailers across the state. He also re-pledged that the new website would be launched that week.

'With the support of the Coast, the criminals that abducted Daniel will be caught ... the people who did this have underestimated the level to which Daniel's disappearance has affected the community and business leaders,' he said. Denise, too, spoke on behalf of her family, saying that finding the men who took her son could stop another child from being taken. Her comments and photograph appeared on the front page of the *Sunshine Coast Daily*: 'Let us send a message to Daniel's abductors and others like them that you'll be found and made to account for your actions.'

Denise's father, Kevin, thanked the Queensland Police Service, singling out a few officers for extra praise. 'You should be so proud of your police force on the Sunshine Coast,' he said, adding it was the police who kept them going in the first week that Daniel disappeared. 'They stayed with us day and night virtually, just took us into their hearts – it was just unbelievable.' For Bruce and Denise, it was a day of firsts. They had never been to a fundraising event before; until now they hadn't known this kind of thing existed. Once again they were overwhelmed by the community support. It was visible – hundreds of people had turned up, and they were all standing shoulder-to-shoulder with them.

Greg Daniels later put the success of A Day for Daniel down to 'community outrage' – the inconceivable had happened, and the community was not going to sit back and accept it.

* * *

As Bruce had hoped, the community indignation about what had happened to Daniel continued. The Australian Institute of Sport Swim Team, who had been training on the Sunshine Coast for the past fortnight, took on the visiting Canadian Olympic Swimming Team as a way of raising money for the Crime Stoppers newly formed Youth Incentive appeal. It was their last chance to swim competitively before the Australian Olympic selection trials the following month.

On the weekend that followed A Day for Daniel, Bruce and Denise again made the front page of the newspaper, writing an emotional letter expressing their thanks. Bruce said, 'Finding and punishing those responsible is like lying in bed at night with an annoying mosquito pestering you. You know it is out there somewhere close by, but you cannot see it to deal with it.'

The Red Ribbon campaign continued to attract new audiences. That weekend, a stall at the Sunshine Coast Plaza, helped by an FM breakfast show, sold their full stock of 500 red candles and 900 letterbox ribbons. Many more stall visitors donated gold coins and others freely gave notes, so a further $2600 was raised. The idea behind the candles had come from a local woman whose youngest daughter had once gone missing and whose nephew had started a candle vigil for Daniel as he had done for his cousin. Fortunately the girl had been found unharmed.

Tim Ryan had also been working on more permanent fixtures on the roads to remind motorists about Daniel. As one of Coates Hire's biggest customers, he contacted the state's general manager for the company, Ian Birch. 'I've got this crazy idea about getting some of your electronic signs out. I want every sign you've got,' he said. 'They have to be everywhere and they need to say "Where is Daniel?"'

From 22 February, the signs began appearing: large, black screens with electronic lights on small trailers flashing, 'Daniel. Any info?' and a Crime Stoppers phone number. The first one appeared near the Kiel Mountain Road overpass. Bruce and Denise had been working with Julie Elliott to ask the Department of Main Roads to place a banner there. The electronic sign on the small trailer, which usually broadcast roadworks or traffic hazards, was eye-catching. Similar signs appeared throughout Queensland, in Emerald, Mackay, Gladstone, Mount Isa, Rockhampton, Townsville and Toowoomba. Explaining the company's motives, Birch told the media that he had agreed to Ryan's request. 'We're a big company and a lot of us have young kids – I've got a boy the same age as Daniel. If it happened to anyone in the Coates family, it would be no different,' he said.

Bruce commented that he hoped the people who had done this to Daniel were 'shaking in their boots and thinking it's only a matter of time before someone cottons on to the fact it's them. That's the point of it all – to make them have a guilt complex – and turn themselves in or have someone else do it.'

* * *

By mid-March, 20,000 posters carrying Daniel's photograph and details of his disappearance were supplied to schools, shopping centres, police stations and businesses across Australia. More than 3000 pieces of information had been reported to the police. Many of the posters were done for free. The fighting spirit of Queensland had been ignited. One printer, Rallings, from Brisbane, printed 1.73 million A5 flyers. They were distributed in all Coles stores through the checkouts. Years later, people were to tell Bruce and Denise that the flyer was still on their fridge.

Daniel's name remained in the headlines and Bruce and Denise had renewed hope seeing Daniel's presence everywhere. Some witnesses came forward who had previously remained silent – a fact they now identified with shame. Six mothers whose children attended the local Woombye State School told police that they had seen an old-fashioned blue sedan waiting outside the school on several occasions from September to November 2003. The car had been seen on a Wednesday or Friday around 2.30 to 3 pm in the school's lower car park, which had angled bays and was a hundred metres west of the main entrance. Some of the mothers said they had noticed that the car had New South Wales number plates. One mother said that it wasn't until one of her children brought home a one-page police circular in February and she read the last line asking whether anyone had seen a suspicious blue car that she suddenly remembered not just the car but also the face of the man she had seen. He had scruffy hair and a weather-beaten, leathery face with marks on it, 'not exactly pockmarks' but 'gaunt, sunken and sallow'. He looked, she recalled much later, 'evil'.

Her friend, another mother, had pulled up near her car that day. The first mother had got out to talk to her friend. As they chatted, she noticed that a man was watching the children. She scanned the man's car for any sign that he had children, but there was nothing. She and the other mother discussed him for a moment and then rationalised his behaviour. Perhaps he had just moved there and was looking for his kids. As both mothers loaded their children into the car, the first mother heard the blue car start up and watched it speed off quickly down the lane. She instinctively reached into the glove box for her small notebook and pen. Her children asked what she was doing as she scribbled down the registration number. As to why she hadn't told the police earlier, she admitted she had been suspicious and fully intended reporting it but she had been using the notebook to jot down details for a family holiday in the upcoming September–October school holidays. They had left for the holiday and the blue car had slipped her mind. Nor had she told the school. She kept thinking that, if she saw him again, she would tell someone. She searched everywhere for the notebook but the last time she remembered having it was at a North Queensland caravan park. She was never able to find it.

Yet more mothers came forward with similar information. One said the same man had been 'scanning' the kids as they left the school one day in November and had parked his car erratically. After glaring at him for some minutes, she must have caught his attention, as the man had unexpectedly swung his head to the right. They had locked eyes. He had then accelerated away. She remembered that the car was 'almost faded blue'. None of the mothers had seen the man collecting children from the school. One of the mothers was nagged to go to the police by her daughter, but she told her daughter she felt she didn't have anything much to say.

* * *

More than three months had passed, and, in spite of all the publicity, police had no firm leads. Around this time, Bruce and Denise auctioned off the small investment property in Buderim they had been buying just before Daniel went missing and that had settled the day after he disappeared. Neither of them felt like going through with the original plan of doing up the place to rent it out. Their vision of the future had irrevocably altered. On the day of the auction, two 'hotlaps' – travelling as a passenger in a race car – had been donated for Dean and Bradley at the racetrack at Warwick, 130 kilometres south-west of Brisbane. After taking the boys to ride their laps, they drove the six-hour return trip to Buderim to attend the auction. Fifty people turned up. Painters, cleaners, fencers and landscapers had given their time to do up the property. They all worked hard but, in the end, bidding was slow and the family lost $30,000 on the sale.

The Sunday Mail reported on 21 March that there had been five attempted abductions in South East Queensland since February, some involving children. But for every bad story, a more positive one would appear. A meeting of principals from seven Sunshine Coast schools decided to trial a walk-to-school program, with groups of children walking together to improve students' fitness and engage the community, the *Sunshine Coast Daily* reported. 'Part of the battle,' one of the principals said, 'is convincing parents that it is a safe thing, especially since Daniel Morcombe went missing, but the children will be walked to school by trained and screened walking leaders.'

Meanwhile, the Queensland Premier, Peter Beattie, announced that there would be a second Day for Daniel on 20 April, to coincide with the next sitting of parliament, and urged everyone, MPs included, to wear red ribbons.

On 22 March, Bryan Baker, the principal of Siena Catholic College, died. Bruce and Denise were preparing to go the funeral but, at the last minute, Bruce told Denise he could not go. He was lying on the balcony and had been vomiting, unable to face another public gathering with the knowledge that his son had gone. Denise went alone.

Almost four months after Daniel went missing, Bruce's anger over Sunbus and the company's policy that had led to a refusal to pick up Daniel spilt over into the public arena. Bruce kept revisiting what he considered this major omission on the part of the company. He responded to a reader in the *Sunshine Coast Daily* who claimed that Sunbus was the subject of an unfair vendetta and who was critical of the fact that where Daniel was catching the bus was 'not a stop'. Bruce replied that Daniel would 'still be with us today' if the replacement bus that first approached the overpass had stopped to pick him up. 'Somebody has to be held accountable for what happened,' Bruce wrote. Sunbus management had never sent flowers or a card, or even phoned the Morcombes. The following day, on 31 March, Bruce was the focus of a news article in the *Sunshine Coast Daily*, asserting that the family may pursue legal action. 'The question is whether Sunbus placed our son in a vulnerable position which led to his abduction.' Bruce and Denise were desperately searching for answers, their emotions swinging between anguish and anger.

* * *

On 19 April, the eve of the second Day for Daniel, *Australian Story* screened a program on the Morcombes. It was entitled 'Into Thin Air', from a comment Bruce had made during the filming, which had taken place over five weeks during February and March. It had been Julie Elliott's suggestion that the Morcombes appear on the show. With 1.4 million viewers, it was the second-highest rating the program had ever produced. Thirty hours of footage had been reduced to 25 minutes. Julie Elliott began the story. She revealed that she had broken the cardinal rule of not becoming attached, as this case had made a deep emotional impact on her.

Then the footage moved to Sam Knight: how difficult it had been for Denise to let her into Daniel's bedroom in those early days, which had not been touched since he left – the missing teenager that the whole country was searching for. Like Elliott, she was living with this almost every day and had become close to the Morcombes.

Denise spoke on air about the letters she received from psychics, how they had told her that Daniel was in a local barn close by or in a country town and how any information had to be greeted with hope. Yet, every day, there was nothing conclusive.

Detective Sergeant Dave Wilkinson, the quiet and softly spoken Homicide Investigation Unit officer with a shaved head in charge of the MIR, was also interviewed, behind his desk in a crisply tailored suit. 'It could happen to anyone,' was his sobering message. 'It could happen to any family.' He added that 60,000 bumper stickers had been sent around the country with Daniel's name and face on them in a bid to find an answer.

Elliott ended the program saying that, every day, everyone parted with a phrase: 'We will find him.' Denise, looking straight at the camera, addressed the viewers: 'We have to know what happened to Daniel. Where he is.' Knight's last comment was, 'It's probably the most important job I will ever do.'

Elliott's instincts paid off. More than 200 new pieces of information were received after the screening of the program, bringing the total number of calls to Crime Stoppers to 4000.

A chat room and forum was set up by the ABC following the program with more than a thousand people calling in. One woman claimed she knew who had taken Daniel. However, in spite of the attention, as the weeks rolled on, there were still no fresh leads.

* * *

The following day, the Day for Daniel was held in Queens Park in downtown Brisbane, organised by radio station B105 with Jamie Dunn, the comedian behind the puppet Agro. Bruce and Denise were totally unprepared for the size of the event, and were overcome with emotion when thousands of red balloons were launched over the city. Construction workers blasted their horns as the balloons drifted high above the skyline. Bruce and Denise stood next to each other as they released their balloons from the netting. 'What keeps us going every day is just everything everyone is doing for us,' she told the media. 'It's just overwhelming.' She ended with her now familiar call for action – for anyone to come forward with any information.

Leading up to this 'Day to Remember Daniel', there had been media stories about the shortage of ribbons. Julie Elliott had urged suppliers to stock up. By the time the big day came around, the community support was at fever pitch. 'A Dance for Daniel', a drug-and-alcohol-free event with security and street angels, had been successful, with the ticket sales donated to the Daniel Morcombe Fund. And there were other community contributions. Daniel's face beamed down from the posters, encouraging support. The boy who was shy even when posing for family photographs was now everywhere. Burnside Primary School near Nambour put together a song called 'Ripples of Red Ribbon', inspired by a teacher after she looked at the Grade 3 students' artwork hanging on the music room's windows.

But it was a local 37-year-old mother and singer, Tania Netherway, who had lost a four-month-old daughter to SIDS and who had never recorded a song in her life, who wrote the track that was to become the catchcry and unofficial anthem of the hunt for Daniel. The words came to her in a dream, she said, after dropping her children to school, when she wondered how she would feel if it happened to her. The music, aided by professional musicians, had been used in the program 'Into Thin Air', with footage of the band playing and Tania singing the haunting refrain. Harvey Norman bought the first 5000 copies in anticipation of consumer demand. There had been the usual media scuffle for anything new, with Channel Ten screening a piece on the CD before the ABC program went to air. The CD was launched on 2 May 2004, and Tania Netherway donated proceeds from the sales to Crime Stoppers to fund the search for Daniel.

CHAPTER TEN

DARK DAYS

Bruce and Denise resolved, as they were repeatedly told, to let the law take its course. They were confident that progress was being made because the police repeatedly informed them that they were doing everything possible. Julie Elliott tried her best to move them into a more positive space. Even before *Australian Story* and the second Day for Daniel, Elliott had been working on an idea to leverage more publicity further afield. Although Daniel had been abducted in Queensland, it was still important not to exclude New South Wales. Several witnesses had told police that they had seen New South Wales number plates on the blue car, and police had not ruled out that the suspect or suspects may have come from across the border. Elliott's idea was to drive to Coffs Harbour and Lismore in northern New South Wales to hold press conferences and continue the campaign for Daniel. She planned to target specific journalists to include them on the journey, particularly if they had regional coverage of the cities involved. Advertisements were also planned on radio and television, and the campaign was to be launched by the Queensland Police Service.

The road trip took place at the end of April. During dinner at Coffs Harbour on the first evening, Denise went outside with Detective Inspector John Maloney, who had come down to accompany them. 'Do you think Daniel is dead?' she asked him, watching his face anxiously, searching for a reaction. He shook his head but she could see in the light coming from the restaurant that he was crying. The trip to New South Wales, the extensive doorknocks of 5000 homes in Woombye and Palmwoods, and the support from Elliott and Knight all signified to the Morcombes that the police were going beyond the usual resources for a police investigation. But a nagging thought kept at both of them. In spite of all the effort, and all the emotional support, there were no major breakthroughs. Why?

Later that night, Denise went back to Elliott's room at the motel. Bruce was tired, as he had done all of the driving that day. There was no one there but the two of them. They opened one too many bottles of red wine and, in that space, away from Palmwoods and Maroochydore Police Station and all that was familiar, Denise finally put the words into a sentence. Daniel wasn't coming home. Denise knew that the words she finally uttered were true and she was acknowledging something she had thought for a long time but had never put into words. Elliott knew how much it hurt Denise to say those words. They both cried as though their hearts would break.

The next morning, 29 April, was the first press conference at the Coffs Harbour Police Station. Denise and Bruce had already met with New South Wales Police. Were the multiple sightings of a New South Wales number plate on the blue car the key to the case? Chief Inspector Jason Breton from the New South Wales Police said that New South Wales detectives were now assisting Queensland Police in searching for the blue car. Asked about the progress of the investigation,

Maloney told *The Courier-Mail* that 'a case like this always affects you personally, but we do feel positive about this investigation … some of the information includes reports of people who could be responsible. In many cases, we have found them and interviewed them but they have alibis which have checked out. You would like it to have been the people we are looking for, but it just wasn't the case.'

But who were these people? Bruce and Denise were never sure. They did another media interview at the Big Banana, Coffs Harbour's tourism icon, holding up signage reading, 'Where is Daniel?'. Then they drove to Lismore. Bruce and Denise followed John Maloney and Julie Elliott. At one point, Elliott stopped to take a phone call on the side of the road. It was not until much later that Bruce and Denise realised the significance of that call. One of the POIs – they later suspected Jackway – had been arrested and charged with a serious crime some weeks earlier.

At the Lismore Police Station, a young cadet journalist suddenly called out a question at the media conference, which stopped the room: 'Did you have anything to do with Daniel's disappearance, Mr Morcombe?' Bruce, sitting next to John Maloney, responded quickly, 'Mate, you had better direct that question to the head of the investigation. I was at a Christmas do with 20 witnesses a hundred kilometres away.' For five months, none of the other journalists had ever asked this question. It was the first time either of the Morcombes had confronted this. They shrugged it off.

That evening, they drove back to Palmwoods, emotionally and physically exhausted but feeling they had achieved something. The road trip was a success. Public donations funded two television and two radio advertisements. Denise said, 'There are moments in time I shared with my son Daniel I will never forget. I will never forget the day Daniel was born with his twin brother. I will never forget the day Daniel took his first steps. I will never forget the first words he ever spoke. I will never forget Daniel's first day at school. I will never forget his gorgeous smile. And I will never forget the day my son Daniel was abducted.' Denise cried in between takes but remained clear about her motivation: to target people's conscience, to get them to come forward. Funds of $100,000 raised from the public went towards keeping Daniel on everyone's minds. The advertisements produced one of the biggest public responses since the screening of *Australian Story*.

* * *

Mother's Day on 9 May marked Denise's first without Daniel. Bruce bought Denise a gold locket with a photo of Daniel inside. He put it on the gold chain that they had bought Daniel in Greece. The heart-shaped locket had a photo of Daniel with diamond trimmings on the outside. The only time Denise took it off was when she showered, to protect the photo.

Bruce and the boys tried their best to make a special day of it. One hundred rose bushes lined their driveway. They were Mother's Day gifts from the boys over past years, and together that day they set about pruning them. For Denise, there was a small measure of catharsis in this, and it became a family tradition in later years. Bruce then cooked lunch and they drove to the nearby tourist village of Montville.

But the secrets behind the door that had closed on that fateful day refused to open. Their fears of what had happened to Daniel plagued them incessantly. When Denise woke up each morning, and frequently in the middle of the night, she was beset by those dark thoughts. Throughout the public appearances and a reaffirmation of community support, there was always that terrible truth – Daniel had gone. The persons responsible, in spite of all the resources being thrown into the investigation, continued to evade the long arm of the law. Police issued plenty of warnings to the POIs and others who may not have come to their attention.

Detective Sergeant Dave Wilkinson had told the media, 'These people won't have a lot of rest. They'll have to keep looking over their shoulder for a long time.'

The POI register contained slippery characters living in the shadows of society. Until Daniel had gone missing, Bruce and Denise had never encountered such people nor even contemplated that they existed as they carried out their daily trips to the supermarket, the Plaza, and up and down the Nambour Connection Road. As the weeks turned into months, no names or identities were given. Just progress reports that Daniel's case was still very much a priority.

Privately, Bruce and Denise continued daily to question the police's lack of progress. During the first week in May, they requested another meeting with Detective Sergeant Paul Schmidt, who was in charge of the operational side of the investigation. Schmidt, a man in his 40s, was known to his colleagues as 'Schmidty' and had lived on the Sunshine Coast for many years. The Morcombes were left alone with Schmidt in his office. They exchanged small talk. Then the door opened. A female police officer entered, shutting the door behind her. Bruce and Denise looked at each other, puzzled. They had never seen her before.

Schmidt began to speak. 'You see, there's this fellow who has been helping police. He says he knows what happened to Daniel. He won't give police any more information but he said ...' Schmidt paused, looking at them. 'He would talk to Daniel's father.'

Bruce and Denise were shocked. This was not the kind of information they had been expecting from the meeting *they* had called as they were not usually involved in the intricacies of the investigation. Was this the breakthrough they had been waiting for? Bruce managed to remain composed, as did Denise, but inside their stomachs were churning. Someone who knew about what happened to Daniel? Was Daniel alive?

'I realise this is highly unusual,' Schmidt continued. 'But, after due consideration at high levels, we thought at least we would see if you would consider meeting with him?'

'I will meet him,' Bruce said, almost without thinking. They wanted answers. Anything was worth that. Later, at home, he began to doubt this decision. But, in that moment, there was no hesitation. 'Where is the meeting to be held and when?' Bruce asked.

'At the city watch house at police headquarters in Brisbane,' Schmidt said. 'Tomorrow.'

Bruce nodded, wondering how long police had known about this and how much more they knew. 'So what does he know?'

'Well, he says he saw Daniel after 7 December and that he's prepared to open up, and he may tell Daniel's father information that he won't tell police.'

This was very different to all the other types of news the Morcombes had received: dreamers, storytellers, 'someone told my mate at the pub', psychics, mediums – all the people who had jumped on the bandwagon since Daniel went missing. Police clearly believed it was a first-hand account and a positive identification.

It was a sleepless night for Bruce. The following morning, 13 May, Elliott and Knight picked both Bruce and Denise up early and they drove to police headquarters in Roma Street in inner-city Brisbane. After Elliott parked, Denise stayed with her and Knight. Bruce was taken up to the office via the lift by Detective Ross Hutton, who had been involved almost from day one in the case, Detective Sergeant Dave Hickey, the tough-talking policeman in charge of the homicide detectives posted north from Brisbane, and two other police officers in plain clothes.

'In a moment, you will be walked into an interview room and your conversation will be recorded. Your job is to see what he knows,' explained Detective Hutton.

Bruce was given no suggestions on what to talk about or which questions to ask. Ross Hutton walked him up to the next door along the passage. Bruce felt very nervous. As they approached the door, Hutton explained: 'You can't get out [of the room] from the inside. It only opens from the outside. When you want to go, just say "I'm leaving" and someone will come and get you. Bill Dooley [pseudonym] is inside. He does not know you are here.' And, with that, Hutton opened the door.

Bruce walked inside and the door clicked behind him. He had entered a thick-glassed booth about the size of a phone box. It contained a seat and a small, fixed desk. Opposite him in a mirror-image booth to his was a man sitting on the desk with his back to him. Bruce breathed deeply. A solid glass wall was between them. Although the sound was muffled, he could see the man perfectly.

As soon as the door had closed behind Bruce, Dooley, a man in his 30s, turned around slowly, with the manner of someone accustomed to being questioned. He was pacing himself. Bruce had time to see the look of shock cross the man's face as he clearly registered who his visitor was. He got off the desk and sat on the chair. His hair was neat but with a long fringe that was combed back over the ears on both sides. They looked at each other. Nothing was said at first, then they began making small talk. Bruce knew the scarcest details about the man in front of him, which made conversation difficult. Then Bruce brought up Daniel.

The man ducked and weaved.

'I've actually seen your boy in Merthyr Road in the Valley,' he began. Fortitude Valley is an inner-city suburb of Brisbane known for its seedier side. Daniel, he said, was in a car on 8, 9 or 10 December in the Valley with a man named Rogers and another man called Adam.

'Was he all right then?' Bruce asked, forcing the words out.

'Yeah, he was just lying there. Daniel was lethargic but he was alive.'

Bruce kept the questions rolling, trying to mask his reaction to what the man was saying. 'Who owned the car?' 'What colour was it?' 'Where was Daniel? Front seat or rear?'

The conversation was stilted and difficult, but the man was polite. He addressed Bruce as 'Mr Morcombe', even though Bruce called him 'Bill'.

When asked for specifics, Dooley would answer, 'Not sure.'

The picture of Daniel lying in a car in what the man described as a drugged state was the most disturbing thing Bruce had ever heard. This man was talking about his son. But this was a one-off opportunity. Keep pushing, Bruce told himself. Don't take your eyes off the ball. It was a macabre conversation – one that was to haunt Bruce for a long time.

Bruce would change the subject to keep the conversation going but then return to the purpose of the visit. 'Do you know what happened to Daniel?'

'It's really difficult, Mr Morcombe. You can understand it.'

'We just want to take Daniel home, say goodbye to him, with his family.' He knew he had to change his tactics, so tried to engage him in small talk about the weather, family and football. And then he chanced a question about Dooley's family. He looked the man straight in the eye, and recalled a detail from the briefing. 'You had a sister.'

'Yeah, I had a sister who died 12 years ago. She was murdered,' the man said quietly, his voice breaking slightly. 'I know exactly where you're at. When I see the car on the TV, I think of you and your wife and your family. I've got family too.'

Unwittingly, Bruce had exposed a weakness. He saw the man was close to tears. No one would help solve his sister's murder, he said. He had no respect for police because of that. Emotionally riled, he told Bruce he was 'filthy' on a particular detective who he claimed had framed him for murder. He said when his mother died he had been unable to go to the funeral as he had been in jail.

They had been talking for around 30 minutes. Bruce felt more in control. His eyes were still pinned on the man in front of him. Occasionally, he would bring up Daniel again, gaining strength to ask the one question he never wanted to ask.

'Is he dead?'

'Yeah, he's dead,' the man said. 'I'm not going to upset you by giving details of what they did to your son.'

Ninety minutes had now passed. There was a long pause. Bruce had run out of questions that the man was prepared to answer, but he was reluctant to leave. He asked Dooley several times if he was leading him up the garden path. Was the man full of lies or did he know? Bruce wanted to revisit the man's story one more time. The car, the clothing, the drugs, the house Daniel had been taken to. Bruce felt anger rising within him. 'You have not been much help,' he said. 'I came here because you told police you would talk to me. I'm leaving.'

Bruce got up to leave. The man sat there with his arms folded, his head slightly bowed. The door opened as though by magic, as he'd been promised by Hutton. Bruce walked out and was ushered into a room next door. Hutton and the other officers had been listening to everything that had been said. Bruce allowed himself to smile out of relief. He had tried his best. He had remained composed. Mission complete.

'What did you think?' Hutton asked. 'Was he lying?'

'Yes,' Bruce answered after a pause of several seconds. The way Dooley had responded to questions and his body language spelt evasiveness to Bruce.

Downstairs, Denise looked at him anxiously. 'What happened?'

Bruce saw the expectation in her eyes, the same expectation he had had before meeting with this man. 'Nothing new, I don't think. Nothing that will help.' They got back into Julie Elliott's car for the drive back north to Palmwoods. Bruce slumped in the seat, mentally exhausted.

* * *

The Morcombes' mental torment was far from over. False leads dangled provocatively. As though it was not just enough to lose their son, members of the public made up stories about Daniel's fate. While the case brought out the best in the community, it also brought out the worst. Not long after the Bill Dooley interview, a 23-year-old university student, David Charles Brine, studying Media and Communications, was charged with sending an email to Crime Stoppers saying that he was using Daniel as a toy and treating him like a pet animal, stating he would injure him if he was not paid compensation. The claim was a hoax, and the man was identified by tracing the email back to the internet cafe from where he had sent it. In January 2005, Brine was jailed for two years, to be suspended after four months, after pleading guilty in the District Court to making a threat to kill in a document.

But it was not all darkness; there were powerful advocates on the Morcombes' side. Father Jan was nominated for the mateship category of the Pride of Australia Medal, which recognised 'loyalty and goodwill and the true-blue spirit of pulling together to achieve a common good, especially when times are tough'. A new officer at Palmwoods Police Station, John Latham, was competing in the Great Endeavour Car Rally and wanted the 120 participants to display 'Where is Daniel?' bumper stickers. A Sunshine Coast company began selling identification kits for $5 to allow parents to make records of their children's fingerprints, photographs and DNA swabs following Daniel's abduction. And, on 15 May, the Brisbane Lions wore red armbands to show their respect for Daniel when playing against Carlton to a crowd of 35,000 at the Gabba in Brisbane. Bruce, Dean, Brad, Sam and Steve

Knight, Tim Ryan and Greg Daniels borrowed a minibus from the Palmwoods Hotel to go to the match. It was a special night, highlighting the fact that the community were not going to forget about Daniel.

* * *

As the six-month mark since Daniel's disappearance approached, there was nothing to reassure Denise that her son was still alive. She could never forget the flame from the baptism candle going out while the other two burnt brightly on the twins' birthday. Daniel had gone. She and her mother had known at that moment, but Denise had pushed that thought deep within her, each day summoning the expectation that today would be different. This day he would turn up. The pain dragged as though her heart would break in two. There was no joy in life. That she would never see her boy again was too horrific to contemplate. It was better to imagine receiving a letter that said Daniel was waiting on a street corner and she could come and pick him up – to hold out that hope, however hopeless it might be.

If he had died in a car accident or from an illness, the end would be certain, even if devastating. She and Bruce at least could visit their son at a cemetery and grieve. As it was, Daniel had vanished. Nothing and no one could find out what had happened to him, no matter how hard everyone tried. The people who knew what had happened were silent. Every Sunday at around 1.30 pm, a gloom would settle on their Palmwoods household as they remembered the day that had taken their child from them. Plucked from a normal family life, Daniel had disappeared into the unknown. These thoughts plagued them incessantly. They had not been there to protect him from the unspeakable things that might have happened to him.

The tidy bedroom that Daniel had left instead of his usual teenager's mayhem became a shrine to his memory.

Denise had even kept the rubbish Daniel had left in the bin in his bedroom. His Christmas presents remained wrapped, including the silver motorbike clock he had sneaked a peek at before Christmas.

Julie Elliott knew that Denise no longer believed that Daniel was coming back. Each day, Elliott lived knowing she was unable to fix the pain. The boundaries she usually put in place around police work had well and truly been crossed. Daniel had even begun appearing in her dreams. In one dream, she saw him standing at her front door. There was another figure with him and she became frightened. She wanted to bring him inside, and that woke her up. When she awoke, the dream was still vivid, but she chose not to tell Denise about it and add to her worry. Police work was tough. But this was the toughest brief she'd been given.

Bruce had channelled his grief into believing that some good must come from the terrible thing that had happened to Daniel. He wanted desperately to try to prevent this happening again, for those scum who had taken his son to decide not to next time. But underneath the desire to do good was his competing desire to punish the person or people responsible for Daniel's disappearance. Deep down, he knew this was not the message to get across to the public. It was a continuing conversation he had with himself, restraining his vengeful feelings. Elliott and Knight had told him this kind of talk would fuel the capital-punishment debate and turn the public's attention away from the main message – to find out what had happened to Daniel. Only that stopped him from venting his anger publicly.

On 7 June, the six-month anniversary of Daniel's disappearance, Bruce and Denise again visited the shrine under the overpass. There was also another press conference. There had been 5500 leads, Detective Schmidt publicly announced, while adding that the police were still missing 'that vital clue'. Both Bruce and Denise were also admitting that there was little hope Daniel was alive. 'The case is now listed as a suspected murder, and we've started to come to terms with the fact that Danny's not coming home alive,' Bruce told the media.

Meanwhile, Daniel's face appeared on 250,000 milk cartons in supermarkets across Queensland and New South Wales, courtesy of a local dairy company. Bruce and Denise went to the launch at the dairy, and it was a sad experience seeing Daniel's photo on the milk carton. Nevertheless, the public face of the investigation meant Daniel's face was always prominent.

Witnesses kept coming forward. Anthony Nash, a 55-year-old man, gave his statement on 3 June. He told police he had left home at about 2 pm with his wife, Sandra, to go to nearby Forest Glen, further south on the Bruce Highway, to buy a Christmas tree. Coming from Palmwoods, they had driven over the top of the Kiel Mountain Road overpass, around the second roundabout near the Christian Outreach Centre and were turning right on the roundabout to join the Nambour Connection Road. Nash was just reaching the stop sign on the feeder road before connecting to the freeway when a speeding car coming towards them almost crossed over to his side of the road. The driver looked as though he was out of control. His arms were flying everywhere as he struggled with the wheel. Nash described him as being in his early twenties with 'wispy blond hair'. He thought later that he might have had some facial hair. There were two other people in the car, he thought – one in the front and one in the back – and they were not wearing seatbelts as they were moving around a lot. The car, he said, was blue, and was an older type of sedan with four doors.

Gary Mitchell gave his statement the day after Nash. He told police he was also driving across the overpass after visiting relatives that day in Nicklin Road, where Daniel used to ride motorbikes. Mitchell said he knew what time they had left their relatives' place – 2.02 pm – because he had asked his wife the time. Entering the Nambour Connection Road and approaching the give-way sign, he had trouble seeing the oncoming traffic as a sedan was parked under the bridge in the shadows and off the shoulder of the road. He had to pull out slightly to get a better view. Although the car was in silhouette, he had noticed a man leaning on the passenger side. About three metres away and closer to the side of the road was a young person facing the man at the car. He thought there was someone further up on the embankment behind the young person. He said he had never seen a car parked there before. He had also seen a white van parked near the truck sales yard. The continuing documented accounts of the blue car was unsettling.

* * *

At one of their regular meetings, Inspector Maloney said to Bruce and Denise, 'I'd like you to come and talk to the police to say thank you and keep them motivated. Why not come down to the MIR and have a chat with them?' A meeting was set for 9 June. Bruce made the MIR team a certificate of thanks, signed by all of the Morcombe family. It featured a photo someone had sent them from one of the balloon releases they had done in Daniel's memory.

When the Morcombes entered the MIR for the first time, they could not help but gaze at the photos all over the walls – sketches of suspects and folder after folder piled on desks. They walked among the sketches, looking at each other. Was there anyone there they recognised? But they shook their heads. It was quite daunting and surreal to see a physical representation of all the work that had been going on. The room was full of police. They chatted to some of the officers and it was clear how hard the investigators were working. Bruce gave a speech and Denise cried when he handed over the certificate.

CHAPTER ELEVEN

PERSONS OF INTEREST

Detective Constable Ross Hutton was in charge of the list of POIs, the initial list of which had been generated from police records of known paedophiles in the area. However, few POIs had search warrants taken out against them. There was no particular rule about which POIs went on photoboards or were shown to witnesses, even if they did resemble the artist's sketches or a COMFIT.

The beautiful Sunshine Coast and the peaceful, rural setting of Palmwoods were tarnished forever as Bruce and Denise slowly discovered that places they'd driven past regularly were actually what Bruce called 'honeypots of activity' revolving mostly around drugs and paedophile activity.

One was the Sunshine Coast Motor Lodge and the other the Woombye Gardens Caravan Park. Police informed them that many people on the wrong side of the law, such as drug dealers and manufacturers, as well as people of no fixed abode, lived there.

Of the list of almost one thousand POIs, many were easy

to exclude, even if their explanations were disturbing. For example, two men in their twenties gave the alibi that they had been photographing young 'nippers', boys learning surf skills, near the Maroochydore Surf Club at the time Daniel disappeared, and they had photographs on their camera to prove it.

Bill Dooley, who became the number one POI, although he had no recorded history of offences against children, remained under watch. There was one POI, however, who had slipped off the radar: Brett Peter Cowan.

The Christian Outreach Centre, founded in 1974 by a former Methodist minister, had a reputation for including marginalised people in its congregation. Cowan's aunt, Jenny Philbrook, and her husband, Keith, were pastors there. Jenny Philbrook had always regarded Cowan, the third of four boys, as the black sheep of the family. In 1998, Cowan had met his wife, 24-year-old Tracey, at a barbecue the Philbrooks hosted at their house. Tracey was also a Christian, believing in forgiveness and salvation. Cowan admitted to Tracey, after they started going out, that he had been in jail and that the crime involved a young child in a caravan park in Darwin. He even showed her some documents from the court case with some lines blanked out that he said were too awful for her to read. Cowan revealed that he had been to jail four times. But Tracey saw good in Cowan, and they married a year after meeting.

Cowan remained something of an outsider. Although he claimed he went to church on Saturdays, Sunday mornings and Sunday nights, the Philbrooks noticed he rarely attended, although occasionally he went to the Tuesday prayer meeting. An exception was when his son was born in July 2003, and Cowan showed him off to the parishioners.

Cowan liked the parishioners and people who went to the Christian Outreach Centre because they believed in salvation. It was part of their statement of faith. They accepted what he had done, and he could talk more openly about his past. They took him for who he was. While out one day he was interviewed as a vox pop by a television station. Presenting with combed hair, parted in the centre, he smiled continually saying he had seen the error of his ways and become a Christian. Some things still niggled him, such as the whole idea of 'unforgiveable sin'. Was there such a thing? Once, a pastor had told the congregation that there was not. But Cowan knew from his Bible readings – he thought John I or II – that there was, and that the only unforgiveable sin was to deny the Father or the Spirit.

In April 2004, around the same time that Bruce and Denise were releasing red balloons into the sky in Brisbane, Trevor Davis, one of the Christian Outreach Centre's parishioners, decided to give the troubled Brett Cowan a chance to create a new life for himself. Trevor Davis felt sorry for Cowan. He had employed him for odd jobs over the years and considered Brett and Tracey Cowan friends. Davis told Cowan that he didn't wish to know about his past. Nevertheless, he was always careful not to allow him access to his children. The new start was a mark of Davis's faith in Cowan that he could make something of his life. After all, he was the father of a young baby now. Davis bought a small business, Suncoast Sandblasting for $50,000, owned by Kelvin Kruger on whose property Dean and Daniel used to ride their bikes. Davis planned to give it to Cowan to make a fresh start in life. Cowan was supposed to pick up the truck for the business the day after Davis made the deposit in April. But he never turned up.

On 10 June 2004, Cowan left Tracey Cowan – three months pregnant with their second son – in the middle of the night with no warning. He moved to Moranbah, a mining town three hours west of Mackay in central Queensland, where he had met another woman, Hayley McDonald (pseudonym), while working there on one of Davis's jobs.

McDonald had five sons. Four of them, then aged 10, 11, 12 and 17, were living with her. Five months later, Cowan confessed to McDonald that he had served a jail sentence for touching a boy in Darwin in the 1990s but told her he had been 'cured' after doing a course while in jail. McDonald was angry but believed she could trust Cowan, as he had been forthcoming with the information.

* * *

By the seventh month of the investigation, the police had 37 colour photographs of blue cars – in police jargon, vehicles of interest, or VOIs – in what they called their 'Car Room'. Photos of the cars were also superimposed onto photographs of the abduction site. Twenty-four witnesses were asked to pick one of the cars as being similar to the one they had seen that day. Only four had been unable to nominate a particular car. Two of the witnesses had seen the blue car in Shires Road, the service road running parallel to the Nambour Connection Road close to the Kiel Mountain Road overpass.

Kenneth Bryant, 74, had been crossing the overpass at Kiel Mountain Road and was on the roundabout heading down to the Nambour Connection Road, approaching Shires Road, somewhere between midday and 2 pm on the day Daniel disappeared when he had to brake heavily. A faded blue, boxy car he thought was an early-model Ford Falcon crossed the road in front of him after coming off the highway and headed down Shires Road at speed.

Sarah Gullo had also seen the speeding blue car. She had been leaving the Christian Outreach Centre at about 1.30 pm, she thought, and got in her car to drive onto the Nambour Connection Road. She said she was about to join the highway when a car came speeding off it towards her. She described the car as being old-fashioned, light-blue or silver in colour, and she remembered that there were two people in it.

Police stopped hundreds of motorists on 13 June to see if they could shed light on the blue car, but nothing was forthcoming.

That same day, which was on the Queen's Birthday weekend, Bruce, Dean and Brad went to the 'Winternationals' drag races at Willowbank. Denise's father, Kevin, accompanied them. He and Monique had come up for two weeks. It was a family tradition to attend this event annually, though this year would be the first time they attended without Daniel. A re-enactment of Daniel's disappearance played across a big screen.

While the boys were at the drag race, Denise and Monique attended Julie Elliott's 50th birthday party. Denise had bought her an address book and some silver teaspoons. Julie was fond of Denise's parents and would call Kevin 'Have-a-chat' as they often had a good joke and laugh together. On the way to the party, Denise and Monique called into Elimbah, a suburb in the Moreton Bay region north of Caboolture, to choose a puppy they had been given by a breeder that they were to pick up later. They called the little black Labrador Max. Bruce was a fan of the television program *Get Smart*, so, as they already had a Chief, Max seemed a natural choice. When Max was brought back to the house, he saw Mittens and immediately chased him. Mittens ran up the curtains and they came crashing down on both of them. There was a newcomer in the house.

The following day was taken up being filmed by *60 Minutes* at the Mary Valley Railway's Race Against the Rattler, another annual event where teams of runners would race against an old steam train. A special team of boys ran for Daniel, all wearing red T-shirts and a baton with the exact number of red ribbons for the days Daniel had been missing. The team included Inspector Mike Condon's nephew.

Before Kevin and Monique returned to Melbourne, Bruce and Denise had a barbecue in their front yard, inviting Greg Daniels and his wife, Genevieve, Sam and Steve Knight and their family, Julie and her then fiancé Warren, as well as Denise's girlfriends Denice, Debbie and Chris. It was the first time they had entertained in a long time, and was a sign they were becoming friends with the police they were closely involved with.

There would be another chance to recharge their batteries in June, when Bruce, Denise and Brad went to Tasmania for an escape. The tickets had been bought before Daniel went missing. Bruce and Denise had planned that Kevin and Monique would look after the boys and they would have a week away on their own. But they decided to take Brad and spend some quality time with him. They stayed in Richmond, not far from Hobart. It was the first break they had taken since the media blitz began the previous December.

When they arrived home, Bruce turned to Denise. 'What was it you liked so much about Tasmania?' he asked.

'That nobody recognised us,' she answered straightaway.

Bruce nodded. He too had noticed the difference. It planted a seed in his mind.

* * *

The case continued on, unsolved. Detective Inspector Mike Condon prided himself on the clear-up rate for murders in Queensland's North Coast region. In his job, he dealt with an average of 55 murders a year. Before Daniel, there was only one unsolved reported murder dating back to 1984, plus two missing persons thought to have been murdered in 1998 and 1999.

In July, Condon requested a review of the 2000-odd job logs documented over the length of the case. He also raised whether the COMFITs of the man seen under the overpass would be released to the public.

On 25 May, 20 extra detectives had been assigned to the case. There was continual discussion in the MIR about which POI to focus on. A new POI (POI21) emerged. Someone reported that a friend, who had once lived in the same caravan park as him, had said, over a beer and a smoke of marijuana, that he had a fob watch inscribed 'From Dad'. Furthermore, the man drove a blue Sigma sedan similar to the one police were looking for, as well as owning a number of white vans.

Another new POI, numbered 'POI20', was a 62-year-old man who owned a van. In early July, after being the subject of questioning by police, he committed suicide, although police said it was not related to Daniel's case.

On 15 July, police focused on the Big Pineapple on the Nambour Connection Road as a place of interest. They wanted to find out whether Daniel had been seen there the day he disappeared or whether any of the employees had seen anything suspicious while travelling to and from work. They discovered there was no surveillance system in place and there was only one payphone at the entrance. No calls were registered as having been made that day.

* * *

On 4 October, Dean's 17th birthday, the police announced a reward of $250,000 for any information leading to Daniel's whereabouts. Police Minister Judy Spence and Police Commissioner Bob Atkinson had been discussing it for a few months. The amount settled on was the highest ever offered in Queensland, more than double the previous $100,000 record. It caused more calls to flood the Crime Stoppers phones. It was offered along with an indemnity from prosecution, depending on the person's involvement, for anyone who might have known what had happened but was too frightened to come forward. A few days later, on 7 October, the Eagle Boys pizza company announced it was distributing Daniel's picture nationwide across two million pizza boxes following the earlier initiative of putting Daniel's face on the milk cartons.

There was still new information coming in from the public. On 12 October, a questionnaire was distributed with the assistance of the Department of Education to 5000 homes in Woombye and Palmwoods. More than half were returned with information that had to be logged. And still more witnesses came forward. Nine days after the questionnaire was distributed, Claude Hamilton, who worked for the Maroochydore council as a motor mechanic, told the police that he had not wanted to become involved, but his secretary had phoned the Nambour Police. He said he was driving his Toyota Hilux ute south along the Nambour Connection Road towards the Palmwoods turn-off somewhere around 1.10 or 1.40 pm on the day in question. As he approached the overpass, he had seen a car on the opposite side of the road to him. Two males and a child were standing near it. The first man was at the open rear passenger door with his arms resting on top of the doorframe, and the second man was about two metres away from him and directly behind the child's back facing towards Nambour about a metre away from the child. The boy was standing between the two men, facing the man at the car door and appeared to be talking to him. The other man was standing behind the boy but not doing anything. Hamilton described the car as a 1983–84 Nissan Bluebird four-door sedan, which was a faded silvery-blue colour. His statement was duly logged and filed with the other statements. But in spite of the information, there was still nothing that would lead to an arrest – nothing that might lead to Daniel's whereabouts.

CHAPTER TWELVE

THE FIRST ANNIVERSARY

On Sunday 21 November 2004, *Seven News* presented a one-hour special called 'Finding Daniel', fronted by Kay McGrath and produced by Peter Doherty. The program featured a live cross to Bruce and Denise in a Sunshine Coast suburb, who asked viewers to show their support by simultaneously shining a torch or turning on the outside light of their porch, and the lights of the neighbourhood would be screened on television.

Of course, there was also no guarantee that everyone *would* turn on their lights. But, on cue, as McGrath gave the signal, the Morcombes were gratified to see lights springing on everywhere. The community was there for them.

The program's second half focused on the investigation, with footage of the car boards in the MIR and then cutting to McGrath's co-presenter, Rod Young, inside Crime Stoppers, where phones were being manned, waiting for viewers to call. There was footage of detectives taking swabs from people living in 63 caravan parks stretching from Redcliffe across the Sunshine Coast to Gympie and police saying that the swabs would be stored for the life of the investigation. Inside the forensic laboratories, cigarette butts were dissected as scientists worked through evidence found at the abduction site. Then there were interviews with the Morcombes and early childhood footage of Daniel singing 'Humpty Dumpty' on Christmas Day 1992, visiting Currumbin Sanctuary and Movieworld on the Gold Coast, and catching a fish at a trout farm.

Denise described Daniel as 'shy' and 'stubborn – if he wanted to do something, he'd go and do it'. Bruce floated the idea that perhaps Daniel's disappearance was the result of a robbery gone wrong, as Daniel had been well dressed and looked like he might have had money or other valuables on him, but Denise gave her views firmly: 'I feel it was planned. I think they came out for the day to pick up someone who was innocent.' Bruce's determination flashed across the screen. 'We need to teach these people some manners and that day will come.'

By far the most newsworthy aspect of the program, however, was the broadcasting of three sketches that were released as an 'exclusive' to the television station. The sketches had been drawn by Senior Sergeant John Garner – the man who had designed the COMFIT system back in 1993 – in the first few weeks after Daniel disappeared. Around 34 COMFITs were to be generated from witness descriptions during the investigation. Some produced both COMFITs and sketches. The sketches and COMFITs had sat up in the MIR for almost 12 months. Now, the police selected what they deemed to be the three most credible of Garner's freehand sketches of the man under the overpass and presented them to Channel Seven as 'new material'. The drawings were based on the accounts of witnesses Abby North, Barry Kelsey and Andrew Jackson, and they depicted a man of 25–40 years old, with a lean to muscular build, about 185 centimetres tall, with a gaunt face and dark-brown, wavy hair.

In the media hubbub that followed, Inspector Condon continued to maintain that the sketches were a breakthrough in the case, telling the media that numerous interviews had been conducted over the past 11-plus months to ensure they were accurate before they were released. 'This is a significant step in this investigation which has been complex and difficult,' he said. 'It's been difficult in getting the sketches as accurate as possible, but we are now satisfied that these are the most accurate sketches.' No mention was made in any of the media reports that all three had been drawn in the first few weeks after Daniel disappeared.

* * *

Several years later, even Brett Cowan would admit there was a resemblance between him and one of the police artist's impressions. At the time the program went to air, he was still living with Hayley McDonald and her sons in Moranbah, again the subject of police attention and the subject of a search warrant for allegedly stealing from his employer. Detective Sergeant Pownell from Moranbah, who exercised the warrant on 30 November, was immediately struck by how much Cowan – with his flat skull, widely spaced eyes, weather-beaten face and unkempt hair – resembled the sketch of the man wanted in the Morcombe case. Pownell took a digital photograph of Cowan, noting that the most recent one on file apparently dated back to 1996. It was never clear whether King's earlier photograph had been filed.

The sketches had an immediate effect, moving the investigation forward. Someone else recognised Cowan. Two days after the Channel Seven special, a man rang Elliott, convinced the person in the sketch was Brett Cowan. He not only named Cowan but also provided his old address at Alf's Pinch Road. The man said that he knew Cowan had been in prison in Darwin and told Crime Stoppers that, three or four years beforehand, Cowan had offered his son and nephew money to 'suck his penis'. As to the search conducted on Cowan's Pajero, there had been no follow-up on the tape strips, which had been used to check for the presence of blood, that were taken from the front seats and the bench seat in the rear of the vehicle. The tests had been sent by police to the Queensland Department of Health. But it was not until seven years later that it was discovered the tests had been stored but never examined. The DNA analysis, likewise, had never been carried out. Cowan seemed to have luck on his side. Nothing was immediately done about the link identifying him as resembling the man from the sketch.

When one of the mothers who had seen the strange man at the school saw the sketches, she leapt to her feet, pointing to one of them and saying to her husband, 'That's exactly the guy.' She rang the police immediately. Years later, the mothers, who wished to remain anonymous, still remained plagued with guilt that they had not come forward earlier. Inspector Condon conceded to the media that the mothers' descriptions of the car had 'sufficient consistency' with the car other witnesses had seen under the overpass and that the women's descriptions matched those of one of the men seen under the overpass.

By noon the day after 'Finding Daniel' was screened there was a total of 700 calls to Crime Stoppers. The phones were so busy that calls had to be diverted to police stations nearby. Maloney described the response as 'outstanding'. Bruce, too, told the media that the information they received was 'crucial and identifiable'. 'We're encouraged by it. We hope we're getting to the pointy end of the investigation.'

Looking at the three different faces of the man in the sketches who may have been responsible for her son's disappearance, Denise felt physically sick. Here might be the man whose unknown face had haunted her thoughts and dreams for nearly a year, the man who had snatched her son. For Bruce, the man's features represented a human face to vent his pent-up anger on – the man he had sworn would not get away with his crime. 'At least,' Bruce said to Denise in the car one day, 'you can look at these sketches two ways. Who does he look like? But who doesn't he look like? The first answer could leave you disappointed. The second is helpful if you start eliminating people. For example, it was clearly not a woman. So that eliminates half the population. It was not a person over 40 or under 20. It was not a person that was overweight. It was not a person that cared about their appearance. Basically, by doing this it narrows the possibilities. That can eliminate everyone we know personally.'

Around the same time, Channel Nine's *Unsolved Mysteries* program showed photographs of a noose that Bruce kept in the barn with a sign stating 'Swing You Bastard'. Bruce admitted on air that he had wanted to put up the sign under the overpass but had not wanted to get the public offside. Denise, too, said that neither of them had wanted 'people to see our angry side because they aren't going to want to help us if we're angry'. She added, 'But we have got feelings.' It was the first time they had admitted what was discussed at home away from the media spotlight.

* * *

As the weeks passed after 'Finding Daniel' with still no firm lead, the hope Bruce and Denise had felt evaporated. They seemed to be no closer to putting a name or names to the person or people who had taken their son in spite of the release of the sketches. They had discussed a strategy of being positive and supportive towards police. They did not want to do anything that would affect the investigation but after all the resources that had been expended on the case there were still no answers. Why?

Unofficially, several names had been mentioned to both of them. Although they still had not received the list of the people that Maloney had mentioned on the New South Wales trip, whose alibis had been checked out, they had been hearing unofficial names since February 2004, and these included Jackway and Cowan. They had also been told that Bill Dooley was a POI, and that he and his associates were constantly in the mix. Bruce and Denise's ears pricked up. They wanted to know more, but nothing more was forthcoming.

At a meeting with Inspector Maloney, the Morcombes had asked if they could help in any way. 'Do the police need more public appeals, media attention?' Bruce offered. Maloney replied, 'We possibly have the pieces of the puzzle, but at this stage it is not obvious to us. We cannot see the answer. But, it is not unusual that when we go back and do reviews we will find that clue.' It was this kind of comment that gave Bruce and Denise confidence that the police were working to some sort of plan.

There were still reports of blue cars. Even Bruce and Denise had been reporting blue cars to Crime Stoppers. On one occasion, they had been returning from conducting franchisee training in Brisbane when they were passed by one. They decided to speed up and take a photo of the occupants. They were clearly on the edge and suspecting everyone. The sudden disappearance of their son had turned them from easygoing Sunshine Coast residents into inhabitants of a different realm. Bruce was to joke with one journalist that the only two people he knew hadn't abducted Daniel were himself and Denise.

Bruce was always ready to take in any new information. As their public profile increased, they were more frequently approached by people when they were out and about. Sometimes these people had already been to police. One woman stood out to Bruce. She approached him at the Forest

Glen shops, a precinct off the Bruce Highway heading south from the Nambour Connection Road. She said she had already spoken to Detective Sergeant Dave Wilkinson. She invited Bruce to her house. Up until then, Bruce had never visited anyone outside of a public place. The woman had asked that Denise not attend, as what she had to say was 'too graphic'. She had seemed friendly.

When Bruce drove up to her house, he saw that it was neat and tidy and that she lived on acreage. He pulled up a chair at the kitchen table, then inwardly grimaced as the woman began with the words 'My dream ...'. He managed to restrain himself for half an hour while she told him stories about some local sheds and what had happened to Daniel. She told him that Daniel had drowned in a bath. Bruce steeled himself to sit through more of her observations before thanking her and leaving.

Everyone, it seemed, had a theory, and the Morcombes had already heard plenty of them. Sometimes, they would be handed a note with information or a name and phone number asking for a call. Many believed they knew where Daniel was buried and gave graphic descriptions of what happened to him. Their descriptions ranged from constructions such as sheds and water tanks to trees, lakes, dams, streams and other natural landmarks. Bruce would usually take notes and forward them to the police.

Sometimes, as with the lady he had met in Forest Glen, the details were horrific. One lady spoke of a chainsaw. Another mentioned an excavator digging a hole to bury Daniel. Yet another spoke of how Daniel was dismembered by a circular saw and pieces of him were disposed of in sand at Kings Beach, Caloundra. Bruce was astounded at how many of these stories came from women. His rational self explained their motivation. Even though the material was disturbing, it was provided in good faith. He accepted they were trying to be helpful and always thanked them.

At home, in the safety of their inner sanctum, though, he struggled with the images they conjured, some of which he spared from Denise. How could they remain normal human beings after listening to these stomach-churning tales? Each time, he would steel himself, hoping that he might get some evidence as to what had happened to his son.

One day, Bruce went into Dick Smith's in Maroochydore and bought the smallest voice recorder he could find. He took to concealing it in his top shirt pocket to record conversations. Some day, someone might say something important. He never gave up listening. Afterwards, Bruce would load the recorded interviews onto his desktop computer. He gradually began collecting a database of these conversations, no matter how offbeat. He would occasionally cringe at the dramatic change in him since the disappearance of his son as he followed yet another strange lead in the hope of finding him. He was playing the role of investigator in one of the police shows he watched on television.

Once he turned up at an address in Nambour after a man said he could help him. He knew the area well from his days of operating Jim's Mowing but he was cautious. He had started another strategy. Before attending any of these meetings, he would check the street on Google Earth and find out what he could about the house layout and sheds, how close the neighbours were in case he might need to flee. He would often arrive early, preparing himself in much the same way he would approach his other business, to give himself time to make an assessment. On this particular occasion, he sat in the car for a few minutes. His heart was pumping. The property was a battleaxe block with a long driveway. Should he go up or shouldn't he? He decided to do it. After all, that's why he'd come here.

At the end of the driveway, he switched on the recorder and knocked on the door. It seemed like a funny side entrance, more a rear door than the front door. There was no answer to his repeated knockings, even though he had deliberately slammed the car door to alert whoever was inside that he had arrived. He had even taken the precaution of speaking briefly to the neighbour out the front; if anything happened, they would remember seeing him there.

There was a pool in the front yard and Bruce thought that perhaps this was the way to the front door. The pool fence was a high, timber one. Before opening the gate, he looked through the sawn hole used to unlock it. Sunbaking next to the pool was a middle-aged, naked man. Bruce thought, My god, what is this place? He rattled the gate loudly and, still looking surreptitiously through the hole, saw the man hastily wrapping a towel around himself.

Bruce wasn't sure what to do. He quickly recovered himself just as the house door opened. He recognised the new person who answered as the man who had first approached him, and he introduced himself. The other man reappeared, now dressed, and the three of them sat around the kitchen table and spoke for an hour inside. The man who had contacted him turned out to have a lot of legal knowledge, and he spoke about official cover-ups and a paedophile ring and why the investigation was heading nowhere fast. Again, Bruce thanked them and left.

Later, he spoke to Sergeant Tracey Barnes, and she told him that the man he had visited had already been spoken to by the police. The naked man was, at that time, a POI. That was deeply unsettling for Bruce. He was now speaking with people on the wrong side of the law. And it was a constant concern for his welfare that further burdened Denise.

* * *

'Finding Daniel' had aired 16 days before the first anniversary of Daniel's disappearance. Bruce and Denise had wanted to mark the anniversary with something more than just an acknowledgement that their son had disappeared. The fact that a whole year had passed with Daniel still missing seemed inconceivable to them.

Neither of them wanted the public memorial service to be any kind of closure in the search for their son, but they both wanted it to be a step towards healing, both for the community and for themselves. Both of them disliked the word 'closure'. The search for Daniel was 'unfinished business', Bruce had said. They were also clear that they did not want a memorial service to be a 'goodbye' to Daniel.

The event was set for 10 am on 7 December at St Catherine's Church in Siena Catholic College. Denise – with the help of Bruce, Julie Elliot, Sam Knight and Dave Wilkinson – had made 2000 mass cards with a candle and red ribbon attached. On the front was a photograph of Daniel in his school uniform, with the date of his birth beneath it plus another date: 'Disappeared 7.12.03'. Inside was a message and a prayer. School students handed them out silently to the large crowd, which spilt out from the church to the balcony, the foyer and outside into the grounds. Tim Ryan had organised marquees and a big screen to be set up for those who could not fit inside.

It was raining that morning. Denise believed Daniel was talking to her. The rain represented his tears. Over the following years that they searched for him, there would be other strange unexplained episodes such as televisions that stopped working. That morning, as they headed for the service, the clock at home stopped at 8.30 am. When the Morcombes arrived at the church, they saw the size of the turnout: over 1500 people in all. Many of Denise's family made the trip north from Melbourne.

Father Jan had helped to pick the verses, psalms and songs for the hour-long service. The first song was the 'Galilee Song'. Gospels and the Lord's Prayer were read. Daniel, Bradley and Dean's baptism candle was relit by the boys' godparents: Denise's brother Damien and his wife, Kerry; Bruce's brother Scott and his wife, Shelly; Denise's brother Paul and Denise's friend Christine. A flame was then passed around the crowd by the students to light everyone's candle.

Both Bruce and Denise had decided not to make a public statement. Instead, their words were captured on a DVD which was filmed at their house by Gareth Lee, a local cameraman from Channel Seven. They had both watched it several times at home so it would not upset them as much on the day. The 13-minute DVD was screened as planned, with Tania Netherway's song playing, to those inside and outside the church.

Denise spoke first on the DVD. She said that Daniel's name was written on her heart forever:

> There is never a day when I do not search for your face. Somewhere, everywhere, anywhere, I see a turn of the head, a back that reminds me of you and I hurry to look more closely only to feel despair again, because of course it's not you. Are you lying in some lonely place, dead or lost? My heart reaches out to you and I try to touch you there. I breathe warm breaths towards you and pray that you will know. I call to you in your lostness and long for you to hear my voice of love. Are you held captive by someone? We would give anything to see you, just to see you once more. I imagine that you are somewhere close. And that torments me, as I believe I should be able to see you. I imagine that you're far away and my soul weeps over the distance between us. I imagine you're part of someone else's family and, on better days, one part of me hopes beyond hope that you are. The other part of me hurts to see you belonging to someone else when we long for you as our own ... There is no place where my love will not reach you. There is no time when I will forget you. As I go on, I carry you close to me, my love, as part of the ongoing of my life.

Bruce said that the family was often asked where they got their strength from. 'We get it from Daniel,' he said. 'It is of great sadness that we are all forced to say goodbye without being able to have him close by, and to lay him to rest with a prayer. But we know he can hear us.' Bruce urged everyone not to dwell on the question of 'why' as the answer could not be altered. 'We can only change and influence the future. All of us here today have gained strength from Daniel. We take home with us the memory of a loving son, a trusted friend, and a good kid who enjoyed life. We are better people for having Daniel come into our lives.'

Denise said the family had all discovered strength they did not know they had. 'Daniel has touched so many people, people who did not even know him. What is truly ironic about all the recognition, support, help and publicity he has attracted is that he was such a quiet boy. Shy but polite were his traits. He was not an attention seeker, yet he has been the focus of national media and in thousands of families' hearts for a year now ... His likeable manner, sparkling eyes and beaming smile captured in photo after photo meant that he was seen as a son that the ordinary Australian family could relate to ... tragically, he was under Bruce's and my parental wing for less than 14 years, but he was ours, is ours and we had many a great time together.'

Brad and Dean both spoke about missing their brother and what he meant to them. The sweet voices of Siena Catholic College students, many of whom knew Daniel, sang hymns. For the first time, Bruce broke down in a public gathering. Father Joe Duffy told the congregation, 'Daniel's wonderful smiling face is better known on the Sunshine Coast than any film star, any sports star, any celebrity ... and I have a gut feeling the person we need to get information about Daniel from is not far away.' Father Jan told the congregation there was 'no room for darkness' and that the candles lit for the service would be carried to families at places of work and shopping centres to provide safety for all the community's children.

By the end of the service, many people were sobbing and others in tears. Denise had run out of tears. There was no casket there to mourn her son. This was not a funeral. She felt drained and exhausted, even though she had appreciated how lovely the service had been. Later that day, invited guests of around 110 adults and 40 children joined the Morcombes for the official opening of a plaque to Daniel under the overpass. The plaque would accompany the poinciana tree that had been planted for Daniel nearby on 27 October: red to symbolise the missing teenager. Poincianas bloomed in December, the month Daniel had gone missing and the new tree represented the large one that grew in the Morcombes' garden in Palmwoods. Daniel's plaque identified his abduction site and around the words a red ribbon had been etched.

The SES blocked off both southbound lanes on the highway for the ceremony. Father Jan carried out the official opening and blessing. Bradley and Dean then tied red ribbons around the poinciana tree while Father Jan watched. Daniel's cousins Katie, Jamie, Emma, Elissa, Tom, Jessica, Emily, Michael and Ashlea also tied ribbons onto the lateral branches of the tree. Dean wore dark, wraparound sunglasses and Bradley was his usual silent self. About 80 people went on to the Palmwood Bowls Club in Nicklin Road for drinks. As the night progressed, Denise did not want to go home and face the fact that, in spite of the service, Daniel was still missing. Denise, Elliott, Knight, Claire Foster from *Australian Story* and Sue, Denise's bridesmaid, were driven by police car to Marooychdore. They went to a bar for some drinks. Elliott had booked a unit nearby. That night, Palmwoods had a power surge. Half of the lights at the Palmwoods house went out. The next day, Bruce decided to watch the cricket. Out of the five television sets they had in the house, the only one that worked was in Daniel's room. It was another of the many strange electrical quirks that seemed to occur around significant dates to do with Daniel's disappearance.

* * *

Following the anniversary, Bruce and Denise were exhausted. In one year they had become different people, and they needed to take stock and find a way forward. They decided to release a public statement to the media that they would no longer be available to comment on Daniel's case unless some new information came forward. A villa at Couran Cove, north of the Gold Coast on South Stradbroke Island had been donated to them for the weekend after the memorial service. Bradley and Dean came too, and they had fun on jet skis.

After they got back, Denise visited a local tattoo studio with Elliott called Ink Attack. She wanted something permanent on her as a tribute to Daniel. She had a red ribbon tattooed on her ankle. The rest of the family pledged to follow suit.

Bruce and Denise had been told by a councillor at Caloundra City Council, Anna Grosskreutz, about a charity motorbike 'Ride for Daniel', which was set for 12 December 2004. Grosskreutz was herself a Harley-Davidson rider, and the event was planned by another biker named Ray Harris. They had already apologised that they would not be there. Attendance was mainly word of mouth. As the Morcombes settled back to watch the event on the news that weekend, they could hardly believe their eyes. One and a half thousand people straddled their motorbikes heading off from the Ettamogah Pub, the cartoonish tourist attraction on the Bruce Highway on the southern end of the Sunshine Coast, to travel 110 kilometres north to Noosaville and then back to the pub again, all as a fundraiser for Daniel. Bruce's brother Scott, and his wife, Shelly, took part. It was a clear demonstration that the community was calling for action and wanted a result. The message they were sending was that crimes against children were not acceptable.

PART THREE

Parallel Lives

CHAPTER THIRTEEN

FOUNDATION FOR THE FUTURE

Daniel's memorial stood surrounded by gifts from wellwishers. There were garlands of flowers, paintings, teddy bears and even a faded red T-shirt with the letters 'R.I.P.' all under the gloomy shadows of the overpass. Any motorist passing by could not have failed to notice. After facing their second Christmas without their son, Bruce and Denise decided that they owed it to Daniel to keep speaking to the media to try to find out what had happened to him.

They had suffered a physically and financially exhausting 2004, but somehow they had to continue. As they drove past the public tributes under the overpass in early January 2005, Denise suddenly spoke up. 'Let's make sure this never happens to another child or family.'

Her remark that morning was spontaneous but timely. There had been discussions of a longer-term plan to make the best use of all of the public donations since the Day for Daniel almost a year ago. Now, accepting they were in for the long haul, Bruce and Denise started seriously considering a more robust approach for the future.

Andrew Parke was the Jim's Antennas national franchisor in Melbourne. He and his wife, Sarah, had recently started the Baby Emma Foundation in memory of their baby daughter Emma Rose, who had died in 2004 from a heart condition. Bruce and Denise began talking to the Parkes on the phone about how they had started up their foundation. In the middle of January, the Parkes flew up from Melbourne to visit the Morcombes for the day, accompanied by Dominic Pellgani from the accounting firm KPMG, who had helped set up the Baby Emma Foundation.

'It was difficult,' Pellgani told the Morcombes right away. They first had to set up a registered charity that was tax deductible. The Morcombes were used to the hard road, though, and this did not put them off. They both believed that the Daniel Morcombe Foundation would be the best way to pay back all of the kindness that people were bestowing upon them and to make use of their public profiles.

There was another motivation: they were continually learning about how the media operated, and it had gotten Bruce thinking about the long road ahead. 'Instead of all the paid advertising we've been doing, we can structure events for the Foundation and then the media will cover them. We can appear on the breakfast shows or whatever and have a media event that will not only keep Daniel in the news – they'll always want to go back to showing his face and back to 7 December – but it will also raise funds for other kids who need help,' he suggested to Denise.

'No child should have to suffer like Daniel did,' Denise responded. This was a mother's cry, and it was something Denise knew she could give voice to. 'They need to know that they are loved. Kids are vulnerable.'

'How could he ever have known that, within an hour of leaving home, he would find himself in a situation he couldn't control,' Bruce said, voicing the kind of thoughts they often discussed. 'We need to help kids realise that these dangerous situations could happen to anybody and teach them what they can do about it.'

'Yeah, and with the internet and everything else going on around them, they don't know what easy prey they are,' Denise said.

Bolstering the positive was not always easy. After Daniel's memorial service everyone had gone back to their lives. For so many people, life *could* go on as normal. In the weeks following the service, Denise had begun drinking. Soon, she lost count of how many drinks she had. She wanted to numb herself, make the pain go away, not to have to think any more. After the service, Denise had been left without a focus and no answers in spite of all the effort they had put into the mission to find Daniel. Every waking hour, she was haunted by wondering what happened to Daniel and whether they would ever know. Her imagination knew no bounds. She would become angry for no reason.

Watching from the sidelines, Bruce knew this was not the normal behaviour of a healthy Denise. He was concerned. The Foundation was the lifebuoy thrown to both of them in an ocean of despair. So much of that first year had been spent searching for Daniel. But, as each day brought no news, their focus had to change to include achievable goals, not constant disappointment.

They began talking about who they would invite onto the committee. Julie Elliott, Sam Knight and Tim Ryan's names came up immediately. After all, they had been through so much with them. 'The Morcombe curse', as Denise would call it, had taken effect in their lives too. Elliott had broken up with her fiancé and Knight had split up with her husband, and would change back to her maiden name of McDowall.

Bruce and Denise made their intentions known in a letter to Greg Beale, president of the Sunshine Coast Crime Stoppers committee, ahead of their 19 January meeting. Bruce wrote, 'We are going to set up a Daniel Morcombe

Foundation. If we could harness the good wishes of the community but donate all surplus funds beyond the Daniel Awareness Campaign to help others in need, then this is a win–win for everyone.'

The beneficiaries of the Foundation were yet to be decided, but Bruce requested that the funds, which had been set up a year ago in response to the public's generosity, should be transferred to the newly established Foundation.

* * *

As Operation Vista continued, with police investigating any new leads, Douglas Jackway's name still echoed through the hallways of the correctional centres throughout Queensland. In 2004, police had re-opened a rape complaint against Jackway from an alleged victim who confirmed that she wanted to have it re-investigated.

In January 2005, a review of facts pertaining to Daniel's disappearance was conducted relating to Jackway's associates and alibis. Police believed that he would not have had time to commit the crime, as the phone records showed that a call was made from Jackway's address in Bertha Street at around 3.30 pm on the day Daniel disappeared to Carrington's house, as well as Carrington's assertion that Jackway and Park had called around to see him at around 5 or 5.30 pm.

The rumours from the jails persisted. Throughout 2005, prisoners continued to either contact Crime Stoppers direct, or ask relatives to let police know they had information. Some inmates repeated overheard conversations between Jackway and other prisoners. One inmate reported Jackway as saying: 'There is no way they're going to find Daniel. I knocked him off.' He added that Jackway had also said: 'Put him in a place where they'll never find him.' Another said Jackway had said Daniel's body was 'up the coast, in a forest'. Several inmates said that Jackway would often watch any coverage of Daniel's disappearance intensely. He had also told some people that he'd changed his hairstyle after the sketches were released by police. Some inmates, police decided, were simply seeking parole in 'helping' police and were hoping to benefit from a deal. In early 2005, Detective Sergeant Ian Tuffield from the Organised Crime Investigation Unit undertook a review of Jackway. But the review remained in draft form and was never completed and was undated. Detective Tuffield went on extended sick leave. Meanwhile, there were continued rumours about an association between Jackway and Dooley. One inmate had told police that Jackway had a mate called Bill Dooley. Jackway and Dooley had both been in the Arthur Gorrie Correctional Centre from March to May 2004 in different units, when Jackway was being investigated for rape. In May 2005, Jackway was sentenced to six years jail for that crime and sent to Townsville Correctional Centre. His earliest release date was set as 1 July 2008 and his full discharge was set down as 16 May 2012.

Police stated they did not believe Jackway and Dooley had been associates in December 2003, nor did they appear to have been associates since then, but another inmate claimed he had seen Dooley and Jackway in a house with Daniel, and that Daniel had his feet and hands bound together and was pleading for his life. The inmate said that he had then seen Jackway shoot Daniel Morcombe in the head. These stories cluttered any clear path to hard evidence. Most allegations were hearsay, with little fact to back them up, but there were disturbing similarities in some of the stories and they occupied much of the police resources.

Another POI who, like Jackway, kept cropping up in police files was Alexander Meyer (pseudonym), a formidable-looking 30-year-old man with a large, shaved head, large ears and a pencil moustache. He lived in his family home in Windsor, a northern suburb of Brisbane, having stayed on there after his mother was admitted to a nursing home in 2005. Denise was to describe him later as having a 'face only a mother would love'. Meyer, who had the frame of a basketball player, had been 13 when he was first charged with possessing a prohibited plant. His wide-spaced eyes showed no fear and his mugshot conveyed a disinterested arrogance that left no one in doubt that he meant business. He was said to have a 'dungeon' under his house in Windsor.

Meyer had been on the list mentioned to the Morcombes off the record in 2004. A convicted paedophile had also named Jackway, Dooley and Meyer as being associates of each other. In the many different versions Dooley told the police, he claimed to have known Meyer and his family for years. He said he had seen Meyer in October or early November 2003, just before Daniel disappeared. Meyer, as it turned out, had also sold drugs to Brett Cowan while they were both at school. Windsor was not far from Everton Park, the suburb where Cowan had grown up. Meyer had also been in the Arthur Gorrie Correctional Centre in 1996, when Cowan was serving time there for the violent rape of the boy in Darwin in 1993. Dooley had nominated Meyer in 2004 as being one of two other men who was with him when Daniel was abducted. He claimed that Meyer had later held Daniel, who had been drugged at the time, while he was sexually assaulted by the man Dooley was accused of murdering: 73-year-old Donald Rogers. Dooley's convoluted stories led to more resources being spent investigating his allegations. In March 2004, Dooley had taken police to Rogers's body. Rogers's remains were off Steve Irwin Way not far from the Bruce Highway. Dooley denied murdering him saying Rogers had died because he didn't have his diabetes medication. Dooley was later charged with Rogers's murder.

In November 2004, Dooley had also nominated Meyer as being the one responsible for disposing of Daniel's body before he asked the police questions about the options available to him for indemnity. Later, Dooley claimed that Rogers's car had been used to dispose of Daniel's body.

On 15 February, he gave another interview at police headquarters. He was then taken by detectives to the Sunshine Coast where he directed them to a pine plantation between Steve Irwin Way and Beerburrum Road. This was close to where he had taken police to show them Rogers's body. This time, he showed them a dirt road opposite Male Road that ran alongside Steve Irwin Way, saying that Daniel's body had been left there, as he had been in the car when it happened. He also showed detectives where the blue car had stopped under the overpass and pointed out where Daniel had been standing. Dooley claimed that the blue car had stalked Daniel after he had been seen under the overpass by three men when they were returning from a drug dealer in Yandina further north. Daniel, he said, had been snatched by Meyer who came up behind him after another occupant in the car kept him talking. Daniel was thrown into the car screaming and had banged his head and was 'terrified'. Dooley denied the third person in the car was Jackway. In one version, he had said one of the occupants was an older man and that he had claimed Daniel was his son. He said Meyer had shaved his head when he had seen Daniel's case in the news. On 17 and 18 February, a senior constable from the Victorian police and her cadaver dog was sent into the area. Later, SES personnel also conducted a search, but nothing was found. Later Dooley took detectives to a bike path along Breakfast Creek at Bowen Hills, a northern suburb of Brisbane, saying that was where Meyer had disposed of Daniel's clothes. But a search by police divers found nothing at that site. Days before police drove Dooley to the Sunshine Coast, they also received information that an inmate of the prison had been approached by Dooley on 10 January while at the Brisbane City Watchhouse. Dooley had told the inmate that Jackway and 'another person called Alexander' had killed Daniel and that Dooley had helped to burn the car afterwards. Dooley had drawn a map of where the car had been left near Gympie, north of the Sunshine Coast and asked him to remove the burnt car as he had believed the inmate was about to get bail. Dooley had also told the inmate the following day that Daniel's body was near where the car was. Later, however, Meyer denied these allegations, saying Dooley was just playing games with the police because he hated them. In these cloak and dagger games, police had to sift out the truth.

* * *

On 23 February, Bruce and Denise began sending feedback to Brett Winkler for the logo he was designing for the Foundation. They had chosen some fonts that they liked, which resembled children's writing, and they liked his idea of a ribbon too. The Foundation was beginning to take form.

Easter that year fell on 27 March. Dean had been down in Melbourne and Denise and Brad flew down to meet him. They drove to Robinvale on the south bank of the Murray River in northern Victoria and camped there over Easter with Kevin and Monique. Then Dean and Denise drove Dean's van back to Queensland. From that date on, Bruce helped Dean with his new Jim's Tree Lopping franchise, committing to helping him for one year.

On 1 May, Tracey Cowan, by then aged 29, gave her first formal statement at Maroochydore CIB. Cowan was clearly a key POI given his own admission that he had driven past the abduction site twice at the time Daniel disappeared yet it had taken police 18 months to formally interview the person police believed at that time was his only alibi. A week earlier, police had also requested a list of phone calls made from Cowan's house at Alf's Pinch Road.

While the investigation continued under wraps, the launch of the Daniel Morcombe Foundation on 6 May 2005, a Friday morning two days before Mother's Day, made more media headlines. Glenis Green was there for Brisbane's *The Courier-Mail*. Knight and Elliott were there too, and Tania Netherway, who had written the song for Daniel. Denise sat flanked by Bruce and Inspector Maloney at a long table. The launch coincided with the new television advertising campaign, which would run for two weeks and was funded by around $90,000, raised from public funds. The campaign featured 1500 advertisements screened on Queensland networks, including police sketches of the man believed to be involved in the abduction and images of a suspect blue sedan seen near the bus stop. The fob watch Daniel had been carrying also featured in the ads, as it was hoped someone had seen it or bought it second-hand. Bruce told the media that the commercials would draw particular attention to Queensland's highest reward – announced the previous October at $250,000 – and possible indemnity from prosecution if any information led to the apprehension and conviction of Daniel's abductors.

'We're not lying down, we're not going away,' Bruce said. 'We've just got to get that additional information that just might break somebody's alibi or find an additional snippet of news that will lead to solving this case.'

Bruce admitted what he and Denise had spoken privately about many times – that Daniel had met with foul play. 'It appears, from all information, that our son was murdered,' he told the media.

Julie Elliott reported that the police were confident those responsible would be brought to justice. 'Police have got different people of interest that they are still following through on,' she said. 'But obviously someone out there is sitting on a piece of information.'

When questioned about what he believed, Bruce said, 'We can't change what's happened and we actually don't know what's happened, but one can only guess and that's possibly your worst nightmare.' Then he added, bringing home the message they really wanted to convey from this media conference, 'But we can influence the future, which we're hoping the Foundation will do, and perhaps educate other children that there's evil out there. The Foundation is really about trying to find some good from a terrible situation. And we want to raise awareness about this through education programs in schools.' Bruce said that they hoped to raise more than $1 million in the next few years through the Foundation, which could help such programs.

There were the inevitable tears, in spite of focusing on the positive. Glenis Green threw a question that took Denise by surprise. 'This Sunday will be your second Mother's Day without Daniel. How do you feel and what will you be doing this Mother's Day?' Sitting at the long table, Denise began to cry, aware, as she did so, that the police and media had got the response they wanted. A grieving mother again. While describing how she could not share that special day with her beloved son, she recovered to say, 'We've always got hope. If we didn't have hope, we'd just give up.'

Ever on the lookout for a news angle, Peter Doherty, from Channel Seven, had noticed the tattoo for Daniel that Denise had on her right ankle. Even though it had been there since December 2004, it became 'news'.

The following Saturday morning, Elliott phoned Denise. She said that Glenis Green's question had really upset her, and Denise agreed.

* * *

The first committee meeting for the Foundation was on 18 May 2005 at the Morcombes' kitchen table. Denise had made sausage rolls and other hors d'oeuvres, and they opened a bottle of wine.

206

It was unanimously decided that the logo for the Foundation was to be a red T-shirt, since that was what Daniel was last seen wearing. The words 'Daniel Morcombe Foundation' would be in childlike writing beside it. This, Bruce and Denise felt, brought back the message that Daniel was a real boy, wearing a red T-shirt. Red was already symbolic from the red-ribbon campaign. It had come to mean one word: safety. The objectives of the Foundation were simple and amounted to three things: to educate children regarding their personal safety (including abduction); to assist victims of crime, particularly where the crime involved children; and to continue the search for Daniel.

At subsequent meetings in the first few months, there was no sign of the name being registered. They were told by a public servant from the Office of Fair Trading in Queensland that they could have 'Daniel Morcombe Trust' but not use the word 'Foundation', as it had a different connotation in law and meant that the income-tax-deductibility factor would be difficult. But the Morcombes were determined. 'Foundation' as a word meant a lot to them. They contacted the then Queensland premier, Peter Beattie. In August, they learnt that their chosen business name had finally been registered. They later heard that Beattie had reportedly intervened, saying that the Morcombes had suffered enough pain.

In those early months, neither Bruce nor Denise could fully appreciate how much of a lasting legacy the Foundation would provide. Concentrating on such positive goals warmed a small place in their hearts and provided hope. The Foundation became the battle cry. They were waging a war against those who had chosen to live in darkness, arming those who were vulnerable and defenceless with weapons to fight back. The Foundation helped them cope with what seemed the hopeless task of finding Daniel. Every day, they grew more and more determined to make the world a better place.

May 2005 also saw the launch of the AMBER alert in Queensland, the state's child-abduction-alert system. It was the only one of its kind in the country and its introduction was in recognition of what had happened to Daniel. The scheme, modelled on a successful North American system responding to the abduction and murder of a child called Amber, flashed alerts on television and over the radio if a child was suspected of being abducted. The alert recognised the need to work quickly when a child was in danger to combat those with ill intent.

* * *

Bruce and Denise continued to be kept at a distance from the intricacies of the police investigation. Bruce understood this, even though they waited every day to hear that police had nailed someone. When Cowan's photo was shown to them, neither of them thought much of it. It was just another query. They knew, without asking, that they would be told nothing further even if they did raise the question: why this man? At around the same time, Cowan's mobile and landline phone records either side of the day of Daniel's disappearance were being investigated. Meanwhile, some aspects of the police investigation became public. After 100 detectives doorknocked 900 homes and businesses within three kilometres of where Daniel went missing, they made a discovery of a burnt-out and partly submerged blue sedan on 25 May, abandoned in a creek not far from where Daniel disappeared. That got Denise's heart beating fast. It was the biggest doorknock in Queensland's police history. But, there were still no solid leads. The car turned out to have been dumped well before Daniel disappeared.

But the public support continued. Calling into the hairdresser's one weekend, Bruce was asked by the woman cutting his hair if he could give her a new bumper-bar sticker for her car, as her other one had faded. These were the small requests that kept them going.

Bruce maintained his philosophy of believing that any lead was worth following in the search for Daniel. He had a call one day in the middle of 2005, while he was at the Foundation home office, from a person who wanted to meet him as he said he could help find Daniel. The voice on the end of the phone sounded like an older man. He spoke quickly and seemed nervous.

Bruce suggested they meet at the Aussie World car park in front of the Ettamogah Pub on the Bruce Highway at Glenview. He chose this location because he knew there were cameras and security on site, just in case things did not go to plan.

He left home early one Sunday morning with a piece of pipe in the boot of his car for protection, now another part of his investigative kit. He also checked that his voice recorder was working and placed it in the top pocket of his shirt. As he entered the large car park, he could see another white, older car that was stationary with a man sitting inside. Bruce glanced around, assessing his safety, as he parked next to the white car. He flicked on the recorder discreetly in his pocket. The man was thin and short, possibly around 55 years old. Not an imposing figure, thought Bruce, relieved. Right away, he saw that the man was distressed. Within seconds of his arrival, the man burst into tears. He came over and they shook hands. With the man still sobbing, they exchanged names. Bruce suggested they sit in his car. Bruce would never sit in anyone else's car, for safety reasons. The man wanted to show him a place down the highway where he said that, on Boxing Day 2003, he saw suspicious people and activity happening. He had been driving north that morning, returning to Gympie after spending Christmas Day with family in Brisbane.

They drove about 25 kilometres south, about halfway to the Caboolture/Bribie Island turn-off. Suddenly, the man said, 'Stop here. Look, that's the spot.' Bruce saw a dirt track that peeled off and was accessible from the highway. Pine trees were in seemingly endless rows, kilometre after kilometre.

The man said he saw three or four men with a couple of cars. One had a trailer on it. He said the men were in the process of winching an older, square-shaped, blue car onto the trailer and they looked nervous. Bruce drove further south and did a U-turn at the next opportunity. 'I was in the right lane,' the man told him. Bruce also moved into that lane. He was travelling at about 70 or 80 kilometres per hour. He looked out of the window but it was not all that clear because of the trees.

He had seen enough, and made the judgement call that it was not relevant.

He returned the man to his car and they went their separate ways.

A couple of weeks later, the man rang again. 'I have seen the same cars,' he said.

Only listening to be courteous, Bruce agreed to being posted some photos. The photos arrived plus notes on people the man claimed were drug runners and criminals in Gympie. Bruce downloaded the conversation onto his computer and filed all the material the man had sent.

It had led him nowhere, but it could be important later on.

CHAPTER FOURTEEN

NEVER GIVE UP

Nerang Police Station, in Cotton Street, Nerang, just off the main artery of the Pacific Highway, has a provincial feel, with its unassuming size, small, red-brick facade, tropical vegetation set back from the road and its generous pedestrian frontage. There, on 6 July 2005, in the presence of Detective Senior Constable Mark Wright and Detective Senior Sergeant Tracey Barnes from Maroochydore CIB, Brett Cowan was finally brought in to officially recount his version of his movements on 7 December 2003.

At 3.45 pm, when the interview began, he agreed to being electronically recorded and gave his latest address as Bonnydoon Road, Uki in northern New South Wales. He told police that he'd been born in Bunbury, Western Australia. Barnes gave him the perfunctory warnings – that he was not under arrest and was free to go, and that he had the right to remain silent but that anything he might say would be recorded and could be later used as evidence against him. Cowan was told he could call a solicitor and was asked if he wanted anyone to be there with him. 'No,' he replied.

His answers were prefaced with many 'ums' as he again recounted what had happened that day, stating he had rung up his 'boss's father' to borrow a mulcher that morning and that he had gone to Nambour to pick it up. He agreed it would have taken him around 30 to 40 minutes to do the trip one way and that he had been at his boss's father's place for around 10 to 15 minutes. He was emphatic that he had not seen a boy standing under the overpass on the Nambour Connection Road on his return journey when he drove past at around 2.05 pm before returning home at about 2.30 pm. He remembered seeing a broken-down bus at the Woombye turn-off. When he drove past, he said, there had still been people on the bus.

Barnes asked him whether he'd seen the sketches that had been released.

'Yep,' Cowan answered.

'Seen 'em on TV?'

'Yep.'

She asked if he thought he looked like any of them.

'I thought one of them,' Cowan answered.

'Has anybody said anything to you?'

'No, nobody. One of them actually looks more like my brother than looks like me.'

He later admitted he'd been involved in abducting young boys in the past, and said he had done a sexual offender's course at Moreton Correctional Centre and that had taught him 'other ways of thinking'. 'I don't wanta be hurting kids. I've always said ... um ... that I've always loved kids ever since I was small ... but I just took it that bit too far.' He volunteered that his present girlfriend, Hayley McDonald, knew about his past and that she had five kids, aged 18, 17, 12, 11 and almost ten.

It was Wright's turn to intervene. Playing the classic good cop/bad cop, he told Cowan that police had a problem with his timing on what he was up to the day Daniel disappeared. 'You understand why?' he asked pointing out that Cowan had driven past the Kiel Mountain Road overpass at exactly the same time as other witnesses had seen a boy and other things such as a car. Cowan told them he had seen nothing. 'We've got a number of calls saying Brett Cowan looks like this sketch, which is of interest to us ... We'll put the cards right on the table. The fact that you've been responsible for similar styles of things in the past, opportunistic stuff, and we've got you in the area ... we can't write this off and say, "Well, it's definitely not Brett Cowan ..." until we can get our times right or something extra that's going to say, "Well, this is why he was home at 2.30," because this is the best we can get from Tracey ...' In closing the interview, Barnes asked Cowan, 'Would you tell us if you did this?' Cowan answered, after a pause, 'Probably not.' With that, the interview ended.

Apart from her statement, Tracey Cowan had provided an Indirect Personality Assessment Questionnaire on her former husband. She painted a picture of a man who had been dominated by his often-absent father and was frequently rebellious towards him, who constantly lied and embellished the truth. She said Cowan picked up trades without a problem, and smiled easily and liked gardening. But, she said, his chosen reading material was pornography, and he watched action and violent movies. He enjoyed the computer game SimCity, and spent his money on cannabis and his car. She had never seen him commit an act of violence, but he continually became angry, she said. He would be competitive with his mates over who could drink the most, smoke the most or tell the dirtiest story. He had been sad only once, over the death of his grandmother, and had not shown any sadness after the break-up of their marriage. He rarely sat still and needed to be occupied, and he was often impulsive. As far as how he interacted with children, she said he was 'lovey dovey' and that he had always liked them and was 'a big kid'. He rarely showed remorse if he had done something wrong – such as the time when he drove the car dangerously when she was pregnant.

Barnes and Wright conducted further interviews including one with Trevor Davis, the son of Frank Davis, who had the mulcher. Davis explained he had hoped to give Cowan a second chance at life, even though he knew he had offended against children, and he volunteered that he employed him for several years on a casual basis.

On 17 July, Barnes and Wright interviewed Keith and Jenny Philbrook, the pastors at the Christian Outreach Centre and Cowan's uncle and aunt. The Philbrooks had taken in Cowan after he was released from jail in Darwin and had visited him twice in prison in 1997. They said that Cowan upon his release had told them he had 'given his heart to God' but, that he had continually lied to them and broken any ground rules they set up. He had also stolen money from them, although they conceded he was a good worker. He had moved out of their home into Alf's Pinch Road in the late '90s and shortly after that had married Tracey. Tracey had later told them that, during her marriage to Cowan, he had talked to her about having thoughts of reoffending.

Barnes and Wright also called in to Clayton's Towing Service but were told there was a record of only one job that Cowan had done for them, and that was on 9 December 2003 at 2.30 pm. However, Mike Clayton, the owner, said it was not uncommon for new staff to work with experienced employees by doing 'cashies' without it being recorded.

The same month that Cowan was being interviewed, the MIR decided to request assistance from the Federal Bureau of Investigation (FBI). The request went through Gregory Groves from the FBI's legal attaché in Canberra. The FBI requested photographs of the path Daniel had taken from the Morcombes' house to the abduction site, as well as the sketches of people seen near the site that were released to the public in November 2004. The FBI also requested a timeline of events and a summary of witness statements, all of which were forwarded to the FBI's Behavioral Analysis Unit.

* * *

On 13 August, Water Police descended on Cowan's former home at Alf's Pinch Road, sheltered by macadamia trees in the grassed paddocks behind Beerwah. SES workers turned up and began wading through the marshy lands behind the house.

It was almost two years after Daniel's abduction. They found nothing.

On 1 September, Barnes and Wright attended the Uki address near Murwillumbah and spoke with Hayley McDonald. She said that about five months into their relationship, Cowan had told her about the boy in Darwin in 1993 and said he was now cured after attending a course. When asked if she was worried about him living with her sons, she said that she had trusted him implicitly and that she had talked to her children about them telling her straightaway if anything untoward should happen. She said a recent domestic at the house between her 17-year-old son and Cowan, to which the police had been called, was just her son being jealous of 'Mum's boyfriend'. Cowan had since told her about the interview he did with the police in July and that he had also been questioned about touching a boy after a wedding. He said that he believed his ex-wife had told the police about it.

* * *

To the outside world, Bruce and Denise always somehow managed to focus on the positive. By Father's Day on 4 September, the negative thoughts, however, were outweighing the positive ones. Denise was still drinking heavily but could not confront the problem. She felt frustrated and sad, isolated and alone. It felt like everyone else was getting on with their lives. The immense frustration of never finding an answer to what happened to Daniel weighed heavily. Straight after handing Bruce a gift for Father's Day, she said, 'I want a divorce.' His answer was: 'Not while you have these problems.'

It would have been easy in many ways for both of them to walk away. But that was not what either of them was made of. They had to find a way through the problem, Bruce thought. He refused to walk away when she clearly needed help. Denise went to see a clinical psychologist who had carried out regressive hypnotherapy on some of the witnesses earlier on in the case. He spoke to her about 'Functional Truth'.

'Think of the worst-case scenario of what has happened to Daniel and deal with that in your head,' he advised. 'If you ever found out whatever happened to Daniel, it won't have been as bad as you thought.'

Taking his advice she dreamt up all kinds of scenarios to add to the horrific stories that had come from the public. After the visit with the psychologist, she sat down and wrote a letter to Bruce:

Dear Bruce,
I saw [my psychologist] today and I think it was worth it.

He told me what I am going through is a part of the grieving process. He thinks I am about three-quarters the way through it. He said I know Daniel will never come back, I have told myself that with my Functional Truth and I am working on that.

He said my anger and trying to self-destruct is part of me trying to be independent, and that is normal, but I can't be independent because I am being held back. I am being held back because I have too much to do here with our own business, and Dean's and other reasons.

He said someone who is looking for a job, wanting to start a Foundation and starting to write a book is not going to kill herself. He said I am too strong.

He couldn't believe that we have never had any medication of any kind to help us. He said he forgot to ask us.

He drew me another map of where we are in our marriage. It shows you being practical with procedures, for example tea ready at 5, go to bed at a certain time, feed the horses at this time, do this at that time. He said that this is the outer core and I have passed that and don't care. I am into the core trying to work out directions and purposes and unity and identity. That does not mean moving house, he said, that is just trying to forget everything.

We need to be friends and discuss what we want.

If this can be a start it may help.

Love, Denise

Bruce penned a reply to Denise. They had to look for positive things to keep them going, he wrote. And their challenge remained: to focus on finding Daniel and holding the family together.

For Denise, when she couldn't speak the words, she wrote them. At this time she also wrote a letter to Daniel, not to be opened until she was ready.

Her drinking remained a challenge, but it lessened over time.

* * *

On 26 September, Barnes and Wright travelled to Melbourne. They had an address for Tracey Hanevald, Cowan's old girlfriend who had been with him in the caravan park in Darwin when he was convicted of the sexual assault of the six-year-old boy. The address they had been given was in Cleek Avenue, Oakleigh, in the south-eastern suburbs of Melbourne, a nondescript suburban street with '50s-style, one-storey houses with ample backyards and a generous nature strip. But, upon arriving at the address, they were told by a woman that Tracey, who was now the girlfriend of the woman's son, had driven to Perth. Later that evening, Tracey returned Barnes's call from Perth and said that, when she had heard about the Daniel Morcombe case, she had always wondered if Brett Cowan was involved. She said she would send information to the police about her earlier relationship with Cowan and agreed to be interviewed later.

* * *

On 29 September, the Foundation set the date for the first 'Dance for Daniel' as 4 March 2006. It was to be at Twin Waters and would have a theme of Red Tie. There would be donations and prizes. Wristbands and temporary tattoos and stickers were all being used as fundraising efforts, and a motorbike rally was planned. There would be an auction of all sorts of prizes, including memorabilia. Another Day for Daniel was planned for 25 November 2005. This was to be the first run by the Foundation, and therefore the first 'official' one. There was plenty of work to do. Bruce and Denise ordered 10,000 red wristbands bearing the words 'Child-safety awareness'. A printer made stickers of the Foundation logo and temporary tattoos of it would be on sale. The Morcombes began emailing Queensland schools one by one to let them know about the Day for Daniel. Each school was sent an order form for wristbands. By the time the day dawned, nearly all the wristbands had been ordered. There was still a lot to learn, however. Many of the wristbands were returned unsold.

September was also the month when Brad and Dean broke their silence on the loss of their brother, for Foxtel's *Crime Investigation* television program. The boys rarely spoke about Daniel at home, keeping their grief to themselves.

Meanwhile, as the Morcombes watched the television news, memories flooded in. Another teenager from Perth, 14-year-old Blake Reynolds, who had been abducted, had been found 20 days later in a house in south-east Perth. Police ruled out a link between his abduction and Daniel's, even though the two men who were arrested had been named POIs by Operation Vista. Denise promised that the Foundation would help the family and the boy recover from such a traumatic experience but the family declined any help.

Dean's 18th birthday came around on 4 October 2005. He had come home with a tattoo on the inner side of his arm. Denise had been expecting Dean to get a tribute to Daniel inked into his skin at some point, as they had all discussed it, but she was not prepared for the poignancy of Dean's choice: three red roses with the words 'Never Forgotten' in a banner, with three candles, one of them blown out. Denise burst into tears. Later, over several sessions, Dean had Daniel's cheeky grin drawn on his bicep. Dean designed the tattoos himself. He would draw the place where he wanted the tattoos on his arms beforehand and then visit the tattooist. On his upper left arm, he added 'Never Give Up, Never Give In', written in a banner with roses flowing to the lower tattoo. He got the idea at a Dance for Daniel, listening to Police Commissioner Bob Atkinson, who was quoting Winston Churchill. Although he was not religious, he also had praying hands tattooed on his forearm, representing all of the people who were wishing Daniel was all right and who had lent their support to the family.

* * *

On 16 October, Tracey Hanevald was eventually located for an interview. She told Detective Barnes that she had met Cowan when she was in Nambour in 1991 and that they broke up after he had a relationship with another woman. In 1993, she had gone to Darwin with a girlfriend and met Cowan after he had contacted her mother saying he wanted to resume the relationship. She had been at the caravan park with Cowan when the boy was sexually assaulted and reported that Cowan had behaved strangely afterwards. Once the boy had been found, Cowan had said to her, 'Let's leave Darwin' adding that as he had a record and there were police everywhere, he did not want to get into trouble. She had accused him of 'hiding something' and he had said their relationship was over and he would leave without her. Shortly after that, he had confessed to police. She said she had seen Cowan in the interview room at the local police station and asked him whether he had done it, and he had said he had. She had withdrawn some money he owed her. She had not seen him since.

* * *

Bruce was busy working with Dean in the field, so as the Foundation's first Day for Daniel neared, Tim Ryan drove Denise around the towns of the Sunshine Coast. Together, they delivered posters and wristbands to the schools and shops that had ordered them. They called into Crazy Clarks in Nambour and bought moneyboxes. While Tim drove, Denise stuck stickers of their logo on the moneyboxes. During one of these trips, they dropped into Sunland Shopping Centre in Caloundra to deliver a parcel to the doughnut shop. As Denise approached the shop, she was caught mid-stride. Inside was Sam, Daniel's schoolfriend who had gone to the movies with him on that Saturday in 2003. She immediately became teary. Sam was a stark reminder of what it might be like to turn the clock back, a young man the age Daniel would have been now if he'd lived. Tim, seeing her distress, took the parcel from her and delivered it to the shop instead.

They also called in to Australia Zoo. At the front counter, Denise asked, 'Would you consider taking a donation tin and maybe some of our stickers?' It was their first meeting with the Irwins' PA Nicole, and heralded the beginning of a supportive relationship with Terri Irwin and her husband, Steve, and their children, Bindi and Bob.

By 18 November, all wristbands had gone except for some at the Nambour Plaza and the Kawana Shopping Centre. Denise made sure some were kept for the committee.

The Day for Daniel ran on 25 November as planned, and was the Foundation's first of many Safety Awareness Days. It was a great success. It was Jenny McKay, the local councillor in the Maroochydore Shire, who came up with the idea of the 'Walk for Daniel'. It was decided to hold it on the same date as the Day for Daniel and to start at the duck pond at Palmwoods and finish at the Memorial shrine under the Kiel Mountain Road overpass on the Nambour Connection Road. Everyone was asked to wear red – either a red ribbon, T-shirt or socks. A clash of commitments meant Denise could not join Bruce and Jenny for the event. She drove past the duck pond just as the walk was starting. The masses of red shirts and balloons bobbing in the skies said it all. They were marching for Daniel in force. She was very upset that she couldn't be there, but she had a radio interview to do at the Siena Catholic College with 92.7 Mix FM. The Maroochydore mayor addressed the hundred or so walkers about the community spirit to find Daniel, and then they released the balloons. Bruce thanked the walkers and vowed they would never give up.

* * *

When the second anniversary of Daniel's disappearance arrived, Bruce and Denise, and Dean and Bradley, opted to stay out of the spotlight. It was left to Julie Elliott to tell the media, gathered around Daniel's memorial shrine under the overpass, as cars and trucks rushed past on the Nambour Connection Road, 'This case has received the most calls and jobs logged of any in Queensland Police history.'

Detective Inspector John Maloney gave another assurance that the mystery of Daniel's disappearance would be solved, no matter how long it took. 'It's sad we haven't solved it in that time but with these investigations you certainly don't mark it by time,' he said. He told the media that a dedicated core of ten officers were working full-time on the case and that 14,000 job logs had been entered so far.

Earlier on 7 December, the Morcombes had visited the shrine at the overpass to place their own bunch of roses before attending the 7 am service at St Mary's Church in Buderim, where they were met by friends.

Brad had now finished Grade 11 and had told Bruce and Denise that he was not going back to school. Well, find a job, they responded. He applied for an apprenticeship with Mallets Foundry in Kunda Park as a moulder. He was to stay there for about six months before he got his first job in the fencing trade, initially as an employee, then as a private contractor. Brad was entering adulthood. On 19 December, all four of the Morcombes flew to Hamilton Island for Brad's birthday and decided to spend Christmas there. The visit was their fifth, but it was their first without Daniel. It was a mistake. In trying to create new memories, they kept encountering the old: the Easter-egg hunt they had done, the diving and swimming, the face painting and the buffet breakfasts. They never returned. At exactly one second to midnight on Brad and Daniel's birthday, Bruce's watch stopped. Later, he found it could not be repaired.

CHAPTER FIFTEEN

THE LABYRINTH

The Morcombes' life was one of sharp contrasts. They lived parallel lives. Working for the Foundation, they were rewarded by joyful faces and providing value to the community. Their relentless search for Daniel, however, dragged them into a seedy underworld where they had to to confront a community of outlaws who evaded society's system of justice. Jail, it seemed to them, instead of being a deterrent, provided an opportunity for like-minded criminals to network, particularly for paedophiles housed in jails specially set up to cater for them. A January 2006 survey by *The Sunday Mail* claimed that three in four Queenslanders wanted convicted child-sex offenders to spend the rest of their lives behind bars. Often these offenders were well versed with avoiding prosecution. Even if they were successfully convicted, judges opted for a lenient sentence, allowed by soft laws allowing prisoners who were often multiple offenders, such as Jackway and Cowan, to be re-released into the community to offend again. In the face of no concrete leads from the police investigation, Bruce never relinquished his vigilante role of pursuing every lead to track the people or person who had abducted his son.

One day, Bruce received an email from a prison officer who said he had information on Daniel. He arranged to meet him at Caboolture train station, which was halfway between Brisbane and the Sunshine Coast, as the man was from Brisbane. As usual, Bruce was looking for a meeting place that would have a security camera trained on it. Arriving earlier than the agreed 9 am, Bruce wanted to assess a good location in full view of the car-park camera. Time ticked by but the man did not arrive. Several times, he drove around to other areas of the car park in case the man was waiting elsewhere. He finally left at 10 am.

After a week of trying, Bruce made contact with the man again. The man apologised. 'Look, just give me what you have on the phone to save time,' Bruce said. The man described a place near Ipswich that had been a quarry but was now closed and three-quarters full of water. He said it was very deep and was known in the underworld as a dumping ground for 'all manner of dodgy dealings'. Stolen cars, guns and bodies were down there. The man said he had heard a story that Daniel had been rolled up in a rug or piece of carpet and put into the boot of a car. The car had been pushed into the water and had sunk to the bottom. The quarry was known by locals as Green Lake, the man said.

'How did you find out this kind of info?' Bruce asked.

'Oh, as a prison guard, I hear lots of stuff,' the man answered.

Bruce passed the information on to police. They did take it seriously and even began pumping out the quarry. He and Denise waited fearfully for news. However, this idea was abandoned because of safety concerns: as the water level dropped, the walls became unstable and often caved in.

There were many aspects to the investigation that the Morcombes knew nothing about. Back in late October 2005, police had been contacted by Sameha Ibrahim, a woman of Middle Eastern ethnicity who had a spiritual and alternative therapies business. She also conducted tea-leaf readings. Ibrahim said she had met a woman called Alise Smythe (pseudonym) after Smythe had attended her business premises on Sandgate Road in Nundah, looking for a GP for a sore on her arm. Ibrahim had answered the door. So had begun a strange relationship.

Smythe was already known to police. Smythe's sister and niece were also closely linked to Alexander Meyer. They had interviewed her a number of times in early 2005 after police had heard she claimed she was in the car that abducted Daniel. It was not until she was in her mid-thirties that Smythe descended into hard drugs and the decision was apparent in her sad eyes and ravaged, once-attractive features. Even those closest to her said that she lived in a paranoiac fantasy world and was prone to making up stories even to her own children. She had also claimed that Meyer confided in her that he had been responsible for Daniel's abduction. Meyer, whom she had dated in high school, had allegedly told her that he had wanted to commit a 'thrill kill'. She also said that he'd told her he would get rid of the body 20 minutes from the Maroochydore train station in red dirt near a thin pine forest. What to believe? Maroochydore has no train service.

The names she produced in telling the stories, however, were the familiar names already nominated to police as people who were responsible for abducting Daniel. Sameha Ibrahim told detectives that Smythe had told her that Meyer, Dooley and another man, who had already been identified as a POI by Operation Vista investigators, had abducted Daniel Morcombe. This man was also a known associate of Bill Dooley. Smythe had also told Ibrahim that she had found a pair of black, red and white shorts and a pair of white shoes and track pants that she said belonged to Daniel at Meyer's house in Windsor. She had given them to Ibrahim, who she regularly met with.

By 2006, however, Ibrahim told police she was frustrated by their lack of action. She began contacting a psychic, Michelle McQuirk, from Townsville, as well as local and state members of parliament, including the deputy mayor of Caloundra, Anna Grosskreutz, who had helped organise the Ride for Daniel, along with organisations which focused on the sexual abuse of children such as Bravehearts Inc.

* * *

The first Dance for Daniel was held on 4 March 2006. Michael Carr, Peter Cupples, Steady Eddy, Tania Netherway and Angry Anderson performed. Band of Blue, the Queensland Police Service seven-piece band, wowed the audience, as operational police officers across the state joined in on guitar, vocals and drums. Kay McGrath, the Queensland Channel Seven newsreader with a 20-year history of child-safety charity work, was introduced as the patron of the Foundation.

On the Monday night after the dance, the highs and lows of their existence came crashing down on Denise. On the one hand, the incredible success of the Dance for Daniel; on the other why they were having the dance at all – Daniel was lost.

Denise took all the sleeping pills she could find, mixed with alcohol. She went to bed hoping she wouldn't ever wake up, but she did.

Bruce was furious. It was time for a reality check. 'Too many people care about you to let them down,' he said. And: 'we have to find Daniel.'

His words got through. Denise never went down this road again.

By Easter, Bruce had made a decision. He stopped working for Dean at Jim's Trees so he could devote his time to the Foundation and searching for Daniel. He and Denise were now both full-time, unpaid volunteers, working from home.

In mid-2006, Bruce and Denise began doing presentations at local schools, focusing on child safety. These two words were vital to both of them in making a difference in the wake of what had happened to Daniel. It was a steep learning curve, as they had no training in public speaking. The first school was Nambour Christian College, followed by Kuluin Primary School, Burnside Primary School and Nudgee Boys' College. They were unprepared for the directness of the questions. 'Do you think Daniel is dead?' one student asked. But they learnt valuable lessons from these first presentations and were uplifted by the students' honesty. Bruce and Denise could tell almost right away by their eye contact with the children that they were interested and engaged in the message they were communicating. Linking Daniel's real story to their lives with safety messages was a unique approach, and it seemed to work. One of the first presentations they did was filmed, and they used it on the first version of the DVD *Foundation Red*. The DVD starred Peter Overton, Brett Lee, Jamie Dunn and Agro, the Muppet-like character from Channel Seven, and focused on teaching children what to do in unsafe situations.

Meanwhile, from Victoria, on 12 July, Kevin and Monique Beavis spoke of their grief about the continuing search for Daniel in their local paper, *Leader – Whitehorse Gazette*, saying they had given up hope he was alive. 'I can't cope. He loved me so much and was always so close to me,' Monique said. She added that Denise had changed forever since Daniel was abducted.

'I wouldn't wish anyone a day in my shoes,' Mr Beavis said. 'When I think of him, I smile a lot and laugh a lot, and I hurt a lot.'

In June, July and August, Bruce and Denise completed 30 school visits across South East Queensland, spreading their child-safety message. Their confidence in what they were doing was growing every day. They felt a real purpose in what they were trying to achieve, pushing boundaries for themselves and the schoolchildren to revisit Daniel's story with a new direction. Their belief in what they were doing carried them forward. Helping others gave them a focus – something to get them through each day. Warning children to be observant and to be aware of potential danger without scaring them was a fine line to tread. The challenge was to approach each school as though it were the first, and to come up with a presentation style that was consistently powerful and would last past their short time on stage. It can happen to anyone, even in broad daylight, they said, and Daniel's story illustrated this beyond any shadow of a doubt.

Meanwhile, the search for Daniel continued. Their next briefing on the case, at Maroochydore Police Station on 7 August, with John Maloney and Greg Daniels, left them both disheartened and more convinced that they might never know what happened to Daniel. The original investigators were disappearing into other tasks as life moved on. Greg Daniels had accepted a promotion to Inspector and was to transfer to Townsville. Sam Knight and Dave Wilkinson, key players in the early days, had both left. The Morcombes' most trusted police contacts were diminishing day by day. Elliott was still a great support, and Denise had helped her pack up her house in Caboolture when she moved to a two-bedroom unit in the northern Brisbane suburb of Ascot. But she was not directly involved in the investigative side of things.

They were told that there were no new leads and were informed that things were likely to wind down by Christmas. They had always feared the day when the investigation would grind to a halt and be shelved as a 'cold case'. Publicly, they had always remained committed to the police and the MIR team, deciding they had no choice as they wanted police to remain focused on finding their son. 'We are on the same side with the same target and the same prize' became their catchcry.

Bruce continued to make notes of some of the POIs that he knew by name: Bill Dooley, Jackway and Cowan. Two lines of enquiry had got nowhere, as the POIs or their associates were dead, he wrote in his diary. Both he and Denise had already begun discussing the next option: a coronial inquest. They had begun searching online to gain a better understanding of the process and under what circumstances an inquest might be called. It was yet another challenge to overcome, but they were determined in their crusade to find Daniel.

* * *

Alise Smythe had got back in touch with the police. She said she had reliable information but would only provide it to a particular detective: Ian Tuffield. Tuffield had been involved in the review into Douglas Jackway and also in the last interview with Dooley. By this time, Smythe had been arrested for several property offences. But she failed to turn up on the appointed day to talk to Tuffield and, on 17 July, was remanded in custody at the Brisbane Women's Correctional Centre (BWCC).

On 10 August 2006, a lawyer contacted police to say his female client Alise Smythe had told him that Daniel's body was buried within 200 metres of the body of pensioner Donald Rogers, who had disappeared a week after Daniel and whose body had been found in the Beerburrum State Forest after Bill Dooley had taken police there. Dooley had been charged with his murder. On 24 August, Smythe was collected from the BWCC and taken to the Goodna Police Station. This time, she told police that she had been a passenger in Bill Dooley's dark-blue car on Sunday 7 December 2003. Meyer and Smythe's ten-year-old daughter were also in the car, she said, and they were driving to the Sunshine Coast for Meyer to buy drugs. She also said she remembered Meyer saying they were 'looking for one'. She said that, at some point, Dooley stopped the car, but that the engine was still running and Meyer got out and walked off. Shortly after this, a boy she believed to be Daniel Morcombe entered the car and sat next to her on the passenger side. She thought she remembered him talking about running away to Sydney and wanting to go and visit a relative. Then they arrived at Meyer's street, where some men were waiting, and Dooley drove the car under the house. Smythe said she and her daughter stayed the night at Meyer's but she did not see Daniel Morcombe again.

At the end of this interview, Smythe was taken to the Nambour Connection Road, where a taped 're-enactment' took place. On several occasions, police drove past the location where Daniel was abducted but she did not identify it in spite of Daniel's stone memorial being clearly in view. Finally, she indicated the area under the overpass. She told the police that Dooley had stopped his blue car at several places along the Nambour Connection Road near the overpass and that they watched the boy before approaching him.

While investigating the truth of Smythe's claims, police searched the phone records to her house. The records showed that, on the day Daniel disappeared, her children's father, who was in jail, had rung three times and asked to speak to her but the children had said each time that she was asleep. Her 14-year-old son later told police that he could recall his mother being home on 7 December 2003. Smythe's daughter denied going to the Sunshine Coast with her mother, saying she had only been there once, on a school trip. She said her mother had told her about Meyer, Dooley and another person being responsible for Daniel's abduction and that she had also said that Daniel had been drugged and overdosed and had died in a bath but they had ended up reviving him. For the Morcombes, this was the most horrendous description of Daniel's fate that they had heard so far.

* * *

Wolston Correctional Centre stands next to the Brisbane Women's Correctional Centre at Wacol, 23 kilometres south-west of Brisbane. A high-security 'protection prison', it houses up to 600 paedophiles and high-risk prisoners. Inside the walls of the $127 million, state-of-the-art building, dubbed by one blog as a 'Wally World', paedophiles, known in jail as 'rock spiders', share space with police and jail informers. It is in establishments such as Wolston that convicted paedophiles continue or start new networks. Although offenders pledge to reform their ways in its rehabilitation programs, some paedophiles use the programs to network, and then ensure these networks continue outside of jail. Many of the associates that police were to track in the muddied waters of the Daniel Morcombe investigation had met each other in jail and continued their associations in the outside world when released.

Douglas Brian Jackway had spent most of his adult life in such centres, and, after being found guilty of an earlier crime, committed in 1991, of raping a nine-year-old girl, he was back inside Wolston. Danielle Richardson had visited him in jail a couple of times and had written him letters, but she denied writing the handwritten letter that arrived in August 2006 addressed to 'Doug Jackway' and intercepted by jail authorities before being passed on to Operation Vista. It read (errors in original):

> Doug, I can't handle it anymore. Daniel Morchams Picture is in the Paper, it's on TV, I see him when I sleep, all the time, I going off my head what we done to him, I have to clear my conscience soon I say you so the same, I will go to the Police soon you are in Jail now what dose it matter if you stay there you killed that poor kid. His Parents need to know.

The letter was fingerprinted but no prints were ever found. Danielle Richardson voluntarily provided her fingerprints, as did Stephen Park and relatives of Jackway, and they all denied writing the letter. It was not tested for DNA as the stamp on the envelope was a printed one and the envelope was taped not licked. It was later conceded by police that the chemicals used to fingerprint the letter also damaged the chances of obtaining DNA.

When Barnes and Detective Senior Constable Glenn Elliott interviewed Jackway on 31 August, he denied all knowledge of who could have sent it to him. He said the only people who called him 'Doug' were his family and friends, as most people called him 'Jacko'. He said he did not think it was his older sister's handwriting.

* * *

Bruce and Denise, largely unaware of these developments, continued directing their energy into the Foundation. The Daniel Morcombe Foundation designed special merchandise boxes that held wristbands, tattoos and stickers. They would drop these boxes off to the local shops in Palmwoods, Woombye and Nambour. Schools were beginning to order merchandise. Sometimes, volunteers would help pack the orders and distribute them. It was humble beginnings but they did not have the funds to do it any other way. They used their own car and were still working as volunteers.

The launch of the Foundation's first child-safety DVD was to coincide with National Children's Week at the Australia Zoo on 20 October 2006. Bruce and Denise had been working hard on the DVD which had a variety of media personalities and sporting heroes talking about child safety. They also wanted to give a private message from their family. They had a small operating budget for the DVD but generous support. They hoped it was a significant contribution in their commitment to keeping kids safe and could be used by schools and other community groups to spread the word.

On 4 September, Bruce sent the script to the Irwins, who had become strong supporters of what they were trying to achieve. They had not yet met either of them. Steve Irwin was going to do a segment on the DVD. That morning, Denise could hardly believe what she'd heard. Julie Elliott rang to tell them Steve Irwin had died from a barb from a stingray. The Irwins had been so supportive to them in their tragedy, and now Terri, Bindi and Bob had lost Steve.

* * *

On 6 September 2006, Sameha Ibrahim was again interviewed by the police. Word had got to police that Ibrahim was visiting Smythe in jail and that she had been in contact with Deputy Mayor Grosskreutz and Ray Harris, who had organised the 2004 Ride for Daniel. Ibrahim told detectives that Alise Smythe had claimed that Daniel was abducted to extort money from Donald Rogers. She said that Dooley and Meyer had apparently stolen $250,000 from Rogers and allowed him to have sex with Daniel to ensure his silence. Smythe had also told Ibrahim that there were two vehicles involved in the abduction and that one was a white van.

On 29 September Smythe was sentenced to two years imprisonment for property offences. In early November, Ibrahim told police that Grosskreutz had been visiting the women's prison to speak with Smythe and that Smythe had told Grosskreutz that Daniel had been buried near a white house used by Meyer's brother, which was near the road that led to Bribie Island. Police were also told that Grosskreutz was conducting searches there with other people.

* * *

The Queensland Police Headquarters in Brisbane has an impressive frontage with a modern, cylindrical front and grey exterior, with rows of windows fronting onto Roma Street in inner-city Brisbane. On 14 September 2006, Brett Cowan turned up there accompanied by his father, Peter Cowan. Police had received information a few months earlier that Cowan had been questioned about his evasiveness to police when answering questions about Daniel's disappearance during a custodial battle for Cowan's sons involving his former wife, Tracey. He had allegedly said there was time unaccounted for because he was meeting his drug dealer that day. The two men were taken to the Homicide Investigation Unit office. Detective Constable Mark Wright and Detective Sergeant Aaron Walker were later joined by Detective Sergeant Dave Hickey. Wright had been at Cowan's 2005 interview at Nerang Police Station as well as being one of two detectives who had called into Alf's Pinch Road after King and Martyn's visit. That the police failed to caution Cowan about his legal rights to remain silent in this 2006 interview was to become an issue later. In the small talk that began the interview, Brett Cowan noted to his father that there were three cameras. Cowan Snr observed that signing in and out was like being in an army barracks. Then they bantered about whether Cowan was wearing his father's socks. 'They're older than mine. Mine are the same age but you wear yours longer,' Cowan Snr said. Then the interview began.

Cowan divulged that he had been living at home since the previous Christmas and that he had been employed building horse floats. Asked by Wright whether he still had his white Pajero, he said he had sold it as it would have cost $10,000 to get a new motor and gearbox. He said a mate of his on Russell Island in Moreton Bay now owned it. Wright began chatting about four-wheel-drive vehicles, asking Cowan's advice as to how you could get permits to take the four-wheel drives onto the beach and to go through forestry areas. He slipped in a question: 'What about Coochin Creek and all that down at Beerwah?' Yes, Cowan replied, he'd been camping down there with an old mate of his quite a bit. He also offered that he used to go four-wheel driving at the top of Alf's Pinch Road and down fire trails and up to a place called Bald Knob.

He was quizzed on his personal life. He told police that his break-up with Hayley McDonald was 'amicable'. He said he had a new girlfriend who was older than him and that she was French and her name was Pagan. He had met her at Mission Australia five months ago and she had two boys aged 14 and 17. He said he only saw his kids once a month at the weekend. One was aged three and the other two. They were picked up by his mum and dad from Maryborough, where Tracey lived, on a Friday from the police station and dropped off on the Sunday. He said his children loved 'bopping' on the dance floor at the RSL.

Eventually, Wright got around to the same question he'd asked at Nerang Police Station: the issue of timing on the day that Daniel disappeared. Since the last interview, police now had more information. When it was put to him that he had visited his drug dealer while out getting the mulcher, Cowan immediately bristled. 'I'm not gonna give youse the names.' Wright countered, saying that 'this is the homicide squad, not the drug squad. We wouldn't give a flying rat's arse, to be honest'.

'Yeah,' Cowan replied, sounding unconvinced and clearly angry with the way matters had gone at the Family Court. He was highly critical of his ex-wife. At this point, Detective Sergeant Hickey arrived. Hickey, with his formidable build, had a daunting presence, heightened by a hawk-like gaze. He immediately asked Cowan to pull his chair closer as he was 'hard of hearing'. Cowan obliged.

Wright asked whether Cowan's father was aware of what had been discussed during the last record of interview at Nerang Police Station. Peter Cowan said that he was and declared that he had been 'shattered' the first time he had heard about his son's past. Wright reminded him that he was only there in the capacity of an 'interview friend'. Peter Cowan acknowledged this, saying he knew he had no say in the interview.

After a preamble of Hickey asking Cowan for details of his address and where he worked, Wright went back to where he had left off. He asked Cowan what he could tell them now about the unaccounted-for period of time in his alibi for 7 December 2003.

'That I was at my dealer's place,' Cowan said immediately.

It was the admission the police had been waiting for.

The dealer's name, he told them, was Sandy Drummond, and she lived in Beerwah. He said he visited regularly, and each time he would stay for half an hour or so and that he would buy pot. He rattled off the phone number of Sandy and the man who lived with her, Kevin.

'You must have rung them a lot,' Hickey observed.

'Oh, I'm just good with numbers ... phone numbers and that,' Cowan countered.

Cowan was asked why he had covered up for Sandy Drummond after he agreed he knew she'd been busted before. He had no answer for this. Then Wright took him through the entire morning of 7 December 2003, beginning with a dial-in from his internet connection from his home at Alf's Pinch Road for an hour and a half commencing at 12.05 am. Cowan said he would have been looking at porn. Then, again, the internet had been activated from 1.50 am for almost two hours. Phone records, prepared on 20 April 2005, would show that on 4 December 2003, he was on the internet for over two hours from 8.30 pm; on 5 December 2003, for over one hour from 9 pm; on 6 December 2003, for over three hours from 9 pm; then again, on the morning of 7 December 2003. But then Cowan's activity on the computer stopped.

They went through in some detail the exact route Cowan would have taken from Frank Davis's house to Perwillowen

Road in Nambour to pick up the mulcher. Cowan said he had to pull off the 'chute' to fit the mulcher in and had tied the door with rope afterwards. He then relayed the roads he would have taken to get home.

'When you were going through Woombye, what did you see?' Wright asked.

'Um, there was the bus.'

'Can you describe it to me?'

'Ah, it's one of those Sun Coast ... whatever them little blue buses are ... um ... had people in it and there were people standing around ... um ... that was about all ...'

'When you say people standing around it, how many people do you think?'

'Um, there was only a couple standing around, I think.' The driver of the bus may have been one of the people standing outside, he added.

'... what do you think the bus was doing?'

'Ah, we assumed it was picking people up.'

'We ... you say "we" assumed?'

'I said I would have assumed.'

'Oh, so you didn't have anyone with you going back?'

'No.'

Walker then took over the questioning, going through Cowan's religious beliefs and his feeling of anger towards the pastor preaching about unforgiveable sin.

'So do you focus your own way without going to church, I suppose?' Walker asked.

'Um, I'm more into Pagism [sic],' Cowan replied.

He said he had played Ouija boards and had once called Hayley McDonald 'Sparrow', and she had been 'spun out' because her great-grandfather who had died was the only one who would call her that.

Walker went back to Cowan's past. It was a confronting past, he suggested. Cowan agreed and told them he had told his aunty and uncle and parents everything about it from the jail in Darwin when he was doing a sexual offender's course. He said he felt 'comfortable' in the church community as they accepted him.

Walker asked him whether he had told his father everything about what had happened. '… obviously, Dad's here and I don't want to discuss things with you that perhaps Dad hasn't heard before. Like, is that the case? Are you, have you been open with your father?'

'Yep.'

'I'm talking specifically about the Northern Territory.'

'Yep.'

'How long ago was that now?'

'Ninety-three.' Cowan said parole had been good and he'd served two and a half years.

'When you left prison at the time, did you have confidence?'

'Yep.'

'And how do you feel now?'

'Still good, knowing that um … it's been used against me in this family court thing but um, I can't say I'll never reoffend.' He said that Tracey had used this statement he had made before against him when he was seeking access to his children.

'Why does an offender say they can't say they'll never reoffend again?' asked Walker.

'Well, you've done it once. What's stopping it from happening again?'

'Well, I ask you that question.'

'Thought patterns … stuff that I didn't consider that I'd learn out of the course …'

'… How can you explain what happened in the Northern Territory?' Walker asked.

'I can't explain it and I can't explain the one previous to it.'

'But … why not? Have you not searched yourself for, for that answer?'

'Yeah. Um, I think that if everybody knew why they did something like that, it'd be easier to …'

'But it wasn't an explosive … there was a lead-up. Did you … when you reflect on it now you feel a build-up to it …'

'Not really. It was sort of, it's the wrong word to use but convenience.'

'Yeah.'

'It was, um, wrong time, wrong place.'

'Wrong person.'

'Ah, every person is the wrong person for that to happen to. But, um …'

'Do you agree it was an opportunity?'

'Yes. Yeah, that's the word I was looking for.'

He said he did not blame drugs for causing his urges but that drugs such as acid and speed did help dissolve any boundaries he might have felt. He said he did not want to have anything to do with those drugs because of this.

'… Sometimes I … um … see a kid and think … oh … you know … sexy or something like that. But I don't look at kids as sex objects any more. I look at them as kids.'

He said this was because he had done the training program for 12 months in jail and then four or five times after getting out.

He told them he had been tipped off that police would be knocking on his door after Daniel disappeared as they were going through a list of prior offenders.

Walker then asked abruptly: 'What do you think happened?'

'What do you mean?'

'With respect to Daniel Morcombe?'

'I don't know,' Cowan said, then added, 'Hmm, obviously he's gone missing, but other than that I don't think anything of it.'

'Everyone has an opinion.'

'Opinion. I don't know. I hope he's still alive somewhere. That's what I think or that's what I hope, anyway.'

They discussed the case in Darwin and Cowan took them through his version of that day. He denied that he had injured the boy or had choked him saying he had just left him on top of some cars that had been 'bulldozed into a pile' and that the boy's injuries must have been caused by a fall prior to him wandering into a service station. Cowan's girlfriend told him everyone thought he had been hit by a car based on the severity of the injuries. Two days later, the boy had identified him as carrying out the offence.

Cowan admitted he had a few associates he had met on the internet through chat rooms and that his sign on was Longdong69 and that he sometimes frequented gay chat rooms.

Hickey was back to the day that Daniel disappeared and the details around the drug deal.

Cowan said that Sandy Drummond always put the bag of dope onto kitchen scales. He would then get it off the scales, put it in a clip bag and stash it in his pocket. He said he had been at Drummond's house for around 20 minutes, and that his place was about a minute and a half from hers. He said that, after visiting her, he went home and took the mulcher out of the car and began mulching. He did not go inside to see Tracey. Eric Fragos, his neighbour, had stuck his head out and came over when he had finished.

He denied ever going near Woombye State School. He said the only car he and Tracey had was a white Pajero. He did have a blue Nissan XR Turbo but it was unregistered and not driveable.

Wright then asked about Cowan's relationship with Tracey Hanevald. Cowan said they had had a good relationship, but that he had initially broke it off when they were living in Nambour and then he travelled to Darwin with another woman, called Roma, in 1993. She had ended up smashing his records, Pink Floyd and *Tubular Bells*, because he left her to get back with Tracey. He had got Tracey to come up to Darwin from Perth on a bus and had convinced her to come back to him. Only two months after they were back together, he sexually assaulted the six-year-old boy in the caravan park. Cowan admitted that he and Tracey had good sexual relations and he could give no reason why he did what he did to the six-year-old boy.

Wright then went back to his earlier life. Cowan said he'd first smoked pot when he was 11 and he'd got into cigarettes when he was seven or eight. Wright asked again about the incident in 1987, the first sexual offence for which Cowan had been arrested.

'What happened prior to that in your life ... that you would ... you would think that was fine?'

'Um ... I've never been molested,' Cowan said. He agreed he had a good relationship with his father. '... I was rebellious against Dad during my teenage years and everything because he was away a lot and, um, just he'd discipline when he'd come home. It was the best upbringing I could've hoped for because now I know where Mum and Dad are coming from.' Cowan said he had been sexually active since he was about eight. 'Not sex or anything but touching, looking.'

Again they returned to asking him about other partners he had. Wright said they needed these details to find out whether he was telling the truth, as, if he wasn't telling the truth about that, why should they believe him about Daniel? Wright continued, 'The other thing that we've, that you must consider and what we will be considering – and we'll have bosses looking at and overviewing anything we've spoken about here this afternoon – is the fact that both occasions: with young John [not his real name] and at the end of it you basically choked him and said don't tell anyone and that's it ... With Ben [not his real name], scientific evidence tells us it was substantially more trauma to him, the threat against that child to say don't say anything ... if we were to choose to put your experiences into what we know about Daniel

Morcombe, it takes that extra step. Both John and Ben could identify you and say, "That's him. This is the bloke that did something to me." But progressively the trauma or the threat to those children got worse. We then go to Daniel Morcombe who is, who we believe is dead, who can't say, "That's him."'

'Yep,' Cowan said.

Hickey stepped in. 'What do you think – and I'm only asking you what you think – what do you think happened to Daniel Morcombe?'

'I think he was abducted. Other than that, as I was saying to Mark before, um, I hope that he's alive somewhere.'

A minute or two later, Peter Cowan spoke. 'Can I speak?'

'Sure,' Wright said.

'Brett, do you know anything at all, son?'

'No, I don't, Dad.'

Peter Cowan said he could see where the police were coming from.

'Um, can I just ask was there any sort of things in the dirt around where young Daniel was or anything like that? Sort of where he was dragged?' Peter Cowan asked the policemen.

'There was indications of …?' Wright asked.

'A scuffle …?' Peter Cowan said.

'… an incident. Uh, I won't go so far as to say that. Um, I can't really, can't …' Wright said.

'Okay,' Peter Cowan answered.

'A lot of times what we do is we don't disclose a lot of what we know,' Wright explained.

'Yeah. Yeah. I understand,' Peter Cowan conceded.

'We leave that to the end, until we know we've got the right bloke,' Wright said. The detective added that the boy in the caravan park may well have been suffocated to the point of unconsciousness and left for dead.

'And I restrained myself here tonight but I just thought I'd ask that question,' Peter Cowan said, adding about his son, 'And I know this guy is pretty well up front with me.'

'Yeah.'

'We've had our good times. We've had our bad times and I've had some times when I've bloody well belted the piss and pick handles out of him. But you know that was part of it, I suppose, growing up ...'

As the interview drew to a close, Hickey asked of Brett Cowan, 'Mate, just with what's happened with Daniel. Is that an unforgiveable thing, if he's been abducted and murdered?'

'In whose eyes?' asked Cowan.

'Well, that's what I mean. In your eyes?'

'In my eyes, um, my eyes yeah. I don't believe in killing anybody and, as the Bible says, you know, eye for an eye, tooth for a tooth, yep.'

Hickey said they would be checking on Sandy Drummond and her husband to verify Cowan's story.

The interview finished after three hours.

* * *

At the time Daniel disappeared, Sandy Drummond was living in Beerwah with a man named Kevin Fitzgerald and had been living in the house for a number of years. Drummond was known to police for several previous offences, mostly around the possession of a dangerous drug and utensils. On 15 September, she told police that she had met Cowan through her daughter. The day after the Cowan interview, Tracey Barnes conducted a record of interview with Drummond. Although Drummond confirmed Cowan would call in to see her regularly, she would not divulge that she sold him cannabis. She also said she could not recall exactly whether he had called in on Sunday 7 December 2003 or not. Cowan still lacked an alibi for the crucial times that day.

CHAPTER SIXTEEN

A SCRAP OF RED

Bruce and Denise had always believed that one day someone would ring them out of the blue with vital information. Someone would tell them something, surely, prompted by their conscience. On 20 September 2006, that day arrived. Bruce and Denise were attending Steve Irwin's memorial service at Australia Zoo. Five thousand people came to remember the man who had attempted to change the way people thought about conservation. Invited VIPs included Australia's 25th Prime Minister John Howard, and a host of familiar national and international celebrities.

Deputy mayor of Caloundra Anna Grosskreutz was also there. As Denise headed to the car park after the service, Grosskreutz approached her. Bruce and Brad were hurrying up ahead as Brad had to get back to work. Grosskreutz explained that she needed to talk to them both urgently. For some time, she had been in contact with someone called Sameha Ibrahim who had some strange stories to tell about Daniel that she'd heard from another woman named Alise Smythe. Grosskreutz also mentioned Dooley's name. Denise immediately pricked up her ears. Grosskreutz said police had a notebook from the 'Sameha' person that had not been returned and that they did not seem to be pursuing this information.

As soon as Denise got into the car, she told Bruce about the strange conversation. 'There's got to be something in this,' Bruce said immediately. 'Especially if she mentioned Dooley's name.'

Over the weeks ahead, they got to know Grosskreutz – and her partner Russell Eggmolesse, known as 'Eggy' – better, while planning the next Ride for Daniel. Grosskreutz handed them a folder and later began telling them the stories that she had heard, horrific stories that would greatly disturb them for a long time.

Grosskreutz's stories returned them to imagining what might have happened to Daniel in the hours or even days leading up to his death. Grosskreutz gave them an address in Windsor that was Meyer's house and told them there was a dungeon downstairs where Meyer had been violent with past girlfriends. She also spoke of his sordid, drug-induced behaviour. They felt sick to the stomach. Over the years that Daniel had been missing, they had heard these same names over and over again: Dooley and Meyer and Jackway. Police had already been told by Dooley that Jackway and Meyer had been in jail together. Grosskreutz also had two maps, both originated from Smythe, that she said were supposed to identify where Daniel's remains lay. As horrendous as it seemed, it was the first time that many of the missing pieces of the jigsaw seemed to fit together.

The Morcombes' relationships with senior investigating police officers continued to fray as more information was revealed to them by Grosskreutz. When Bruce told Senior Sergeant Paul Schmidt, at a routine briefing, that he had heard rumours that Daniel had been codenamed 'Birthday Cake', Schmidt raised his eyebrows. Bruce took it to imply that Schmidt thought he was losing his mind.

* * *

Publicly, Bruce and Denise maintained the same measured approach with the media. The launch of the child-safety DVD, entitled *Foundation Red*, went ahead on 20 October at Australia Zoo. Addressing the audience, Denise said, 'The tragic passing of Steve Irwin has touched us all. He was a passionate family man and communicator ... Preparations were taking place for Steve and Terri to be filmed for a contribution on the Foundation's DVD. Steve's energy and personality will be greatly missed.'

Bruce and Denise wanted the DVDs to be provided for no cost and to be posted free of charge within Australia, primarily targeting schools. But as the DVDs became public, orders also came flooding in from concerned parents, grandparents and community groups. Their first order, for 10,000 copies, was stored in the barn at Camellia Cottage. Denise told the waiting media that the DVD would have a positive impact on children and families, and help keep children safer, as often they did not know what to do when danger happened. 'If it's not right, then tell someone,' she said.

Bruce added that the message on the DVD was targeted at children aged eight to 13. He said that $25,000 was to be donated from the Foundation to a separate bank account dedicated to child victims of crime.

On 31 October 2006, Bruce announced that the Walk for Daniel, started the previous year, was to be an annual, national event, coinciding with the Day for Daniel. The Foundation was really raising its profile. It had become an incorporated company, with a corporate brochure and still with its well-known patron, Kay McGrath.

On 3 November, staff at the Logan Central Police Station donned red instead of blue to help raise money for the 2006 Day for Daniel. Less than a week after the walk, they led the Bravehearts Highway Thunder Convoy for Kids on the

Gold Coast, aimed at highlighting the need for authorities to do more to protect kids. The 500-plus-vehicle convoy along Queensland's M1 highway included trucks, cars and motorcycles. The cars carried white flags and balloons, and speakers called for the protection of children against sexual attack. Braveheart Inc's executive director Hetty Johnston told the media that one in five children would be sexually assaulted before the age of 18 and that all children were put at risk when jailed sexual offenders were released back into the community. She claimed that Queensland's judges were not fully utilising their powers under the state government's *Dangerous Prisoners (Sexual Offenders) Act*, which allowed the justice system to keep dangerous paedophiles behind bars even after their sentences had finished. 'We've had 22 prisoners assessed as being a serious risk and dangerous, and put forward to the Attorney General for continuing detention, and only six of those have been contained.' Her words echoed in the Morcombes' ears. Had the state let them down?

* * *

Since Daniel Morcombe's disappearance, Siena Catholic College had seen many children come and go, but 11 November 2006 marked a special day. It was the day Daniel would have graduated from the high school.

Graeme Hight had known he had to acknowledge Daniel on what would have been a special day for him. Hight had come up with the idea of a waiting chair. He knew one of the school's families whose parents made such furniture, so he approached them. Without any rehearsal, on the day of the graduation, all 134 students in the graduating class stopped beside Daniel's chair as a natural mark of respect for the boy whom nobody had forgotten. A brass plaque on the chair stated simply, 'Daniel's Chair, For Our Friend Daniel Morcombe, Seniors of 2006'. One of the girls had tied red ribbons on either end of it. This year, his class were also wearing red ribbons in his honour. Speaking to the media later, Graeme Hight said, 'It did cut a few of the kids deep and some of the girls walked away in tears from it all.'

Bruce and Denise had declined to attend the graduation, stating it was too difficult for them. On the weekend before the big day, however, they had gone down to the school to see the chair, peering into classrooms until they found it. They both imagined what might have been if Daniel had not disappeared.

November also marked an important date in their personal calendar. Bruce and Denise bought a holiday cottage in Tasmania. Bruce had been looking on the internet since the trip he, Brad and Denise had made in 2004. He had finally found something he liked. It was a property on three hectares of undulating grassland that had a number of outbuildings and beautiful views across the D'Entrecasteaux Channel to Bruny Island. They called it Bay Lodge. Bruce had flown down a couple of times to look at houses and impulsively bought it before Denise had even seen it. It was another project – to restore the house and grounds to its former glory. When Bruce showed it to Denise for the first time, she was as forthright as usual, saying, 'It's a beautiful escape, but there's so much work to do.'

* * *

On 22 November, police visited Smythe at the BWCC with her solicitor, but she refused to speak with them unless she got indemnity from prosecution. Ibrahim meanwhile went to visit Smythe and smuggled into the jail a request for indemnity, which Smythe signed. In late November, police heard from yet another person to whom Smythe had been talking. This time, it was the counsellor at the BWCC, who reported that Smythe had said not only was she in the car with Dooley and Meyer when Daniel was abducted, but that Meyer had taken her to the burial site, which she said was on the road to Bribie Island before the bridge that connected the island to the mainland.

On 1 December, Grosskreutz told Bruce and Denise about her recent visit to Alise Smythe at the BWCC and how Smythe had told her that the police refused to believe her.

Grosskreutz was determined not to give up, however. From that point on, she and her partner Eggy were convinced that police had them under surveillance and were monitoring their phone calls. Eggy was a biker, too. The Morcombes thought of him as a 'gentle giant of a man' who treated Grosskreutz with kindness and 'like a lady'. They were not surprised when they were invited to their wedding a couple of years later.

It was time to act upon what they had been told about Daniel's final hours. Grosskreutz told them that she and Eggy had already been to the Bribie Island site, but had not told the Morcombes they had found a scrap of red material which they had left at the site, on one of the tracks leading into the bush. Bruce and Denise visited Grosskreutz at the Caloundra city council chambers. Grosskreutz looked up from behind her desk.

'Would you like to come with us and do some searching?' she asked.

'We have to go,' Denise said. 'This is it.'

'Tomorrow,' Bruce said. 'It's Saturday. Will that suit?'

Nothing could be more important than this.

* * *

Bribie Island Road is a busy highway linking Bribie Island to the mainland. It joins up with the M1, the main artery between Brisbane and the Sunshine Coast, near Caboolture, south of the Glass House Mountains. On Saturday 2 December 2006,

249

Bruce and Denise met Grosskreutz and Eggy at their Beerwah home before they all drove to the Sundowner Hotel car park on the Bribie Island side of Caboolture. They parked and waited a short time for the others to arrive. There was another man with them, a prison guard from the BWCC. Grosskreutz, Eggy and Ray Harris had already visited the site.

Bruce and Denise had in their possession Alise Smythe's childlike drawing. It showed a dirt track that crossed a depression or creek. Mounds of soil or uneven ground were also marked, along with some pine trees and a curious cross-shaped stick that looked like a marker. Close by, on the map, was a white house also mentioned by Smythe.

Having all driven to a location near Bribie Island, they stopped at the spot that Grosskreutz and Eggy had been to before. After walking down a track into the bush, Bruce immediately identified the white house, which was close to the search area.

'I'm gonna check it out and knock on the door,' Bruce told the others.

Someone remarked, 'I'm not going.'

As he walked towards it, he had a familiar sense of unease. It was a Queenslander on stilts. He walked up the rear stairs. Whoever opened the door was bound to recognise him. How do I handle myself, he asked himself. Get on with it. The same familiar internal battle raged as he faced a potentially dangerous situation. One step after another, he climbed the stairs. He rattled the door. There were toys in the garden. Bruce knocked again. There was no one home.

When he got back to the others, Grosskreutz and Eggy were pointing out where the Morcombes should search. They had broken a branch and left an arrow where they had found the red material. Bruce was acutely aware his mind would let him see what he wanted to see. Everyone was mesmerised by the task in hand.

The area was clearly a dumping ground, Bruce thought, for lazy sods who preferred a quick fix to taking their garbage to the dump. There were mounds of soil and rubbish everywhere, including a blue tarpaulin, mattresses and old tyres. They poked in the various piles. What kept occurring to both Bruce and Denise was that the place resembled terrain where POI Bill Dooley had said Meyer disposed of Daniel – perhaps not the red soil but definitely the pine trees. Now this woman, Alise Smythe, had named the same people as being responsible for Daniel's abduction, and she had even claimed she had been in the car with them. They were both certain that, after hearing so many stories, this time they might be getting close to the truth.

'What's that there?' Grosskreutz said, pointing to a log that was next to a tyre.

Everyone gathered around and someone lifted the tyre. Denise saw it immediately – unmistakably a piece of red material. It was almost too much for her. Lodged in the soil, a small four-centimetre-long fragment was exposed. Clearly, there was more hidden in the earth below. For a split second, both Bruce and Denise wanted to start digging. Was this Daniel's final resting place? Had they found him? Was this his weathered red T-shirt? Their emotions said 'Dig'. Their heads counselled caution.

They carefully flicked away at the soil and leaf litter with a crude stick, exposing more material to a depth of a couple of centimetres. The red cloth seemed fragile, as though it had been buried there for a number of years. Bruce and Denise looked at the others.

'No, I don't think we should dig any more,' Bruce said. 'We might make a mess of it. We might contaminate vital evidence.'

There was a moment of soul searching. For three years, they had waited to find where their son might be buried. Now, they could be standing at the actual spot.

'Let's ring Julie,' Denise said immediately. 'She'll know what to do.'

Julie Elliott immediately passed on the news to the Homicide Investigation Unit. She was on duty that day and hastily drove to meet them.

Several police officers, including a scenes of crime officer, arrived not long afterwards to conduct a search. One made it clear that he was not impressed. They asked Bruce and Denise to take off their shoes and took samples from the soles. Everyone was told to wait some distance away from the search site. A cadaver dog had also been called in. Another couple of hours passed, then finally some news. Police had exhausted their search of the area, even digging down some 70–80 centimetres, but all they could find was more red clothing. This had been bagged and was bound for Maroochydore Police Station. They were advised that the dog did have a reaction to something, but it was considered a false alarm. After sitting around in the hot sun for most of the day, the Morcombes, Grosskreutz and Eggy and the prison guard left and went their separate ways.

That night, the Morcombes stood together smiling. They were special guests at the Palmwoods Christmas party, held at the local sports oval. In spite of the startling events of the day, they found it a healthy distraction but no one guessed about the traumatic happenings earlier that day.

* * *

On 7 December 2006, Bruce and Denise marked the third anniversary of Daniel's disappearance by delivering a media statement. Finally, they said, they had decided to sell their home in Palmwoods. Dean had left home and was working full-time. Bradley was about to turn 17. It was time to take this important step. They would always keep Daniel's pony, Bullet, they told the assembled media.

'I've still got Daniel's clothes packed up and stored away,' Denise said. 'There's even stuff of his still in the ironing basket that I haven't been able to face.'

But that same day, Bruce called a markedly different media conference. Fuelled by all of the rumours he had been hearing, he had revisited the idea of the front door, placing it again under the overpass, next to Daniel's memorial plinth. On it were six handwritten questions revealing, for the first time, the family's belief that Daniel had been taken by paedophiles and that Daniel had been given the codenames 'Christmas Cake' as well as 'Birthday Cake'. There was a different tone and focus to the usual media interviews that Bruce had given in the past. He was visibly angry. He said he and Denise had heard all sorts of theories, including that Daniel had been drugged while in a car and that he was alive for some time after his abduction. Bruce said he'd been prompted to put these questions into the public arena.

During the media interview, Bruce mentioned that there was 'a man of interest' to the investigation whose sister had been murdered. He also made reference to knowing about a 'forest track' where Daniel's body might be.

As far as he was concerned, the message was aimed at one man in jail: Bill Dooley. Bruce's aim was to make Dooley 'put up or shut up'. Behind the scenes, police investigators had been split as to Dooley's versions. Some believed he was involved. Others believed he had made it up. Sergeant Schmidt had attended the media conference too. After taking one quick read of the questions displayed on the door, he took Bruce aside and gave him a dressing down.

Bruce responded, 'Everything we receive, we forward to police. Much of it you already had – but some information we received privately matched up perfectly with what you also have.'

There was a tone in Bruce's voice that said he was someone to be reckoned with. Something had clearly shifted.

He was not looking for a fight. Just the truth. But it was time to make a public stand. The Morcombes would not lie down. If it was a test of wills, then they would win, Bruce was thinking. That night on the evening news bulletins, Bruce remarked, 'Whoever is responsible is the most hunted person in Australia.'

* * *

Police were clearly perturbed about recent events and Bruce's media conference involving the door. That same day, John Maloney released a statement. 'I want to make it clear we will not be stopping this investigation,' he said. Schmidt added that up to 20,000 pieces of information had been received from the public since Daniel had vanished. The announcement was clearly meant to appease the Morcombes as well as to put forward the best picture of the police investigation.

The next day Bruce and Denise called in to the Maroochydore Police Station to hand Smythe's indemnity request, which they'd gotten from Grosskreutz, to Operation Vista detectives. As they were leaving the building, Bruce received a text message from Sameha Ibrahim. She suggested they arrange a meeting. Still full of the strange energy of the past few days they decided to make it that evening. And so it was that at around 5.20 pm they pulled up outside a small white weatherboard house in Ashgrove. A straggly tree sat outside the front and the nature strip was overgrown. The house, like the others in the street, was set back from the road. This visit to Banks Street was to be the first of many. He had a story concocted. If someone asked him what the pipe was for, he was going to say he was buying a fitting for it. Their life had taken a surreal turn. Ibrahim came to the door and ushered them in. She introduced them to her partner, Gary. The room they sat in was small with a coffee table and magazines and a lot of clutter. Bruce and Denise sat in the lounge chairs in the corner. They took notes and listened. They learned more details about Daniel's alleged abduction, including who was in the car, what had happened to him and where he was buried. They also learned that Daniel may have been killed in a house close to Meyer's house in Windsor; possibly on the north side of Windsor where someone said to be related to Meyer lived. They also heard about a house in Kelvin Grove with an easement at the front and a big door where Daniel was supposed to have been drowned in a bath before being revived, as well as a flat behind a butcher shop with a white door and a motel called Big Bed that was said to be a brothel.

Daniel's abductors had codenamed him 'Birthday Cake', she said, not just 'Christmas Cake', as they had previously been told.

Ibrahim told them they were on the right track during their search the previous weekend, but that Daniel was buried only 20 metres to the rear of the house and that he was wrapped in a white sheet before he was buried. She also gave them a basmati rice hessian bag with clothes that Daniel was said to have worn after he had been abducted. Inside were a pair of tracksuit pants and shorts.

The following day Bruce typed an email to Detective Sergeant Tracey Barnes. It read:

> It may be wise to avoid possible contamination of the site behind the white house and that some thought be given to investigate this area further as a matter of urgency. Perhaps with Alise's assistance.
>
> Denise and I had no trouble understanding Sameha's accent. However, everything is based on hearsay. I believe Sameha is telling the truth. But whether she is told fact or fiction only time will tell. But for what it is worth it is my opinion that this story is plausible and although some parts can be ruled out it is based on fact.

* * *

Two days later, on 12 December 2006, Bruce and Denise dropped off the hessian bag to Maroochydore Police Station.

On 15 December, Bruce and Denise again met with Schmidt. It was a brief meeting. 'Has anything been found forensically from the examination of the red material?' Bruce asked him.

Schmidt paused. 'I still have it here,' he replied. 'It's in my desk drawer.'

Bruce and Denise looked at him, wide-eyed. This turn of events had not even occurred to them.

They left crestfallen. The police at least needed to eliminate the material, they thought. After the excitement of finding potential evidence, Schmidt's response had sent them back into the land of guesswork. Later, a police report stated that the material had in fact been examined at the centre and compared with an identical T-shirt to the one Daniel had been wearing. It was determined to have been different material.

* * *

Over the rest of December, the location of Daniel's possible resting place haunted both Bruce and Denise. They did not know that the police had conducted a fifth interview with Smythe the day after their own meeting, in which she had repeated her claims. At night they would lie awake thinking of their son lying in a rubbish dump off the Bribie Island Road. No one wanted to do anything about it. One day, they jumped in their car and drove back there. This time, it was just the two of them. They hadn't even packed a shovel. Bruce wanted to look more closely at the white house, especially after what Ibrahim had told them. The vegetation behind the house was jungle-like and difficult to climb through, but they were charged with emotion.

'Here's a likely spot,' one of them would call. 'Look, a bit of a clearing. D'ye think it's been disturbed in the past?'

They were soon on their hands and knees, digging with their bare hands. It was not sand but soil. They were both convinced they were in the right place. They would take turns to dig a single hole while the other rested. It was hot, sweaty work. Using the butt of a large stick, they toiled away feverishly for more than half an hour. In despair, one looked at the other.

'We're going mad. This is ridiculous,' Bruce said, holding out his arms to Denise. 'Come over here.'

They hugged, almost in tears, looking at the pathetic hole and assessing their equally pathetic state of mind.

'Let's go,' Denise said. The decision was united. They were not going to find Daniel.

They cleaned up as best they could and headed to the nearest shop for some lunch. They were so thirsty. At the Ningi Bakery, only a couple of kilometres down the road, they were recognised by staff as soon as they ordered.

'So what brings you down this way?' one of the staff asked.

With a smile, Denise replied, 'Enjoying the day with a walk.'

* * *

Brad got an added birthday present on 19 December when he passed his driving test. It was another milestone but it made him think of Daniel, who should have been there beside him.

The Morcombes spent that Christmas at Scott and Shelly's house, Bruce's younger brother and sister-in-law. The following day, Bruce and Brad began the drive to their Tasmanian property, boarding the *Spirit of Tasmania* on a daytime crossing from Melbourne to Tasmania. They had packed their things in a green station wagon they had bought locally. It was to be their workhorse car in Tasmania. Inside was the *Forget-Me-Nots* painting by Kendall Perkins-Brakels that Tim Ryan had given them. Bruce and Brad painted and decorated their Tasmanian retreat. They visited Hastings Caves. That year also marked the passing of Chief the dog, who had been Daniel's best friend. Chief died of old age.

CHAPTER SEVENTEEN

TINY STEPS TO BIG STRIDES

For some months, Denise had been walking up and down the undulating hinterland around Woombye, with the Blackall Ranges a dark silhouette in the distance. This vista was one of the things that had inspired Bruce and Denise to buy Camellia Cottage – a sense of space around them which had been lacking in their other homes. Sometimes, Denise would walk alone on the concrete pathway that ran parallel with the Woombye-Palmwoods Road, following in the footsteps of her son's last walk. She never stopped thinking about him. Her walks, though, this time, had a purpose apart from being enveloped in dark memories. She and Julie Elliott had made a pact to walk the Milford Track, in the Fiordland National Park, in the far south-west of New Zealand's South Island. They had talked about it late the previous year at a coffee shop near the Roma Street Police Headquarters. Elliott had suddenly announced she was doing the walk. 'Would you like to come too?' she had asked Denise.

Denise knew what Elliott was trying to do: get her to stop thinking about Daniel as much and to have another focus. She was secretly excited but then began thinking of how unfit she was. 'How long is it?' she asked Elliott.

'Fifty-six kilometres.'

'And carrying a backpack? That's way out of my league,' Denise answered.

When she got home from Brisbane, she told Bruce and the boys. They had all looked at her as though she were joking. One of them said, 'You can't even walk to the letterbox.'

It was the kind of remark that got Denise going. She was determined then to do the walk.

Elliott had thought it was a great idea and was pleased at how enthusiastically Denise embraced it. Denise began walking rain, hail or shine. Sometimes on the weekend, she and Bruce would walk the five- to six-hour route from Baroon Pocket Dam in Montville to Kondalilla Falls. While not walking around Palmwoods and Woombye, Denise would train with Elliott in the streets around her unit in Ascot or climb Beerburrum Mountain, or Mount Ngungun in the Glass House Mountains, or sometimes Mount Coolum, a dome-shaped mountain rising 208 metres on the coast. At the peaks of these mountains, she would look out across the terrain, always wondering where Daniel might be and whether she would ever find him.

Denise had never had any success attending counselling, and Bruce had not even bothered, other than once when he had seen someone briefly with Denise. On bad days, especially in those early years, Denise had rung Elliott threatening to take her life. 'You can't do that,' Elliott would say in her no-nonsense voice. 'You have Brad and Dean to think about, and you have to get on with it. And Bruce.' It was the only message that she knew Denise would listen to. For Elliott, such talk brought up feelings of powerlessness she had experienced when unable to avert the final act that her husband had chosen. The heartfelt grief of being so close to a woman who could not get any answers, in spite of all of she and Bruce had done, was soul destroying. Denise had made about six visits to a counsellor in Brisbane, but, in Elliott's eyes, counselling had not been right for Denise. 'I don't see the point. How would they know how I feel?' Denise had said when Elliott asked how it went.

Bruce seemed more stalwart, able to rationalise mood swings. Neither of them would ever give up the search for Daniel. Elliott knew that in her bones. In the earlier years, before she moved to a unit in Ascot, she had still been travelling back and forth from her acreage at Caboolture. This added to the stress of being involved in a case that never seemed to end. Usually now, though, she only came up if there was some need, but she remained very close to Denise. She had seen her soldier on through each painful day. There were good days and bad days, and in the early years they had shared most of them. They never forgot their private pledge that one day they would find Daniel. That day, Elliott said, she would be there to give Denise a hug.

* * *

'No Stone Unturned', a second *Australian Story* television program on the ABC, screened on 25 February 2007, almost three years after the first show, 'Into Thin Air'. It hit a similar nerve with viewers around the country. Terri Irwin, less than six months into her own tragedy, introduced the segment. This time, the Morcombes had their own website. After the program aired, they had 61,000 hits. Featured on the episode was footage of Bruce and Denise walking through the bush near Bribie Island and talking about Alise Smythe's information about the abduction of their son.

'When somebody rings you and says, "I know where your son's buried and I know the people that have done this," I mean, as parents anybody would sit up and say, "Tell me more," Bruce told the cameras. 'It just stood out. There were names that these people were telling us that we had heard over the last three years – and there were places that we had heard of and we just tried to put two and two together, and we hoped that this source of information would actually lead us to Daniel and his abductors.'

Denise told viewers that Daniel had always said he wanted to be a vet and that, even a long time after he had vanished, she still forgot he wasn't there. Two years after he had gone missing, she had seen one of the chickens they kept at Camellia Cottage doing something funny. Walking up the path to the house, she was thinking, 'I'll tell Daniel.' Halfway up the path, she stopped, tears in her eyes. 'I can't.' Daniel was the one who was always happy for cuddles, who would whisper, 'I love you, Mum,' she said. Denise told viewers that Dean and Bradley had not wanted to talk about their brother. They had thought it was strange that she wanted to often look at photos from his birth up to when he disappeared, which is why she had been so surprised when Dean had got the tattoos of his brother on his arm. A year later, Brad would follow suit, on 28 January 2008 getting his own large tattoo on his right calf of roses and candles with a scroll around them, with lettering saying simply, 'Daniel'.

* * *

The Novotel Twin Waters Resort in Ocean Drive is on the opposite side of the Maroochy River to the Horton Park Golf Club, where the first golf-day fundraiser had been held. On 3 March, at the second Dance for Daniel, the Band of Blue, Beccy Cole and James Blundell performed. Steve Irwin's shirt, which had been donated for auction the previous year, was redonated and sold for $18,000. The Foundation also received two anonymous donations on the night: a cheque for $30,000 and one for $15,000. The night had brought a good injection of funds into the Foundation.

* * *

Bruce had wanted to leave Camellia Cottage and all of its painful memories for some time. But, for Denise, it was closing the door on a past she was not ready to forget. After the Day for Daniel the previous year, however, and now that she was in training to get fit, she had finally succumbed. She did not show much interest as to where they might move. Instead, it was Bruce who tackled the task of finding a new house, with his usual no-nonsense, hard-headed, businesslike approach. He made a list of what they needed. As maintenance on the old home was an issue, this time he wanted a brick home with aluminium windows, single storey and with no neighbours. If possible, they also wanted room for the ponies.

After making the hard decision to move the previous year, Denise had already started packing Daniel's items into boxes. Nothing from his room was thrown away. She kept his old school shoes, undies, shorts and shirts, as well as old books, knick-knacks and stuffed toys. Some of his clothing may be important after he disappeared as police wanted to compare sizes and brands, and who knew what they might need down the track. Bruce had suggested not keeping anything without sentimental value, but Denise was too emotionally attached to even the smallest piece of paper that had belonged to the son she now believed would never return. It was too precious to throw away. She put many of the smaller things inside the wooden box he had made in Grade 9, and she also kept all his unwrapped Christmas and birthday presents, plus the card that he had bought for Bradley's birthday but had never been able to give him.

Packing was horrible. Denise tried to stay mentally removed from the task. Staying in Camellia Cottage had been a commitment to Daniel. If he ever walked down that long driveway under the canopy of trees and was somehow able to explain the years of his absence, his family would still be there. But, as they started to move through the fourth year since he had been missing, even Denise admitted that she could no longer sustain that hope.

* * *

The Milford Track is in one of the most remote parts of New Zealand. The terrain, compared to the more settled eastern coast, is primeval rainforest and swift rivers that have survived multiple ice ages. Water, wind, rain and ice continue to reshape its contours. When Denise and Julie Elliott arrived at Christchurch International Airport on 13 March 2007, it was freezing and pouring with rain. Had she trained hard enough, Denise wondered, looking out at the grey streets. She had certainly given it her all, using a personal trainer, walking eight or nine kilometres every day and losing 20 kilograms in the process.

They flew to Queenstown on South Island and completed an induction course. Denise regretted packing so much. Elliott had even packed her make-up kit. Denise's personal trainer, Janine, had given her four little material bags with a red ribbon tied to all of them. They met up with two friends of Elliott's who had flown together from Brisbane. Denise gave them a bag each to tie to their backpacks. They caught a boat to the top of Lake Te Anau and then did a short walk of two kilometres to the first night's stop.

On day one, Denise struggled with her backpack, as it didn't fit properly and bounced on her hips, but all of the hard work in training served them well. On day two, the weather was far better than expected, with only a few flakes of snow when they walked from Pompolona Lodge to Quinton Lodge. The Mackinnon Pass was the hardest part, with its high elevation and zigzag track. The following day, Denise had blisters, and Elliott occasionally had to wait for her on the track. With a few bandaids, Denise was back on the move. Day four was an eight-hour walk of around 21 kilometres over tracks and rocky hills where avalanches had fallen. There were pegs along the track to let the walkers know the distance they had covered. At the end of the walk, at Sandfly Point, there was a sign saying '33.5 miles', with a pair of old, broken boots tied to it. They were sore and exhausted, but they had made it.

* * *

Windsor is one of Brisbane's northern suburbs intersected by the major highway heading up to the Sunshine Coast. Brett Cowan had grown up in the nearby suburb of Everton Park, less than ten kilometres away to the north-west. Further west again was Keperra, the suburb where Alise Smythe had once lived. Her house was later burnt down.

Bruce had no trouble identifying the house in Windsor, with its lawn almost waist-high. He and Denise had driven past there a couple of times before. Once, he had even poked his camera between a crack in a fence to take a photo of the back of it. This time, he parked his car and sat for some time outside. Denise's trip to New Zealand meant she was away for a fortnight. He had been planning the visit for some time. This house was Alexander Meyer's family home. An old Queenslander, it was by far the most derelict house in the hilly street. Its weatherboard exterior with peeling, beige paint showed it was clearly a house that had not had any attention for years. But it was not the state of the house that Bruce had come to look at; it was the room below where there was said to be a dungeon. It was in this room that his son was supposed to have been kept and even tortured. Built on stilts in traditional Queensland style, the property had enough room beneath it for a car to park there. A small driveway with two cement lanes led to the garage door.

In the search warrant executed in March 2005, police had found nothing because the house was too filthy inside. A total of 32 items were taken from the house. Several had been tested for DNA, but nothing of significance was found. The upper level was a living area. The room down below was solid brick with only one door and a single window. Was this the so-called dungeon that Bruce had heard of? Bruce certainly believed Meyer capable of such a set-up. Meyer would not pay a security deposit or provide identification, thus Energex records reveal that power was disconnected on 31 October 2003 and not re-connected until 29 December 2003.

The house immediately to the left of Meyer's as you faced the street had a neat, white picket fence and was immaculately kept, freshly painted in pale yellow and with a newly tiled roof. Opposite, the houses were similarly well looked after, with landscaped gardens. The one directly across the road had a poinciana tree out the front.

Bruce swallowed slowly. He sat watching the bottom of the house, intent on willing it to give up its secrets, trying to block out the horror of what might have happened to Daniel if he had been kept captive there. Here he was again, inhabiting this crazy world where people led lives he had never even read about, never knowing who to trust and whether anything anyone told him was true. He was tackling it in the only way he knew how, by ensuring no stone was left unturned.

He had not even mentioned this visit to Denise. She had already been through enough, especially with all the searches on Bribie Island Road and all of the confusion that had brought. Why subject her to this when, for the first time in the years since Daniel's disappearance, he had seen a smile on her face as she headed across the Tasman bound for Christchurch. He knew the walk that she and Elliott had planned was arduous, and it was her first chance to get away from it all. The last thing he wanted was for her to be concerned about him playing super sleuth in the suburbs of Brisbane with highly dangerous criminals. So no one knew he was here. He could just drive away.

Many of these things went through his mind until he finally got enough courage to get out of the car and walk up the path to the front door. At least he was in full view of the street and it was broad daylight. He knocked loudly, intent as usual on the rehearsed words he would say if the door opened. Startled, he heard the sound of a car. It was the neighbours backing down their driveway from the house next door with the white picket fence. He saw immediately what decent people they were. When there was no response to his knock on the door, Bruce approached their car. The woman had tears in her eyes, as she had recognised him and they had known instantly what he was doing there. The man, too, was close to tears. It took a couple of minutes for them to compose themselves. They seemed so pleased to see him.

'Would you like a cup of coffee?' the woman asked gently.

Bruce shook his head. 'I have to see first-hand how these people lived,' he said, although he knew he probably didn't need to explain himself. 'Can you tell me if the police have visited?' he asked.

'Forensic was here for about three days,' the man told him.

Bruce felt a huge sense of relief. Something had been happening.

The couple told him then about the years of agony living next to the house next door. How drug addicts would roll up at all times of the day and night. The incessant noise. How they would try to keep their spirits up by making their own house a haven. To find out that it might be the place where Daniel had been held captive had been too much for both of them.

It was not until later that Bruce was told by police that Meyer had moved out of the house two weeks previously.

* * *

Bruce had been searching through hundreds of homes online but only visited nine of them. The purchase, as he was to recall later, was one of convenience. There was no emotional attachment involved. One of the nine houses Bruce visited was on the Palmwoods-Montville Road, a continuation of the Woombye-Palmwoods Road once through the small village of Palmwoods. The house was on a bend three kilometres beyond the village and past a banana plantation. It was set back from the road and had a visitors car park at the start of the main driveway. Low-lying shrubs and trees screened the house from the road, and a timber picket fence in need of repair lay between the large nature strip and the garden. Surrounded by rural properties, it was a single-storey, four-bedroom house with a red, corrugated-iron roof. It ticked all of the boxes.

Denise had signed the contract for the sale of Camellia Cottage before heading off. When she returned home on 1 April after her fortnight in New Zealand, Bruce had three properties to show her. Denise didn't really care which one they bought, she told him. They went to look at the shortlist on Sunday morning. The house at Palmwoods-Montville Road felt comfortable. She said three words to him: 'This will do.' They signed the contract that day and the settlement was on 31 May.

In the global world of real estate, the couple who bought Camellia Cottage were from the other side of the world: England. They had seen the house on the internet, having fallen in love with Australia some years before. Unlike most Australians, they had never heard of Daniel Morcombe. Bruce was not surprised at their emotional connection to the house. It was, after all, like an English country cottage, complete with outhouses and landscaped gardens, surrounded by tropical paradise. The new owners' dream was to turn

Camellia Cottage into a venue for weddings. They bought ponies, Katie, Shambala and Lily, but Bruce and Denise kept Bullet and Sorrento, Bella and Coco, both born after Daniel disappeared. Later, Daniel's bedroom would become the place where the brides got dressed before the ceremony.

On 17 April, a red hibiscus named the Daniel Morcombe Hibiscus was planted at Australia Zoo. Glass House Mountains breeder Allan Little had created it especially, and the plant had been bought at a silent auction at the last Dance for Daniel. The bidder donated the plant to the Australia Zoo as a permanent memorial to Daniel, where it was prominently displayed with a small plaque. 'It's something that will live on – it's so people don't forget Daniel,' Bruce said. 'People will continue to fight. Even when we have the answers, this will be here as a reminder for other people.'

* * *

On 8 May, at a strategy meeting for Operation Vista, it was decided to set up a meeting with the principal officer of the Crime and Misconduct Commission to see if the commission could organise coercive hearings to force some of the POIs and associates to give evidence. The hearing began on 26 November. On 9 January 2007, when Alise Smythe had been interviewed for the sixth time, having been picked up from jail by detectives and driven to various locations, she gave yet another version about what had happened to Daniel. This time, she said he was kept in a unit in Annerley, a suburb south of the Brisbane CBD. The unit had reportedly belonged to Rogers, the 73-year-old man Dooley had been accused of killing, and who had been supposedly held to ransom after having Daniel delivered to him for sex. Smythe said she had been told this by the father of her children.

Smythe was also taken back to Bribie Island Road but could not identify the track where she had claimed Daniel had been taken to. When told about the fact that her daughter could not have been with her in the car when Daniel was there, as her daughter had said she had only been to the Sunshine Coast once, on a school excursion, Smythe became visibly upset. She denied ever signing an indemnity letter sent to the previous Attorney General. All of these stories had to be followed up, by the police but also by Bruce and Denise. These stories had been woven into their imagination of their son's final moments. The pine trees, the red soil, the same names. Were they the ramblings of drug-addled criminals who were morally bankrupt and would stoop so low as to make up stories of a boy who had been abducted and was missing, believed murdered?

* * *

From experience, the Morcombes had now learnt to focus on light and hope. Their annual events were a big part of this. On 10 June, the third Ride for Daniel saw 5000 riders forming a 45-kilometre-long cavalcade and riding through the Sunshine Coast hinterland, starting at the Big Pineapple and ending at the Ettamogah Pub on the Bruce Highway. It raised $50,000. That same month, they moved into their new house. Brad moved with them. Dean had already moved out. Packing had been one thing for Denise, but seeing the empty rooms in Camellia Cottage when the furniture removalists came made it worse. The house seemed so bare. In the emptiness, she could feel Daniel there and she felt like she was abandoning him.

The new house seemed bereft and lonely compared to Camellia Cottage. It had no family memories, but that was precisely why they had moved. It was a conscious decision to make new memories, like their decision to buy the shack in the D'Entrecasteaux Channel in Tasmania. It was their chance to turn the page – not to have 'closure', because they both firmly believed that day would never come. Each time that someone, however well meaning, mentioned that word, they would both shake their heads decisively. No.

They moved into the new house in Palmwoods on 31 May, bought new furniture and planted a cutting of Daniel's Hibiscus near the back door.

* * *

The Daniel Morcombe Foundation was growing, but harnessing this interest required a commitment of several hours a day. Emails were continuous, not to mention the letters through the post. There were concepts for artwork to decide upon, fundraising meetings and planning for events. Keen to shape the Foundation, Denise preferred to tackle many of the administrative tasks. They revamped the Foundation website: one part was on the Foundation; the other on the investigation. Unwittingly, this focus mirrored their lives, split in two. They inhabited two worlds. In the August newsletter for the Foundation, Bruce posted that their online shop would be up and running soon.

Around the same time, Bruce and Denise decided to send the *Foundation Red* DVD and an introductory letter to all Queensland schools. The Foundation could not afford to hire a company to do a mail-out, so Denise asked Sam McDowall to help. She and Sam went to the Department of Education website and cut and pasted every address into a spreadsheet. There were 1870 schools in Queensland. Denise and Bruce sat down for days making labels and putting the DVD inside, along with newsletters and Day for Daniel posters. They used a room in their new house. The whole bedroom was full of parcels. Gradually, schools began making orders for Day for Daniel merchandise.

The Foundation was already putting its money to specific work. After donating funds for the rehabilitation, travel and accommodation expenses for a boy who had been bashed during Schoolies week in 2005, and who later made a full recovery, the committee donated money to other individual cases. Funds were put towards a new off-road bike, helmet and boots for a young boy who had been abused. Around the same time, Bruce and Denise announced the Foundation would be assisting Laurel House in Maroochydore and Laurel Place in Gympie. Both organisations provided specialised counselling support, information and education for child victims of sexual abuse within the Sunshine Coast and Cooloola. The Foundation bought toys and games and covered travel expenses to help children who had been victims of crime in some way.

Denise and Bruce's work was beginning to be recognised. Accolades were coming from as high as the current and future state premiers, Peter Beattie and Anna Bligh, Prime Minister John Howard, Queensland Police Minister Judy Spence and Queensland Police Commissioner Bob Atkinson. These influential leaders also recognised what Bruce and Denise were doing as parents for their son Daniel.

On 13 August, they received an email from the father of a boy who had been abused 'at the hands of a trusted friend', thanking the Foundation for donating a bike. The man wrote:

> We can only say that we believe that you wonderful people
> have been an amazing part of God saying to our son that
> he is loved and cared for, not just by his God and his
> family, but the community at large. There have been lots of
> tears, smiles and head shaking around here today. How can
> such pain as we have in some small way shared with your
> family over the past few years come to be expressed in such
> wonderful care for others.

As always, though, the dark side dogged their paths. Bruce met up with a man who lived in Nambour who introduced him to his landlord, a man who had got a PhD late in his life. The man had already made a report to Detective Sergeant Dave Wilkinson back in March 2004. He spoke of a Nambour drug and paedophile ring that picked up boys in a van using other kids as bait to draw the victims into the vehicle. The van had a link to a blue car that was at an elderly man's house outside of the town. The elderly man did not use the car but his son had visited from Melbourne and used it. He did give one name of a computer science teacher who had raped a nine-year-old girl. Bruce traced the name to a man who looked after boarders at a Catholic college in Brisbane. The meeting lasted 45 minutes. Was there a wider network masking the truth about what happened to his son? It was not the first time he had thought this.

* * *

In September 2007, a young woman walked into Ferny Grove Police Station in north-western Brisbane. Approaching the counter, she said she had some information for the police, explaining it was of a confidential nature and related to the Daniel Morcombe case. Constable Matt Bower took names of people she claimed were involved in Daniel's abduction. The names had come to her from someone else, she explained. One of the people the woman nominated as kidnapping Daniel was someone called 'Cohen'. She gave his tow-truck registration number. It was later traced to Brett Cowan.

The woman also told Officer Bower that the person she described as 'Cohen' resembled the police COMFIT picture. Two days later, a man approached the same police station and nominated Brett Cowan, or Cowen, as being involved in Daniel's disappearance. He gave a registration number and said Cowan was involved in a child porn ring and that he resembled images of suspects shown on television.

And there was more detective work going on behind the scenes. Grosskreutz and Eggy had received another map from a jail source in the BWCC. Someone had apparently overheard Smythe talking about another location for Daniel's remains. Coincidentally the spot was also off Steve Irwin Way, the same main artery where Rogers's body had been found and also where Dooley had taken police back in 2005, telling them that was where Daniel's body had been taken. Since the episode at Bribie Island, they both felt relieved to have turned over the information they had received to Bruce and Denise who were now speaking directly to Ibrahim and Smythe. Grosskreutz and Eggy had visited the new site twice. It was north of Australia Zoo, whereas Rogers's body had been found south of the zoo. They had discovered an old Bluebird car nose in the bush, concealed from the road. What was more alarming was they saw old bits of carpet at the back of the car with what appeared to be blood on them. They took photos of the car and showed the new map to the Morcombes.

Bruce went to check out the place. Steve Irwin Way was the only road named on the map, but there was a dirt road and a BP service station also marked. Bruce was convinced the dirt road was Old Caloundra Road. A scrap dealer had also been marked on the map, opposite the service station. Bruce remembered the large phone number advertising free collection of car bodies as the number was on the body of an old Toyota Celica – Bruce thought a 1973 model. His first car – that he had taken Denise out in all those years ago – was a 1975 Celica and it had a similar shape. It was the sort of car you did not see too often. The map showed a dirt track that crossed a depression or creek. There was some uneven ground and a curious cross-shaped stick that looked like a marker also drawn on the map.

Once at the location, Bruce found a pine tree that had been cut in half some years previously, leaving just the stump along one track. A sapling of a pine tree was doing its best to grow from the decaying stump. It only had a couple of lateral branches but they stood around a metre tall. Could this be the cross marked on the map? Bruce wondered. He even removed the sapling while poking around the stump but nothing was there. Always by himself, Bruce spent several half-days looking for the exact place. Up and down different dirt tracks, he was looking for any signs that this was where Daniel had been taken. After walking through endless bushland and along bush tracks and driving on unsealed roads, he found nothing.

Not long afterwards, Bruce handed the map to Tracey Barnes out the front of Maroochydore Police Station. Barnes pressed him about where he had got it. He did not want to say, but, after she accused him of withholding evidence, he told her.

When Grosskreutz and Eggy returned to the site, about a week later, the car had disappeared but they saw the place where it had been. The carpet, too, was gone.

* * *

The Foundation's third Day for Daniel took place on 31 October 2007. Speaking at the beginning of the walk, which now began at the Suncoast Christian College, formerly the Christian Outreach Centre, Bruce and Denise said it represented the fact that it should be safe for young people to walk in the streets. 'We encourage people to think of Daniel and his colour of identification – red – and wear red, whether it's a red shirt or shoes or tie, to serve as a reminder that child-safety awareness is important,' Bruce said.

On 26 November, secret coercive hearings began before the Crime and Misconduct Commission involving the questioning of some POIs identified by Operation Vista investigators.

On 7 December, the fourth anniversary of Daniel's abduction, Bruce and Denise found that the rock area around Daniel's memorial seemed to have been disturbed. There were flowers and toys that had been tossed around. Bruce wrote to the Operation Vista investigators. It could have been the wind, he wrote, but that was unlikely, as a vase and flowers were left standing and other, heavier objects were strewn around.

Meanwhile, Bruce and Denise's country retreat in the green, sloping hills in the south of Tasmania had lived up to their hopes as the refuge they both needed. Tasmania provided a rare chance of anonymity. A trip to the local corner shop did not result in stares or handshakes and the unavoidable hug. They could slip into the hardware store at any time without anyone noticing. They decided to spend Christmas there that year.

Dean and Bradley flew from Queensland on Christmas Eve to join their parents. Dean had a new tattoo on his hand: the word 'MEMORIES' written across his knuckles. Kevin and Monique also flew down that year, to join the family for Christmas lunch. Damien, Denise's brother, his wife, Kerry, and their two children, Michael and Ashlea, caught the *Spirit of Tasmania* from Melbourne to Devonport and drove to their holiday home.

Bruce and Denise bought ten Santa suits at a discount store for $5 each and decided it would be a lunch condition for everyone to wear one. The unpredictable cooler Tasmanian weather helped as they sat around the table full bellied and merry in their suits. It was to become a family tradition for whenever they had Christmas in Tasmania. There were other light-hearted moments among the sadness as they remembered Daniel. When removing the Christmas tree, Bruce decided that he was fed up with re-decorating it each year and of having to pick up the Christmas baubles that kept dropping from it throughout the festive season.

He decided to hot glue every decoration to the ornamental tree, ready for next year. This became another family joke. Entering into the spirit of things, Brad and Dean also got up to mischief by turning about-face some of Denise's displayed Franklin Mint cat plates in a glass cabinet. The food items in the pantry were also rotated 180 degrees, a departure from the norm as Bruce always kept labels front and centre in the cupboard.

CHAPTER EIGHTEEN

OPERATION GOLF
AVALON

Operation Golf Avalon began on 8 January 2008. Its aim was to thoroughly re-examine all of Douglas Jackway's alibis. Other than the partially complete draft review in 2005 by Tuffield from the Organised Crime Investigation Unit, Jackway's alibis had never been systematically investigated. It was Jackway's friend Carrington who had helped throw doubt on Jackway's involvement in Daniel's abduction as he claimed Jackway had phoned him from his Bertha Street house at around 3.30 pm the day Daniel disappeared which meant Jackway could not have been in the Sunshine Coast and would not have had time to abduct Daniel. Carrington was a convicted paedophile with a substantial criminal history including sexually assaulting a boy en route from Bundaberg to Sydney. New timelines were drawn up by homicide detectives using provable facts such as phone records and arrest dates. Each alibi had his or her own timeline, to be compared with versions from other alibis. Covert and overt strategies were put in place, including using listening devices.

The investigators assessed the known facts. Video footage confirmed that Jackway and his young male friend Park had called into the BP Express at Goodna at 5.03 am on 8 December 2003 and Jackway had withdrawn $10. Police had noted in the original investigation that Jackway did not have a mobile phone at the time he was interviewed, and it could not be proven whether he was telling the truth, as there had been no ability to track Jackway's phone history.

A list of the phone calls made to and from Jackway's house in Bertha Street showed eight calls had been made to Carrington's house on 7 December, from 40 minutes after midnight through until 3.30 pm, some only lasting a number of seconds. There was a call from Carrington to Jackway's landline at 1.03 pm. Carrington had made reference to all of the calls in his statement apart from three, and these were the shorter calls. Whether it was always Jackway who had either phoned or answered, however, was not conclusive. Carrington admitted it could have been either Jackway or his de facto. Jackway, too, had told police that both he and Danielle Richardson would call Carrington from the Bertha Street house.

Police also re-interviewed Vincent Tournoff on 27 January 2008. Tournoff had had a previous de facto relationship with Richardson and still had a good relationship with her children. He said he had spoken with Jackway the morning Daniel disappeared for about two hours and he changed his original account saying that he'd probably left the Bertha Street house before midday, not between noon and 1 pm, as he had called into the newsagency to get bread and milk, and it closed at midday on Sundays. Jackway, he said, had left the house before he did. Police visited the Goodna newsagency and confirmed that it did shut at midday on a Sunday.

As part of the 2004 Tuffield draft review, investigators had tracked down Park, who was then in Alice Springs and still with Carrington. Park then revealed that Jackway was, in fact, away from the Bertha Street house for four or five hours, a different version from his original account which maintained Jackway was only gone for a short while. When contacted four days later, however, Park changed his story again and reneged on this comment, saying he didn't want to talk about it.

Detective Senior Constable Emma Macindoe, on the review team, concluded that the evidence against Jackway was circumstantial, but exactly where he was when Daniel went missing and who he was with had not been satisfactorily answered.

* * *

No matter how many times Cowan's file disappeared into the archives, like Jackway, Dooley and Meyer, his name would not stay out of the investigation. On 8 January 2008, Detective Sergeant Tracey Barnes completed the POI report into Brett Peter Cowan. Barnes was a police officer for 26 years, and had been involved in Daniel's investigation almost from day one, including as the key role of reader. Barnes contacted the Department of Main Roads Traffic Management Centre about the monitoring of cameras between Beerwah and Nambour after finding out that Cowan believed he had been filmed by overhead traffic cameras when he had driven under the Kiel Mountain Road overpass that day. Sergeant Barnes learnt that there were three cameras on this route and one was at the Kiel Mountain Road overpass. But none of them was operating in record mode.

* * *

By the end of January, Bruce sent his usual email to Barnes and John Maloney:

Hi Tracey and John,
Now Christmas is behind us Denise and I would like to
be briefed on Daniel's case and what directions it may take
over the balance of 2008.

I'm thinking of early next week if that fits in with you.
Please let me know.
Regards
Bruce Morcombe

It was a reminder that the Morcombes would never give
up. Bruce had left enough time after Christmas to retain
politeness but the email had a sting in its tail. Bruce wanted
evidence of progress. Barnes replied that there was nothing
new to follow up. Not to be dissuaded, Bruce emailed back
almost a week later, adding that he did not want to upset the
investigative work but:

As we mentioned on 19.12.07 we have offers from 2 x
Private Investigator firms (service free of charge) and also
another businessman who wants to offer a $1,000,000
reward. I have delayed these options until the time is right.
I think that time is fast approaching but we always work
with you and not in a negative manner.

I suppose I need to know if you have any issues with
me moving these options forward. Also, when is the
Coroner's Report being completed? When is the MIR
being transferred and downsized to a skeleton staff? What
is happening with our friends at the Woombye Caravan
Park? Any news on further Crime and Misconduct
Commission involvement?

* * *

The Morcombes continued to receive emails from all sorts of
people, from ordinary folk wanting to help, to those who were

clearly delinquent and psychics hell-bent on offloading their dreams. On 11 March, Bruce received a call from someone who said he had spoken to a prisoner who did not want his name mentioned but that the prisoner used to play chess with Bill Dooley. The prisoner said that Dooley had drawn a picture of a small brick building, resembling one built by Telstra or perhaps a power station, and had said that it was in a pine forest on the North Coast. He had put the initials 'D. M.' on it. The building had barbed wire around it and a creek bed/gully/floodway in front of it. There was long grass in front and a sign nearby warning people about 'debris'. The person who contacted Bruce said it could be interesting to see if the area was where Dooley had dumped Roger's body.

That month, the third Dance for Daniel was again held at Twin Waters. Band of Blue played and Ross Wilson with the Urban Legends were the highlight, playing a variety of hits including many Daddy Cool and Mondo Rock classics, such as 'Eagle Rock', 'Cool World' and 'Come Said the Boy'. Someone bought one of the Rolling Stones guitars for $36,000. There was one condition – that the guitar be hand-delivered the next morning to the buyer. At 5 am the following morning, Denise was up and searching through all of the auction merchandise that had been packed away the previous night, eventually finding it. It was worth the effort.

* * *

Julie Elliott and Denise hadn't trained as hard for their next expedition that Easter: the five-day, 65-kilometre Overland Track in Tasmania, through the heart of the Cradle Mountain–Lake St Clair National Park.

Beginning in Cradle Valley at Cradle Mountain, they really felt the lack of training. They had flown into Hobart just before Easter and stayed for two nights at Bay Lodge. They had then driven to Evandale, south of Launceston, and met up at the walkers' base to check their gear. The first day, a blizzard came in as they were walking around Dove Lake. The whole group put on their wet-weather gear and started up a very steep section of the track towards Marion's Lookout, using the chain attached to the walkway for balance. Afterwards, looking at the photos, Denise and Elliott wondered how they ever reached their room that night. Denise had thought she would go flying over the edge along with her big turquoise pack.

On Easter Sunday, Denise and Elliott climbed – or rather scrambled – over rocks, some bigger than themselves, to get to the top of the 1617-metre Mount Ossa, an optional sidetrack. The weather warmed up enough to strip off into T-shirts and show bare arms to the lukewarm sun. Elliott and Denise posed for a photograph at the top of Tasmania's highest mountain, both dressed in their fleece waistcoats, a triumphant smile on their faces. In the distance, Cathedral Mountain was a silhouette on the horizon.

* * *

The new Daniel Morcombe Foundation office at 1/10 Aerodrome Road, Maroochydore, was a commercial space of 105 square metres that was once a takeaway food outlet, but it suited their needs. The blurring of boundaries between the Foundation and their family life meant the move was necessary. They had moved in January, having signed a three-year lease the previous December, with the option of extending for a further two years, a mark of their commitment to their new life.

Peter Boyce continued to be enormously helpful as a committee man, also providing pro bono legal advice. Tim Ryan and Sam McDowall had both resigned, and Robin and John Pearce, a retired schoolteacher, became committee members in the middle of 2008. Pearce's educational background would prove invaluable in structuring educational policy, as well as with the foundation's newsletters. Robin Sherwell, a friend who had been helping Denise since 2006, while they were still at Camellia Cottage. She had worked part-time for them when they opened the office in Aerodrome Road.

The Foundation was now able to receive visitors. And a sign out the front with the now recognisable T-shirt logo prominently declared the Daniel Morcombe Foundation was here to stay.

* * *

On Good Friday, with Denise away in Tasmania, Bruce was sitting in the back area of the office near the photocopier when the phone rang. Unusual, he thought, given that it was a public holiday. Nevertheless, he picked it up.

'Oh, hello, Bruce.' The woman gave her name and continued. 'You don't know me, but I have some information you might want to hear relating to Daniel's abduction.' It was the same woman who had gone to police at Ferny Grove, but Bruce did not know this at the time.

What she said next chilled Bruce to the bone: the same names listed again.

'Where are you?' he interrupted.

'I'm about to go into the Maroochydore Police Station. Why?'

'I'm in Aerodrome Road – only around the corner, just two minutes away. I'll come and see you.'

He saw the woman sitting on a bench outside the Maroochydore Police Station. Being Good Friday, there was no one else around. She looked to be in her late twenties. She had dark hair and was well dressed and respectable, compared with many of the people he had so far encountered. Bruce parked his car, walked over to her and asked her if she was the woman he was there to meet.

They sat down and Bruce began taking notes on the names the woman had been told by her source. He recognised some of the names. Then he watched her go inside the police station and gave her a wave. 'Ring me when you're done,' he said.

Bruce returned to Aerodrome Road. Two hours passed while he pondered the notes he had made. No phone call. He got up and jumped in his car, heading for the police station. Just as he approached the front door, the young woman came out. Bruce recognised the police officer she was with – he was one of the investigators on Daniel's case and his name was Graeme Farlow.

Farlow nodded to Bruce, saying, 'It's not what you think ...'

Outside, Bruce spoke to the woman for about ten minutes before they went their separate ways.

Bruce had also made some more visits to Ibrahim's house in Ashgrove. Once, he called into the nearby McDonald's, thinking that at least he would be caught on the cameras in case he went missing. He met Alise Smythe there and they spoke for around two hours. He could see how much her memory had been damaged by her drug usage, but he believed there was something in what she was telling him. He went over and over the stories involving Meyer and Dooley.

* * *

Denise and Bruce usually steered clear of psychics. Bruce had his share sometimes when he unwittingly ended up chasing information at some stranger's house, only to find the 'information' was based on a dream. Denise, however, simply passed notes or emails of that nature on to the police. Not long after Denise returned from the Overland Track, however, Tracey Barnes received a message from someone on the Gold Coast saying she had an appointment with a well-known psychic from the United Kingdom and she asked did Denise want to attend. For some reason, Denise decided to go. She and Bruce travelled to Southport on the Gold Coast to meet up with the woman and her husband. The woman had brought two blank cassettes to record the session. They met in an office in Southport that had a reception area. Bruce waited outside.

'[The psychic] has no knowledge about Daniel, not coming from Australia,' Denise was told by the woman.

Denise listened to the psychic explain that he conversed with the spirit world. 'Do you know a person named Mary?' he suddenly asked.

Denise did have an Aunt Mary who had recently died, but she was thinking to herself that most people would know someone called Mary. It was a common name.

Suddenly, the psychic started speaking again. 'I can see a young boy,' he said.

Denise was startled out of her scepticism.

'He has a sore head. He's saying, "Mum, I know you are smoking cigarettes."'

The session ran for an hour.

Denise began to believe he was speaking with Daniel and listened carefully. After the session ended, she agreed to come back the following Monday afternoon. She wanted to find out more.

Before a second visit to him, Denise and Bruce stopped in to say thanks to the woman and her husband, as they had paid for the session as well as setting it up. The husband casually mentioned that he had been talking to the psychic about Daniel. Denise immediately felt let down. So, the psychic did know about her son. During the second session, he spoke about Daniel getting into a car with a man with work clothes on. He spoke about a laundromat and the coastal town of Gympie, and a particular sign that gave the distance in kilometres. On the way back home, they drove up the Bruce Highway heading for Gympie. Denise really wanted to believe what she had heard. They wanted to find out whether the sign existed – something to show that the psychic had been telling the truth. They drove up and down the Bruce Highway a couple of times, but there was no sign. Back home, they listened to the recording together but they found themselves questioning each other about what facts the man had revealed and whether any of it could be proven. Really, there was nothing that either of them could latch onto. Denise felt the whole exercise had been a waste of time.

* * *

Around the end of April, Bruce and Denise met with John Maloney and Tracey Barnes at the Foundation office on Aerodrome Road, for an update on the investigation. As usual, nothing much was forthcoming. Bruce then handed Maloney a copy of his diary notes from the Libby Taylor meeting, which he had typed out. Maloney looked at the list dispassionately. There was a pause in the conversation as they both read it. Maloney looked up. 'There's one new name on the list. Several we have already investigated.' He continued, 'It can't be this one, Lenny Fraser. He's dead.' Taylor knew Meyer, having been introduced to him by a mutual friend. She also said that Meyer and Cowan knew each other.

Denise also told them about her meeting with the psychic. Another dead end.

By this time, Operation Golf Avalon investigators had re-interviewed Carrington and Park, who were living together in a flat on Lusitania Street, Newtown. Police had installed a covert listening device in the flat, which captured Carrington attempting to find out from Park why he had told police so many different versions of what had happened that day. Park was interviewed on 13 April, but he was still vague about the details. He did say, however, that he had continually lied to police about being in Jackway's company all day, and that he had done so because Jackway told him to. The older man had a big influence over him, he revealed. He said Jackway had gone out at midday on 7 December and it wasn't until much later that they had visited Carrington. That night, he was recorded saying that Jackway was out of his company for four or five hours that day, a vastly different picture to what police had initially believed.

The following day, Carrington was interviewed. The only deviations from his original account were that he said he had also received a phone call from Bertha Street from Park that day asking for money, and that he could not be sure if it was Jackway who made the call at 12.29 pm. After returning home, Carrington had discussed more details with Park, and it was decided that Park would tell the police the truth. They continued talking about it, and Carrington wrote out a timeline of Park's memory of events that day.

When re-interviewed on 15 May, Danielle Richardson's story had also altered. She said the information she had given police about her and Jackway arguing most of the day was not correct. She revealed that Jackway had left the house for a long period of time – in fact, most of the afternoon. Jackway had asked her to tell the police that he was at home that afternoon and at some point he had told her, 'Stick to what you said.' She said she had agreed because she was scared of his temper. She said she didn't believe he had committed the crime and when he told her police were trying to accuse him of it she had thought he was innocent. She claimed that, in 2007, when police approached her about the letter that was sent to Jackway in jail to see if she'd written it, she had told them then that Jackway would have had time to go up the coast.

Operation Golf Avalon investigators timed the 133-kilometre distance from Bertha Street, Goodna, to the Kiel Mountain Road overpass as taking one hour and 24 minutes travelling within the speed limit. The round trip would have taken two hours and 48 minutes, which according to the times Jackway's alibis had originally provided gave Jackway nine minutes to find Daniel, stalk him and abduct him.

Like a pack of dominos, the various versions supplied by Jackway's alibis began to fall. Park was interviewed again on 23 May 2008 and provided a handwritten document to investigators in which he denied absolutely everything he had said in previous accounts. This time, he said he had continually lied to police about being with Jackway all day on 7 December 2003. After visiting Park's mother and putting fuel in the car, Park said that Jackway had left him at Bertha Street that morning and driven off saying he was 'going to a mate's place'. Jackway, he said, had been away for five or six hours and had returned in an agitated state and gone to his bedroom. He said they had both visited Carrington around 5 or 5.30 pm.

Park also told police that two days later Jackway had come downstairs in the house at Bertha Street and called out for him. Jackway had told Park that the police would be looking for him. When Park asked why, Jackway had replied, 'They are gonna think that I've done it.' He also told investigators that Jackway had provided him with an alibi and that he had further threatened him into ringing his mother to say they had been over on 7 December, not on 9 December. Park also said that the phone call to Carrington's house at 12.33 pm that day was made by him and not Jackway. He said that when Jackway returned from the coast he had two $50 notes on him, which was the amount of money Daniel was thought to have had with him that day, but which Jackway claimed he had got it 'from a mate'. The car had to be refuelled in Goodna the day after Daniel went missing, Park said, even though petrol had been put in it the previous day.

* * *

Was there more than one offender? As Bruce and Denise puzzled through the many names they had encountered on the journey to find Daniel, this was a question they kept asking themselves. On 7 May, Bruce wrote to Tracey Barnes asking whether there was any evidence that Jackway knew Dooley.

On 26 May, Bruce wrote a letter to Gerry and Kate McCann. The previous year, their daughter Madeleine – born seven months before Daniel went missing – had disappeared from their holiday apartment in Portugal while her parents dined nearby. Bruce offered to help them in any way, explaining how their son, too, had been abducted. Originally suspects in her disappearance, the McCanns later received damages for false allegations of their involvement. Bruce wrote:

> My wife, Denise, and I have watched the painful path you
> are travelling and we often relive some of those emotions
> again with you. Our sympathy goes out to you both and
> we wish you well in your endeavours to find some answers.
> I know you would receive mountains of mail from good
> family people around the world plus many, many from
> every dreamer and psychic whose intentions are to be
> helpful but we know only too well muddy the water and
> confuse the investigation.

Bruce explained how they had set up the Daniel Morcombe Foundation three years ago and that neither of them had found it possible to re-enter the workforce: 'It has been a hard grind but you learn to take a few small steps forward each day. The Foundation has enabled us to have a focus and purpose as it adds meaning to those days.'

After providing them with the Foundation's web address, Bruce said he and Denise would like to meet the McCanns when the time was right: 'It is possible that our combined efforts can make the world a safer place for children as well as generate potential new leads.'

This tentative token of friendship was to blossom later into a mutual respect and understanding.

* * *

Bruce and Denise were still mulling over the list of names provided by the young woman Bruce had met up with outside Maroochydore Police Station. Bruce asked Tracey Barnes via email whether police were aware of the person who the woman had nominated as her source. Barnes replied saying she had interviewed her two weeks earlier, having been requested to by Graeme Farlow. She said that the person who had supplied the names had been involved in the drug scene and had heard many rumours, but that none of them could be substantiated.

This person claimed to have direct knowledge that Brett Cowan and Alexander Meyer were known to each other. She also believed that Cowan was a paedophile. She claimed that she knew Smythe but had not associated with her for many years.

Barnes said that the woman also claimed to be something of a psychic, as she could 'feel' things. 'My impression of her,' she said, 'was that she felt deeply concerned about what had happened to Daniel (she has children of a similar age) and was passing on every piece of information she had heard that may assist the investigation.'

Neither Bruce nor Denise had given up on the idea of a coronial inquiry, involving a Coroner ordering and adjudicating an investigation into the cause of Daniel's death and which may also inquire into the police investigation. Bruce emailed Julie Elliott on 2 June stating he thought any coronial report from police would take until 2009 to prepare.

He said that, although Maloney and Barnes were 'more open than some time ago', he still did not know all of the names being investigated. He added again that he and Denise had been approached by a businessman offering a million-dollar reward saying that Maloney had not encouraged it:

But from where we sit, as long as it does not damage DMF [the Daniel Morcombe Foundation's] reputation and Vista work it may be worth a shot. We probably need to sit down and work out issues.

* * *

By 6 June, more than 18,000 job logs had been recorded since Daniel had vanished. The media conference held to document this was like so many media conferences that had gone before. Inspector Maloney told the public, 'We have detectives working on it on a daily basis, and we are still following up leads and information coming in from members of the public and other sources, as well as reviewing what we've got,' he said. And he added the same plea: 'We still need that one vital piece of information.'

* * *

On 8 June, the Ride for Daniel attracted 7000 riders in a record-breaking ride, a sevenfold increase from its first incarnation. At the head of the procession, Denise rode pillion behind Eggy. Bruce, Dean and Brad were on trikes. This was now the 'largest and loudest' annual motorbike ride in Australia. Again, the riders set off from the Big Pineapple to the Ettamogah Pub. The stream of motorcycles stretched 30 kilometres along the Bruce Highway. Before the ride, Denise gave a passionate speech, saying it was time Daniel's abductors were caught.

'It is time for it to be put to rest,' she said. 'The police have been fantastic. They have a team of police who won't give up. We'll keep pushing until we get answers. Someone has the answers. We need them to talk … they can't keep things like that quiet forever.'

As the cavalcade rode past Daniel's shrine, Denise could not hold back. 'Just awesome,' she said, tears in her eyes.

The Foundation itself was also going from strength to strength, and they were reaping rewards. Throughout June, July and August, the Foundation was responsible for making the Maroochydore Police Station child-witness room a friendlier and more inviting place, by giving it a makeover and supplying reading books, colouring books and DVDs. They also assisted a child on a school camp to Canberra. Through the Queensland Homicide Victims' Support Group, they helped a program called 'Kids in Need' as well as other sexual-abuse or counselling-service programs for children. The Foundation assisted in other ways too, such as by paying for school fees and uniforms, speech therapy, computers, driving lessons and books. Some of the children receiving these gifts had suffered sexual or physical abuse or had witnessed a crime being committed on a family member, in some cases murder.

In August, Bruce and Denise flew down to Tasmania for a break and on 4 August, at the Sacred Heart Catholic Church in New Town, an old, stone traditional church in a historical suburb only kilometres from the CBD in Hobart, the Morcombes and Denise's parents took part in a service packed with parishioners. It was National Missing Persons Week. Their Daniel Morcombe Foundation Tasmanian supporters had invited them to a mass. The service focused on young people aged under 25, and Father Brian Nicols dedicated it to Daniel. Bruce and Denise met Jessica Reidy, a Tasmanian police officer from the Missing Persons Unit who was an avid supporter of the Foundation. She was organising the first Tasmanian Walk for Daniel on the Day for Daniel planned for October 2008. The walk was planned to start at the Salamanca Markets and pass near the famous Constitution Dock, where the Sydney to Hobart yacht race ended. When it was held two months later, it was a cold, wet and windy day. Hundreds of schoolchildren participated, all dressed in red.

In September, Bruce and Denise travelled to more schools to spread the word about child safety. Children were encouraged to wear red during their visit and to write in red pen, as well as being shown the *Foundation Red* safety-awareness video. Later that month, the Morcombes flew to Adelaide as part of a national tour to seek support for the Day for Daniel, and to meet up with representatives of various state education departments and child-safety departments around the country. The Morcombes had a pre-organised meeting with Emeritus Professor Freda Briggs from the University of South Australia. Denise and Bruce were both pleased when she acknowledged their efforts in child safety. She had international contacts, having worked as a consultant to Avon and Somerset Police in the United Kingdom for a child-safe program, and proved to have invaluable knowledge in the area of child safety. They both gained a lot from meeting her. From Adelaide, they continued on to Perth, Hobart and Melbourne.

In October, a private detective from China left a message on the Foundation's mobile number, saying he 'had some clues to help with the case'. Bruce, as usual, passed this on to Tracey – another lead to nowhere. The detective would ring Bruce's mobile every few weeks saying he had information on blue cars.

* * *

Just a few days into October, a letter arrived at the Morcombes' home. Inside the envelope was a three-page handwritten letter from the McCanns. Kate McCann wrote general chitchat about family and Madeleine's investigation and went on to say:

> I just wanted to thank you for making contact and for your kind words. You, unlike most people, will be able to appreciate the pain, anxiety, anger and the awful, indescribable existence of 'not knowing' when your precious child is abducted without trace. Daniel looks beautiful and it is good to hear (and also encouraging) that you have managed to stay strong, survive, and to continue the search for Daniel as well as help educate and support other families. Like yourselves, we feel we need to do everything we can to try and find Madeleine, and virtually every 'child free' moment we have is used for this purpose. It's hard to switch off knowing that your 'baby' could be out there, waiting for you.
> Take care,
> Kate and Gerry McCann

Dean's 21st birthday was on 4 October 2008. That evening, the family gathered at a local Italian restaurant called Cala Luna in Alexandra Headland, on the coast. Bruce and Denise had dropped off a birthday cake and a 21st helium balloon before Dean arrived. Another personal milestone without his mate Daniel. Dean had organised a camping trip with his friends that weekend in Kenilworth, a small inland town in the upper Mary Valley, in the Sunshine Coast hinterland.

* * *

Tracey Barnes admitted that the police, too, were frustrated by the lack of progress. Bruce told Tracey after meeting with the Assistant Police Commissioner that they would announce the private reward in seven weeks, after preparing a legal document for sponsors. He said he was keen to work with police on an announcement venue, call number, posters, website, email address, and Queensland Police involvement in the media conference to announce the reward.

Heading up to the fourth Day for Daniel on 31 October, *Woman's Day* ran a large story on Daniel's case with a focus on the family. *WHO Magazine* also ran one the same week. Both magazine articles focused on maintaining the hunt for the abductors and on how the family was coping. To support the Day for Daniel, the Morcombes had done an animated television commercial, which ran nationally. Bruce and Denise visited Cairns, Townsville, Adelaide, Perth and Hobart. They had decided to take the child-safety-awareness campaign to a national level and to make sure Daniel would never be forgotten.

Publicity was always a double-edged sword, however. It brought the 'loonies' (as both the police and Bruce and Denise dubbed them) out into the open. The public email address listed on the Foundation website meant the Morcombes would increasingly bear the brunt of it. Earlier that year, Bruce had received an email asking him to place an ad for a 1977 Volvo for sale for $7000 under the name Paul, and after doing that he would be contacted by someone. Some weeks passed with no contact, and then he got an email from the person saying he feared for his life and he had information on 'the car, the people, what they were doing, why they were doing it, where they were living, and drug habits'.

The email went on to say that despite their fear, this person would come forward, but for a reward without delay. They suggested Bruce place another ad in newspaper classifieds to make contact.

Bruce was told that the ad might take some hours to appear. He was not sure whether this person wanted to meet to discuss a reward for information. Tracey's advice was to steer well clear, but Bruce decided to contact him, leaving his private mobile number. Again, several weeks passed, but then the man agreed to meet with Bruce. Bruce approached Tracey again. She agreed to step in, and went to meet the man at the prearranged place in Golden Beach, a suburb of Caloundra. She came back to report he had supplied nothing that was helpful and she'd told him never to contact the Morcombes again.

More than 500 Australian schools took part in the fourth Day for Daniel on 31 October. The Australian Federal Police National Missing Persons Coordination Centre joined to make it a day of remembrance and recognition for Daniel. Hundreds of red balloons were released by Bowen school students to mark that fateful day five years beforehand. About 350 students from Bowen schools took part in a Walk for Daniel at the state high school's main oval.

* * *

On 1 December, the million-dollar reward was launched, comprising $750,000 from a private consortium of Brisbane businesspeople and the $250,000 already offered by the government back in 2004, which made it the largest reward offered in Australia. The reward was for information leading to the arrest of the person or persons responsible for abducting Daniel Morcombe.

Crime Stoppers fielded all calls. It was decided that the reward would only be offered for six months, expiring on 31 May 2009. Atkinson also offered a pardon for anyone involved in Daniel's disappearance in a minor way if they divulged information that would lead to a conviction. But, in spite of the hefty promised payout, most of the information coming in was from people who had already contacted the police, who wished to ensure that their information had been obtained and investigated. A large volume of calls was received from psychics who wanted to add to their original testimonies. No information of any significance came forward.

Two days after the fifth anniversary of Daniel's disappearance, Denise received a standing ovation from students at the Mareeba Primary School when she visited to deliver a laptop computer. She flew up to Cairns to deliver it in person and returned the same day. The school's name had been drawn from a competition run by the Daniel Morcombe Foundation. The children were dressed in red and, standing there, Denise knew something positive was coming out of their efforts. Their mantra about child safety was spreading far and wide as another year without Daniel came to a close.

CHAPTER NINETEEN

LOOKING FOR ANSWERS

More than five years on, Bruce and Denise were seriously questioning the idea that one day they would get answers. The repeated mantra no longer worked. In spite of the police resources thrown behind Australia's biggest manhunt and reportedly the largest reward on offer in Queensland, there was no real clue to lead to a breakthrough. To the public, they retained a positive outlook. But, as they entered 2009, a number of issues simmered. It had begun with the way they had been treated by police when they first discovered Daniel was missing and had built, as the years went by, into serious doubt as to why there were no answers. Reward posters were displayed throughout Queensland jails, probation offices and parole offices. Bruce and Denise had also made some A3 and A4 laminated posters pleading for information and promising a reward of a million dollars plus indemnity from prosecution. They had asked local shops in the Palmwoods/Woombye area to display them.

They had a hunger to contribute personally. As the months slipped into years, and the years threatened to turn into a decade, there was always the threat of a 'cold case'. These two words sent a chill through both of them. That the answers to their son's disappearance could be put in the too-hard basket was their worst fear. Bob Atkinson had continually reassured them that Daniel's case would 'never, ever' be let go while he was commissioner, but what about when he stepped down?

Meanwhile, they continued to plough their energies into the Daniel Morcombe Foundation. At the start of the year, through the Kids in Need program, the Foundation bought beds, mattresses and curtains for the young brothers and sisters of twins who had been murdered. The school presentations continued, and the 'Day for Daniel' fundraising events increased in number.

The Ruby Room of the Caloundra RSL, catering for 500, became the venue for the fourth Dance for Daniel on 7 March. Tropical Cyclone Hamish brewed off the coast, disrupting travel plans for those attending. Guests came from as far away as Melbourne, Townsville and Bowen. Even Denise's 87-year-old uncle, Michael Beavis, attended all the way from Ocean Grove, Victoria.

Bruce and Denise's speeches detailed how the Foundation had spent more than $400,000 helping kids to keep safe, including child-safety initiatives and supporting young victims of crime. During his speech, Bob Atkinson assured Bruce and Denise of his enduring commitment to find Daniel. It had been another hugely successful event, leaving Bruce and Denise marvelling at what could be achieved with a community behind them.

* * *

Bruce had never forgotten Bill Dooley and their encounter almost five years earlier at the Roma Street Police Headquarters. The anxiety he'd felt meeting someone who claimed to know what had happened to Daniel was etched on his mind. In 2006, Dooley had been sentenced to life imprisonment for the murder of 73-year-old Donald Rogers, but the following year the Court of Appeal quashed his conviction. At the start of his retrial, Dooley pleaded guilty to manslaughter. The Crown alleged that Dooley had withheld Rogers's medication for diabetes to extract his PIN number for his credit card before dumping his body in a pine forest just off Steve Irwin Way not far from the Bruce Highway in the Sunshine Coast hinterland and burning his car to avoid detection. He had then allegedly spent $30,000 from Rogers's account. Dooley refused to admit that he had murdered Rogers, claiming that he had died from natural causes and was affected by heroin, but he had still pleaded guilty to manslaughter and was due to be sentenced.

Each day, Bruce would scour the law lists for the Supreme Court searching for his name. One day, he was rewarded: *R v. Dooley*, 10 March 2009. He wanted to sit in the same room as the man who had lied to his face. The morning of Dooley's appearance before Justice Fryberg, Bruce got into his car and drove to the court complex in George Street, Brisbane. Arriving early, he sat alone for 20 minutes, the only other people inside being court staff attending to water jugs and recording equipment. Then, two correctional-service officers suddenly appeared. Between them was Dooley.

Bruce was still the only person in the public gallery. He stood up and looked straight at the man he had come to see. Dooley looked momentarily shattered when their eyes met. He was representing himself, having sacked his previous counsel. Bruce was convinced Dooley thought he was there to protest against the downgrading of his charges. Recovering, Dooley quipped with the guard, 'That's Bruce Morcombe. Here to see me?' Bruce got some satisfaction seeing Dooley squirm.

The arresting police officer arrived and approached Bruce, and they had a chat outside. When they returned to the courtroom, around 20 minutes later, Bruce saw that there were virtually no seats left. It was packed with 25 school students. The only vacant places were a few directly behind Dooley, which meant he would be separated from him by only a glass partition, no taller than a common pool fence. Bruce tried to decide what to do. Then he saw Dooley look at him. Stuff it, Bruce thought. That's why I am here. He sat down directly behind Dooley, who half-turned. 'How are you, Mr Morcombe?'

'Good,' Bruce said, not wanting to cause any fuss in the courtroom. He thought of Dooley feeling the heat of his angry breath on the back of his neck.

After a while, as nothing was happening, the schoolkids got up and left. Bruce decided to leave too. His mission was accomplished. As the door swung open out of the courtroom, one of the kids approached him: 'Why are you here, Mr Morcombe?'

'You could say it's a payback for what happened to my son, Daniel,' he answered, unashamed to tell the truth.

He got back into his car and drove home. Four hours of driving for one hour in a courtroom, but he felt vindicated. The Morcombes are on a mission. Don't get in the way. That was the message. Two days later, Bruce emailed Tracey Barnes requesting a meeting:

Not much news our end but I feel we need an update on where the investigation is at. I note that Dooley had his sentencing last Monday? Can you please tell me what is happening with him? The Commissioner underlined his commitment to solve this case at our Dance. Which was nice.

I look forward to your reply.

Regards

Bruce

* * *

Bruce always thought outside the box. Ideas were buzzing around his head for a unique strategy to engage the public's interest before the private-reward offer was due to expire. He came up with a 'Frankenstein' car. He wanted to get one vehicle matching the various descriptions of the blue cars seen under the overpass the day Daniel disappeared and then blur the edges a little by swapping, for example, Holden Commodore tail lights with Toyota Corolla ones, and putting mirrors from a Bluebird on the body. He began searching the net for car-wrecking yards. On 12 March, he wrote to the police outlining his idea.

Detective Schmidt was horrified and strongly voiced his disapproval. With such opposition, Bruce settled for a three-dimensional life-size model of the man seen next to Daniel based on all three COMFIT sketches released by police back in November 2004. Given that the technology existed to produce something quite lifelike, and remembering the idea that germinated when he saw the police mannequin as a poor replica of Daniel, Bruce had begun googling back in July. He had turned up a business in Brisbane. It would cost $1000. The woman who ran the business told him that she did not want her studio mentioned, in case people came around to visit her. After an internet search and a number of meetings over several months, a clay bust was completed. Bruce and Denise staged a media event on 6 May, placing the model under the overpass. Denise said that, when she first saw it, the replica looked so real it gave her the creeps. The model was shown that morning on the *Sunrise* show. The following day, Crime Stoppers received 82 calls.

Detective Superintendent Maurice Carless had taken over from Inspector Maloney. Bruce and Denise thought he was a methodical, businesslike and gentle person. Detective Superintendent Carless told them that after the

303

model was released in the media more information had been sent to the police over the internet and that it had been one of the best public responses the case had received in recent years.

There was other media interest too. Channel Seven's *Sunday Night* had been one of the programs Bruce had in mind for profiling the clay model. The producers decided instead to run a special feature on Daniel's case. Bruce emailed police at Operation Vista advising that the program's producers had information regarding red material, Christmas Cake and New South Wales vehicles. 'I have told JJ and Tracey Barnes before that the media is full of rumours,' he wrote. 'About a year ago, a Channel Ten journalist nominated Jackway to me as someone of interest to police.'

On 14 May, Rory Callinan, the researcher from the *Sunday Night* program, and the presenter, Ross Coulthart, turned up at the Foundation office in Aerodrome Road. They wanted to focus on police investigative errors such as the time it took for POI sketches to be released, how long it had taken for Daniel's disappearance to be entered into the system and the protracted wait for any clues. Bruce and Denise had always been concerned that, if they took a negative stance against police, it might affect the investigation. So, instead, they talked to Coulthart and Callinan about potential leads, including Jackway and others, as well as their suspicions over gaps in people's timelines and unreliable alibis.

The producers decided to focus on Jackway. After a bit of digging, they managed to find news footage of the car chase he was involved in from Noosa in November 2003 just before Daniel disappeared. They wanted to showcase Jackway's knowledge of the Sunshine Coast and the fact that he had done his schooling there as well as having lived in Tewantin to the north. Callinan tracked down a couple of witnesses who had given car descriptions as well as speaking to witnesses who had provided facial descriptions of people they had seen before, during and after 7 December 2003. Bruce wrote to the police with the information:

> Unsure what if anything is of value. They certainly had nothing I had not heard before and these days is almost common talk in the community. My hunch is that they will run with something, likely with accounts from locals. This has never been covered before by media. They seem to be on a trail that the car's description as blue may be slightly wrong in that they believe it is badly faded blue making it almost grey/light blue. This is not new to us but they felt it worth noting more strongly.

* * *

Mid-May, Bruce and Denise flew to Darwin to raise awareness about child safety and what parents needed to know, as well as taking part in the Bikers United Against Child Abuse (BUACA) ride that Saturday. There were around 500 riders on the 50-kilometre ride from an inner-city Darwin park to a sporting oval. The bikers were friendly and keen to chat. Denise had already written letters to the principals of all Northern Territory schools, inviting them to take part in the Day for Daniel. The Morcombes' approach to students had subtly changed over time as they tackled the best way to get their message across the country, not just Queensland. By initiating contact with the schools of each state, they found they were usually able to generate local media interest.

* * *

The inaugural International Missing Children Day took place on 25 May 2009. It was the first time there had been a consolidated global effort to recognise the plight of missing children. Nine countries from four continents took part. While their parents flew to Canberra, Dean and Brad stood in for them for the first time at a fun run at Moffat Beach in Caloundra with the Foundation trailer. The day was windy and the track threatened to be closed, but the boys did a great job handing out information about the Foundation. Everyone was kind to them.

From the lawn of Parliament House, Denise addressed an audience that included Australian Federal Police Commissioner Mick Kelty, Minister for Home Affairs Bob Debus, and high-ranking Australian Federal Police officers about their journey to find Daniel. Balloons with missing children's faces from each member country floated above the crowd. One included a picture of Daniel. Bruce and Denise had tears in their eyes as they watched the white balloons soar over the top of Capital Hill and Parliament House. Daniel's story was joining that of other children across the world who had likely met a similar tragic fate. His plight had crossed international boundaries, much like Madeleine McCann's. Through Bruce and Denise's initial contact, there had been several other emails from the McCanns. The two couples tried to keep each other's spirits up from each side of the world, hopeful that one day they would meet.

Denise's niece, Mia, was also born that day.

* * *

As Denise and Bruce touched down on the Maroochydore tarmac on 31 May after their trip to the nation's capital, they were oblivious to recent events. They had not even heard of his name. On 27 May, Paul Eugene Carrington was found dead in his flat on Lusitania Street, Newtown. The autopsy revealed the 56-year-old, an associate of Jackway's, had died from coronary atherosclerosis. The same day his body was found, Jackway was interviewed in jail by Detective Senior Constable Emma Macindoe, one of a crack team of homicide detectives reviewing the Operation Golf Avalon investigation. By a strange coincidence, Jackway's name, which had been protected as a POI in the case, was about to be broadcast on national television on *Sunday Night*. Jackway was about to be outed.

Bruce and Denise had briefed Commissioner Atkinson on the show's content, and Macindoe decided to bring Jackway's interview date forward upon seeing the promos for the upcoming television program and becoming alarmed it would jeopardise her enquiries. Before the show went to air, the police hurriedly showed several witnesses a photo-identification board that included Jackway.

Four days after Carrington's sudden death and the re-interview of Jackway, Channel Seven aired their exclusive story, naming Jackway as the person who 'could hold key information' into the disappearance of Daniel. Jackway, the show backgrounded, had been released only weeks before Daniel disappeared. The program interviewed a former friend who said that Jackway had disappeared for several hours on the day Daniel vanished. A mother from the Woombye State School also identified Jackway as having similar facial features to a suspicious man she saw near the school in the months leading up to Daniel being abducted. On Monday morning, after the show was aired, Bruce and Denise turned up at the Foundation office to find its posters and advertising stripped from the office windows. Police sent around detectives to conduct tests for fingerprints.

On Monday 1 June, the day after the television program screened, Bruce and Denise called a media conference. Standing on the steps of Maroochydore Police Station, they addressed the bevy of cameras and microphones. 'We understand police took more than 300 calls to Crime

Stoppers last night, which is a phenomenal effort,' Bruce said. 'They're really pleased, and we thank the community for continually searching for answers. The police haven't identified to us the quality of those leads.'

Bruce said the information that could eventually crack the case might not be obvious at the start. 'It may well be a piece that on its own looks like nothing, but when linked with two or three other bits weakens an alibi or identifies a vehicle – or something like that. The past 24 hours has just been enormous and we had circled 31 May as a potentially crucial day, as the last official day of the one million dollar reward. So we felt that if money was the motivator for someone with information they really had to do it then – we had it in our mind that they would leave it to the last minute.'

The reverberations continued throughout the week. On 2 June, *The Courier-Mail* ran a poll asking readers, 'Do you think Daniel's body will ever be found?' On 5 June, Bruce gave more details to the media about Jackway's movements, focusing on the period before Daniel's disappearance when Jackway was getting his car back from the holding yard in the Kunda Park Industrial Estate after it was impounded by police. He said Jackway's impounded car had two punctured tyres after the police chase and that he may have gotten tyres from a stolen car to replace the ones on his car. He said the held car was only a few kilometres from where Daniel had gone missing. 'It was a wet Friday afternoon, there's a bloke changing wheels – it's the sort of thing people might notice … might remember,' he said. 'The description of the car police are interested in in connection with the case is blue and possibly square shaped. Jackway had been driving an old blue Commodore.'

A few days later, Bruce gave a further interview. 'What we are looking for is our son's body,' he said bluntly, stung by the fact that the large reward had still failed to produce answers. 'It is not as if it's a pot of gold. These are really difficult emotions to wrestle with, but the point is if we can find Daniel's remains, it will be a relief.' At the same time, Bruce was careful not to overstate the importance of Jackway in the investigation, even hinting he was more interested in a few other names.

On Friday 5 June, Bruce sent an email to Bob Atkinson detailing 12 specific questions, all relating to Jackway and a variety of associates. Bruce and Denise needed answers. Bob was good enough to ring personally and he worked through Bruce's questions one by one on the phone.

The next week, the *Sunday Night* program aired a follow-up to the Jackway story, showing 'Amy', who said she had been raped by Jackway. 'When I heard about Daniel Morcombe and Douglas was out at the same time, he had the same car, he was travelling up and down from Brisbane to the Sunshine Coast, I really thought he did it,' she said. The program included more recent photographs of Jackway than the teenage shot of him screened the previous week.

* * *

At the fifth annual Ride for Daniel on 21 June, Bruce and Denise spoke loud and clear: crimes against children are the worst of the worst kind of crime.

'Our Ride for Daniel makes a highly visual statement that crimes against children have no place in modern Australia,' Bruce said. 'Demonstrations like this show child predators they have no friends and nowhere to hide.'

In the midst of the crusade to find their son, Bruce would often pass by Daniel's photograph in the kitchen and whisper, 'Sorry we let you down, but we are still looking.' He wished he'd kept more mementos of the boy who had not lived to be an adult: Daniel's naive artworks, his Father's Day and Christmas cards. He kept a few things in folders, but he wished he'd kept more, to hold onto Daniel. You keep a card for a week and then it falls into the bin and the moment's lost, he thought. It's only when your child is no longer there that you hang onto things, as though somehow that will bring him close. One thing Bruce had kept was a piece of timber with two key hooks that Daniel had made for him in Grade 2. Had he been a good father? He would not rest until Daniel's killer or killers were brought to justice. As Daniel's father, Bruce saw one of his essential roles as 'putting an old head on young shoulders', passing on life skills to your son whether it was a carpenter or mechanic passing on trade skills or a sportsman passing on sporting skills or a father being a role model in a family unit. He was determined to maintain the rage, to ensure his son's killer or killers were found. He knew Denise was too.

The police had tried hard but they had not solved one of the most brazen of all crimes: to snatch a child in broad daylight. Whenever Bruce or Denise mentioned involving the Coroner to some of the investigating police officers, they still seemed resistant. Bruce had the impression that it was because, to police, an inquest implied a failure on their part and suggested that someone needed to check their work. For the Morcombes, however, it was never about a failure of duty or a blame game. It was about thanking the police for all the work they had done but having a fresh look at the material by trained professionals with more powers than them. The State Coroner, Michael Barnes, could compel people to answer questions, and there was a big stick: perjury charges could be laid if anyone lied at the inquest.

The police's excuses in this matter began to make Bruce's blood boil. For around 18 months, the Morcombes had heard that the Coroner could not receive a brief while the investigation was active. A couple of calls a week from the general public meant it was still active. In the middle of 2009, at one of the regular meetings with Schmidt, Bruce said, 'We need to draw the line at a date and finish the brief to that date. If new material comes in, then so be it.'

On 24 June 2009, Bruce took matters into his own hands and wrote a letter to the State Coroner, Michael Barnes. He asked for fresh insight into the case, especially focusing on the continuing names that cropped up as POIs. An inquest presented the opportunity for a fact-finding mission with wider scope than other court hearings, Bruce wrote. He and Denise had been fed morsels of what was happening but had no real idea of the extent of the investigation.

Two days later, a reply was forwarded from Acting State Coroner Christine Clements:

> I note there already has been an extensive Police investigation and that you and your family have shown extraordinary fortitude and persistence to maintain investigation by police and encourage the public to provide information. I will formally request the Police to provide their report and then consider how the coronial jurisdiction may assist you and your family.

Bruce told the media that it was time to 'apply the legal blowtorch' to a few POIs. He said recent publicity had outed several 'key persons', which had spurred the family's decision to approach the Coroner. 'Most of that information is not new to us or new to police,' he told the Australian Associated Press. 'We've been able to keep those lines of enquiry out of the public arena, which police always say is helpful to the investigation. Now that they're in the public arena, it's time for the State Coroner to apply the due legal process to work through Daniel's police case file and see what he can make of those persons of interest.'

He said he hoped the Coroner's power to speak to several key people 'at the pointy end of the investigation' under oath would lead to a breakthrough in the case. As to when or if the coronial inquiry might happen, Bruce said he hoped it would be held over the next few months but that it could take up to two years. 'The Coroner won't pick this file up and say we're on next week,' he said. 'But we're expecting that it will happen around mid-next year. We always appreciated that it would be the Coroner's call and his call only.'

State Coroner Michael Barnes responded through the media saying that while he was acting as Chief Magistrate he was unable to progress the request. He would return to his official role the following month. Then he would have to wait for police to complete an investigation report. He assured the media he would be acting independently from police and government.

On 6 August, they received an email from Barnes's assistant Daniel Grice, saying a meeting had been set up with the State Coroner on 20 August at 10.30 am. Bruce emailed Mike Condon telling him about the developments.

Bruce approached lawyer and Foundation committee member Peter Boyce about the prospect of an inquest. Bruce told him that he and Denise would be there to represent themselves if it went ahead. 'That wouldn't be wise. You have no experience in the legal system,' Boyce politely said. 'I'm happy to read the material and appear for you.' The offer turned out to be gold. Without Boyce's experience and incisive questioning techniques and attention to detail, the inquest might well have been a lost opportunity.

Meanwhile, on 7 July, Queensland Premier Anna Bligh came out publicly supporting the Morcombes in response to their plea for an inquest. While stopping short of urging the State Coroner to go ahead, she said she understood why they would want to explore every avenue in their effort to solve the mystery and hoped an inquest would help. 'The plight of the Morcombe family, I think, has touched the heart of every parent,' she said. The Morcombes felt buoyed by the words of the premier.

Bob Atkinson came out the following day with a similar vote of public support. 'Bruce and Denise Morcombe have just been outstanding in terms of their strength and character and the way they have engaged with us over the five years since Daniel has been missing,' he said. 'We have no difficulty with the prospects of a Coroner's inquest.'

* * *

After the fierce battle for the inquest, the usual dark and light played through Bruce and Denise's lives. There was something to look forward to. The band Dean played in, Ablaze Withsin, fronted by Steve Polwarth, was to play at the Globe Theatre in Fortitude Valley in inner Brisbane as one of the bands in the 'Rock 4 Daniel' event to raise money for child protection. Musician Kate Bradley organised the fundraiser. Ablaze Withsin had scored plenty of gigs in South East Queensland and were grand finalists in the 'Loud 08' band competition. The gig at the Globe Theatre, however, was the first time they had played for the Foundation. For Dean, playing heavy-metal bass guitar was an emotional release and here he was helping his brother. He was committed to practising every single day for a couple of hours and his dream was always for the band to become a full-time career. Around this time, Bradley decided to move out and live with his older brother.

Detective Chief Superintendent Mike Condon confirmed to the media that Operation Vista investigators were working on a report for the Coroner: 'I'm loathe to put a time limit on it because we want to make sure it's right ... From a coronial point of view there is no doubt it is a substantial report, one of the largest I've come across in 25 years of plainclothes [police work].'

Wanting to see for themselves what had consumed police for all these years, Bruce requested a copy. The answer was an emphatic no.

* * *

Denise carried the mobile phone with the advertised phone number for the Daniel Morcombe Foundation. The number was a harrowing link with the outside world, as neither she nor Bruce ever knew who would be at the other end. Bruce had a number that was not known publicly. Whenever there was a discovery of human remains, one of them would receive a phone call from a high-ranking police officer. Out of consideration for the Morcombes, police had undertaken to talk immediately about the discovery in case they were Daniel's. One phone call was more alarming than others.

Bruce and Denise received a call from Condon. A jawbone had been found in the pine plantations near Toorbul on the mainland across from Bribie Island. It was a young adult male. Daniel had been 12 days shy of turning 14 when he was abducted. Now, over five and a half years had passed. Could he have been kept for all that time and this bone belonged to him? Highly unlikely, Bruce and Denise thought, but until forensic tests were carried out they had to wait.

Six weeks had gone by and still no answer. And there was still nothing by the tenth week. They had their first meeting with the Coroner at around this time, so Bruce raised the matter with him. Michael Barnes said he was surprised it was taking so long and that he would follow it up. Within a couple of days, the Morcombes received an answer: negative. They were both relieved, but at the same time their hopes were dashed. They still had no answers.

* * *

Bill Dooley's name was still never far from the investigation. This time, it was not Dooley who directly contacted police but a French-born private investigator named Daniel LeGrand, from a company called Ausworld Investigations.

LeGrand had spent almost a year covering the case and went public claiming he knew the location of Daniel's grave.

After contacting Bruce via email, they arranged a Skype interview. LeGrand had some quite specific questions for Bruce: was Daniel circumcised; did he have a scar from an appendix operation or something similar; did he have a birthmark running from his chest to over his shoulder; was he wearing boxer shorts instead of underpants. The answer to every one of these questions was no.

'I've been told Daniel's remains are actually buried in a five-kilometre radius of his disappearance,' LeGrand said. 'They are buried in red dirt, possibly close to an old hangar or large shed.'

His information, he said, came from one Bill Dooley. He said Dooley was hopeful of getting out at Christmas and pronounced that 'something big' will happen in Daniel's case soon. He also said there was new information from a woman who had a police record who claimed Daniel was buried near a boat shed at the end of Roys Road and he wanted to go with police to search as he had further details to offer. The woman had told LeGrand about a paedophile ring that had links to Fortitude Valley and Fraser Island. Bruce suggested to Condon that Tracey Barnes contact LeGrand to take the matter further. A couple of days later, Condon emailed back saying that the woman Bruce had named was known to the MIR and that the Roys Road area had been previously searched with no result.

* * *

Bruce's 50th birthday was on 29 August. Bruce, Denise, Dean and Brad flew to Lord Howe Island for a week, where they went walking, snorkelling in the lagoon, playing golf and feeding the metre-long kingfish in the protected shallow waters at Neds Beach. They had dinner at Pine Trees Lodge and stayed at Somerset Apartments, and Denise organised a cake. Denise bought Bruce a gold watch, and Dean and Brad paid for a fishing trip for the family. Before leaving the island paradise, they approached the Lord Howe Island School and gave them some DVDs, newsletters and information about the Daniel Morcombe Foundation having brought material in their luggage. The short break was what they needed: to step off the treadmill of administration about the inquest as well as media attention and the continual work for the Foundation.

In September, it was back to public engagements. On 6 September, they took to the road for Child Protection Week, touring central Queensland. They visited Bowen at the invitation of Constable Michelle Vico. In true country spirit, Michelle had made a huge cardboard sign in the shape of a T-shirt and attached it to the two-metre-tall mesh fence. On it was simply written 'Meet the Morcombes'. It was a sight that still makes Bruce and Denise laugh. From Bowen, they continued on to Townsville, where Senior Constable Bernadette Strow, whom they'd met the previous year, had arranged for them to speak at the Police Academy to cadets and senior police officers, and to several thousand students over two days. The women were to become a continuing source of support for Bruce and Denise.

Three days later, the Morcombes received the news that the police brief was expected before the Coroner within three weeks.

* * *

Julie Elliott had been floundering for some time, still feeling deeply inadequate that there was nothing she could do to provide an answer in the search for Daniel. There were other things happening in her personal life. Her mother was diagnosed with ovarian cancer. She knew she was becoming more and more isolated from her friends and family. No one could help her. And this relentless case seemingly couldn't be resolved. She didn't like the fact that she wasn't able to stand up to what was happening. After much thought, though, she decided to stand down from the Daniel Morcombe Foundation committee in October. She was replaced by Gina Van Wezel, from the Bank of Queensland, and Tracey McAsey, a local businesswoman with vast event-management experience. But she left with a promise. 'If they ever find Daniel, I'll be there to get my hug,' Elliott said to Denise. A few months later, she left the police force to begin a new career as a marriage celebrant as well as conducting funeral services.

* * *

The annual Walk for Daniel, the opening event of the Day for Daniel, had averaged 525 walkers over three years since it began in 2005. By 2009, there was a 50 per cent increase in people participating. It was the walk that Daniel never made home. Symbolically, the walkers were completing the journey for him. Bruce's speech began, 'It is now 2155 days since Daniel was last seen just 100 metres from here.'

For the first time, every state had a school participating in the event. It was proof that the interstate visits were working well in tandem with the concentrated mail-outs. All the way across Australia, children united to embrace personal safety. Denise and Bruce stressed that 'the DFD', as it had become known, was not a memorial day but 'a day of action to educate children on how to keep safe'. They both believed that, by linking Daniel's very real story to safety messages, children would no longer be complacent, thinking 'This will never happen to me'. Everywhere the Morcombes went when they visited schools – in assembly halls and school playgrounds – they saw interested faces before them, absorbing those important life skills. More than 15,000 free copies of the

DVD *Foundation Red* had been handed out. The Foundation website had received more than a million hits in the past 12 months. This in itself was a remarkable achievement to end off the year.

They both got a sense of satisfaction from their work at the Foundation, however, Bruce never took his eye off the ball. On 6 November, as the year drew to a close, he made an impassioned plea to the state government for convicted child rapist Douglas Jackway to be jailed indefinitely. Bruce was aware from media reports that Jackway's release from jail for rape was imminent.

There had been more cloak-and-dagger activity with Daniel LeGrand again phoning Bruce around 20 October. This time, he was saying he had contact with someone in jail who knew Dooley and who had told him a whole lot of stories, including allegations that there had been a paedophile ring involving police and a priest. LeGrand had also told him that Daniel's body had been moved three times, which is why he had not been found. Bruce did not believe what LeGrand had been told. A journalist from *The Courier-Mail* then rang him and said he was going to do a story on LeGrand's allegations.

Mike Condon, now detective chief superintendent of State Crime Operations Command, had written to Bruce on 26 October saying there was some progress on the coronial report. The Homicide Investigation Unit had finished its part and the report had been forwarded to the Sunshine Coast for their investigators to add to it. He advised that the report would then be forwarded to the Coroner's office within two to three weeks. So followed a number of emails between Condon and Bruce, with Bruce continually requesting updates.

On 18 December, he reminded Condon:

> at the time of the 6th anniversary, Denise and I again
> supported the QPS [Queensland Police Service] efforts

publicly and over the entire journey in the media we have never stepped out of line with any negative comments, expressed our frustration at the lack of progress or identified information that was provided to us in confidence.

Two days later, Bruce went as far as suggesting that the delays in the police report to the Coroner were because it had identified some error in the investigation that was now being 'cleaned up'. 'If a stuff-up has been found, I would rather be told about it now than to find out months down the track.' Condon reacted angrily, saying that Bruce's comments about a 'stuff-up' were unfounded.

CHAPTER TWENTY

DIGGING DEEP

In the fractured life they led, the dark undercurrents threatened to swamp the Morcombes. Social media had played its part in the hunt for Daniel but with social media came the backlash. Early in 2010, one Facebook site started by a Brisbane student under the group categories 'Just for Fun' and 'Totally Pointless' began posting that they would give Daniel back if they gained one million followers. Denise was outraged, as was Bruce. She set about tracking down the administrator, who had buried his identity. She wanted to confront him about his actions. She began checking out the admin settings on the offending Facebook page. She found a name and checked the boy's Facebook profile, taking lists of several of the friends. They were reportedly boys who went to Caloundra High or Marist College, a Catholic boys' school in Ashgrove, Brisbane. She contacted the principals of both schools. A week later, she found out that the Caloundra High names were false but that the administrator attended Marist College and was in Grade 12.

When approached by the principal, Peter McLoughlin, the boy said he had done it as a joke. He was immediately suspended and was going to be expelled. He was also going to be charged by police and would have had a criminal record. The story leaked to the media and the bogus site was inundated by messages from the public furious at the boy's behaviour. McLoughlin apologised in an email to Denise, stating, 'I am shocked, dismayed and ashamed that you have had to endure this torment.'

Denise asked police to help her take the Facebook site down. They contacted Facebook but this took time and the damaging material was still online. Prime Minister Kevin Rudd joined the fracas, saying that following a number of these incidents he was considering appointing an online ombudsman to deal with Facebook pages that were defaced with pornographic and offensive comments. Eventually, the site was taken down. After a few weeks, Bruce and Denise asked Bob Atkinson to drop any charges against the boy. Instead, they emailed the boy's parents asking for an apology, which they received. Then they asked to meet him. One Saturday morning in March, the boy turned up with his mother at the Foundation office in Aerodrome Road. Denise made him sit down and watch a montage of photos of Daniel that they played at the dinner dance the week before. The boy was in tears and apologised. He told Denise he wanted to do law. Denise asked him to help promote the Day for Daniel at his school that year. She was pleased when, true to his word, he did.

There were other niggling things – the most important of which was the pending inquest. Bruce had already written to Condon early in the new year requesting an update on the police report to the Coroner. He emailed Condon again on 14 February 2010, his patience at breaking point:

> Am I getting the mushroom treatment or can you please
> tell me what's going on? Why have I heard nothing in

16 days? In less than three weeks I will be at a function with the Police Minister and Police Commissioner. I would have thought that some priority would have been given to supplying me with an update of the police report for the Coroner. We met with the State Coroner on 20 August last year. It will be six months since that meeting next week. We were led to believe the report was close to completion back then … Please give me more than 'certain matters are being looked at …'

Condon replied the next day saying that, 'as witnesses' in the inquest, there was a limitation as to what he could pass on. 'As Daniel's parents this will no doubt frustrate you,' he wrote. 'I constantly remind my staff and myself for that matter to walk in the shoes of yourself, Denise and your family … We remain committed to a resolution and will never give up on the belief that someone someday will give us the piece of the puzzles that we need to prosecute those responsible.'

* * *

The Dance for Daniel, now billed as the Red Tie Gala Dinner, was being recognised as the premier charity night on the Sunshine Coast. An event planner was used for the first time. Tracey McAsey, only days away from having her second child, worked tirelessly to make sure it was a night to remember. There was a Buddy Holly show and the auction items were the best ever, with holidays in France, flights to Hong Kong, tours to central Australia and accommodation at Sanctuary Cove and the Whitsundays. The Foundation auctioned a Don Bradman item and a Pat Rafter US Championship match racquet. Raffle prizes included a diamond pendant worth $5100, a Barack Obama-signed book, a U2-signed guitar and Buddy Holly memorabilia. Footage produced by Kay McGrath and her colleagues at

Channel Seven told stories of the child victims of crime who had been helped by the Foundation on the road to recovery.

Committed to focusing on the positive, Bruce and Denise often referred to two distinct periods in their lives: family life with Daniel and the time since. Their lives now bore no resemblance to that prior to December 2003. But, despite a whole range of negative thoughts, they had pledged to try to do something positive every single day. Speaking engagements were an important part of that. In April, Bruce and Denise addressed students at the Business Liaison Association's Grade 11 and Grade 12 Legal Students' Conference at the School of Law at the Cairns campus of James Cook University. Bruce was blunt. 'Let me continue by dispelling a myth,' he told the students. 'Television shows like *CSI*, *Cold Case*, *NCIS* and others are pure entertainment. They bear no slither of fact or resemblance to our experience. They are pure fantasy with an extremely simple storyline.' He could see the students were sitting up and taking notice. It was all part of getting their message across about child safety and the dangers of complacency.

On 16 April, Bruce received an email from Mike Condon confirming that the police report for the Coroner was being completed for the Coroner, 'who will now determine the way forward. It is likely he will write to you of his intentions'. Sure enough, later that month the police had finally handed over four large boxes to the Coroner, Michael Barnes. Accompanying the boxes was the covering report mentioned in Condon's email and two volumes of appendices. The police brief covered six and a half years of material, compiled during the last 16 months by Detective Sergeant Tracey Barnes and checked by Paul Schmidt. The boxes included electronic data. There were 10,000 pages of documents.

Meanwhile, there was a political scuffle when the then premier, Anna Bligh, changed the *Child Protection Act 1999* by adding a section banning the publication of information which may identify a child victim of crime. Bruce told the media he was opposed to this. He warned it had the potential to damage police investigations and it would severely restrict the ability of family members to harness the enormous community energy they had experienced first-hand.

'I think the impact is obvious in a case like Daniel, where it's been important for the public to be made aware of the circumstances and background of that case,' he said. 'I can only speak in Daniel's case, but I think it is the media's ability to galvanise public disgust at that particular type of crime that creates such huge momentum to ensure that the case is solved and is not forgotten.'

* * *

The coronial inquest was Bruce and Denise's first chance to gain an overview of the police investigation. Advised by Peter Boyce, they approached Michael Barnes to ask for permission to view the police report.

After receiving an invitation, Bruce and Denise visited the Coroner on 12 May at his brightly lit office in the Magistrates' Court complex. The room's furniture was cherry red, and there were abstract paintings on the wall. It was their second visit, but this time there was more at stake. Would he call an inquest? Senior counsel assisting the Coroner, Peter Johns, and Daniel Grice, were also present. As they sat down, Bruce and Denise noticed the boxes on the floor and on a nearby desk. Barnes gestured to the files, saying he had no problem about them having access to what was inside, with a few provisos. He confirmed at the same time that the inquest would go ahead. They both smiled in relief, thinking that the report looked extensive.

Michael Barnes was outspoken in his belief that Coroners should intervene during the early days of criminal investigations to prevent them becoming cold cases. So passionate was he about this coronial role, he was known in court circles as 'Cold Case Barnes'. He was well aware that after a crime had been committed, police were often busy working on other cases. A Coroner, however, and other lawyers could carefully examine every assumption and conclusion made. Coroners were hamstrung, though, if police did not choose to bring the cases to them and in this case it was the agitation of the parents that had brought the inquest to him. Only five per cent of all deaths ever reached the inquest stage in Queensland. Barnes had been appointed around the time that Daniel first went missing and, unwittingly, the Morcombes had found an ally in helping them unravel the lies and red herrings in the search for their son.

Barnes explained to the Morcombes procedural matters relating to the inquest. He said he had an issue releasing some of the material because it exposed the methods police used, as well as naming past sex offenders and informants, but that there may be a way around this. They talked generally about the POIs. Bruce explained he had driven all the way from the Sunshine Coast to Brisbane and back to see Dooley in court.

Barnes suggested that one way around sensitive information in the files was that addresses and contact details could be deleted from the report to protect witnesses' privacy. He also suggested that perhaps Bruce and Denise might come down to the police station to read the material and not take any of it away.

'Do we have a date for the inquest at all?' Bruce asked. 'So we can get prepared?'

'I think perhaps the first two weeks in October,' Barnes answered.

Bruce and Denise looked at each other. It was more than they had hoped for. Now they would have almost five months to read all the report documents and prepare targeted questions to be put before the Coroner's Court.

'I don't think Brad and Dean need to give evidence as their statements were clear and complete,' Barnes explained. 'And another thing ... I am concerned about the content in the report and the effect it might have on you.'

Turning the focus of the conversation away from themselves, Bruce added, in his usual analogous way: 'Well, we have 32 trees in front of us and we are shaking each one to see if something falls out. Odds on that working are small.'

'Yes,' Barnes replied. 'How we go about calling witnesses and divulging information and contacts is our biggest problem but we need to maintain a process that is strong and robust enough to find the truth.'

* * *

Four days after the meeting with the Coroner, on 16 May, they flew to Melbourne for the christening of Denise's niece and nephew, Mia and Jack. Denise was godmother to Jack. Around 30 family and friends attended. Everyone wanted news, but Bruce and Denise said nothing to anyone about the latest developments. Only Brad and Dean, long-time confidantes of their parents were told.

Denise, too, was becoming more outspoken about their futile wait for answers. Their trip to Melbourne had coincided with Law Week. The following day, they both addressed a group of boys enrolled in Legal Studies at the Salesian College. The schoolboys, who had been studying the case, sat there in stunned silence when Denise told them how police had no evidence as to who abducted Daniel. 'Has Daniel's abduction affected your faith?' one boy asked Bruce, who answered by saying they did not attend church as much as they used to but they were better people than before.

Then Bruce and Denise spoke to the students at the Mary Magdalen School in Chadstone. The message, as always, was to focus positive energy on a bad situation by keeping upbeat. They told the students they were like Daniel in that they were not looking for trouble. But, in Daniel's case, trouble found him. You might think, they said, 'That could have been me.'

* * *

On 25 May, Bruce and Denise were guests of Home Affairs Minister Brendan O'Connor at International Missing Persons Day in Canberra. The launch focused on parental abductors of children, particularly those taken across international borders. There had been more than 650 such cases in Australia in the previous year. Bruce and Denise met Australian Federal Police Commissioner Tony Negus at the launch. The Foundation had already donated funds for a return flight to Europe and $1000 cash to a man named Ken Thompson, who had been fighting for the return of his son in 2008. Ken had handwritten a 'thank you' card after receiving the funds and had proudly displayed the Foundation logo on his clothing.

Denise told the media it was the first time the Foundation had undertaken such a project. After receiving the funds from the Foundation, Mr Thompson cycled 6500 kilometres across Europe in search of the son he last saw in April 2008, when his mother took him overseas. Thompson's son was eventually found in Amsterdam after the police received a tip-off paving the way for their reunion. It was a euphoric ending to a two-and-a-half-year search.

* * *

The boxes from the Coroner's office arrived at the Morcombes' home in Palmwoods on 27 May. Denise immediately passed them to Peter Boyce, and his staff photocopied and numbered every page and divided the POIs into separate folders. 'Read it. Highlight areas of interest and stick-tag the pages,' Boyce told Denise. 'Have Bruce write a report once he has read the files and send it to me.' Denise hastily couriered three large boxes to Bruce, who decided to read them in the peace and quiet of their Tasmanian retreat, knowing that what he would find between these pages would torment him for years to come. He read for 16 to 18 hours a day, and it took him four to five days. He worked methodically through each POI, learning all sorts of new things he had known nothing about. He did not know about the blood being found in the sheets at the Sunshine Coast Motor Lodge around the time Daniel went missing, nor did he know of the many interviews police had conducted with POIs and associates, particularly with people such as Dooley and Smythe.

He took notes as he went, flagging things on the page and scribbling reminders to himself. It took all of Bruce's determination to keep reading. There were theories about how long Daniel had remained alive, how he had died and where his body lay, how he was restrained, the position he was in the rear of the van, illustrations of knots and even a suggestion that he had been assaulted after he was murdered. And the previous criminal history of the people involved made Bruce's stomach turn. Several names, phone numbers and addresses were blacked out.

Sometimes, he had to just walk away and look out to the ruffled waters of the D'Entrecasteaux Channel and Bruny Island in the distance, seeking reassurance that all life was not like the dark filth between these pages. He had never been exposed to such a depraved bunch. The POIs and associates were capable of anything. He had made a list of 86 questions in a ten-page-long email, which he forwarded to Peter Boyce and Peter Johns, assisting the Coroner, on 28 July. Jackway was his key POI but he also listed eight others, including Brett Cowan. Five of the questions he listed were specific to Cowan.

After Bruce returned home with the brief, Denise began reading but threw away the files in disgust. 'Sick,' she said to Bruce. 'It's absolutely disgusting.'

The first pages were filled with boast after boast of what various people had done to Daniel. The previous crimes committed on other victims by many of the POIs were horrifying.

* * *

On 25 June, given the growing interest in the impending inquest, the Foundation began its official Facebook page.

On 10 July, Bruce and Denise were completing filming for the revised version of the *Foundation Red* DVD, made possible by the Foundation's fundraising and a grant from the Australian Federal Police. The DVD was planned to be released to coincide with the start of National Child Protection Week and made available to order free of charge on the Daniel Morcombe Foundation website. They were talking to Jessica Watson, the 16-year-old who had sailed around the world single-handedly and who was doing a segment on the DVD about safe texting practices, when the call came through that the inquest date was set.

Bruce and Denise kept working on the DVD until all the new segments were finished. Then they went to their Maroochydore office to meet the media. The inquest was only two months away – to be held on 11 October. For the first time, Bruce publicly discussed his emotional reaction to the weighty police files:

We, as ordinary parents on the coast, were shocked at the prevalence and number of the predators not just on the Sunshine Coast but also right throughout society. You think your kids are safe until something like this happens, and then you just scrape away the fabric of society and you realise … the number of desperate people out there is quite shocking. And perhaps what some of these people get up to is equally shocking. I'm the father of Daniel and I'm really just trying to appeal to the person that may be responsible, or know who is responsible, that you would hate to sit where I am and see people lying to my face … that's the number one thing we're trying to get out of the case: what happened and where is Daniel?

Bruce told the assembled reporters, 'What Denise and I and the family want is to find where Daniel is, so we can lay the poor boy to rest as he deserves, but also to apprehend the offenders in this crime and see that they are punished.' He said that the family had given up hope of finding Daniel alive. 'You have to run with that decision perhaps as a comforting thought, as strange as it sounds. If he was held longer than six and a half years, you wonder, if he is dead, is that more peaceful than being locked in a dungeon and being abused? We're aware of some of the persons of interest … their criminal history, and it's not pleasant. We're really dealing with some terrible low-lifes. The family is bracing for the long legal path ahead, which could take years before a prosecution. There's a hell of a long way to go. We get up in the morning knowing that and go to bed knowing that.'

The new DVD officially launched a week later at the Australia Zoo, as part of Child Protection Week. The venue was especially fitting as it featured an appearance by Terri, Bindi and Bob Irwin, talking about personal safety.

* * *

Two days before the opening of the inquest, Bruce told *The Courier-Mail* that he was 'quietly confident' it would lead to the discovery of his son's remains. For the first time, they could more properly judge how police had handled the case. Bruce said that he and Denise had always held onto the hope that the investigation would one day provide the answers they so desperately wanted. 'We're trying to remain positive, I suppose, and always work cohesively with the police,' he said. 'Interview after interview and event after event, we always say we're a team.' The implication that this might not be entirely true hung in the air between them and the watching media.

PART FOUR

Closing the Net

CHAPTER TWENTY-ONE

THE INQUEST BEGINS

The State Coroner, Michael Barnes, had set down five days for the inquest and a further four days if necessary. The police brief contained a summary of 33 POIs, which included phone records, movements and criminal history for each of them. More than 20 witnesses were expected to appear out of the thousands of people already interviewed during the investigation so far. There were 17,840 job logs. Eighty-four eyewitnesses had seen Daniel the day he went missing, mostly on the busy Nambour Connection Road, and they had variously seen a blue car, a white van and one, two or more men near the Kiel Mountain Road overpass around the same time and on opposite sides of the road. Detective Sergeant Tracey Barnes had written a 71-page summary report, based on a 10,000 page police brief.

The Maroochydore Magistrate's Court was only a short distance from the entrance to the Sunshine Plaza, where Daniel had been heading that fateful day, and was next door to the Maroochydore Police Station.

When the rain came on 11 October – the first day of the inquest – Denise sensed Daniel's spirit in the skies. It was two months before the seventh anniversary of his disappearance, and there was finally going to be a public airing about the investigation into his whereabouts. She knew that it always rained when Daniel was angry or something big was going to happen.

On day one, Peter Johns, assisting the Coroner, outlined the case, which he described as 'the biggest investigation in police history'. Johns said that the purpose of the inquest was to find out if Daniel was dead, and if so, when, where and how Daniel died, as well as looking at the adequacy of the police response to Daniel's reported disappearance and the adequacy of the ongoing investigation, given that there had been 'some public criticism' about it. Johns also requested the Coroner ban publication of the names of any of the POIs because it would be 'grossly prejudicial' to name them. Barnes agreed he would do so when Johns raised them individually. It was agreed that the 33 POIs would be referred to by a code for each: POI1 to POI33. Peter Boyce had only been given the full list of POI codes that morning. Johns also told the court that 14 people, some of whom were associates of POIs, had been summonsed in 2007 to give evidence before the Crime and Misconduct Commission.

Barnes, addressing the Morcombes, said he was aware how distressing the proceedings would be for them and invited them to request a break if necessary.

The first witness was Bruce. Watched by Denise, Dean and Bradley, he retold those vital hours after Daniel's disappearance. He described the 'casual approach' taken by police when he and Denise had first reported Daniel missing and how they were told to go home about 7.30 pm on 7 December 2003 and wait for him. Bruce also explained how they had been told by a police officer that a missing person's report would not be filed until the following morning and that the officer had appeared confident that Daniel was going to turn up in spite of Bruce and Denise saying his disappearance was 'completely out of character'.

Bruce also told how he had visited the police station some years later with clothes that Daniel was said to have been wearing and some red material. Bruce recounted, 'I felt as though I was delivering something troublesome, that I was a nuisance.'

When Schmidt gave evidence, Boyce read out police policy requiring that a missing person's case be activated if there were concerns for the welfare of a person, or if it was out of character for them to be missing. 'If you interpret policy literally, Daniel ought to have been reported as a missing person. These are your rules, aren't they?'

'Yes, that is correct,' Schmidt said.

'And sometimes when officers don't follow these rules, they can be disciplined?'

'Yes,' Schmidt replied.

Schmidt had earlier told the court it appeared the officer who initially spoke with the Morcombes did not immediately file a missing person's report because there had not been sufficient information to elevate the case to this level.

During the second day of the inquest, Ross Edmonds, the bus driver who had failed to pick up Daniel, gave evidence. This was the first time Bruce and Denise had seen the man who was one of the last to see Daniel alive. Edmonds ignored both Bruce and Denise as he entered the court and steadfastly stuck to the fact that he'd been ordered not to stop. They had waited seven years to see him.

'It would have taken you no longer than 30 seconds to stop,' Boyce put to him.

'Exactly right, mate, but that's what I was told to do,' Edmonds replied.

Jeff Norman also gave evidence, saying that he had seen no one when he drove under the overpass a few minutes later in spite of being told someone was there. He told the court that Edmonds had been told not to pick up passengers but that he would not have been reprimanded if he had stopped to pick up Daniel as, in those days, there was no policy about picking up children waiting beside the road. Nowadays, the policy was for bus drivers to pick them up regardless of whether they had the fare.

Other witnesses repeated the accounts they had originally given to police of what they had seen that day. Schmidt had already told the court that the evidence given by passengers on the bus, in particular, was largely consistent, in that their accounts supported that there had been only one man under the bridge standing a number of metres behind Daniel, or leaning against the overpass structure, and there was no car nearby. Dozens of other witnesses both before and after the bus had passed reported seeing a blue car and one or two men near Daniel. Seven had reported seeing a white van.

By Wednesday, day three of the inquest, Peter Boyce turned up the heat. Given that the inquiry addressed the adequacy of the police investigation, Boyce took every opportunity to interrogate the police. Boyce asked them whether they had ever checked the phone records from the Sunbus company following Jeff Norman's evidence that a woman had called at 3.30 pm on the day Daniel went missing, sounding distressed, asking if a boy had been reported missing after not being picked up from the Woombye bus stop. She had not left her contact details. Boyce said it was abundantly clear that the police view that Denise had made the phone call was wrong, as she had not known Daniel was missing until some time later.

When Sergeant Tracey Barnes got into the witness box, she admitted that this was an oversight. Barnes confirmed that Daniel's case had been the 'largest investigation in Queensland history, involving losts of intel [intelligence] gathering]'. She confirmed she was the author of a 71-page report which gave an overview of the investigation and described how she had been with the Break and Enter Squad when she had received orders on 8 December 2003 to join the team investigating Daniel's disappearance. Initially involved as one of the investigators, on 1 March 2004, she was given the role of 'reader' in the MIR room, which involved reading all of the job logs from police investigators to see whether any further action was needed. Her role for six or seven years was to read the job logs, decide whether further action was required, then if further action was required, she would either assign it to the same investigator or a different officer. If she decided no action was needed, she would sign off the job log and it would be filed. Later, when questioned by Boyce, she agreed that decisions for re-investigation were solely her responsibility if she was the reader.

She admitted that she had also been involved as a reader from 8 December to 1 March but had not read all of the statements when she returned from leave. She said an exhibit officer had also been employed. Anything that needed forensic examination would be placed on the forensic register, which a regional forensic coordinator maintained. There was also a Scenes of Crime officer who supervised the collecting of evidence at the scene. She said a full set of Daniel's fingerprints had been compiled and that the National Automated Fingerprint Identification System had been used in the investigation. Sergeant Barnes told the inquest that data from 14 cell towers, which transmitted in the area of the abduction site, was downloaded and that close to 1600 calls had been made around the time Daniel was abducted. Barnes repeated that the buck stopped with whoever was appointed reader at Operation Vista as to whether an investigation was taken further. She said that Detective Senior Sergeant Schmidt was responsible for the overall strategy of the investigation. Asked whether she agreed that Daniel's case should have been referred to the

Homicide Investigation Unit as a 'cold case' investigation, as set out in a letter from Schmidt to the inspector in January 2010, she answered, 'I agree that the investigation should be the subject of a review.' She said she would not have read the letter recommending a cold case as she would not have had access to it.

She defended her decision and that of a colleague not to send off the clothes the Morcombes had brought to the police in 2006. 'There was no reason for it,' she said. 'The person who handed the clothes to the Morcombes had obtained them from someone who we believed had no credibility in relation to the information that she had been receiving.'

Barnes also defended the six-week gap on doorknocking around Eudlo Road, about ten kilometres south of Palmwoods, after a witness had come forward to Crime Stoppers on 20 April to say she'd seen a blue car being driven erratically on that street with a man in the back punching his fist into something under a white sheet. The witness had not been interviewed until a month later. 'It may have been a number of factors impacting on why that took so long to organise ...' Barnes responded, 'maybe a lack of resources situation, or investigators were involved in other matters that may have been given a higher priority.' She added that, on a daily basis, there were hundreds of pieces of information coming in ... it was a case of 'prioritising tasks'.

When questioned by Boyce, she said she had not really read the report from FBI Agent Beasley from the Behavioral Analysis Unit at Quantico as it was not part of her duties, nor did she do an overview of all of the POIs. Asked who took on that responsibility, Barnes replied, 'The investigators would come back to the briefing, we'd discuss interviews that (Ross) Hutton or someone else had with the POI and decide whether further investigation was required.'

On the fourth day of the inquest, there was a new face at the bar table. He introduced himself to the court as M. D.

Nicolson and said that he was the Queensland Police Service solicitor and that he was appearing for the commissioner. Boyce privately wondered whether Nicolson's presence was owing to his questioning about the adequacy of the investigation. If so, the case had become adversarial: it was the Queensland Police Service pitted against the Morcombes and their counsel whereas it was supposed to be an inquest into the death of a 13-year-old boy.

When Barnes was recalled to the witness box to continue her examination by Boyce, she was quizzed about how the photoboards worked during the investigation. She said she only knew of photoboards relating to Dooley, Meyer, Smythe and Jackway. Boyce asked her whether anyone reviewed whether new POIs had their photos put on photoboards. She answered 'not to my knowledge' and that she believed such a procedure would 'muddy the waters'.

Detective Senior Constable Ross Hutton was called on day five of the inquest. He told the court that he had been involved in the case since the day after Daniel went missing and had remained involved for a further five years. He outlined details of seven of the POIs who had been linked to having blue cars in the area. His role, he said, entailed attending to job logs and later compiling POI reports on individuals. Hutton said there were no specific guidelines as to who would become a POI.

He confirmed that Jackway was the first POI to come to police attention, having done so on 9 or 10 December 2003. Hutton had also been involved in the Jackway investigation, including being there for the first search warrant. The detective said that Danielle Richardson had volunteered as the interview progressed, on 9 January 2004, that Jackway had 'probably done it' but, at that time, she had told police that he had only been absent for an hour and a half on the day Daniel went missing, which Hutton said would not provide enough time for him to have committed the crime. He said that Richardson had admitted she had later changed her account of how long he had been away from the house.

Boyce raised the issue of Jackway being interviewed in front of Stephen Park, about his whereabouts the day Daniel went missing. Hutton responded that police had gone in with 'a relaxed manner', without conducting a formal interview, so they could obtain information.

Outside the court, Bruce said he and Denise did not hold a grudge against the Queensland Police Service and were satisfied that the hearing was uncovering potentially crucial avenues for investigation. 'We're getting closer,' he said. 'We're chiselling away, and I'm sure what's been revealed today and over the preceding days is a clue that there's more information than perhaps some of the associates [of the persons of interest] would be aware of.'

When the inquest reconvened ten days later, on 25 October, another solicitor had appeared at the bar table, Mr C. R. Gnech from the Queensland Police Union, advising the court that he was representing Sergeant Munn and Senior Constable Paul Campbell, the first two police officers Bruce spoke with on 7 December 2003. It was yet another example, Bruce thought, of how embattled the police felt.

Sergeant Munn told the inquest that he did not consider that Daniel fitted the police definition of a 'missing person'. However, he had agreed to broadcast the details to all police units on the Sunshine Coast, asking them to be on the lookout for the teenager. 'The thinking was, when I was speaking to the Morcombes, it was still daylight, or twilight … there had been no set time for him to be home [and] he was nearly 14 years of age,' Sergeant Munn said. 'In my opinion, there was nothing that the Morcombes had provided to me, information-wise, to give me any fears for his safety or concerns about his welfare, which is the judgement I have to make to proceed it to a more formal investigation.'

Operation Golf Avalon had taken 18 months to review the case against Jackway. Detective Macindoe was one of six detectives from the Homicide Investigation Unit asked to investigate, and she told the inquest that she had looked at it with 'fresh eyes', as she had no previous involvement with the case. She agreed that the 'bookend' phone calls made between Jackway's and Carrington's houses at 12.29 pm and 3.33 pm, if true, meant that Jackway would not have had time to abduct and murder Daniel. Macindoe said, however, that Park consistently claimed that he had called Carrington from Jackway's house in Bertha Street, Goodna, at 12.33 pm to ask for money and that Jackway wasn't there. Macindoe agreed that, apart from the phone calls, there was no evidence that tied Jackway to being in Goodna between 11 am and 4.30 pm and Carrington had said that both Richardson and Jackway would call him from the house in Bertha Street so Jackway may not have made the calls.

Macindoe confirmed that, in his final version, Park said he had not been with Jackway for most of the day and that, when Richardson was further questioned, she acknowledged that Jackway had been missing for up to three hours.

Questioned by Johns, Macindoe confirmed that covert strategies had been in place for Jackway and that it was always intended he would be reinterviewed, but that the date had been brought forward because of the publicity from the *Sunday Night* program. She had four days to prepare an interview plan, after the advertisements for the upcoming show were being aired.

She added that she did not think Jackway was capable of telling the truth 'even to simple questions' and that he would often give three or four different answers to one question. She also agreed with Michael Barnes that there was evidence that four or perhaps five people had been pressured by Jackway to give false alibis. However, Macindoe also agreed there was nothing to connect Jackway with being on the Sunshine Coast when Daniel disappeared.

'But there are a number of circumstantial matters, aren't there?' said Johns.

'Yes.'

'That would lead you to a great deal of suspicion about what he in fact did on that day, 7 December?'

'That's right. What he was doing and who he was with and where he was.'

She said that Carrington was the most consistent alibi and that, when unknowingly under surveillance, he had helped Park to go over what he remembered. She agreed with Boyce that there were several times when Jackway wasn't happy while being interviewed by her and that he had asked her to leave at one point. Jackway had also told her he was punched on the nose by a fellow inmate over his alleged involvement in the Morcombe case, and she had later confirmed that this was true.

Macindoe also said that she had checked whether any of the POIs had been associates of Jackway's and that she had specifically worked on Dooley and established there was a connection. She said the review team had not been provided with any material on Jackway's associates. Instead, they had gained information by going through his jail records, as well as previous addresses.

Cross-examined by Nicolson, Macindoe said that they had not sought to get DNA from the letter sent to Jackway in jail because the procedure used to test the letter for fingerprints had destroyed the chances of obtaining it. Bruce had always believed that Jackway was the number-one suspect for abducting his son. He had also worked out that Cowan, Dooley, Meyer and Jackway had all made reference to going to a female drug dealer on the Sunshine Coast the day Daniel disappeared, and he had passed this insight on to Peter Boyce.

Newspaper headlines on day six of the inquest screamed that the Queensland Police Assistant Commissioner would be called to give evidence. This meant there had been an escalation of the handling of the case to the highest levels within the force. Other media reports noted that there had been 100 calls to Crime Stoppers following the inquest being opened.

After establishing that Denise did not ring Sunbus at 3.30 pm, records of calls made to the Sunbus office in Maroochydore on the day Daniel disappeared were finally checked, revealing three incoming numbers an hour either side of the time nominated by Jeff Norman from Sunbus as when the call came through. The first had been from a private landline, the second was from a motel in Noosa and the third was from a mobile phone. There was no further insight into who might have made the call that day. The first number was excluded by police; one of the six people staying at the motel confirmed she may have rung Sunbus; and the owner of the mobile phone said he may have rung Sunbus by mistake as he was attempting to reach another bus company to take him to the airport.

Detective Ross Hutton was back on the stand again, setting out Dooley's many versions of his alleged involvement in Daniel's abduction. Hutton said that, after Dooley led four detectives to the Beerburrum State Forest and down a series of bush tracks to where Daniel was supposed to be buried, he later admitted to lying about the location because he feared that he would be charged. Hutton said it had been extremely difficult to ascertain Dooley and Meyer's movements on the day Daniel disappeared because they had regular use of mobile phones that were registered in false names and they had provided police with so many different versions.

On 28 October, Detective Sergeant Mark Wright took the stand, and went through how Brett Cowan had come to the attention of Operation Vista and outlined the versions Cowan had given of his movements that day. When questioned, Wright said one of the sketches of Cowan had been only 'vaguely similar' to him. Asked by Nicolson whether there had been 'every effort' put into investigating whether Cowan was involved, Wright answered, 'That's correct.'

Boyce quizzed Wright about the forensic tests of Cowan's car. 'Police attended Clayton's towtruck company and located Cowan's car, took digital images of it and the tyre tread?'

'Yes.' Wright went on to say that he'd never seen the forensic report.

'Now, is it fair to say from your report that there's more factors that exclude Cowan than include him?' questioned Nicolson.

Wright answered, 'Yes.'

Detective Senior Constable Glenn Elliott went through a similar process over Alise Smythe's involvement in the investigation. Elliott described her recollections as 'very much drug affected'.

On 28 October, the day the inquest was due to be adjourned, Mr Johns presented a list of POIs whom he believed should be called to give evidence. He nominated Dooley but not Meyer, nor Smythe, nor some of the others who had already given evidence at the Crime and Misconduct Commission in 2007. He nominated Jackway to be interviewed, along with his associates. He suggested a skilled counsel was needed to question Jackway. He also suggested Cowan be called. 'Of all the persons on the list he is the only one in my submission, we can say with some confidence, was definitely at the scene of Daniel's disappearance ...' Johns also pointed out that Cowan had not been required to give evidence so far under oath. He then named other POIs – POI32 and POI33 – who had nominated themselves as being involved in Daniel's kidnapping.

Boyce called for Dooley's associates to be summonsed. He submitted that this meant ten POIs in total should be called to give evidence. 'If we don't call relevant persons of interest, in my submission that's really only doing half the job that needs to be done in this process. And from my clients' point of view – and that's the whole of the family – they have a keen interest, your Honour, in making sure that they have, for the very first time, the opportunity to hear the evidence come from those persons of interest who we've spoken so long about and to make sure that the whole process is open. And they have a real interest in making sure that those persons of interest who made admissions against their interest, that they're here as well.' Boyce went on to tell the inquest that, 'POI5 [Jackway] heightens my clients' interest immensely'. He submitted that all of Jackway's associates be called. Boyce also asked for POI6 and POI7 (Cowan) to be called so the Morcombes could be 'satisfied' that Cowan was telling the truth. He should also be interrogated as to what else he saw when he drove past the overpass that day, Boyce said.

But no one was prepared for what Nicolson had to say when he got to his feet. He submitted that no POIs should be called at all. He queried the forensic purpose of calling the POIs and 'whether this examination of these persons of interest are likely to assist – in addressing the issues subject to the inquest'. Nicolson questioned whether the POIs would give 'credible' or 'reliable' evidence to assist with the inquest. Working through the individuals, he argued that Jackway had already been the subject of an extensive review and that many of the others had already given evidence to the Crime and Misconduct Commission, which had the same powers as the Coroner's Court to enforce witnesses to tell the truth.

When Nicolson resumed his seat at the bar table, Bruce was still processing this shock recommendation from Nicolson. He could hardly believe it. Boyce, too, was dumbfounded by the submission. Denise, Dean and Brad couldn't believe what they heard. Later, Bruce made an appointment with the Police Commissioner about their concerns.

Michael Barnes indicated that he had issues with the security available at the Maroochydore court if the POIs were called to give evidence and suggested, instead, the hearing be moved to the Magistrates' Court at 363 George Street in Brisbane's CBD.

* * *

On 29 October, the Day for Daniel provided a distraction from the gruelling days in the courtroom. More than a thousand schools and businesses registered, with 500,000 schoolchildren participating across the country. Bruce told the media, 'We estimate that perhaps that's half a million school-age children who are now safer when they get home today than when they left to go to school, and that's a really positive thing.'

Federal parliamentarians also joined in, urged on by the Honourable Peter Slipper MP, who addressed parliament on the matter. Parliament was a sea of red on the Day for Daniel, as politicians wore the colour to show their support, including then Prime Minister Julia Gillard and then Opposition Leader Tony Abbott. Even the small mining towns of Collinsville and Scottville, 90 kilometres west of Bowen, 'painted the town red', and Collinsville had a school disco.

On the annual Walk for Daniel, Denise's father, 79-year-old Kevin Beavis, tore through the banner to begin the walk. He and Monique had flown up for the Day for Daniel and attended the walk on the Sunshine Coast. There was a record crowd of 1000 people, and Kay McGrath arrived in the Channel Seven chopper.

In the last newsletter of the year, Denise published a letter of thanks from a parent who described how her nine-year-old boy had walked to the corner store, about 300 steps from their home, and was waiting for his brothers outside the shop when a man pulled up and asked him to get in his car. The boy had stepped back immediately and later said that he remembered hearing about this from a talk about Daniel Morcombe.

This reverberated especially with the Morcombes because they had already begun thinking of a signal that children might use to alert passers-by that they were in urgent need of help. Bruce and Denise had discovered there was no such signal in use anywhere in the world. Many of the witnesses in Daniel's case had said they might have stopped but were not sure whether Daniel was in danger or not. 'At the end of the day, you have to have a simple sign, but a sign that is not mistreated or abused or perhaps confused with something else,' Bruce said. 'Upon reflection, when Danny was raising the stick in his hand to hail that bus that didn't stop, was he in fact trying to hail the bus, or was he saying, "Help! Please pick me up. There's a dude behind me about to grab me."'

* * *

On 3 November 2010, Denise turned 50. Bruce had organised a surprise: a penthouse in Mooloolaba. He drove her to the unit. 'We're going to have a look at it,' he said.

Denise knew Bruce's hobby was looking at real estate. She reluctantly went upstairs. Inside, he turned to her: 'I've booked it for three nights and your parents should be here soon.'

It was the surprise that Bruce had hoped it would be.

Over the next three days, Bruce had old friends of Denise's around for dinner: Denice, Debbie and Chris, her friends since 1994. Bruce's brothers and sister also visited. They had met these friends when their children had been in pre-school together, and had been the closest of friends before Daniel went missing. In recent years, they'd seen less of each other, so this reunion made for a wonderful night. The conversation flowed just like old times.

The following day, Peter Boyce drove Bruce and Denise to Roma Street for a meeting with Bob Atkinson. They wanted a review by the Homicide Investigation Unit of all of the POIs who had not appeared before the Crime and Misconduct Commission or had a review done previously.

* * *

Michael Barnes had rejected the submission from the Police Commissioner's representative that no POIs be called. He announced that six of them would be giving evidence when the inquest reconvened in December. 'In my experience, the forensic process whereby a number of competent counsel contemporaneously engage with the issues and the witnesses almost always results in new evidence coming to light,' Mr Barnes said, adding that three of the six were in custody for 'heinous crimes'.

The following week, it was confirmed that some of the top criminal barristers in Brisbane would help to question them. Bruce welcomed the move to 'go all out with the best legal minds' now that the inquest had reached its most critical stage. 'These are difficult characters to deal with and we knew that specialist people would be needed to question them … to unsettle them,' he said.

* * *

As if there wasn't enough going on, Bruce and Denise were told on 1 December that the landlord at the Foundation's premises in Aerodrome Road intended increasing the rent from $25,000 per annum to $32,000. Given the financial climate and the number of empty shops and offices in the area, they felt this was unreasonable. While searching the internet, they came across an investment property that they had owned about six years previously. It was the two-storey, metal-clad, imitation-weatherboard house in Amaroo Street, Maroochydore, right next to the Sunshine Plaza.

Underneath was an area ideal for storage. Upstairs were two air-conditioned rooms. At the back was a small kitchen and bathroom. Denise immediately arranged for an inspection.

Being a corner allotment, the house had rear access to a gravel car park, but the best feature was its prominent location at the entrance to the Sunshine Plaza shopping centre and all the big stores. The neat box hedges that surrounded the property and gave it such a distinctive feel had been planted by Bruce. The place seemed just right. The Morcombes had even organised all of the electrical wiring and knew where all the power points were. The premises also had the capacity to allow for the Foundation to grow. They signed a two-year lease immediately.

* * *

Brad and Anna had been dating for a year. Anna had been a year below Dean at Siena Catholic College and a year above Bradley and Daniel, and knew both of them. They had met at the Sands Tavern in Maroochydore. Anna was working at the homewares store, Spotlight. The weekend before the inquest reconvened, Anna threw a surprise party for Brad's 21st birthday. They celebrated early so that guests could focus on the festivities and not the pages and pages of media coverage of the inquest which were bound to come in the week ahead. In a continuing downpour of rain that had started around mid-afternoon, 50 guests turned up to the back patio of the Morcombes' house. Brad, who had grown his hair long since he was 19, would cut it short the following week. The band Dean was in, Ablaze Withsin, played live music. At 8.30 pm, Bruce gave a speech thanking everyone for coming, but especially thanking Brad's friends for supporting him for so many years. Everyone knew in their hearts that there should have been a double 21st that night, but nobody needed to say it.

Bruce and Denise had commissioned a painting for Brad's present. It depicted an aquarium with five Mexican fighting fish, representing the five members of their family. At the bottom of the tank were 21 pebbles and, through the aquatic vegetation, in a subtle image reminiscent of Bradley and Daniel's shared hobby, two sets of eyes looked back at the viewer from the other side of the aquarium. Brad loved the painting.

* * *

There was continuing media attention after the revelations at the inquest. In a large feature in *The Courier-Mail*, Denise said, 'I've always said the day we find Daniel is the day we can start to grieve.'

'Even if they're telling lies, I hate them for [that] and destroying our family [again],' Denise added. 'Hurting the boys, hurting Bruce, hurting everyone.' Yet the deepest ache, she said, was long ago planted by the most monstrous unknown: the space between Daniel's kidnapping and presumed death. 'What the hell did Daniel go through?' she asked.

Bruce, in his disarmingly frank style, added, 'If he was grabbed and put in a vehicle, what would he be thinking? You put yourself in that position. It would be terrifying.' He said they had heard so many versions of how he had died: 'He was shot, he was strangled, he was hit with an iron bar, there was a heroin shot – an overdose. But to kill the lad, all we've ever said is, "I wish it was quick." If he's gone through three, five, even seven days of physical rapes and torture … and … was he fed? You know, it's just disgusting. The time between abduction and death is worse than the actual death.'

Bruce said he remained quietly confident of a significant breakthrough. 'We know this is an ongoing filtering process,' he said.

* * *

When the inquest reconvened on 13 December, it was at the Brisbane court complex. This time, there was another senior counsel appearing for the Police Commissioner: a man called A. J. MacSporran. Without much ado, Bill Dooley was called to the witness box. He entered via a side door to the court and sat in the glassed-off box wearing a suit and reading glasses. To Bruce and Denise, he looked the picture of health. Craig Chowdhury was also new. He was engaged as counsel assisting the Coroner in addition to Peter Johns. He immediately began a combative line of questioning, pouncing on any of Dooley's denials. When Dooley admitted he had not seen Daniel in Merthyr Road in New Farm, an inner-city suburb of Brisbane, on 10 December 2003, Chowdhury asked, 'Why did you say that to Mr Morcombe?'

'Look, I had no idea of the repercussions that the whole thing would cause … I coloured the picture. I had no idea that police would put me in front of Bruce Morcombe. I had no idea that would occur.'

'Did you think, "I'd better come clean and say, 'Look, mate, I've been taking the police for a ride'?"'

'Absolutely,' Dooley answered.

'So why then did you say to this poor man who's lost his boy, "I've actually seen your boy in Merthyr Road"? Why on earth would you say that to him?'

'I don't know.'

In between the questions, the court replayed the tape of the conversation between Bruce and Dooley in 2004. At the point where Dooley said there was a difference between a 'junkie' and a heroin addict, because a junkie would have no morals, Chowdhury asked Dooley: 'What, do you have morals do you?'

Dooley responded, 'Here we go.' Later, he added, 'Certain morals.'

Dooley's version of Rogers's death was that it wasn't murder. He was matter of fact. 'When he died in that car, I didn't know what to do. I panicked, right? And being a career criminal, if you like to put it that way, I certainly wasn't going to the coppers and say, "Listen, old mate's just carked it in the car", so of course I dumped him.'

Dooley told the court that the real murderer of Daniel would give evidence later in the week and that he was a fellow inmate at the Wolston Correctional Centre who was also a POI in the case. Dooley said the man would tell the 'chilling story about how he abducted, raped and murdered 13-year-old Daniel'. He said that this time he was telling the truth.

POI33, alluded to by Dooley, had, in fact, given a 'disturbingly detailed account' to police of what had happened to Daniel. POI33 said that his 'older male lover' (POI32) had snatched Daniel from a bus stop and sexually assaulted him. Over the years, he admitted his own involvement and he said they had both dumped Daniel's body in the Brisbane River. But by the end of the first week of the reconvened inquest, POI33 had his confession picked apart as being full of 'inconsistencies and lies'.

That afternoon, Alexander Meyer took the stand. He told the court he was employed as a removalist. He denied he had anything to do with Daniel's abduction but admitted to knowing Bill Dooley, saying he had only met him after Daniel went missing. He admitted to using heroin regularly around the time Daniel disappeared and confirmed there was a downstairs room in the house in Windsor that had no windows and was built of besa bricks and could be deadlocked, but denied the room was called a 'dungeon', although he confirmed that his brother called it that. He also admitted that he had 'slapped' his girlfriend around and that they had used that room as their bedroom. Meyer also said he found credit cards, some belonging to Donald Rogers, at the house but denied ever having met Rogers. He also said there was no truth in Dooley's stories that he had disposed of Daniel's body and denied telling Alise Smythe that he wanted to carry out a 'thrill kill'. 'I'm not a murderer, sir,' he told MacSporran in cross-examination.

After listening to more stories, Bruce described them as 'disgusting human beings'. He said that the week's evidence 'demonstrated how difficult the many accounts made it for police over the last seven years'.

* * *

On the seventh anniversary of Daniel's disappearance, seven helium balloons were placed under the Kiel Mountain Road overpass. Each balloon had a note attached from Bruce and Denise to remind Daniel he had not been forgotten. The location was adorned with red flowers and a plaque featuring a poem.

Bruce said that the anniversary remained as hard to endure as it was when he first went missing. 'It's not so much easier [with time], especially with the coronial coming around,' he said.

Just prior to Christmas, Bruce and Denise moved the Daniel Morcombe Foundation office to the new premises in Amaroo Street, Maroochydore. One of their keen volunteers, Charlie Wetere, and his daughter assisted with a truck and van to move the furniture and stock.

Bruce, Denise, Dean and Bradley spent Christmas Day with Bruce's family at Scott and Shelly's house, along with their cousins.

On Boxing Day, Bruce flew to Tasmania, as he wanted time to read more files for the reconvening of the inquest, specifically relating to the six POIs being called. Denise stayed home at Palmwoods. She was getting accustomed to being alone for weeks on end while Bruce read the police brief.

Another year was drawing to a close.

CHAPTER TWENTY-TWO

HORRID CREATURES

The cyclone season in Queensland traditionally runs between November and April each year, when the lows build up within the monsoon trough. From January 2011, it was clear that there would be a tumultuous start to the new year, with rain falling steadily across the state and no signs of it abating. February was to bring Cyclone Yasi, a Category 5, the worst of the cyclones, with winds of up to 290 kilometres per hour. It hit 1596 kilometres north of Brisbane, crossing the coastline at Mission Beach and causing massive devastation.

In early January, the Foundation office flooded downstairs. A lot of stock was ruined. Denise worked hard to move the boxes onto shelves. Brad and Dean joined in with mops and buckets to clean up the mess. Bruce was still in Tasmania.

More than seven years after Daniel had gone missing, on 20 January, Mike Condon, now Assistant Commissioner, pulled in between 30 and 40 detectives from across the State Crime Operations Command to sift through 5000 job logs in the investigation. Addressing the media, Bruce suggested the review might have happened because of a November meeting with the Police Commissioner, Bob Atkinson. 'We raised some concerns about the investigation as well as some suggestions and they were taken in good faith,' he said. 'Certainly, what we were interested in was Daniel's case not becoming a cold case without a serious review of all of the high-priority job logs.'

Asked about the resumption of the inquest, Bruce said, 'We've got two very ugly and suspicious people that are being called. We just need to load up every piece of weaponry we've got to fire very specific questions.

'It might just have to do with a timeline, a movement, a car or something that didn't come to light earlier ... Or let's just hope they find that one mobile number that holds a clue and bingo.'

In January, all of the Morcombes had been shown a photo of Brett Cowan by Detective Grant Linwood and asked whether they knew him. Denise wondered whether Cowan, being a sandblaster, was known to Kelvin Kruger, who had the steel-fabrication and sandblasting businesses on Nicklin Road, Palmwoods, where the boys would ride their motorbikes. Linwood made notes. It was never too late to review the facts. Denise had, after all, included in her statement of 8 December 2003 the information that the boys rode their bikes at Kruger's.

* * *

On 9 March, the Morcombes read the newspaper headlines with a sense of dread. A 13-year-old boy, Declan Crouch, had gone missing without trace from his home in Cairns. The boy had returned from school to his home in the northern suburb of Machans Beach. He had left his school uniform and bag in his room and then vanished. A week later, in a sinister déjà vu of when Daniel had disappeared, a mannequin was placed near Declan's house, and SES volunteers began searching bushland looking for any signs of the missing boy. Two weeks later, the case became the biggest missing persons investigation since Daniel's disappearance.

Bruce told the media, 'It's not a pleasant club we belong to, but if we all stick together, we can perhaps help each other through.'

There were regular updates in the news during the search for Declan that continued to haunt the Morcombes. By the end of March, there were reportedly 130 sightings of him.

* * *

The Foundation's sixth annual dinner-dance fundraiser took place on 19 March, with more than $65,000 raised from the auction and raffles. Three hundred people attended in what was to be a landmark charity event for the Sunshine Coast. After marking the latest achievements of the Foundation, including noting that more than 3000 copies of the revised *Foundation Red* DVD were delivered to schools free of charge, Bruce and Denise showed a collage of headlines from the inquest.

On 21 March, Bruce and Denise, with committee member Brett Winkler, conducted trials at schools to evaluate their distress signal for children. They had been considering two options. Option A, 'Daniel's signal', was a lower-case 'd' made by the right arm vertically stretched and the left arm kinked at the elbow above the head. To show urgency, the palm at the top of the 'd' opened and closed in a blinking fashion. 'Daniel's cross' involved the arms stretching above the head and forming a cross at the wrists, and again the hands blinking, opening and closing. They chose the cross and registered it as a trademark before having it reviewed at Griffith University. 'Daniel was in some sort of distress and, if people had known that, maybe they would have stopped or taken more notice of what was happening,' Denise told the media service Australian Associated Press.

Bruce added, 'They're both simple for a child or person in distress to use and recognisable for passers-by and not confused with a child waving to a friend or stretching arms.'

* * *

When the inquest resumed on 28 March, Danielle Richardson admitted to the court that she had lied to police for five years about the whereabouts of Douglas Jackway on the day Daniel went missing. She said that, after a fight, Jackway had left the house in the morning and had not returned for 'a long time'. She had lied because she both loved and feared him.

Park, too, two days later, admitted he had withheld information because Jackway had threatened to 'smash him' and his family. After stepping down from the witness box, Park walked across to where Denise, Bruce, Dean and Bradley were sitting. 'Man, I'm sorry I couldn't help more,' he said.

Each day, Bruce pored over the evidence, meticulously noting a list of questions for Peter Boyce, who too had done countless hours of preparation, to put to upcoming witnesses.

Behind the scenes, police too were busy. A plan was being hatched. One of the detectives, Grant Linwood, had an idea and it was targeted at one particular POI: Brett Peter Cowan.

On 30 March, day 17 of the inquest, Jackway gave evidence. He was a stocky, heavy-set, powerful man with almost shaved blond hair and an attitude that seemed bitter and angry as he began his evidence. To Bruce and Denise, he seemed more than capable of having carried out some of the horrific acts he was said to have committed. Most of all, they wanted to know whether he had done something to their son.

His evidence lasted most of the day. He confirmed he had grown up on the Sunshine Coast and had been at Tewantin

Primary School before attending Noosa District State High School but had been expelled. After going through his early history, Jackway told Peter Johns that he had two tattoos on his left calf. One said 'hectic' and the other said 'hatred', which he said was jail slang.

Johns took him through his earlier offences. Jackway told the court that he had taken heroin before the Gladstone offence in 1995. Questioned about his alibis on the day Daniel went missing, he confirmed that he knew Stephen Park, denying that they had a father–son relationship but stating they were 'just friends'. He said he had met Carrington at Woodford Correctional Centre and that he had called him soon after he got out of jail in November 2003. Carrington had come around for Jackway's birthday and he said that it was on this occasion that Park had met Carrington. Jackway claimed he had two mobile phones but that neither of them had SIM cards. One of them had been in the glove box of his car.

Jackway gave details of how he had got into a chase with police shortly after getting out of jail for the Gladstone offence after being intoxicated and getting asked to move on by a security guard in Hastings Street, Noosa. After paying Clayton's Towing Service $225 for the impoundment, he had gone to pick up his impounded car from Avian Street, Kunda Park, and had borrowed a jack from the Rebel Motorcycle clubhouse opposite. It had been raining heavily. He said he had cleaned his car thoroughly because there were prawns all through it after he recovered it from the yard, as there had been a bucket for bait left on the back seat.

Johns took Jackway through the events of 7 December 2003. Jackway said that Danielle Richardson had arrived home early on Sunday morning with a man called Stuart and that he suspected she was cheating on him. He said he had followed this man in his car up the motorway with a fishing knife and that he threatened to kill him. When he saw the man using his mobile phone, though, he had been concerned he was ringing the cops, so he had made a U-turn and gone back to Bertha Street. He confirmed Vince Tournoff had come around later that morning, but said that Tournoff had told him that Danielle Richardson was no good for him. Jackway agreed he often shoplifted from Supacheap Autos, listing all of the items he'd stolen, including skull knobs, a wooden racing steering wheel and a stereo, as well as nine lanterns from another shop. He said he and Stephen Park had gone to Carrington's place twice on the day Daniel went missing and that later he had gone to a park near the boat ramp at Goodna for two hours and spoken to Danielle Richardson about their relationship. He said he had then slept at Bertha Street and had left early the next morning, on 8 December, for court. He said he could not recall exactly when he had gone to Park's parents' house but agreed it might have been Sunday.

Questioned by Johns, Jackway said he did not accept Carrington's version that he had only called in to see him once that day, late in the afternoon, even though in his earlier statement on 16 December 2003, Jackway had initially said he only went there once in the late afternoon. He said he used to give Carrington his dad's watch as security when he borrowed money from him. His dad had died in 1999. When questioned by Johns, Jackway said that it was Danielle Richardson who had made the phone call at 3.33 pm from Bertha Street on the Sunday Daniel went missing. He later acknowledged that this phone call was the crucial call to confirm that Jackway was in Goodna soon after Daniel was abducted. He said he would have been at Carrington's house at that time.

Winding up his questions, Johns said, 'You know that during these hours where you've given us a version but Stephen and Danielle say that they can't place you and Paul can't place you, so, during these hours, you're driving an early-model blue sedan?'

'Yeah.'

'[Do you know] from media reports that there is a large amount of evidence that an early-model blue sedan was seen very close to Daniel Morcombe?'

'Yes.'

'When he was abducted?'

'Yeah.'

'There is good eyewitness accounts from at least one of the people who saw a male person standing near Daniel that that person had a tattoo on their inside left leg?'

'Yeah.'

Johns quizzed Jackway about the timing of him turning up the day after Daniel went missing and his car breaking down near the abduction site. 'I'd suggest you are one of the very few people out of jail at that stage who have shown the capability and the inclination to snatch a young boy from a very public area in daylight. Do you accept that there's not too many people getting around who have a history for that?' Johns asked him. He later added, 'You are one of those few people. We'll hear from another one tomorrow ... it's surprisingly common that – when these crimes happen, the person that commits the crime returns to the scene of either the kidnapping or murder ... and, of course, on your own evidence, the following morning you've managed to find yourself hundreds of metres at most from the scene of Daniel's kidnapping ...'

Further questioned by MacSporran for the Queensland Police Service, Jackway said he could not recall whether he made any phone calls to Carrington the day Daniel disappeared or not. When Boyce got up to cross-examine him, Boyce asked what time Jackway had left the house in Goodna on 8 December to drive north for his court appearance. Jackway said it would have been about 7 am and denied that it was any earlier in spite of the CCTV footage at the BP petrol station in Goodna capturing images of him and Park at around 5 am.

Boyce questioned Jackway about only having mobile phones that had no SIM cards. Jackway admitted that he told police that he had one mobile phone but that the credit had run out, and he said that was a lie. He said he had met Bill Dooley while at Wolston Correctional Centre. Dooley was an 'inter-jail bookie' and Jackway had asked him to place a bet on the horses.

Boyce suggested Jackway had lied when telling police about his whereabouts.

'Yeah.'

Boyce said to him bluntly, 'You've told many lies.'

'Yeah.'

'... there's just no explanation for your lies, is there?'

'No.'

The next morning, 31 March, Sandy Drummond, Brett Cowan's professed drug dealer whom Cowan had claimed had seen him the day Daniel disappeared, gave evidence. Drummond said that she had first met Cowan at her daughter's flat when he was selling fireworks. She told the court that she could no longer be sure that she had seen Cowan on 7 December 2003. She said Cowan had rung her after police had visited her, asking questions about dropping in that day. She had asked him why he had told police that he had dropped in. He had told her he was coming to see her but she had never seen him again after that.

Brett Peter Cowan, POI7, was then called. Unlike Jackway, Cowan entered the court through the normal public door, causing a stir in the public gallery. His long hair was worn loose down his back and he had a long-sleeved shirt on his lanky body, light-blue jeans, white runners and white socks. He had a strangely disquieting presence, speaking softly, seemingly unperturbed by being under public scrutiny, his manner playing down the consequences of why he was there. Before he had even entered the room, Denise had felt a shiver run down her spine. He sat in the witness box and stared at the Morcombes with a smirk on his face. Denise turned to Bruce and said, 'Oh my god, it's him.'

Cowan told the court that he now lived in Western Australia and that he had three sons. His youngest son had been taken by the Department of Corrective Services as the boy's mother had married again and moved to America. That son was now living with Cowan's elder brother and his wife, who were his 'kinship carers'. Cowan said it was better for his son that he did not live in the same state. Cowan was frank about his past. He said he had started molesting small children at a local swimming pool when he was still in primary school. He told the court he completed two courses for sexual offenders while in jail. The court was told that a psychologist had described POI7's defence strategy as 'denial and minimisation' when confronted by anything. The inquest heard that POI7's previous sexual offences had been 'unplanned and on impulse'.

After being released on parole from the offence in Darwin, he told the court he had married and started going to church, but that he was later accused of molesting his 15-month-old niece. '[My wife's] parents came around and said they'd been praying and that God had told them that I'd touched my niece,' he said.

'What did you say to that?' Johns asked.

'I kicked them out of my house,' he replied. He said his wife initially believed him but that their marriage soon started to crumble. He said he also cut ties with the church because he believed the pastor had 'mispreached about unforgiveable sins'. Later, he smiled as he described his reaction to becoming a person of interest in the case. 'I had nothing to do with Daniel's disappearance at all,' he said. 'As I said to the police, and I'm sorry if it sounds bad, but I thought it was funny that they thought I had something to do with it.'

'Why was that funny?' asked Johns.

'Having to do something in half an hour, and get rid of, you know, or anything like that ... I don't think that's possible,' Cowan said.

He went on to explain that he was only interested in 'six-to eight-year-old boys', which was another reason he thought it 'funny' he had been nominated as a POI in Daniel's case. Continuing to answer Johns's questions, Cowan said he always carried Vaseline in the glove box of his car as he had sex with various male and female partners. He admitted he had this in Darwin, on the Sunshine Coast, in Moranbah and Murwillumbah. His answers were punctuated with smiles, which disgusted Boyce, Bruce and Denise, as it appeared to them that he was boasting about his sexual preferences.

Boyce had seen a lot of criminals since he started in Nambour as a lawyer in 1977. But he had never before run into such an entrenched level of criminality. Throughout this inquest, he was encountering people who had been imprisoned for long periods of time, who would spend a month or two on the outside and then be sent back to jail. They were institutionalised. They had no idea how to live in society, and they were publicly supported before being released to commit further crimes. Before the inquest into Daniel's death, Boyce would have never agreed to indefinite sentences. After the inquest, he abruptly changed his mind. There was a 'level of prisoner' in this case that he had encountered who never bothered with driving licences, never paid for groceries and never gave a second's thought to satisfying their own sexual desires. Cowan was one of these people, Boyce thought.

Cowan told the court he was being truthful about claims that he visited Drummond in the area for 'at least 30 minutes' on 7 December 2003, even though she had no recollection of him dropping by. He also claimed that he showed his alleged drug dealer and the man living in her house, Kevin Fitzgerald, the mulcher he had collected that morning during the visit. Johns told Cowan that his alibi was worthless and then questioned him about his previous offences, including the 1987 offence when he had lured a boy into a toilet block. Cowan admitted that he used drugs and had injected amphetamines. Johns went on to question him about the 1993 offence when he assaulted the six-year-old boy in the Darwin caravan park. He confirmed many of the details put to him but denied causing injuries to the boy or choking him, only admitting that he had put his fingers up the child's anus. After being questioned by Johns, Cowan admitted that, for both his previous convictions, he had committed the crime in a 20-minute/half-an-hour time period. He also admitted that he had only confessed to the crime in Darwin because police had told him that semen had been found on the six-year-old child's underpants.

Johns suggested to Cowan that it was rare for a boy under 18 to be kidnapped from a public area and his perpetrator never to be found, asking Cowan how many times did he think this had happened in his lifetime. Cowan replied, 'I don't know.' Johns answered, 'This is the only time and do you understand that as of December 2003 you were one of the very few people in Queensland if not Australia who had a proven history of kidnapping and sexually abusing young boys after taking them from public areas?'

Johns quoted court records from the Northern Territory case from a forensic pathologist who had examined the boy from the caravan park and had reported, 'The description of the anal canal as containing similar black contaminants is suggestive of penetration by an object which was itself contaminated. The presence of fragments of loose tissue with the anal canal is consistent with this penetration, having torn off fragments of the epithelial lining of anal canal. A smooth, rounded, blunt object would be unlikely to produce this form of injury, whereas a more irregular object would cause such injury.'

'So yet another doctor who is providing evidence that just doesn't seem to match up with what you've said happened. Do you accept that?' Johns put to Cowan.

'It happened in a bushfire area. My hands had crap and black shit all over them,' Cowan replied.

Johns continued, 'The boy had sustained a punctured lung which the medical report had attributed to suffocation ... Fifteen minutes or so later you went back and had a shower. You returned to normal activity after the shower, the same as in the case in Brisbane; you returned very quickly to normal activity.'

Later, when asked about his four-wheel-drive activities, Cowan told the court that he often went four-wheel driving and had gone to state forests, including a forest off Roys Road off the Bruce Highway, and that he had camped at Coochin Creek and had once become bogged there.

Johns warned him that this would be his last chance to give his account of what had happened in Daniel's case. 'I am suggesting to you that Mr and Mrs Morcombe, who are sitting right there, who have been without their son for seven years, deserve better from you than this ridiculous alibi that you've come up with.'

'Well, it's the truth.'

Johns accused Cowan of being an accomplished liar and pointed out that he bore a striking physical resemblance to witness accounts of the man seen close to Daniel on the day he vanished. He also put to Cowan that he had driven twice under the overpass around the time that Daniel had gone missing: 'When you were driving down the Nambour Connection Road approaching the Kiel Mountain Road overpass, you saw Daniel. Of course you saw him. To have us believe that you didn't see him is like suggesting to us that a snake might slide past an injured mouse and take no notice ... Of course he attracted your attention. And, as such, you parked your vehicle right near the Christian Outreach

Centre that is an area you know so well. That's what happened, isn't it?'

'No.'

Johns further put to Cowan that he had spent 20 minutes talking to Daniel and that, when the bus passed by and did not pick him up, he had convinced Daniel he would give him a lift, and that Cowan had later disposed of his body when driving his tow truck around the Sunshine Coast.

Cowan denied this.

'You assaulted him and, in the course of that assault, you either accidentally or intentionally killed him,' Johns said. 'I say that you intentionally killed him, because on the previous two occasions it's very annoying to have the victims come and identify you. That's the circumstances, isn't it?'

'No, it's not.'

'And if that wasn't intentional, Mr Cowan, today is your opportunity to tell how an accident might have occurred.'

'I had nothing to do with Daniel's disappearance,' Cowan replied.

When MacSporran got to his feet, he began, 'If you didn't know before, you now surely understand why you are a prime suspect for this abduction and suspected murder?'

'Yes.'

MacSporran went through details about how Cowan loaded the mulcher into the car. Cowan agreed he had tied it on to the Pajero. MacSporran asked Cowan, 'You routinely carry rope in your car?'

Cowan replied, 'Yes.'

During Boyce's question time, after the morning tea break, he brought up the sketches police had done during the investigation. Boyce asked Cowan to look at them. 'You say you have been told you look like one of them. Which one?'

Cowan chose one and held it up to the court next to his head. It was a surreal moment.

Boyce then brought up previous interviews Cowan had had with police about drugs and the triggers that lead to his offending. Cowan responded, 'They [the drugs] f— your inhibitions up. You know your boundaries; they stuff your boundaries.'

'And in 2003, you were a heavy user of cannabis and have continued to do so?' Boyce asked, to which Cowan replied, 'Yes.' Boyce then asked how many cones Cowan had on the morning of 7 December 2003.

'Two or three cones,' Cowan replied.

'And then another cone before you go to Frank's?'

'Yep,' Cowan replied.

'So you were stoned.'

Cowan: 'Yeah.'

Boyce: 'And you were stoned when these other offences occurred?'

Cowan replied, 'Yes, sir, and I'm stoned now.'

'Okay. When did you have your last intake of drugs?'

'About 20 minutes before I was picked up this morning.'

'What did you have?'

'Three cones.'

Cowan explained that he had been smoking bongs in his Brisbane motel room and he had brought the drugs with him from Western Australia. Later, Cowan revealed that Alexander Meyer's mother used to supply him with drugs when he was at school for three or four years, and they would smoke in the Meyers' downstairs room, which was a bit like a dungeon. Later he told Peter Johns during re-examination that he had last seen Alexander Meyer at a house in Keperra around six years ago, when he was with Hayley McDonald. Cowan denied knowing Jackway.

Outside the court, Bruce said they were relieved to return to their Sunshine Coast home after the harrowing week at the inquest. 'We've had a gutful of paedophiles and druggies and scum, but that's what we're dealing with,' he said. He described Cowan as a 'sexual freak', telling reporters he thought there was a 'definite chance' Cowan was responsible for his son's disappearance. He said Cowan's admission he was drug affected in court was bizarre. 'He'd been in the witness box a day and a half. He only had ten minutes to go,' he said. 'It seems very bizarre and clearly he has no respect for the law.'

Both Bruce and Denise expressed dismay and scepticism at the series of coincidences cited by both Jackway and Cowan in their explanations about their proximity to the scene of Daniel's disappearance. 'We've had our mind set on POI5 and when this one walked in yesterday and looked exactly like the sketches ... I don't know,' Denise said. 'It's just so confusing; there are just so many [paedophiles]. I can't believe Daniel could be so unlucky on the day.'

* * *

Qantas Flight number 767 from Brisbane to Perth left at 8.10 pm on 1 April. Brett Cowan had been waiting at the airport for four hours for his flight after being dropped off by police following his evidence at the inquest. He was already seated in 42A when 'Joseph Emery' arrived and sat down next to him. Emery was in his 30s, an athletic man with a rough-looking mohawk, tanned skin and piercing eyes. They began chatting easily enough – the usual talk between strangers trying to find common ground forced by circumstance to spend several hours together. Cowan told Emery that he was a sandblaster and painter. Emery told Cowan he was moving to Perth and had booked a motel for a couple of nights as he wasn't sure where he would stay. Cowan suggested the caravan park where he was staying in Orange Grove, a south-eastern suburb of Perth.

When they arrived at Perth domestic airport at 11.30 pm West Australian time, Cowan introduced Emery to the

woman who was there to pick him up. 'This is Trace.' Emery
shook the proffered hand. Later, Cowan was to say that he
thought Emery might be a plant from a television station
trying to get an inside scoop on him after giving evidence at
the inquest. He might have sensed something, but he had the
profession wrong.

Emery's first task when he booked into his Perth motel
was to begin transcribing the notes of the conversation from
the concealed recording device which had recorded their
conversation on the plane. Standard operating practice –
SOP in 'policespeak' – meant Emery always typed up a
summary of the conversation while the recording was
downloading, as it was still fresh in his memory. 'Emery'
was, in fact, an undercover police officer from Queensland.
Cowan had become an unwitting target of what was dubbed
the 'Mr Big' operation. Devised in the 1990s by the Royal
Canadian Mounted Police, the idea was simple enough.
Undercover police acted out a number of different scenarios
to convince the target that he or she was being invited to
join a criminal syndicate and had to be honest about his or
her past before being included in the gang. In return, the
organisation would 'wipe' the criminal's past misdemeanours
to prevent them from jeopardising its activities. Elaborately
played out scenarios, which often ran for many months and
involved money changing hands, were aimed at getting
the criminal to confess to a crime with the understanding
that, by coming clean, he or she would join the gang. In the
United Kingdom and United States, and other countries that
have common law, police are not permitted to use Mr Big
strategies because they are considered an infringement of a
suspect's constitutional rights. But in Australia, although not
widely publicised, the High Court had already adjudicated
that such evidence was not entrapment. The confessions
extracted from criminals while undergoing Mr Big scenarios
were deemed to be admissible, even though one of the High

Court judges remarked in 2007 that he was of the view they would have 'limited life expectancy' given that the criminal community would read about the police tactics in law and media reports.

The next day, Emery rang Cowan, asking him if he knew where he could buy a cheap car. Cowan agreed to help. Emery turned up at his caravan park in his hire car. Cowan had told him to wait out the front as directions to his caravan were complicated. At the car yard, Emery chose a maroon Ford Fairmont and paid for it. Cowan drove it back to the hire-car company, where he picked his new friend up. Later, they began texting as Emery settled into his new city.

* * *

Bruce and Denise knew nothing of Cowan's fellow passenger on board the Qantas flight. It was a secret that was well and truly buried. On Monday 4 April 2011, the inquest reconvened at Maroochydore courthouse. There was now no need for the security, given that the last of the jailed POIs had been called. It was day 20 of the inquest, and some of the other associates of the POIs had started to give evidence.

A man who had been an inmate with Jackway at Wolston Correctional Centre told the court on 5 April that he had heard many rumours nominating Jackway for Daniel's abduction. He also said that Jackway had tried to sell him a car that was similar to the one in which Daniel was said to have been abducted. He had thought this strange.

Detective Senior Sergeant Michael Buckley, who had been senior Scenes of Crime Officer for the Sunshine Coast District when Daniel disappeared confirmed that there had been no scientific investigation of the opposite side of the road to where Daniel had last been seen. He said he was not aware that witness accounts had placed Daniel on both sides of the Nambour Connection Road.

On 6 April, Kevin Fitzgerald, the man who shared a house with Sandy Drummond, told the inquest that he could not recall Cowan coming to their house on the day Daniel disappeared, even though he confirmed that he had been a regular visitor to their Beerwah property. He said Cowan bought drugs from Drummond on at least a fortnightly basis. He would also 'drop in' regularly on other occasions. He said that, most Sundays, he and Drummond would visit the RSL around lunchtime before the raffles were drawn at 2 pm, as Drummond's daughter ran the raffle and they would both usually put around $10 through the pokies. Fitzgerald told the court that he had no recollection of ever seeing any mulcher that Cowan had shown him. It was something he would 'definitely' have remembered, he said, as he had a keen interest in anything with a motor. 'Let me put it this way: I've just spent about two weeks working on a ride-on mower to make sure it's all going like it should, and it's not like I didn't have anything else to do,' he said. 'I'd like to believe that if I went out and looked at that thing, I would still, to this day, know what engine was powering it.'

Fitzgerald said that, although he had been around at the time detectives first spoke with Drummond, they had not asked any questions. The first time he had ever spoken to them was two days ago.

Drummond, when recalled, confirmed that she would usually go down to the RSL on Sundays at around 11.30 or midday.

Detective Senior Sergeant Damien Powell, who headed the Missing Persons Unit, got into the witness box to defend the way the investigation was handled immediately after Daniel was first reported missing. He said he was 'comfortable' with Sergeant Robbie Munn's 'professional judgement call' not to file an official missing person's report on the evening of Daniel's disappearance. However, he agreed that recent procedural changes meant it was now mandatory for officers to immediately create missing person's reports for youths, the elderly and people with mental illnesses. 'It's taken the discretion away from the officer,' he said, confirming that Daniel was not logged as missing until 9.44 am on the morning after he went missing. This was 15 hours after Bruce and Denise had reported Daniel missing to Sergeant Munn at the Maroochydore Police Station.

Later that day, Queensland's most senior detective, Assistant Commissioner Mike Condon, gave evidence, telling the court that more than 500 new POIs were currently being investigated following the review of Daniel's case. He said that, back in December 2003, he had been the detective inspector in charge of the Homicide Group, which included the Homicide Investigation Unit, Missing Persons Unit, Crime Stoppers Unit and the Prostitution Enforcement Task Force. There had been big changes to the way the Queensland Police Service handled missing persons since Daniel disappeared, Condon said. In the last financial year, police had received 3300 missing children reports and only five children, out of all the children who had gone missing since 1977, had never been found.

Examined by Johns about the review process for the investigation, Condon said there had been several reviews beginning with a review of 2100 job logs over a seven to eight month period from July 2004. However, Johns pointed out that this represented only about a third of the job logs for the investigation and asked Condon whether he believed that was adequate. Condon answered that there were 72 standard lines of inquiry which formed the framework of the investigation and that investigating that many job logs may identify some of these lines of inquiry which would link to thousands of job logs later on. Asked about the POIs, he said some had gone through an external review process such as the Crime and Misconduct Commission which included

Dooley and Meyer. He said Jackway and Cowan had been independently reviewed by the Homicide Investigation Unit.

Questioned closely about Cowan's investigation and why he had not been interviewed until two weeks after Daniel was last seen, he said Cowan had not been suggested as a POI until 21 December, and had been spoken to by the police that same day. 'I would suggest that once he came to our attention there was some re-prioritising of our strategies at the time and he was given the level of attention that he warranted. I think that's quite clear from the evidence that, from the 21st onwards, there was ... very much a focus on him and I certainly have no criticism whatsoever about how he was dealt with from that point on.' He confirmed that there had been further investigation after information about Cowan visiting his drug dealer on the way back from dropping off the mulcher had come out in Family Law Court proceedings in May 2006 against his former wife Tracey.

When it was Boyce's turn for questioning, he quizzed Condon about the 200 hours of CCTV footage police had collected from various service stations on highways linked to where Daniel had gone missing, asking Condon why it had taken so long to get some of the footage. The footage had been checked to see if there was any evidence of the blue car described by witnesses or of Daniel.

Condon denied to Boyce that, following the inquest, he had committed more money to the police investigation. 'You may have the view that you've caused it all, but let me tell you that I make decisions relevant to my portfolio and they're certainly not influenced by you or anything else you've said at the inquest.'

Returning again to Cowan, Boyce asked why Kevin Fitzgerald, the man who lived with Sandy Drummond, had not been interviewed. Condon said he did not know, but speculated it might be because he had been deemed 'of no relevance'.

Condon denied that Daniel's case had ever been considered a 'cold case'. He admitted there were matters arising out of the inquest that needed to be reviewed and that the Queensland Police Service was committed to the investigation 'for at least another six to twelve months'. While agreeing that the idea of a 'cold case' had been part of a document prepared by Detective Schmidt, he said this was 'certainly not the view of two senior officers of the region and the command'. Boyce quizzed Condon about the lack of documentation relating to the forensic examination at the crime scene. Condon said he did not know why they had only searched one side of the overpass.

Condon also offered to find out more about why police had not seized Cowan's computer, which contained evidence of him accessing porn sites for four hours, after they first visited him. Asked why police had opposed the calling of POIs at the inquest, Condon said he was concerned it would become a 'circus for individuals' and that they would enjoy their time out of jail for the day and the media would have a field day reporting the multiple versions given by them. He also conceded that police did not investigate the phone records from Sunbus to find out who the mystery caller was on the afternoon Daniel disappeared, and that 'proved to be wrong'.

Condon said he was 'very happy' with the decision he made not to release the sketches and COMFITs until 349 days after Daniel went missing. 'They are a tool to be used at a particular point of an investigation, or not used at all,' he said.

Boyce then asked Condon to comment on the tactics surrounding the initial questioning of Jackway in front of his alibis. Condon admitted it would have been better to question him separately.

Cross-examined by MacSporran, Condon said that Daniel's case was not only one of the largest investigations but it had also been one of the 'most frustrating'. 'We've had some very good information that has simply turned up nothing, or you get to a point where you can't take it any further … We certainly remain committed to solving it. I believe we will. I can't tell you when. That information is either within our holdings or there's a trigger out there that we need to introduce to the public which will cause someone to come forward with a piece of information which would bring the jigsaw together.'

Condon agreed that there was no evidence so far of violence being carried out on Daniel: 'that critical window is missing in the investigation without a doubt'.

At the end of Condon's lengthy examination, the inquest was adjourned to a date to be fixed so that lawyers could make their submissions about whether any further evidence should be called.

* * *

Bruce and Denise had a surprise up their sleeve. During the final court proceedings that morning, Bruce had scribbled an invitation to each of the media, handing it across the long bench seats to the journalists who had been regularly covering the case. It read, 'POI BBQ 11am 7th April at the Foundation Office'.

The media duly arrived as they always did, expecting this time a barbecue lunch rather than a media conference. There were flames, but not under sizzling sausages. A life-size effigy with a clay head and fibreglass body – a composite of three of the witness descriptions of the man seen under the Kiel Mountain Road overpass – stood in the car park at the rear of the Foundation office with a black hood over its head. The model had been gathering dust underneath the office for several months after being displayed in a media exercise under the overpass some time earlier. As journalists watched, Bruce picked up a can of diesel, pulled off the black hood and began dousing the figure underneath. Denise attempted to light the crotch region without success. However, the wig caught fire easily. Flames slowly engulfed the model, Bruce and Denise laughing as the cameras filmed. Bruce called out over the crackle and roar, 'It's doing me good.' Denise, smiling, said, 'Burn, you bastard.'

Bruce said that the act was 'an emotional release of the last seven and a half years. The people who have harboured this bugger. It's a message to them. You've heard us, but it's not right.' He said it was a message to all these persons of interest that have come under a cloud. 'You may well not be involved in Daniel's disappearance, but you're horrid creatures.' He added, 'We can sense it in our bones that someone is getting real close.'

Within minutes, Denise got a call from her father, Kevin, from Victoria. 'I've seen it on the news already. What are you up to?' he asked.

Denise laughed. However odd the act might have been, she and Bruce both got satisfaction.

The wrap-up coverage from the television news focused on the inquest, homing in on two persons of interest, Jackway and Cowan.

Cowan's alibi for the missing 45 minutes of the day when Daniel disappeared was beginning to disintegrate.

The day after Fitzgerald gave evidence saying he could not recall whether Cowan had turned up on 7 December 2003, Emery turned up at Cowan's caravan park at around 11.15 am local time. The television was on in Cowan's van and the morning news was playing. When coverage of the burning effigy story came on, followed by a summary of the case evidence, Cowan, who had shown no interest in what was on the screen, turned abruptly to the television. Emery was watching him carefully. The newsreader described the case as the 'largest' in Queensland's history. 'D'ye think it was?' Cowan asked, turning to Emery, who shrugged.

Cowan was an accommodating host. He allowed Emery to use his post-office box as an address. He took him around places of interest as well as offering to follow up an application for him to stay at the Crystal Creek Caravan Park. The 'rapport building' was going well. So far so good. On 9 April, a trip planned to Fremantle fell through as Cowan wasn't feeling well. But having access to Cowan's post-office box was a good pretext for Emery to keep in contact with him.

Later, commenting on the last few days of proceedings, Bruce described the inquest as fruitful. 'We're interested in policy and there's probably two parts to that. One is what happened to Daniel and what the policy was, whether that was followed to the letter of the manual; but also whether that system has improved, with technology, with management systems, all those sorts of things,' he said. 'As a family, we thought activation of investigation procedures could have and should have happened earlier, but, as we've heard, that was a judgement call, and the Coroner will have his own decision about whether that judgement call was right or wrong. It's a relief that this chapter is closed, and we'll move onto the next chapter, which we hope in the coming months may well be some sort of formal closure.'

CHAPTER TWENTY-THREE

THE UNDERCOVER STING

On 10 April 2011, while visiting the post-office box, Emery noticed a letter addressed to Cowan with 'OHMS' (On Her Majesty's Service) printed on the envelope. It was an application, Cowan revealed, to change his name to 'Shaddo N-Unyah Hunter'.

On 15 April, Emery bought a carton of Crown Lager and called around for a social visit. It was a further exercise in rapport building. Cowan was walking around the caravan park and told Emery he always did that as he had sore legs. The next day, the trip to Fremantle finally eventuated and Cowan, an impromptu guide, took Emery around the restaurants at the waterfront.

Four days later, Cowan told Emery he had been laid off by his employer as he was the last one to be brought on. He had only one more week's rent paid at the caravan park and said he needed cash. Emery replied that he'd found some landscaping work and could lend Cowan some money. 'How much?' Emery asked. 'Two hundred dollars,' Cowan replied, and Emery obliged. Emery said he might be going back east around Easter time, and Cowan offered to drop him at the airport.

Then, suddenly, after such regular contact, Cowan went to ground. Emery tried to contact him to no avail. Finally, on 2 May, he heard the familiar ping on his mobile phone of a text arriving. It was from Cowan: 'Sorry about the f— around. Living down south with family and will be back in touch.' Cowan also apologised about not giving back the money. Emery responded by offering it to him as an Easter present and 'a thank you for helping me set up in Perth'. The loan was becoming an impediment to developing their relationship and the sooner it was out of the way the better.

While waiting for further developments, Emery went around to the caravan park. Cowan had moved out. Cowan revealed later that he had been kicked out because he had named the place during his evidence at the inquest. After telling Cowan he needed to check the post-office box, Emery met up with Cowan on 4 May at High Wycombe Village Shopping Centre at the back of Perth Airport, not far from where Cowan now lived. This time, Emery had a friend with him: 'Paul Fitzsimmons', introduced to Cowan as 'Fitzy'. A short man with long hair which he wore in a ponytail, Fitzy spoke with a nasal twang. His conversation was peppered with the 'f' word. He laughed easily, and spoke in a soft voice. From May through until August, Fitzy would become the most important contact with Brett Cowan.

The next day, Emery told Cowan he could find him some 'easy' work. There was a job between 2 and 4 pm the following day. Was he interested? Sure, Cowan was. Emery was successfully re-establishing the friendship. The carrot had worked.

On 6 May, Cowan and Emery were sitting in the short-term parking at the domestic airport. Cowan had been briefed that they were watching for a man arriving off a flight from Melbourne. Emery had produced the man's photo. Once the man was spotted, they had to make a phone call, he told Cowan. They hung around the terminals at different places. Then they met up again. Mission accomplished. Emery made a phone call. He then drove Cowan back to High Wycombe Village Shopping Centre, their previous meeting place. Cowan was given $150 for the day's work.

Three days later, Emery rang Cowan again. There was more work the following day. Emery told Cowan he would pick him up at Midland Gate Shopping Centre, north-east of Perth. Their job was to collect money from someone who was in debt to the boss. They waited in the car near Jimmy Bean's diner. While they were waiting, Emery got a phone call from a West Australian police officer called 'Dean'. Dean arrived and handed over a wad of money. Emery handed it to Cowan, who counted it, but it was short $2000. Emery got out of the car. Standing next to the passenger side, so Cowan could hear, he told Dean off and said he'd probably be in trouble. Back in the car, Emery asked Cowan if he minded doing 'loan sharking' work. Cowan said that was fine. He was paid a further $150 for the day's work.

On 12 May, Emery told Cowan there was more work but then rang to say it had fallen through. The next job was on 16 May, when he again picked up Cowan at the Midland Gate Shopping Centre. Fitzy was also there. Fitzy told Emery to go and collect the remaining $2000 off Dean. Cowan was asked to accompany Fitzy on another job. Cowan accompanied Fitzy to Fremantle, where they collected $2000 for the crime syndicate from 'Cassie', a madam who ran illegal brothels. On the way there, Cowan told Fitzy he wanted to be known as 'Shaddo'. Later that evening, they met up with Emery at the Burswood Casino and he handed over the $2000 supposedly given to him by Dean. Fitzy asked Emery to drive Cowan home. Cowan gave him Tracey's address in Bullsbrook, a northern suburb of Perth.

Four days later, Emery picked up Cowan again. This time, they drove to Innaloo, inland from the beachside suburb of Scarborough, where Fitzy was. They were to check on a prostitute who was driving a Nissan Pathfinder four-wheel drive that belonged to the crime syndicate. The syndicate, Emery let slip, also controlled the girls who were working as prostitutes. The mission was to find out whether she was working outside of the organisation from Sorrento, a beachside suburb further north. While they were in the car, Fitzy got a phone call telling him to go to a particular motel car park. 'Brooke', the target, was another undercover police officer. As they watched, Brooke left the motel room heading towards her car. Cowan was told to follow her when she left the car and find out which room she was going to. Cowan came back to report that Brooke was probably 'working' as she had gone into a room with a man. They waited outside the motel room and Cowan was placed on watch. When the man left, Fitzy, Cowan and Emery entered the room and Fitzy proceeded to rip into Brooke, accusing her of working on the side. She was given money and told not to come back. They also took her car. Cowan seemed quite happy to fall for the ruse. The Mr Big strategy was going well.

* * *

Unaware of all the drama being played out in Western Australia, on 25 May, Bruce and Denise flew to Canberra for the Australian Federal Police's International Missing Children's Day launch at the Canberra Zoo, returning home that same day. The following day, they boarded a plane for London. Brad and Anna had just completed a Contiki bus tour across Europe, and the Morcombes met them at their London hotel. Denise had always dreamt of visiting the Yorkshire moors, where the book *Wuthering Heights* was set.

All four of them stayed a night in West Yorkshire at a town called Haworth, and Bruce and Denise then walked the 16 kilometres through the moors and countryside until they found the old farmhouse 'Top Withens', the house thought to have inspired the novel by Emily Brontë.

They spent a week in Scotland, then drove Brad and Anna to Heathrow before heading to the West End to see *Les Misérables*. Bruce was transfixed by the song 'Bring Him Home', which seemed to resonate so much with how he felt about Daniel. That night, they returned to the Cotswolds.

The next day, they had a rendezvous with Gerry and Kate McCann in a pub called 'The Dirty Duck' in Stratford-upon-Avon, the birthplace of William Shakespeare. They spoke to Gerry and Kate for several hours over dinner and enjoyed a couple of pints. The conversation centred around comparing both couples' experiences with the media and the police. They were so much in the same space that all four of them were wearing rubber wristbands. Bruce and Denise took off their Daniel Morcombe Foundation bands, and Kate and Gerry took theirs off, and they swapped them in a gesture of friendship and hope. Kate and Gerry signed a red Foundation T-shirt writing on it 'Never Give Up'. This is now framed and hangs proudly in the Morcombes' office.

As they were leaving, Bruce asked Kate whether she had a signed copy available of her book, *Madeleine*. 'We might collect one on the last day of our trip,' he said.

'Well, if you haven't booked anywhere, you're welcome to stay with us,' Kate said.

It was settled. As their trip to the United Kingdom came to an end, Bruce and Denise stayed at the McCanns' house in Leicester for dinner and then spent the night at their home. They had a lovely evening playing with the McCanns' twins, Sean and Amelie, and then talked for several more hours after dinner. Bruce and Denise were very interested in their search efforts, and The Madeleine Foundation and how it worked. Kate gave them a personalised signed copy of her book.

There had only been one dark cloud to mar the holiday. On 2 June, Bruce and Denise, after checking the Queensland newspapers online, read that police divers had found human remains in a mangrove forest near Declan Crouch's home, and that a crime scene had been established and the remains were being identified. They felt for Declan's mother, Ruth. But it was after Declan's remains were positively identified on 11 June that they had received a phone call from the Police Commissioner, Bob Atkinson. Declan had taken his own life.

In spite of being overseas, the Morcombes were sought out for comment on bus policy and procedures and the 'No kids left behind' plan being implemented in Queensland. 'Obviously, we see this as a good thing, because what has been happening to date, they just haven't been able to get right,' Bruce said.

Bruce and Denise then visited North Yorkshire before heading home. Denise especially was dreading the return trip. Mittens, Daniel's cat, had been run over while they were away. It was upsetting to arrive home and know he was no longer there – another part of Daniel slipping away.

* * *

Back in Perth, Emery was being gradually phased out of the picture. In the last few weeks of May, he only had one phone interaction with Cowan. Fitzy, as a 'mid-level' member of the criminal syndicate, was well-established in his own rapport building with the target, all the while recording phone calls and face-to-face meetings, and entering details into running sheets.

On 25 May, Fitzy took Cowan on a job involving an illegal consignment of crayfish that was to be taken to a restaurant in Northbridge, an inner-city suburb of Perth. Another undercover police officer posed as an Asian restaurant owner. Cowan had to move the polystyrene boxes containing the crayfish and put them in the back of Fitzy's car. They then drove to the restaurant. He was paid a further $150. Other 'jobs' included Cowan being asked to photograph a 'bank manager' with a 'prostitute'. He also had to pick up blank passports – this was to impress upon Cowan the reach of the organisation – and pay money to bribe a 'customs officer' at Perth International Airport. Fitzy told Cowan about a man called Jeff who was the West Australian boss of the syndicate, and they met him briefly. On another occasion, Cowan and Fitzy were involved in the burglary of cigarettes in the middle of the night.

On 14 June, another job involved the buying of illegal firearms from a flat in Perth. They picked up three pistols from another 'criminal' called Danny and went up to a hotel room. Later, the pistols were delivered to another 'criminal' at a roadhouse on the Great Eastern Highway. Cowan revealed that he had knowledge of firearms as his dad had been 'high up in the army'. He said that, throughout his childhood, he had access to guns. He also spoke about his white Pajero. It was clear that cars were one of his hobbies. On each of these assignments, though, Fitzy would do the driving.

On 16 June, Fitzy involved Cowan in the pick-up of $10,000 from an Asian 'restaurant owner' and collecting some fake passports. After collecting the money, they went to Coco's Restaurant, a silver-service dining establishment overlooking the Swan River, on the South Perth Esplanade. Emery was to meet them there after lunch. The occasion was to meet 'Jeff', introduced as Fitzy's boss. When the bill arrived, Cowan commented on how much it cost. Jeff told Emery he had been doing a good job, before handing him $10,000 under the table, as well as plane tickets and a passport. 'This is to set you up,' Jeff told Emery. 'Fly to

Sydney and then on to London.' He was told to lie low and Fitzy and Cowan were told to delete Jeff's mobile number from their phones.

Fitzy and Cowan drove Emery to the domestic terminal at Perth Airport. Cowan did not see Emery again. He was later told that Emery had become a liability to the organisation so was being paid off. There were further financial transactions, each one getting more expensive.

On 21 June, Fitzy and Cowan went to a cafe at the District Court and paid $30,000 to one of the 'court officials'. Then they met a 'prostitute' at the Subiaco Oval who gave them takings of $6000, and then there was a job involving ecstasy.

At this point, Fitzy imparted that there was a 'big job' coming up and that Cowan might be asked to be involved. He was told that crime-group members were entitled to ten per cent of any proceeds from jobs, and this one would net Cowan $100,000. He said the job involved a 'large drug transaction'. On 29 June, Cowan and Fitzy drove to Albany, a harbour town in the south of Western Australia, about five or six hours drive from Perth. They had to meet up with someone from a bank and another person who gave them credit cards. Cowan and Fitzy then handed over some empty metal canisters to a 'port manager', who was to return them full of ecstacy pills. He and Fitzy stayed in Albany overnight and the next day returned to Perth, after paying the 'corrupt' port officer $8000. On 6 July, back in the Perth suburb of Claremont, they collected $27,000 from the brothel madam 'Cassie', another undercover officer.

Cowan was then asked if he would like to go to Melbourne for another job to help the Melbourne crime group. They had to take money and jewellery back to Perth. The jewellery was a blood diamond from Africa said to be worth $200,000. The other purpose of the trip was for Cowan to meet the national boss of the syndicate, 'Arnold'. Fitzy, Jeff and Cowan flew over on 13 July. When they met him at the Hilton, he had bodyguards to signify his importance. Cowan was told he was being checked out to see if he was suitable to stay in the syndicate. They collected more money from an 'illegal brothel', picked up the diamond and on 15 July flew back to Perth. Scenario 19 played out back in Perth on 21 July when they collected more money from Cassie as well as exchanging money with a 'corrupt' police officer.

Cowan confided to Fitzy: 'I've been wondering how the other side lived and now I can find out for myself. I've found my calling. I've found the job I've been waiting for all these years.'

* * *

In spite of all the media headlines and recent focus on the case, Bruce and Denise were concerned that their supporter base was slipping. At the request of the Sunshine Coast Regional Council, they gave eight presentations between 1 and 12 August to libraries. During the presentations, they used montages and victim-of-crime vision that they had played at the Dance for Daniel. They felt that the attendees had been given 'an eye-opener'. They were hopeful that the talks meant more schools and businesses would get behind the Day for Daniel and the annual Dance. The numbers were small, however, with only 30 people attending the function at Beerwah and sometimes less at Cooroy, Noosa, Coolum, Maroochydore, Nambour, Kawana and Caloundra.

Bruce wrote to Condon on 11 July asking for the inquest to be resumed 'at the earliest possible time'. The following day, Condon replied telling Bruce that 'investigations are continuing in relation to a person of interest that gave evidence at the inquest'. Little did they know that Condon was referring to the high drama that was being played out across the other side of Australia. On 8 August, Bruce and Denise met up with Mike Condon and Brian Wilkins from the Homicide Investigation Unit at the launch of Missing Persons Week at the Suncorp Stadium in Brisbane, hosted by the Australian Federal Police. Never one to miss an opportunity, Bruce casually asked Condon for any updates on the police investigation. Nothing to report, he was told. Bruce and Denise sighed, knowing the waiting game well. The time bomb was ticking.

The following night, there was a Daniel Morcombe Foundation committee meeting, where Bruce and Denise shared the news that there was only enough money in the Foundation account to cover electricity and the phone for the office, to ensure their funds lasted for the upcoming Day for Daniel.

Foundation projects to be delivered in 2012 included a 'Feeling Safe' internet-safety program with the University of the Sunshine Coast and the Queensland Police Service. They had also decided that the 'No Strings' puppet show would be available on the Foundation website and the 'Daniel's Cross' emergency hand signal should be evaluated. The annual Day for Daniel was to remain the focus of the Foundation's safety education and was to continue as a standalone day, rather than being incorporated into Child Protection Week. As funds were rapidly drying up, it was to be considered as a significant fundraising day.

* * *

In Perth, Fitzy was continuing his rapport building with Cowan. On 22 July Cowan was taken to Fremantle Cemetery where illegal firearms were collected from an undercover police officer. On 26 July, Cowan was taken to an airfield as preparation for the big job and he was told that a big drug haul was being flown in. Everyone was going to share in it. He was sent to the airfield by himself to undertake general surveillance and take photographs to show he could be trusted.

Fitzy met him in the casino car park to talk about the plans and to look at a map of the area. Arnold could fix everything, Fitzy said, on more than one occasion. He could make things disappear. There was a 'golden path' and 'you don't want to f— it', he warned Cowan. Three days later, Cowan was given further surveillance work at the airfield.

On 2 August, Cowan and Fitzy went on another job in Armadale, an outer suburb of Perth, to pick up the canisters. The canisters contained 5000 pills of ecstasy. The man who passed them over was supposedly the wharf manager. Cowan looked inside. The pills were made of chalk, but he suspected nothing.

On 4 August, Cowan shaved his goatee beard, which had been about two or three centimetres long when Fitzy first met him. 'Holy shit,' Fitzy quipped. 'Where's my dirty old man?' He asked Cowan which brand of cigarettes he smoked, and Cowan told him Horizons. Fitzy bought him a carton. There was a short discussion about Cowan's inability to give up smoking. They were meeting 'Craig', a 'corrupt policeman', at the shops in Belmont, in Perth's eastern suburbs. Craig duly arrived and, after some chitchat, Craig suddenly announced, 'There's a subpoena from Queensland for Brett. It's yeah ... do you know about that?'

'No I don't,' Cowan said.

'For Coroner's Court ...' Craig said.

'That's been and gone,' Cowan said.

'No, this is fresh,' Craig replied.

'Fresh, is it?'

'That's something we can fix as well.'

'No hassle with it,' Fitzy joined in. 'Yeah, gotta make sure everyone's all right?'

Craig offered to 'fix it up'.

After Craig left, Fitzy asked, 'What's that about, mate?'

Cowan replied: 'I was living in the area that Daniel Morcombe went missing from. That's how I met f—in'

Emery on the plane back from being subpoenaed over there for the Coroner's Court in Queensland. I know I had nothing to do with it. I'm f—in' … my alibi is a hundred per cent.'

'Well, there's nothing we can't get fixed, but the thing is nothing can come back on us … You've got to be 100 per cent honest. You can't f—in' lie to us,' Fitzy said. His tone was not menacing but his words hung in the air.

'None of these subpoenas will work – if they are sending it out to Brett Cowan, I'm not that person any more,' Cowan said smugly, adding that was why he'd changed his name to 'Shaddo N-Unyah Hunter'.

'I don't give a f— what you done,' Fitzy replied. 'We can make things go away … I talked you up. You're not even … you don't even swear, mate … you just do what I say … we're mates. There's nothing they can't make go away …'

Later, after taking a call from the brothel madam Cassie, Fitzy turned to Cowan: 'You're part of the brotherhood.'

'… this is, you know … the only thing that stuffs me up with you. This'd be the only thing that stops me from comin' in with you …' Cowan said. Cowan then told Fitzy that, if he thought there was another subpoena, he wouldn't have changed his name.

'Why Shaddo Hunter anyway, man?' Fitzy asked.

'Shaddo … Um, oh, my dog, his name's "Shadow" but I've had … like … that name for ages. You know, and I just changed the spelling of it … ah … and Hunter it just … fell there one night. Not long after I got back from f—in' Queensland, I was just sittin' there talkin' to Trace and we were talkin' about it and everything … And it's just like I heard Hunt or something like that on the TV or the radio and I've gone: Hunter. It was just going to be Shaddo N-Unyah.'

'Why N-Unyah?'

'N-Unyah business.'

'Ah, you're a f—ing funny bloke.'

When they met up with Jeff, he also told Cowan he looked five years younger after his shave. Fitzy then told Jeff about the subpoena, with Cowan reassuring him that it had only occurred because he was living in the area at the time Daniel went missing. Cowan also told him any subpoena would be 'null and void' because he had changed his name by deed poll to Shaddo. Jeff reinforced the need for honesty and then asked Cowan, 'You happy to keep boxin' on with the good work?'

Cowan agreed. Jeff told him it was important to take 'baby steps' first. Intent upon proving his loyalty, Cowan assured Jeff that, if there was ever an issue of them being stopped and drugs being found in their car, for example, he would take the rap and say he was a hitchhiker. He told them the only income he was receiving was from Centrelink for sickness benefits, and he had to get an up-to-date medical certificate. There was laughter when Jeff suggested he wouldn't be declaring this income.

After they left Jeff, the talk in the car turned back to the subpoena. 'I had me old man with me the last time they interviewed me and they were … f—in' Homicide Squad in Brisbane … and I just turned around and said to 'em this is the last time, that's it. If you ever want to speak to me again, you gotta arrest me for it …' Cowan said.

It was around 6 pm when they headed back to the city. Fitzy again stressed that this crime syndicate could 'make things disappear' but Cowan had to be honest with them. Cowan said that the worst thing that could happen to him now would be not to receive another phone call from the syndicate. Fitzy talked about how good the 'big job' would be and mentioned Arnold, the big boss, again. He paid Cowan $200 for the day's work when he dropped him off.

'If I've got to disappear, I've got to disappear,' Cowan said. 'As long as I can contact me parents at least once a month, that's all I care about: "It's me, Mum and Dad – how are you going …?"' he tailed off.

On 8 August, when Fitzy picked him up, Fitzy told Cowan the big job was on and they might be going to Kalgoorlie the next day. 'Jeff said to take you as well, so that's pretty cool.' Cowan told Fitzy that he had seen 'Craig' on television investigating a murder, and Fitzy immediately came back with the fact that Craig was 'high up' in the West Australian Police.

Cowan added, 'I'm quite willing to cut all ties to my family, f—in' from Tracey and everything, and f—in' Brett and Shaddo can f—in' die … Death certificate, f—in' dead and buried …' Then he added, 'I haven't been happy like this before … the mateship sort of thing.'

Fitzy confessed he was 'a bit pissed off' that Cowan hadn't told him of his past misdemeanours.

'I didn't know this was coming up. I thought it was dealt with …' Cowan said. When he was told that Jeff had a way of 'knowing everything', he reassured Fitzy he had 'nothing to hide'.

Cowan mentioned cutting ties again. Fitzy countered, 'Don't worry. Arnold will get everything checked out. If you ever get that call from him – probably through me.'

They talked more about jobs coming up and Fitzy raised the idea of Cowan committing acts of violence. 'I'm not big on that but, you know, if it's required it's required at the time sort of thing …' Cowan responded.

Fitzy reinforced the brotherhood structure. 'Everyone gets an equal share … that's why you never have to rip them off or anything.'

Cowan offered again to break ties with Tracey.

Fitzy offered that he wouldn't lose her as a friend.

Then Cowan told Fitzy he had a new phone at home that had a SIM card and was not registered. 'That way you don't have to worry about getting a SIM card. Got it already.'

Fitzy said he didn't 'carry much' on his phone.

The next day, they both headed out to Kalgoorlie. About two hours into the seven-hour drive from Perth, the phone rang and Fitzy answered. 'Yes, just out at Northam now … So Arnold's in town?' He chatted for a few minutes then hung up. 'Arnold wants to have a chat to ya …' Fitzy said. 'Jeff could've rung two hours ago …' he added, sounding a little exasperated, 'before we left Perth.'

'Is that what Craig brought up the other day?' Cowan asked, sounding worried. Then he asked whether 'Kal' had been cancelled.

Back in Perth, they drove straight to the Hyatt Regency in the CBD and into a space in the underground car park. Up in the Swan River Room, Arnold was on the phone, pacing back and forth, the mobile pressed to his ear. It was time for the police to get some answers and time to test the rapport building.

* * *

On Thursday 11 August in the now familiar underworld-like life they led in their pursuit to find Daniel, Bruce arranged to meet with a man recently released from prison. The man had said he had information about conversations that were circling the jails. He wanted to help.

Having driven to the address in Brisbane for a late morning appointment, Bruce arrived an hour early. He parked the car around the corner and looked at the street, which he'd already researched on Google Earth. After a while he entered the property, which was protected by a high timber fence. The man he met was friendly and said he shared the house with a couple of mates. Bruce sat on the couch near the man as recent washing and food plates gave him limited options. The man told Bruce a variety of stories concerning inmates and possible maps of where to look for Daniel's remains. It was nothing particularly new or, more importantly, of substance. Bruce decided to ask if it was okay to video the conversation. The man agreed, so he set up his new mini-camera at a critical vantage point.

An hour later he left and made his way back to the Sunshine Coast. You never know when you might stumble on the truth, he was thinking to himself as he left, always the optimist but not realising how close he was to the mark.

CHAPTER TWENTY-FOUR

'I DID IT'

Arnold came across as an influential, no-nonsense businessman, but his mannerisms, speech and shaved head were every bit the police officer. Cowan, however, did not seem to sense anything untoward. It was 12.35 pm on a sunny afternoon in the Perth CBD. The Swan River was screened from view behind opaque curtains at the Hyatt Hotel.

'Sorting something else out that's causing me a bit of grief,' Arnold was saying into the phone. 'Once I've got this out of the way, I'm comfortable to proceed ... that's not an issue ... I don't know how long this is going to take me ... important so I can decide what to do with other shit ... Still waiting for a bit of info ... once he gives me that stuff ... at the moment a couple of issues to sort out here.'

Cowan walked into the room and sat on one of the couches. A young, blonde-haired woman was sitting on one of the other couches. He was wearing jeans and a bomber-style jacket, his hair back in a ponytail. Leaning forward, his arms spread the length of his knees, his long fingers dangled awkwardly. The girl fiddled with her hair in a habitual way until Arnold got off the phone. Arnold gave her a large handful of money and told her to go and buy herself something.

'How ye going, bud?' Arnold asked, approaching Cowan on the couch with his hand out.

Of all the introductory lines Cowan might have chosen, Cowan told him he was painting a fence.

'A white picket fence?' Arnold laughed at his own joke.

Cowan said he was doing it for Tracey and that it was going to be purple as she loved everything purple. She had a purple aviary. He told Arnold about 'Birdie', his pet ringneck, how he had rescued him when he was working as a tree-lopper and accidentally clipped the bird's wing: '... so I kept him. He was nesting. So he's 12 months old in September. Well, I've had him for 12 months.' His voice had its customary anxious-to-please tone.

'Oh, that's good,' Arnold nodded, sounding a little surprised at the subject of the conversation.

'He talks and whistles and carries on so ...'

Arnold asked whether Cowan collected birds. Cowan shook his head but told him the man across the road did and how he'd like to get a partner for Birdie. 'Yeah, they breed good.'

'Excellent.'

The incongruous chatter changed abruptly when Arnold announced, 'Heard through Jeff, through Paul [Fitzy], you've been doing some good stuff.' Then Arnold threw out some rhetorical questions. 'You're happy? They're looking after you? That there's no issues there because as you know things are moving. You've got no problems? You're happy? No one's forcing you to do anything you don't want to do?' The phrase was the closest approximation to a police caution.

Cowan reassured him he was 'quite enjoying it'.

'One of the reasons I've brought you here, you've got to crawl before you walk ... walk before you run and as you probably know I've got a lot of people in my confines around the country that I pay good money to get good information from.' Arnold was speaking quickly, not waiting for a response.

'And as this thing's progressing, this big job we're looking at, I've been checking you out and there's a coupla' things have come up we need to talk about.'

'Yes, if I'd known I thought it was all dealt with?' Cowan replied.

'Look, I'm here on other business,' Arnold said. 'I'll be straight with you ... but I got some other information through early this morning which has kind of made me postpone all of that stuff so we can sort this out. What do you need to tell me? Is there something you need to tell me?'

Cowan began to reply, but Arnold interrupted him. 'Just let me stop you there before you go on. I'll let you know that I don't care what you've done. All right? I've got no qualms at all. You know, I've dealt with a lot of real bad c—ts and had a lot of real bad c—ts on my books. What they do, what they get up to doesn't faze me at all.'

'Yes.'

'And I'll pay you back as you pay me back.'

'Yes I understand that.'

'Now go on.'

'Because I lived in the area ...' Cowan started to say.

Arnold began to fiddle with his phone as though he had a fit of nerves, perhaps as the words everyone had been waiting to hear were about to be uttered. Or, perhaps he was ensuring Cowan's words were being captured.

'Just let me figure out how to turn this bloody thing off. All right ... system off ... sorry ... go on,' he said.

'I was living in the area in '03 when Daniel Morcombe went missing so I've been interviewed and I was hounded for ages about that and I can guarantee I had nothing to do with Daniel Morcombe's disappearance ... One of my alibis ... was shot to pieces ... And, um, I've lost my two eldest kids due to this as well ... I was brought to the Coroner's inquest ... and I thought that was the end of it ...'

Arnold said he had received information that morning and that he had to keep the gang 'safe and clean as a group because ultimately, you know, if the heat's on you, the heat's on Paul, the heat's on Jeff and the heat's on me ... So what's happened is, from the information I've got ... All right, I'm told you've done the Daniel Morcombe murder.'

'Yep.'

'I'm told that it's dead set that you're the one who's done it. Like I said, it doesn't bother me at all ... I can sort this for you ... I can buy you alibis, I can get rid of stuff ... But I need to know what I need to do, do you know what I mean? So you're saying to me, look I had nothing to do with it – that's not what I've been told. And that brings me in a real dilemma, in a crossroads, because I want to move forward with what we're doing.'

'Yes.'

Arnold pulled himself up off the couch while telling Cowan that he'd heard there was a subpoena coming for him and although he wanted to bring Cowan on board, he had to weigh up the risks.

Behind them, the curtains remained closed. Plush lamps sat on the glass coffee tables. The moment of judgement hung in the air.

'Have a read of that ... That's what I copped this morning,' Arnold handed Cowan his laptop.

'Can you enlarge that?' Cowan asked, explaining that he'd left his reading glasses in his car.

Arnold sympathised, then began reading aloud. 'Ok, what I've got is ... Shaddo Hunter, alias Brett Peter Cowan, is the main suspect in the disappearance of Daniel Morcombe ...' he read out the details. 'My sources told me that there is no doubt he's the person responsible for this event.'

He read more from the email that said that when the inquest reconvened, Cowan would be 'again in the spotlight' and that he should be dropped 'like a hot potato'.

Arnold again asked Cowan how he could sort things out adding that he'd heard he was loyal from the other boys.

'So what do I need to fix?'

Cowan was looking more and more nervous. His head bowed, he looked at the ground, speaking quietly: 'Yeah ... OK ... yeah ... I did it ...' Cowan said.

The words that the police had been waiting to hear for so many months had been spoken, less than ten minutes into their 'chat'. Yet they were uttered so softly it was almost as though Cowan had not said anything.

Arnold responded without missing a beat, as if he heard that kind of confession every day. 'Okay, so you did it. But what I'm saying is I need to take you right back to the whole thing, so that if there's anything like, I don't know, if they've got any DNA at all or that kind of shit.'

'There's no DNA,' Cowan said.

'Obviously they haven't found the f—ing body,' Arnold said, blasé.

'They took my car, they searched my car, did all forensics on my car. They got nothing out of my car.'

'Look, just lead me through the whole f—ing thing, how it happened from whoa to go, and then I'll think about things that we need to sort and fix ... Do you want a coffee or something?'

'No, I'm right, thanks,' Cowan paused. 'I've seen him standing there, I did a loop around and ...'

'Okay, hang on. What time was this?'

'I don't know, about lunchtime?'

'From what I'm told, it's about lunchtime. Where were you going?'

'I was going to my boss's father's place to pick up a wood mulcher.'

'You're going to your boss's father's place to pick up a wood mulcher, yep?'

'Yep. I'd been doing some tree-lopping in our own yard … Picked it up on my way home and there was a broken down bus, the Sunbus broken down, and then I seen Daniel.'

'Did you know him at all?'

'No.'

'Okay, so you've seen him on the side of the road. What did you do, a U-ey or something?'

'No, I went up and around and parked in the church car park and my car was never on the road, so I don't know how they got …'

'Well, I've heard something about a white four-wheel drive that they've seen.'

'Yeah, well, it was not sitting on the highway at all.'

'So you parked behind the church or wherever it was?'

'Yep, yep. I've walked in and sat there.'

'Did you talk to him for long?'

'I didn't talk to him at all. You know, when I got there, I made it just look like I was just waiting for the bus.'

'Okay, fair enough, yes.'

'The bus drove past and that's when I said I'm going down to the shopping centre, do you want a lift?'

'Yep.'

'And he's gone, "Yeah, yep."'

'Yes, so he's missed the bus or something has he, or …?'

'No, the bus drove past because it was given orders not to pick up any more passengers because it was a broken down one and there'd be another bus through.'

'Okay, so you asked him if he wanted a lift and he said yes?'

'Yes, he's jumped in.'

'Where did he sit in your car: the front, the back?'

'Passenger seat.'

'Passenger seat, yes.'

'Instead of taking him to the shopping centre, I've taken him to a secluded spot that I know of.'

'All right, where was that?'

'It's at Beerwah, just off the Coochin Creek.'

'What's it called? That's very important.'

'Beerwah.'

'Beerwah?'

'B-e-e-r-w-a-h.'

Arnold made a show of pretending never to have heard of the place. 'Beerwah. Okay, so you knew the area pretty well, so you've taken him? How far was that from where you picked him up?'

'Half an hour.'

'Half an hour. I don't know the area. I've never really been to Queensland or had much to do with it. Okay, so you've taken him to Beerwah. Have you talked to him along the way or ...?'

'Yes, we just chatted.'

'And no problems ... Like I said, I'm not judging you at all, all right? So ... just tell me what I need to fix. You've taken him to Beerwah.'

'Went to an abandoned house thing that I knew.'

'Do you know exactly where that was?'

'Yes, the end of Roys Road.'

'Ang ... eroys?'

'Roys Road.'

'How do you spell that?'

'Roys Road?'

'Oh, Roys Road. R-o-y-s, was it?'

'Yes.'

'Roys Road, at the end. Because what we might need to do is ... I'll get to that later. We're going to need to get that sorted.'

'There's nothing there. I went back because I just put him under bushes, and I went back to that area.'

'Okay, so you've taken him into the house. What happened in the house?'

'Um.'

'Like I said, I'm not judging you, all right?'

'Yep. I never got to molest him or anything like that. He panicked and I panicked and I grabbed him around the throat and, before I knew it, he was dead.'

'All right. How long did it take you to strangle him out? Do you know? You probably don't think about it like that …'

'It didn't seem long.'

'All right, so you grabbed him around the throat. Was he still sitting in the car?'

'No, no, we were out of the car.'

'So you take him to the house. Whereabouts in the house?'

'Just into … there's no furniture or nothing, just into the first room. When I opened the door …'

'Did he f—ing spit, leave blood, anything, in that room?'

'Not that I know of.'

'What about his clothing? Did he have all his clothing on still?'

'Yes, he had his clothing on then.'

'All right, so you choked him out. He's died in that room. What have you done then with him?'

'Taken him outside, took his … put him into the back of my car …'

'When you say the back of your car, you're talking about the …? It was a white four-wheel drive or something?'

'A Pajero. It was like a …'

'Like a big door in the back? Did it have seats in the back as well?'

'No, I had the seats taken out. The mulcher was in there.'

'All right, so you've laid him in the back of the car. Was the mulcher there still?'

'Yes.'

'Did he touch the mulcher or …?'

'Nothing.'

'Do you reckon you left any prints at the house or …?'

'No, the house is gone.'

'It's gone? All right, we'll get to that in a minute. So you've taken him in the back of your car. How long did this take you, do you reckon?'

'I only had to go like from the house 150 metres … to where I … it's all bush.'

'Okay, all right. So you take him from the house?'

'Because it's an old sand-mining site.'

'So you pick him up from the house, put him in the back of your car and you've driven him 150 metres or so to where?'

'More secluded bush away. It's in a fenced-off area. I was actually gonna lease the property to do sandblasting on. There's an embankment where the sand mining got up to and then it's all been growing over with trees and bush again, and then you've got the old lake, the sand-mining lake … dragged him …'

'Yep, mate, I'm not familiar with the area, mate, so just draw us a little f—ing map so I know what you're talking about, just from like where the house was to where the thing was.'

Arnold produced a sheet of paper and a pen. Cowan leaned further over and began drawing on it on the coffee table. The long hours and months of police work had paid off. Cowan appeared to be absorbed in his role in the scenario and showed no sign of being suspicious about the number of questions that he was being asked. Now the dam had burst, he seemed hell-bent on giving an explanation of what happened that day.

'The end of Roys Road comes in like that, to a macadamia or an avocado farm.'

'Yep.'

'And that sort of spreads out around here like this. There's a couple of sheds and then there was the house …'

'Yes, yes.'

'Where the house is there's a little track that goes off down there through a gate.'

'Yep.'

'Down to a caravan, an old mobile saw mill ...'

'About 150 metres away ...?' Arnold asked.

'Yes ...'

'So, once you've done that, what have you done with him then?'

'I took him out of the car and dragged him down the embankment.'

'When you dragged him, did you leave any, how did you drag him: by the feet, by the arms or ...?'

'I carried him over and threw him over the embankment.'

'Okay, so you threw him over the embankment. How far was that?'

'Metre and a half.'

'Metre and a half down. Has he left any marks or ...?'

'No.'

'Okay, and you f—ing pushed him like the old cowboy movies ...'

'Yes.'

'All right, so he's gone down the embankment about a metre and a half. What have you done then?'

'I went down there and dragged him through. I don't know how far it was, until I found somewhere I thought was ...'

'A good spot?'

'Yeah.'

'So was that sand ... grass, what?'

'Sand.'

'Did he still have all his clothing on? Did you leave anything behind?'

'No, he had all his clothes on.'

'Yep.'

'I've stripped him off, got trees, branches and covered his body with that. His clothes I took back with me and threw 'em into the creek.'

'You threw them in the creek ... which creek?'

'I'm not too sure.'

'Was the creek there, right there, or did you have to ...?'

'No, no, it was on the way home. I had to go across one and it's all secluded like an old logging bridge type thing.'

'Went over a logging bridge down a creek or something?'

'Yes, there's a creek there, fast flowing, and I just threw his clothes in there.'

'You just chucked it in. Did you have to put them in a bag or anything like that?'

'What?'

'One by one or the whole lot. What happened to them?'

'I threw them all in.'

'What happened to them?'

'They sank and floated away.'

'They sank and floated away?'

'None of that's ever been found.'

'You're lucky, aren't you?'

'Yep.'

Arnold changed position several times on the couch as restless as a cat on a hot tin roof. Cowan, in contrast, barely moved, occasionally inching a little further forward with his eager to please face on.

'All right. So, after you've done all that, now I've heard something about a f—ing watch, that he had a watch, some f—ing thing?'

'Yep.'

'Did you have that?'

'It all went in.'

'The whole lot went in? So you didn't keep anything of his? There's no chance anyone is going to find anything of his?'

'No, nothing.'

'All right, so you've left him there under the shrubs? What have you done then?'

'I went home.'

'You've thrown his clothes in the thing … you've gone home?'

'Yep. I did stop at my dealer's place … they're lying when they say I wasn't there.'

'All right, okay, so you did go to the f—ing dealer. Mind you, from what I understand … she's probably that drug f—ed that she wouldn't know what time of the day it was. All right, so you've gone to your dealer's place. After you've thrown the clothes in the river, you've gone to the dealer's house?'

'Yep …'

'You've picked up there?'

'Yep … spent about 15–20 minutes there, which I always did. Liked to spend half an hour or so, so I'm not walking in and out. Went home, went inside, said "G'day" to my wife, went outside and started chipping the timber.'

'So that's the end of that then. Did you go back?'

'About a week … well within that week I went back.'

'Had it hit the press by then, that he was missing?'

'I think so, yeah …'

'All right, so … it hadn't hit the press then?'

'Yeah, like as a missing person.'

'So a missing person, and you're thinking, "Oh f—, I better do something here or …"'

'Just in case, I took a shovel back.'

'So about a week later, you've gone back, you've taken a shovel back in the same car?'

'Yes.'

'Where did you go then?'

'I went down to where I've put him … and I only found a fragment of bone. The rest of it was gone.'

'F—, in a week?'

407

'In a week. The rest of it was gone. There was a patch there, you could tell ...'

'So what do you reckon's happened there?'

'I don't know. There's a lot of yabbies and animals and that sort of thing.'

'All right, so what was left of him?'

'A little piece of bone.'

'No skull, no f— all. So what have you done with that?'

'That was part of the skull.'

'Yep.'

'I broke it up with the shovel.'

'So it's broken up, it's still there?'

'Yep.'

'Because that's going to cause us a problem. We're going to have to go and grab that.'

'No, I broke it.'

'I know, but nowadays they can do wonders with all that stuff and shit. DNA and all that kind of crap. We'll have to. I'll have to get you to fly over there with a couple of boys and sort all of that shit out, all right? We'll sort it out for you. The shovel, you broke it all up with a shovel. Where's the shovel now?'

'Don't know. I took it home with me. Used it in the gardens.'

'As far as you know, is it still there?'

'At the house?'

'Well, it's a f—ing long time ago, I suppose.'

'Yeah.'

'Is someone still living in that house?'

'Someone has rented the house.'

'So the shovel might still be there? You don't know.'

'I left my wife about seven months, eight months after that. We moved from that house to Nambour to another house and then I left her and went to Moranbah.'

'All right. So as far as you know there is nothing of his you've kept that can make you f—ing come unstuck?'

'Yes, nothing at all.'

'And the bit of bone that was left. How big was it?'

'Only tiny.' Cowan made a shape by cupping his hands, suggesting a diameter smaller than a tennis ball.

'That's amazing, hey? So you've gone there to bury it all and that's what's left ... All right. Is there anything else you can think we need to f—ing clear up? Your alibi, this drug dealer of yours: do you still talk to her?'

'No, I haven't been in touch with her ...'

'You reckon we could approach her and pay her some f—ing dollars, or you think we should? I'll have a think about that.'

'She's still into drugs, as far as I know, so she may be approachable on that sort of thing. But it's the boyfriend that's saying he would have remembered the motor and all that sort of stuff on the chipper.'

'What's the chipper got to do with all of this?'

'That's because I did show him the chipper.'

'Oh, you showed him the chipper and he's saying that he would have remembered, but he's saying that he doesn't remember.'

'He doesn't remember.'

'All right, Shaddo. Look, I need to make some f—ing calls and I need to have a bit of a think. What I'll do, I'll get ... Jeff to come back up and they can take you down. Go buy yourself something f—ing to eat.'

'Yep.'

'Let me make some calls and when I've sorted out the calls I'll give you a call back about what we're going to do. Might have to think about putting you up tonight somewhere, get you on a plane tomorrow with one of the boys, couple of the boys and sorting all this shit out, go and have a look and making sure everything is f—ing good. Because if we can sort this out now, it's going to, you know, keep us all happy, right. Anything else?'

'I said to Fitzy the other day about cutting all ties. I've cut ties to me family before. And I've got no problem with cutting all ties to everybody, even to the state of a death certificate, dead.'

'Okay, look, you know I can f—ing fix things. We sent Joe [Emery] away for a while as well. He had a few dramas. It's not an issue, all right?'

'All right. Hopefully he's going all right.'

'I'm sure he's going all right. So have faith in me, all right?'

'Yes.'

'We'll sort this out for you and we'll move on. I might have to put this job back a little bit till we sort this out, but that's not a problem, all right?'

'Nobody else knows that's …?'

'Now it's up to you what you tell them, all right? All they know is I needed to talk to you about something.'

'Yes, it's not something I'm going to tell anybody.'

'No … no, that's fine. You have to come up with a scenario then. Let me have a think about it and we'll sort something out.'

'If Jeff and that need to know that, like …'

'Someone else is going to need to know …'

'I'll leave that in your corner …'

'… because I'm going to have to send someone else with you to sort all this f—ing shit out, all right? So let me have a think about it. Let me get … I'll talk to a couple of my people that've f—ing been giving me some of this info just to see if there's anything else that could get us unstuck.'

'Really it's that half-an-hour alibi, that when she's saying I wasn't there, that's what …'

'Well, we need to clear up if there's anything left there. You say the house is gone now?'

'Yes, the house is gone.'

'What do you mean gone now, like demolished?'

'I don't know it's like a worker's cottage ...'

'No blood, no spit, f—ing ... Did you f— him?'

'No, I didn't touch him.'

'Did you f—ing blow, did you ...?' Arnold motioned with his hand. 'So you left no ... nothing?'

'No, nothing, and even if there was my DNA in the house, I'd been there before with another guy ...'

'Okay, now look, while we're talking about it, is there anything else I need to sort for you?'

'Like?'

'Like anything else you've f—ing done that's going to get us unstuck?'

'No, there's nothing.'

'So no more kids they're going to find missing and looking at you?'

'No, nothing like that at all.'

'All right.'

'I didn't go out that day to molest a kid either, or anything like that, it just happened ...'

'It just happened?'

'It just ... yes.'

'So when you threw this f—ing – I'm just thinking. As you're talking I'm thinking, because there's a lot of shit I'm trying to f—ing sort out here. There's something about this watch, you know, they're missing this f—ing watch. Did you see a watch he had or ...?'

'I didn't.'

'So it might have been in the pocket or some f—ing thing. I wonder if it was heavy enough to sink ... might have to ... you're going to have to show them also where you ...'

'All been floods through there, the amount of time ago it was and everything.'

411

'That's probably in your advantage because what concerns me is the actual f—ing place where you took him, but we'll sort that out.'

'Nobody really knows about that place either so …'

'Yes, we'll sort it all right. And like I said, we're just going to have to put things back a bit. We'll sort it.'

Arnold picked up his phone again. 'How you going, mate? Listen, you want to come back up with Jeff and grab Shaddo and just take him down for a coffee, or a drink or a bite to eat or something? I just got a few calls, got to sort a few things out. No worries. See you soon. Bye.'

He turned to Cowan again. 'At this stage, they don't know anything, all right, so it's up to you what you want to tell them, but I'm going to have to bring someone else on board obviously.'

Cowan nodded.

'… And you know I've built this business up over a long time, and I've got a lot of good contacts all around Australia and internationally, and you know ultimately the heat's on me, the heat's also on f—ing them. So the big, big thing I've got to think of – but if I can't sort this out for you – and I'm pretty sure I can then we can move on, all right?'

'Cool.'

'Want a smoke or something?'

'I've got my cigarettes.'

They both stood up and headed towards the balcony. Out on the verandah, Cowan lit up a cigarette, inhaling deeply. Arnold smoked too. Cowan was back to being slightly cocky, telling him he was 'reasonably confident' they couldn't pick him up. He told the story about changing his name to Shaddo N-Unyah Hunter, that he had 'a puppy dog' in Queensland whose name was Shaddo, giggling as he described the reasons why he chose that name. 'N-Unyah … N-Unyah business.'

'Very clever,' Arnold said, his mouth working at a smile.

He asked Cowan about his Pajero and Cowan told him it was on Russell Island in Moreton Bay, south of Brisbane, and that he had sold it to a mate as it was going to cost him $10,000 to fix it. They bantered on about cars and four-wheel drives, about FJ Cruisers, and how Cowan wanted to get one, Jeeps and Hummers. Cowan's long fingers fluttered as he swapped car talk with his new friend, shuffling from one foot to the other, grinning all the while, a man finally free from his burden.

Arnold brought the banter to a close. 'Go and get something to eat. Try and get you on a f—ing plane tomorrow. Might have to postpone things … keep you on board and sort these problems out for you …'

Before they left the verandah, Cowan pointed to the view. This was the kind of life that he had always coveted, he confided, waving his cigarette to the horizon.

Inside, on the sofa again, Cowan went back to the map of where he took Daniel, marking out the outhouses he had mentioned and Roys Road. He described how he threw Daniel's clothes off a bridge and that they would have drifted downstream and were probably in Pumicestone Passage. They talked more about what had happened to Daniel.

'I didn't even wash my car or nothing,' he said, '… and they had my car for a whole day on Christmas Day.' Cowan said when he got the car back it hadn't even been vacuumed but that there was fingerprint dust everywhere.

'Would he have touched anything?' Arnold wanted to know.

'Only the door handle … When he started to struggle … I was starting to pull his pants down, he said, "Oh no," and he was s … I was standing. He was squatting …' Cowan crooked his arm up, miming himself standing behind Daniel and choking him.

413

CHAPTER TWENTY-FIVE

THE ARREST

With the confession now behind them, Fitzy was summonsed back upstairs by Arnold and he and Cowan went to the basement of the hotel. Fitzy began recording almost as soon as they got inside the car and the mike picked up them fumbling for coins to put in the parking machine. He began driving to the Como Hotel for lunch. On the way there, he probed Cowan about what had happened, all the while secretly recording their conversation. Cowan revealed that the boss might be sending him to Brisbane. Slowly, he began telling Fitzy about what had transpired, adding that now it was only Fitzy and Arnold who knew he had been involved in Daniel Morcombe's disappearance. He became angry when he described to Fitzy how he had lost 45 minutes of accounted-for time because his alibi had become shaky. As Elton John music played in the background, the mike picked up Cowan ruminating over the events of that day. His words came thick and fast, as he marvelled at how fate had dealt him the opportunity that day.

'If I was ten minutes later getting the wood chipper …

He was standing there ... I seen the broken down bus ... I done a U-turn, the broken down bus got fixed and drove past ... knew another bus would be through shortly. The bus drove past us. I offered him a lift ... I went back about ten days after I took him – buried the rest of him, like buried the body ... Nothing there, a bit of bone and that's it.'

Cowan repeated again that, until today, he had told nobody.

Chatting about who might accompany him to Queensland to 'clean up' the mess, he said it would be good if Fitzy was able to come with him. Then he went back to the confession. 'Ever since him, I haven't touched another kid. It was only 'cause he struggled and I panicked. Otherwise, he would still be here today,' Cowan said.

'Did you know him?'

'No, it was a spur of the moment ... and that sounds f—ed up but if the bus hadn't broken down, he wouldn't have been there ... Um, if I'd been in the other lane, I mightn't have seen him.'

'Yeah.'

'Shit like that.'

Cowan bragged about how he hadn't bothered to clean his Pajero, and that they still hadn't caught him even after they took the car in to be checked. He talked again about his alibi. 'I could've been there a lot longer if he didn't panic. I could've been there for an hour doing stuff.' But he said that, in 10 or 15 minutes, he was back in the car driving home. He explained that he had used 'branches and grass' to bury Daniel. 'I don't know how I'm gonna react going back to the same area,' he confessed to Fitzy. 'Mentally or spiritually.'

'Yeah, there was no screaming or nothing?'

'F—ing nothing.'

Fitzy asked whether he had stabbed the boy, and Cowan replied, 'Choked him'.

They talked some more. 'See, this is what pisses me off: all the witnesses say there was two people. There was ...'

'Mmm ...'

'Me and another bloke – there was a white one, nah, blue car, parked there ... Um, everybody said there was a blue car with two blokes talking to him.' Cowan said it was just him and Daniel.

'Always believed when they first came – you know, when the coppers first came around – it was like, "F—, they got me." But none of the traffic cameras picked up on nothin'. And, once again, if they had a picture of him in my car, I would have been f—ed ... But in Queensland they got the law where you don't need a body to be charged with the crime.'

Fitzy asked about the place where he had taken Daniel.

'From where he went missing to where he ended up is 40 kilometres.'

'Yeah?'

Cowan could not stop talking. It was as though the dam had broken. Fitzy hardly asked any questions.

'It's still my route home so ... And I had him seat-belted in my front seat. He got willingly into the car because he thought he'd missed the bus because the bus drove straight past him. He said he was going down the shops ... You know, I've never lied to the police other than I didn't have anything to do with it ... but the other main suspect has threatened witnesses – false alibis.'

Cowan said that the story had not been in the news recently but that there had been a big write-up in one of the Sunday papers after the inquest.

Fitzy asked him about the area where he had dumped Daniel's body.

'Beerwah is an ... um, spread out farming community, yeah ... A lot of tracks ... They lead down to dead-end orchards.'

'Yeah.'

'They have the workers' quarters on it. I knew this place had workers' quarters on it. I do know it is there because I have been in there and I had had me "man fun" in there. In there, I knew it was safe ... f—ing four people can say I been in there, you know, so ...'

'Yeah ... what did he do when you were driving?'

Cowan suggested Daniel sat quietly and spoke little. 'I went in the house and then came back and said, "The missus said do you want a drink before we go?"'

'Yeah?'

'You know, he came inside and I grabbed him ...' Cowan paused. He said if Daniel hadn't panicked and didn't run, he would have had his fun with him and dropped him back near where he'd got him, but that he 'probably would have been caught for it'. Cowan paused again. 'It's my deepest, darkest secret.'

Then there was more discussion about the potential Cowan could earn, and Fitzy suggested the possibility of Cowan driving down the road with $150,000 in his bum bag from their sort of work. Cowan laughed. There was an ever so slight note of hysteria in his voice.

Still at the pub, Cowan's mood was ebullient. He asked Fitzy to play pinball, which he said he hadn't played for ages. The afternoon wore on.

Back in the Swan River Room, when they returned, Arnold was serious. 'The only people that need to know about this need to know about it, right?' he asked Cowan.

'I've told Paul,' Cowan said, using Fitzy's first name.

'You've told Paul everything?'

'I've told Paul.'

Arnold says he was glad as they clearly had a good relationship. Arnold then told Fitzy the name of a hotel in Perth to take Cowan to and said it was booked in his name. 'Lock him down for the night. Book three flights for Paul, Shaddo and Ian. You go to Queensland tomorrow morning. When you get there, give Mal a call – he'll pick you up. Mal doesn't know the full story – just that he has to pick someone up … as we have to sort this shit out.' Fitzy was then paid $5000 to cover their expenses.

Arnold asked again about Daniel's fob watch. Cowan still maintained that he did not know where it was. He said he collected watches but swore he did not have Daniel's.

'Anything else [incriminating] that you can remember?' Arnold asked. 'Prints, saliva …'

'No, nothing like that. Carpet in the back of the car … I had sheets sitting down: the mulcher was sitting on top of the sheets …'

'What colour bed sheets? White sheets?'

'No, floral.'

Cowan said he ripped the sheets up afterwards and used them for rags and tying stakes in the garden. Quizzed further by Arnold, he said did not know whether Daniel's body had touched the mulcher or not and that he had washed the mulcher before returning it.

Fitzy asked whether anything else needed fixing.

'Not unless you can stop my last girlfriend getting custody of my youngest son. He'll be two in December.'

Cowan explained that his brother had kinship custody of the boy and that his ex-wife, Tracey, had custody of his other two boys, and that there were court orders that the boys were allowed to phone him once a week. 'But it's too hard for my boys to understand why they couldn't see Dad …'

* * *

On 10 August 2011, Cowan, Fitzy and another 'crime syndicate operative', Ian, arrived at Brisbane Airport. Ian was a short man with cropped grey hair, more serious than Fitzy. To Cowan, he was the man Arnold had appointed to 'fix up' the mess of his past crime. Upon arrival, Cowan told them he did not want the Queensland police to detect his whereabouts via his mobile phone, so he was going to take his battery out. Instead, he told Fitzy he would use his $10 phone, which he'd had at home and needed a recharge. The irony was that he was in the company of two police officers.

As Ian went to get the car, Cowan and Fitzy discussed the route they would take to the Sunshine Coast. Occasionally, Fitzy would snigger at Cowan's jokes. Cowan, in an expansive mood, told Fitzy he didn't like the baked beans he had had for breakfast. When he woke up that morning, he said, his mouth was open and he was dribbling.

When Ian finally arrived with the rental car – a Toyota Hi-Ace which was actually an unmarked police car – Fitzy suggested that Cowan get in the front so he could navigate. Ian explained to Cowan that he didn't know much about the case, creating another opportunity to mine Cowan for information. He began by asking, 'How long ago did this happen?' Cowan told him when and then went on to talk about how he got married in 1998 and gave him an abbreviated history of his life. As they drove, Cowan pointed out places of interest, as though the purpose of their visit was to take in the sights. They turned off the Bruce Highway at Steve Irwin Way and went through to Beerwah and heading for Cowan's old house on Alf's Pinch Road.

Ian asked Cowan whether his 'missus' knew what was going on.

'She knew I was going up to pick up a chipper that day,' Cowan answered. '... um, but she doesn't know anything about what I actually did. This is the first word I've ever spoken about it ...' He paused.

'Feel all right?' asked Fitzy.

'Yeah, yeah and no.'

It was the typical ambivalent response Cowan gave to questions.

'If you want a break ...' Fitzy said. There was talk of stopping for a cigarette.

'Don't stop in the street,' Cowan said quickly. 'I still know people that live here.'

They talked about Cowan's white Pajero and how it had 300,000 kilometres on the clock. He told them he had put another couple of hundred thousand on the clock after driving back and forth from Moranbah, west of Mackay.

They drove past Sandy Drummond's house, and Cowan described how he would buy a small amount of pot from her. He told Fitzy and Ian that he wanted to take them as close as possible to the most authentic route that he took the day Daniel disappeared and when he drove to get the mulcher from Nambour. The road had changed, he commented as they continued with the drive. The bridge had been built over the railway line near the RSL. When Ian asked about timing, Cowan told him he was 'not 100 per cent' sure on the times he left home that day nor when he returned, but he thought it was 'between one and three-ish'.

'I didn't have a watch on, hardly ever wore a watch … f—in' sandblasting …'

Eventually, they were on the road to Nambour, or 'Namboring' as Cowan told them he called it. 'It's dead, just like a ghost town.'

He showed them the Big Pineapple. 'I had my wedding reception there,' Cowan said. As they drove under the overpass, Cowan pointed out the church on their right. 'That's the church I was married in.'

At the same time as he passed the overpass, he pointed to the side of the road where the memorial stood and then at the church behind. 'That's where I parked my car, picked him up …'

'Did you see him when he was standing there when you [first] went past?' Ian asked.

'No.'

They passed Thrill Hill Water Slides as they headed towards the Woombye turn-off. Fitzy reminisced about how much he used to enjoy going down a water slide when he was little: 'used to get those big long tarps, f—in' water it all down with soap and detergent on the grass at home'.

Cowan pointed out a hill where he'd lost the trailer he was towing and recounted how another motorist had told him he'd 'almost took out a lady and her kids'. They pulled up outside Frank Davis's house on Perwillowen Road in Nambour, where Cowan had picked up the mulcher. Cowan told further tales of past exploits, pointing out other local landmarks.

'You drove back the same way?' Ian asked.

'Yep, same way.'

Driving south back down the Nambour Connection Road, Cowan showed them where he saw the broken down bus at the Woombye turn-off, but said he couldn't recall whether he noticed it when he was on his way to picking up the mulcher – only on the way back. He directed Ian to turn left after they drove under the overpass, pointing out where he first saw Daniel standing close to the road. He described Daniel as 'f—in' cute'.

Showing them where he parked his car in the church car park, Cowan described how back then the spot was once sheltered by bushy trees. Ian pulled over and quizzed him further on what happened.

'There was no struggle, no f—in' screamin' and shoutin' – nothing. He willingly got into my car ... I sat up against the wall, you know, waitin', and um, yeah, when um the bus drove past, he was like, "Oh f—, what am I gonna do?" and I offered him a lift ... Came and got in the car and we left. Went back the same way.'

'And where'd he sit?' Ian asked.

'Front seat. If there was anything found in the car, I wouldn't be sitting here with youse now.'

He said police had called later to his house at Alf's Pinch Road when he was at work at Clayton's Towing Service. He said he had been willing to do 'whatever they wanted me to do'. Asked what Daniel had been wearing, he said, 'red shirt, blue pants, shoes and socks'.

'Carrying anything?' Ian asked.

'No.'

'Where was he going?'

'Going to get a haircut ... goin' into Sunshine Plaza. So I told him I'd give him a lift but I had no intention of taking him to the shopping centre. Like if the bus had stopped and he'd got on the bus ...'

'What were you thinking?'

'I don't really know what I was thinking. I'm an opportunistic offender ...'

They were still parked near the church. Cowan said he did not want to hang around as his auntie and uncle were pastors there. Asked what Daniel had said while he was in Cowan's car, Cowan replied they hadn't talked much. Cowan had been more concerned with where he was going and what he was doing.

As they drove on, he pointed out the traffic cameras on the overpass to Ian and Fitzy.

Ian again asked what he and Daniel had discussed.

'Um ... I just said I've gotta duck home quickly and let me missus know what's going on. He didn't ask where I was goin' ... I had no intention of going anywhere near my wife.'

'So he didn't ask why you weren't going straight ahead to the Sunshine Plaza?'

Fitzy butted in, asking for directions as to where they were going next and Cowan told them. Ian then asked, 'What did he do when you said you were just dropping home ...?'

'He just said, "Yeah ... all right, no worries." Don't exactly know what he said but he was all right with it. Yeah, the bus drove past and the next bus ... you know ... in his mind wasn't comin' for over an hour.'

'You were acting like waiting for someone to get off the bus?'

'Yes. I said, "I'll have to go down and pick her up from town then, you know,"' Cowan replied.

Cowan still maintained he could not remember any particular conversation he had with Daniel in the car except to say 'we were just talkin' and stuff'.

'This is a long way from the shops and shit ...' Fitzy remarked as they turned right after crossing the roundabout to join the Bruce Highway and began heading south towards Brisbane.

'It's only ten minutes down the highway from the Plaza ...' Cowan said.

They drove past rows and rows of pine trees until the distinctive Glass House Mountains came into view. Then they turned off the highway heading towards Kings Road and the site where he claimed to have driven Daniel.

Soon, they took a wrong turn to the left and had to do a U-turn to go back towards Kings Road.

Near the end of Kings Road, where it began to peter out, beside the macadamia farm, Cowan pointed out where the building once stood near the large mango tree. 'And that's where it happened ... That's where I thought he was going to run, and my arm went around his neck and I choked him out. I actually felt that break in there, so ... like in ... that bone thing – that bone that's in – I felt that snap in me arm when I pushed it in below the Adam's apple.' Cowan's voice was still soft, as though describing nothing untoward.

'Did he say anything?' Ian asked.

'When I started pulling his pants down, he went, "Oh no." I actually went into the house when he sat in the car. And then I came out and said, "Oh, me missus said come in and get a drink ..." You know, to make it look good. I went in and came out after that.'

'So you put him back in the car or something?' Fitzy asked.

'Yeah, I put him in the back of the Pajero.'

'Did you have the wood chipper in the back?'

'Was he breathing or nothing …?' Ian asked.

'Nah.'

Cowan pointed out an old mobile timber mill and showed them where he parked his car that day on 7 December 2003. They got out of the car. Showing them a mound of dirt, he said he parked at the back of it, where there were some metal frames. He pointed at some long grass and said that was where he was going to set up the sandblaster for the business that never got off the ground.

Cowan described how after disposing of Daniel's body, he obliterated his tyre marks with tree branches.

'You scrubbed them out?' asked Fitzy.

'Yeah, I f—in' got a branch from the tree …'

Ian pointed to the embankment and the encroaching pine forest. 'What, and you carried him over here?'

'Yeah …'

'Was he big?'

'Not really … Yeah, and I dropped him down there.'

They moved closer to the embankment through the saplings that grew near the edge.

'And then I got down there myself …'

The three men stepped over the embankment. Clinging to the pine trees, they scrambled down until they were on level ground. There was dense bush and branches and clumps of grass on the ground below, and in the distance the dam shimmering. There wasn't as much undergrowth in 2003, Cowan said.

'I dragged him over – like he'd be covered by water by the looks of it now, 'cause the water wasn't there … I didn't bury him. I just put him under branches and shit. I came back about ten days later and found nothing – just one little bit of bone. I had my shovel with me and everything.'

Down on the flat, they made their way across to a body of water. There was sand underfoot.

'It would have been over this side,' Cowan said. 'I haven't been back here ...'

'Where that island is?' asked Fitzy, pointing.

'No ... in where the water is.' Cowan said he had heard that nothing grew in an area where there had been a body. 'There was no bones, no teeth, nothing. There was just what I thought was a bit of skull. Then I crushed it with the shovel and *chop chop chop chop*' – Cowan made vertical chopping motions with his hand – 'crushing it into the ground.'

'None of his clothes were there or nothing?' Ian asked.

'... that's why we're stopping at the bridge on the way back. I took the clothes and everything with me. I stripped him.'

Fitzy asked whether he was feeling all right. 'Yeah and no ... and don't really want to be here ... Yeah, I'm nervous ...' He said he took Daniel's shoes and socks and bundled them all together. He said again he had not seen any watch. He told them his grandparents had fob watches and his mum had one, but he had definitely not seen Daniel's. 'I didn't go through his pockets, though.' On the way back out of the embankment, Cowan pointed to the path he took, saying he was 'dragging' the body 'pretty quick' as well as carrying it.

'Shaddo ... didn't tell me you had to be a commando to do this shit, mate. I like the urban area,' Fitzy quipped.

Back on flat land, Cowan again showed how he had got rid of his tyre marks. 'F—in' smart, hey?'

Fitzy did not respond, momentarily out of the habitual play of camaraderie after hearing Cowan chillingly describe Daniel's murder. Instead, he noted it was 5 pm.

Back on Kings Road again, opposite the macadamia farm, they stood before a large shed next to the mango tree. Behind the shed were buildings linked together like prison cells. 'These were old tobacco-drying sheds,' Cowan said. 'This side of the Steve Irwin Way are pineapple and avocado farms, but on the other side it is tobacco.'

As they were driving, Cowan initially became confused as to which bridge he had thrown the clothes from. They first stopped at a small bridge on Kings Road. Then he directed them to a second bridge in Woods Road, about 400 metres away. Cowan confirmed this was it.

They left the car parked back up the road a bit.

'It all went out the driver's window so ...'

'Did you make sure it wasn't floating?' Fitzy asked.

'Yeah, I don't think it was ...' Cowan peered over the side. A large eucalypt lay across the creek, a short distance from the bridge. 'It wasn't like that before. It was smoother down the other side,' he said. 'It floated and then, as it was floatin' away, it was sinkin'. It's said that, every year that it rains really hard, that bridge goes underwater so ... Yeah, there was no logs or anything across there. It was just water.'

Ten years ago, he told them, some people had drowned when their car had overturned from the bridge and it had sat on its roof. 'They couldn't get out.'

Ian's phone had been beeping. He told Fitzy and Cowan he had to ring Arnold. When he returned, it was to report that Arnold was still concerned about the watch. Cowan again said he did not have it – unless, he said, it fell out of his car but police hadn't found it in his car. He repeated that he hadn't checked Daniel's pockets as he 'wasn't interested in stealing money'.

He described again how he had killed Daniel.

'He didn't say anything?'

'Nope ... Yeah, well, I probably would have been caught in the end if I ... let him go. He could have got me f—in' licence plate ... F—in' when I let him out and f—in' what type of car it was.'

'When you were driving down here, were you going to knock him?' Ian asked.

'No intention whatsoever.'

Ian wandered away again. He arrived back saying, 'Arnold's happy. I just rang him.' Ian told Cowan he would be put up in a hotel.

As they drove out, Fitzy questioned whether Cowan had just driven home after disposing of Daniel's body and clothes. Cowan said he had stopped at his dealer's, as this had been prearranged.

There was silence, then Fitzy spoke. 'Hey, Shadz, why did you take the clothes off the dude?'

'Well, um, I don't know, f—in' … it's red,' Cowan replied. 'Easily seen … Clothes take longer to break down …'

'Yeah,' Fitzy says.

'… and I was unsure if any hair, skin, DNA would be on it of my own.'

'Yeah,' Fitzy responded. 'You've been thinking … that's what I've said about you: you're f—ing smart.'

There was a discussion about lunch and Cowan told them there were lots of boutique restaurants around.

After dropping him off, Fitzy and Ian told Cowan that, the following day, 11 August, he could do his own thing as they were returning to the scene to 'clean up' and make sure there was no evidence left. Instead, the following morning, Fitzy and Ian met up with a Detective Anthony Parsons and revisited the places Cowan had taken them the day before. They were filmed from behind as they did so, the cameraman taking care not to reveal the features of either of the two undercover policemen.

After visiting the scene that morning, Fitzy picked Cowan up just before 1.30 pm, and they drove to a cafe in Redcliffe. Cowan told Fitzy he had burnt the clothes he was wearing, shorts and a singlet, in the family barbecue. '… f—in' cooked tea then threw the clothes in after I got me tea,' Cowan said.

'F—ing covered yourself well,' Fitzy said.

'I thought I was gone, man,' Cowan replied. 'I really thought I was f—in' gone. Like when they came and questioned me … I just stuck to me story. I got me f—in' chipper, came home stopped at my dealer ... I didn't tell them I'd stopped at me dealer's place ... don't dob on your dealer ... Even though they're making out I had no trouble in givin' up other people that smoke and everything, I f—in' didn't.'

Cowan steadfastly stuck to his story that he had not seen Daniel's wallet or fob watch. 'I paid no attention to his clothing. I just took them off ... I stake my life on that one, Paul. I'll put my life up on that. I'll go down ... Mateship too, my job, the whole f—in' lot, man. I'd even put my kids' life on it. I don't have it.'

On the phone to Arnold, Fitzy repeated in front of Cowan that he swore on his life and swore on his mateship that he hadn't seen the fob watch.

'Swear on me kids' life ...' Cowan butted in.

'Swears on his kids' life he has never f—ing even seen it, and he said the same about the wallet ...' Fitzy said into the phone.

'And I don't give me kids' lives up at all,' Cowan added.

'Nah ... nah, f—, man ...' Fitzy replied.

'Other than me mum and dad and my kids and my family, and that's it ...' Cowan continued.

'Yeah ...'

'But, you know, as I said, if I have to die ... I don't see me kids now. I'm not losing out or anything ... I don't speak to them or anything. It just means if I'm still kicking when they turn 18, and I still can't see 'em.'

They returned once again to what Cowan did to Daniel.

''Cause it crushed that and I ... like ... only goin' by CSI and shit like that ...'

'Yeah,' Fitzy said.

'Once that's crushed, that's it an' yeah you're gone ...'

Cowan said that means you are dying through lack of oxygen.

'... That crushes an' the bone in there actually sort of ... it ... it's shaped like, it's shaped like that in your throat but when you crush it, it comes back the other way and blocks off all you … I didn't know anything about it until I seen it on TV …'

Asked about how he had placed Daniel's body, Cowan said 'on his back'. 'And, for some reason, facing east. I only just realised this … Like the way his body was positioned was east-west.'

When Fitzy asked what that meant, Cowan replied: 'Well a lot of people bury their … dead east to west so the rising sun … rises in their face.'

'Were you spinning out?'

'I think I shut down … I just went into f—in' safety mode to protect myself … I wasn't out to kill him, that definitely wasn't on the cards – but if he'd played the game, I would have had a suck, made him suck me off, rah, rah, rah, then taken him. Once I blow … once I blow … I'm not interested any more. So I would've been, "C'mon, let's go." F—in' taking him to the shopping centre … left him … f—in' driven off. I wouldn't be sittin' here talking to you today if that happened either,' Cowan sniffed as though amazed himself at the turn of events.

They talked about how Cowan had later noticed the memorial the Morcombes had erected for Daniel and how his wife, Tracey, had driven the white Pajero and how he hadn't bothered to wipe it down. Cowan commented that he couldn't believe he was talking so 'matter-of-factly'. He told Fitzy that he'd been back once to the demountable, several years later with his then girlfriend, Leticha.

'Was the house there?' Fitzy asked.

'The only house that was there was the worker's cottage. That got my head going again … did the police come and get the demountable? You know … f—in' shit like that.'

Cowan said there was little to connect him to the crime as he'd covered his tracks literally. His tattoos were his only concern, and the only one the police had on his record was the tattoo with a skull.

On 12 August, Fitzy texted Cowan, telling him he would pick him up at around 2 pm. They went to a cafe near Racecourse Road and had a meal and something to drink. For a change, they did not talk about Daniel. Fitzy told Cowan they would probably be heading back to Perth the following day. Ian had been working on 'clearing up the problem' and had told Fitzy to tell Cowan that they still needed to find Daniel's fob watch.

The next day, 13 August, Ian and Fitzy picked up Cowan just before 10 am. The decision to arrest Cowan was still up in the air. What evidence did they have other than the confession? In the end, the decision was made by the upper hierarchy of the Queensland Police Service. They drove to Kings Road on the pretext of looking for the fob watch. Ian parked the car in the clearing at the end of Kings Road. It was around 11 am. The men got out. Immediately, from behind log piles and the bush, four men appeared: plain-clothes police officers Detective Senior Constable Ross Hutton, Detective Senior Sergeant Steve Blanchfield, Detective Senior Sergeant Edwards and Detective Senior Sergeant Graeme Farlow. They approached the car. Cowan, Fitzy and Ian were all arrested. Cowan, as ever, showed no emotion and was quiet from the moment police appeared.

Cowan's mobile phone was confiscated by Hutton. Blanchfield immediately read out his caution. Cowan, pale-faced, said he declined to comment. He was told he was able to make some calls on Hutton's phone. He said he wanted to ring his parents. He also rang a solicitor, and was transported to police headquarters in Roma Street in Brisbane. In the underground car park, while outside the lifts, Blanchfield allowed Cowan to have a cigarette. He watched as Cowan stood against the concrete wall next to the lifts and put his left leg up behind him before inhaling deeply. It was the same pose described by many of the witnesses on the Sunbus that had not stopped to pick up Daniel.

CHAPTER TWENTY-SIX

SEARCHING FOR THE TRUTH

For 2803 days, Bruce and Denise had repeated the mantra 'Today's the day we find out what's happened to Daniel'. It was as much a cry of hope as anything else. When that day finally came, however, in spite of thinking they were prepared, they were totally blindsighted by events, unprepared for the emotional impact.

It was an ordinary Saturday, 13 August 2011. Denise's appointment at 'Cut that Out', the hairdressers in Woombye was for 10 am. That night was their niece Jessica's 21st birthday at Scarborough, a northern suburb of Brisbane. The theme was 'detective' and Denise still didn't have anything in particular to wear. After putting on some washing and sweeping the kitchen floor, Denise grabbed a cup of coffee and walked outside to the back verandah. Looking out at their lush tropical Queensland garden, she noticed a black and white butterfly, about the size of a saucer, on the grass. That was unusual. Usually they were high up on a tree somewhere or sometimes on a bush. Perhaps it had broken its wings? She walked across the grass, bent down and picked it up. It didn't fly away. Carefully, she placed it on to Daniel's Hibiscus which was planted a metre away, near the back door. The hibiscus, a bright luscious red with white swirls, was now about a metre high.

Later, as she pottered in the kitchen, she looked out of the window. The butterfly had gone. Its wings mustn't have been broken after all. The phone rang. It was Mike Condon, the Assistant Commissioner. He was coming up to the Sunshine Coast and thought he might drop in to say hello. He said he would ring before he turned up. Probably a routine call to update them about the police investigation. Denise knew Bruce had been sending him emails.

Inside the hairdresser, Denise sat waiting for her foils to set while her mind ran through the errands she had to do on the way home. She had bought a Royal Doulton crystal photo frame and needed wrapping paper for it, and she still didn't have an outfit to wear. She'd decided on jeans and a shirt and a black felt hat. As she left the hairdressers around 11.30 am, she noticed that the church across the road was having a garage sale. There were old clothes in a pile and on racks. She looked at a few jumpers and skirts and then spotted some old brown pants and a matching blazer from Katie's. All up, they cost $2 – they would make an ideal costume and would go with the black hat. She paid for them, then went to Nambour and bought the gift, the wrapping paper and a card before stopping at Woolworths to buy a few groceries and then heading home.

Mike Condon rang again at around lunchtime. He'd been held up. Denise pointed out that she and Bruce would be leaving at around 6 pm to drive down to Scarborough for their niece's party. Condon assured them he'd be there before they left. Back at home, Bruce put some beers in the freezer for the party. It had been decided that Denise would drive. Dean and Bradley were coming too. Denise tried on the suit – it looked good, though was a little too big. She put on black ankle boots and then the hat. Then she began wrapping the birthday gift. It was getting on for 5 pm. The phone rang again. Bruce answered it.

It was a Channel Nine news reporter, Neil Doorley.

'Is it true?' Doorley asked.

'Is what true?' Bruce asked, immediately alert. 'What do you know?'

But Doorley would not say.

The new iPhone they'd bought for the Foundation then began ringing. Denise picked it up. It was Bob Atkinson, the Police Commissioner.

'Is Bruce with you?' he asked.

'Yes,' Denise said. 'Why?'

'Can you put the phone on speaker?'

She fumbled with the phone trying to work it out so both she and Bruce could hear what Bob had to say. Something had happened. Denise could sense it.

'I can't work out how to do it, Bob,' Denise said, frustrated. 'I'll relay it to Bruce.'

'There's been a man arrested for killing Daniel. They'll be charging him soon.'

'Who is it?' Denise asked, dumbfounded.

'It's Cowan.'

Denise handed the phone to Bruce unable to hear more, her mind in shutdown.

There was a knock at the front door. It was Mike Condon. Condon, who rarely smiled, was especially grave. Bruce opened the door, still on the phone to the Police Commissioner. He hung up and they both walked into the lounge room, Condon sitting on the three-seater couch and Bruce and Denise taking the single armchairs. They now knew why he was there. For almost eight years, they had been waiting to hear these words. After so many false leads, this time the police had evidence. Denise broke down. The news came as a complete shock. Daniel was really dead.

Afterwards, Peter Boyce was the first person to get a phone call from Bruce. He was at a football match where his son was playing. He couldn't believe what he was hearing. Then, Bruce and Denise began the long task of phoning family members, making the call everyone had been waiting to receive. Someone had been arrested for Daniel's murder. They rang Scott and Shelly and said they would not be coming to Jessica's 21st.

As she was speaking on the phone, Denise noticed the first bulletins flash up at the bottom of the silent television screen in front of her: 'Man arrested in Morcombe case'. Soon, there was a live cross. It was indeed true.

Then the phones began to constantly ring, and the texts flooded in. The Morcombes did not pick up or answer any of these calls for at least two hours. Instead, they sat numbly in the lounge room. Brad and Dean came over for a while and then left. It was too much to take in after all these years. After regaining his composure by about 8 pm, Bruce decided to answer the calls. The first one was Queensland Premier Anna Bligh. She seemed close to tears, offering both personal and governmental support for their family. Denise then took a call from Tim Ryan, who was ringing from Hawaii. 'It's fantastic. They've found someone.' Tim sounded exuberant.

Denise started crying. 'That's my son ... How did you find out?'

Tim felt immediately chastened.

Robin Sherwell, a friend who worked at the Foundation, called in and sat with Bruce and Denise for a while to comfort them.

Within minutes of the arrest being confirmed through media outlets, the Foundation's official Daniel Morcombe Facebook page was deluged with condolences and messages of support. 'Like so many others tonight, I am shedding tears for what has been a long, hard journey for the Morcombe family ... and now a harder one is starting ... our thoughts and prayers are with you all,' one message said. But there were other Facebook messages, too, not only on Daniel's page but also on the Queensland Police Service's, unleashing community anger on the man, yet to be named, who had been arrested.

The police media organised a conference to be held at police headquarters in Roma Street shortly after the Morcombes were told. It had a surreal quality to it. Words were flying around that so many people had believed would never be said. 'This is obviously a very significant milestone in what has been a complex and protracted investigation,' Deputy Commissioner Ross Barnett told a packed media conference. There were five charges, he said, listing them in a steady, confident voice: child stealing, deprivation of liberty, indecent treatment of a child, murder on 7 December 2003 and interfering with a corpse. 'Today's arrest is underpinned by the dedication, tenacity and professionalism of every [police] officer who has worked relentlessly on this investigation for nearly eight years. We have repeatedly affirmed our commitment to solving this disappearance and have never wavered in that resolve.' Barnett revealed that the police would be searching an area of bushland in the Sunshine Coast but would not comment further because the matter was before the court.

For Bruce and Denise, the reading of the charges against Cowan at last provided them with some dates of when Daniel might have died. All this time, they had not known how long he had been kept alive.

* * *

Ken King was in Sydney running his own business when he heard the news. He immediately rang Dennis Martyn to confirm what he'd heard. He knew Martyn's feelings on the subject would not have changed over all those years. Martyn confirmed it. King found a cathedral in the city and went in to pray. He felt a curious mixture of relief and regret. He was part of the organisation that had let the Morcombes down. He felt consumed by guilt that the police hadn't done a better job. Cowan should have been investigated more fully back in early 2004.

The temptation for the police, he knew, would be to say that the arrest had taken so long because 'that's the time it took'. But King would never believe that. There might have been a lot of good intentions, but that did not change the fact of how long it had taken to charge the man he believed should have been arrested in the first few weeks after Daniel disappeared. Having so many resources was one thing but, he believed the investigation had fallen down because of the way in which it was handled.

King also felt that both the law and the courts failed society as a whole. Daniel had been murdered because the likes of Cowan and others should have stayed in custody. The sentencing regimes were grossly inadequate. People who committed violent, heinous crimes against children should never be allowed to do it again, certainly not be released after a short time to re-offend.

At 57, after leaving the police force, Julie Elliott had decided there were too many other things to do in life. When the phone rang in the early evening of 13 August, she was making a birthday cake for her granddaughter, who was turning three the following day. It was Bob Atkinson.

'We've made an arrest,' he said.

The emotional toll of the previous years swam before Elliott's eyes. She rang Sam McDowall – someone she knew would understand what the news meant. Their paths had diverged since they were both working on the case, but they were still friends.

The news flashed up on Julie's television screen a short while later. For Julie, it was like an out-of-body experience.

She hadn't cried so much since her mother and father had died. She continued to watch the news, sobbing her heart out. Julie had not expected such an emotional rollercoaster upon hearing that the case was finally coming to an end.

After some time, she picked up the phone and dialled Denise's number. She left a message.

* * *

Plagued by fresh thoughts of Daniel's fate now that Cowan had been arrested, Bruce and Denise could not sleep that night. This news was irrefutable. Cowan had made admissions. Bob Atkinson had told them. The image of Cowan smiling in court, his studied casualness and strange, statue-like composure when he appeared at the inquest would not go away. Instead of an effigy, Cowan was a real person – a man who could give them answers about Daniel's final moments. How would they feel when they confronted him and whatever Daniel had suffered at his hands? They were both unsure about how to deal with this sudden change of events. The day that they had finally heard the news they had been waiting for played through Denise's head.

In the early hours of the following morning, Sunday 14 August 2011, Denise suddenly remembered the butterfly alighting on Daniel's Hibiscus. It had been Daniel giving her a sign that something was about to happen. At 6 am, Bruce and Denise got up. Denise made coffee and they talked haltingly about what to do. Oblivious to the news, Max, their now chunky black Labrador, wagged his tail as he always did, looking for his morning pat.

At 9.30 am, Detective Superintendent Carless and Kym Charlton, the Executive Director of Queensland Police Service Media, arrived. Bruce had decided to call a conference to thank the community and media for all of their support throughout the investigation, and to deal with the media in one go. Denise was trembling uncontrollably. They had decided it was best that she not front the cameras. Bruce thought it was more appropriate to conduct the conference on the nature strip outside their big, black, motorised entrance gates, which fronted onto the road. This would be less invasive.

With one minute to go, at around 10 am, Denise suddenly joined Bruce as he walked up the front path. She had been by his side every other time. She would not falter now. They were greeted by the largest media gathering either of them had seen. Cameras were trained on their every movement. Some of the live-cross vans were parked nearby. Many of the journalists who had covered the case for years were in tears. Both Bruce and Denise spoke for around 30 minutes.

Denise was dressed in a white jersey dress with blue flowers. Pale with shock, she stood close to Bruce, who had his arm around her protectively. Most of the interview, she stared at the ground, the tattoo on her right ankle clearly visible above her slingback shoes. She said only a few words. 'He needs to be buried with dignity.' She added in a quiet voice that she was now being forced to confront the idea that her boy was 'never coming home'.

Bruce, in a long-sleeved, navy shirt, looked far more hesitant than in previous interviews. 'It's a very difficult place Denise and our family find ourselves in,' he said, slowly. 'It's a place you don't want to be in. It's an extremely difficult time and last night was not pleasant at all.' He explained that both Brad and Dean did not want to talk to the media as their grief was a private thing. He then spoke of how influential the coronial inquest into Daniel's disappearance had been on the present turn of events. Without the resurgence of interest and fresh leads, the investigation could have been treated as a cold case, he said.

Media reports had already begun speculating that the accused might be Cowan, in spite of him not being named.

Bruce could only go so far as to say: 'We have already seen the person that has been charged and I'm not sure there is really anything to gain from [attending tomorrow's hearing] other than it being extremely upsetting for us and extending that pain. We know who it is and what he looks like, and we have already given him the glare.'

The legal process, he said, needed to run its course.

Asked whether this meant closure for the family, Bruce responded swiftly: 'Closure is not a word we are very comfortable with and please consider a man has been charged, but our priority as parents is to find Daniel. That's what we are driven to do. We are assured the police service is hard-nosed in finding Daniel and returning his remains.'

Bruce said the family was bracing itself, as it could take several years for the case to be settled. 'We are aware it may still be a couple of years or even longer before this matter has fully run out.' Asked whether they were sure that the police would find Daniel's remains in bushland, Bruce replied, 'They certainly haven't found any of Daniel's remains or anything significant,' before adding, 'We are indebted to the police, who worked extremely hard.' He continued, 'We've said right from day one the person that is responsible picked on the wrong family – we said we would never give up. We're true to our word.'

The editor of the *Sunshine Coast Daily*, Mark Furler, asked whether the Foundation would continue now that Daniel had been found. Without hesitation, Denise said, 'Yes. We have worked very hard for many years. It will continue.'

'Would you like people to wear red tomorrow?' Furler asked.

'Yes, as a mark of respect, we would,' Bruce answered.

Bruce said the Foundation needed help to cover expenses, such as the cost of running its busy website. 'Our pockets are not lined with cash. We need ongoing financial support.' Expanding on why they would not be attending court the following day, Bruce said, 'We try and do things that are positive. It helps us get through the day. That's what is important to us and not seeing some dirtbag in court.'

Bob Atkinson and Mike Condon rang Bruce and Denise throughout the day, giving them updates on the searches that were being set up. Rain had hindered searchers and police were using sandbags, creating small ponds in the swampy ground that were methodically drained.

Denise rang Julie back late that morning. It was difficult for either woman to put into words what they felt. The conversation was brief. 'I need a hug,' Julie said. After so many years waiting for that moment, she needed to greet Denise the way she'd always promised. Denise needed the hug too. They had often discussed the possibility of someone being convicted but Daniel's body never being found, or perhaps the other way around, of Daniel's body being found but not the person who had abducted him. Now, they were apparently on the verge of getting both.

As soon as she entered the house after lunch that Sunday, Julie noticed how shocked they both looked, how little they had known of the lead-up to the news. Bruce was flushed and distracted, and Denise was white as a sheet. Both women clung to each other in the moment they had both described for so long but thought would never happen. Tears ran down their cheeks.

Emails poured in, including one from Ken Thompson, who had found his son, Andrew, after he disappeared overseas:

> A nation is now grieving for Daniel. My thoughts are very
> much with you both, as well as the rest of your family and
> friends. Of course, with Daniel himself. I will be forever
> grateful for the support you gave me in my search for my
> own son while you were still searching for Daniel. The
> nation is now grieving with you during the forthcoming

trial. I trust we can all provide you with the strength that
will be needed to get you through this ordeal.

Family and friends called in as the day blurred into a never-
ending procession of supporters. Many did not understand
the conflicting emotions the news had brought. While
there was cause for celebration that the man responsible for
abducting Daniel might finally have been found, the news
that they would definitely never see him again was a poisoned
chalice.

Later that evening, Queensland's leading forensic
pathologist, Peter Ellis, visited the search site. He had
assisted in identifying bodies after the two Bali bombings
in 2002 and the tsunami in 2004. Ellis's appearance sparked
media reports that Daniel's remains had been discovered,
but the Queensland Police Service immediately released a
statement saying that having a forensic pathologist on hand
was 'standard procedure'.

* * *

On the morning of Monday 15 August, Denise and Bruce
drove to the Foundation office. Thousands of emails, from
every corner of Australia and overseas, had arrived since the
arrest. Often, it was simply people wishing them well, but
an overwhelming number of people also wanted to support
the Foundation with small donations or to buy merchandise.
In the days and weeks ahead, the Foundation would see all
of its previous records – for website traffic, donations and
purchases – completely smashed.

Wearing their bright red Foundation T-shirts, Bruce
and Denise came down the outside steps of the Foundation
office at around 11 that morning to greet the media, followed
by Bob Atkinson, who had driven up from Brisbane to speak
to them about the events taking place. Bruce told the media,

'We still plan to continue the road trip [up the Queensland coast in September to visit 20 schools]. Daniel's legacy is that many, many other kids will be safe from predators, and that is something positive that will come out of this very sad affair. I see the Foundation as a positive thing, and it's our way of saying thank you, and it's just something the family wants to do so other kids never find themselves in Danny's situation.'

He said that, while abduction was extremely rare, unfortunately child abuse was not. 'If we can encourage children who have been abused to come forward and notify police, or the kids' helpline or a trusted adult, then we are doing the right thing by Daniel, and that's what he will be remembered for.'

That same day, more than 50 Queensland police and SES volunteers had once again begun the task of scouring bushland in the Glass House Mountains. This time, however, there was a focus to their efforts. Ironically, they had been searching all those years ago not that far from where Daniel's body was now said to be. Bruce and Denise thanked the SES volunteers and police officers for their hard work.

Denise said she was preparing herself for a long wait for justice, as the accused's lawyer had already said he would fight the charges. 'You learn to be patient,' she said. 'I think over the years you just have to.' Struggling with tears, she said she no longer believed her son was alive. 'On Saturday, I hoped, but that last glimmer of hope went.'

Bruce said that he and Denise were preparing to visit the search site, which he described as 'a muddy jungle', in the coming days. 'We'll find Daniel and bring him home, and I'm sure that's what Australia wants,' he said. True to form, he said that displays of hysterical outrage and calls for vengeance would never bring back his boy. 'At the end of the day, you have to ask yourself: is that being helpful or is that just a distraction? I think it's really important that people's judgement has to be measured, and we have tried to be examples of that.'

* * *

That Monday morning, Brett Peter Cowan appeared at the Roma Street Magistrates' Court. Still not publicly named, but billed as a 'Perth father of three', Cowan was picked out by the cameras of the attendant media sitting next to Detective Grant Linwood in the back seat of an unmarked car, a shadowy figure with straggly hair and a cap.

The public gallery was filled by the media, wearing splashes of red in an unprecedented show of personal support. Cowan's lawyer, Tim Meehan from the Brisbane criminal law firm Bosscher Lawyers, appeared for the accused, saying his client was not required to be in court, but Chief Magistrate Brendan Butler challenged this, telling Meehan that his client had an 'obligation to be here'.

When Cowan shuffled into the dock, he was wearing a prison-issue, caramel-coloured sweatshirt and jeans. His feet were bare and his hands unrestrained. His hair, as before, was loose and fell over his shoulders. He sat with his back to the gallery, dishevelled, a vastly different figure from the man who had been standing on the hotel balcony overlooking the Swan River.

During a hearing that lasted only minutes, Cowan said nothing. He was remanded in custody until the next hearing on 26 September. When the media questioned Meehan outside the court after the brief hearing, some of them noticed he was wearing a red tie. He told reporters that his client would be seeking bail by an application to the Supreme Court. 'My client will be defending the charges,' he said, adding that the accused was faring well. 'In the circumstances, he's doing all right.'

Meanwhile, the president of the Queensland Council for Civil Liberties, Michael Cope, criticised senior police and politicians for praising the police investigation, saying such comments would be more appropriate after someone had been convicted of Daniel's murder.

* * *

The Beerburrum State Forest, some 70 kilometres north of Brisbane, straddles both sides of the Bruce Highway. No light penetrates the dark undergrowth of introduced pines, which extend across 270 square kilometres. Volcanic plugs rise abruptly out of the coastal plains, straddling the bitumen highway unexpectedly in the gaps between the forests and the maze of dirt roads, dead ends and dense bushland. Giant freaks of nature, they were spawned from molten rock spewing from active volcanoes up to 27 million years ago. Captain Cook, the first white explorer, named them the Glass House Mountains after the glass furnaces of his homeland. At the foothills of the mountains among the native bush are military rows of trees punctuated by small townships such as Beerwah, Landsborough and Mooloolah and there are marshes in the forests.

Bob Atkinson had cautioned the media for pre-empting a quick outcome in finding Daniel. 'The search area does form part of a tidal area and it may well be necessary to extend the search area all the way to the coast.'

The fire trails, in between the pine trees, are a playground for dirt-bike riders and four-wheel-drive enthusiasts, but there are also burnt-out cars dumped there. Sand miners over the years have been pillaging the sand from the creeks, changing the topography of the land. When finished, their mechanical appliances often lie abandoned like giant iron creatures in isolated glades. Casual visitors to the state forests are advised only ever to walk in daylight hours. The introduced pine trees have unwittingly created a perfect playground for criminals seeking to hide illegal activities. Even standing on the observation deck of the 20-metre, steel and timber, three-legged fire towers, built to detect the tell-tale plumes of smoke from threatening bushfires, it is impossible to see what is happening on the forest floor.

The demountable building in the cleared area past the pine forests at the end of Kings Road where Cowan had said he had his 'man fun' had been known to the police for years before Daniel disappeared. It was reportedly a place where druggies had parties as well as a homosexual haunt. Two men, later found guilty of murdering another local from the Glass House Mountains, once lived there. Opposite the demountable was the macadamia farm, one of several slabs of land in the area that had been cleared for farming. Other cleared land bore strawberries, pineapples and citrus fruits. With their neat, light-brick houses in small communities, tidy fences, dams and ponies, the local farmers lived in uneasy proximity with the occupiers of the forests. A strawberry farmer once described to a journalist how, one Christmas Eve, the air was rent by pump-action gunfire. The pellets landed on the roof of his property 'like meteors'. The newspaper article dubbed the area the 'Beerwah moors'. Two months before Daniel's disappearance, a 22-year-old local man, Luke Stillman's, burnt-out car was found in the forest. His body had never been found. A victim of one murder had been discovered there with multiple shotgun wounds.

It was to this terrain that Bruce and Denise were brought on the Monday afternoon following Cowan's arrest the previous Saturday. Mike Condon came to the Foundation office after lunch and picked them up. To avoid the media, he took them in an unmarked car through the fire trails and farms, until eventually they entered a controlled search zone guarded by police. The media, gathered at the control site, had been forbidden to go any further, with police tape designating the area of no entry. Condon had told the Morcombes they too would not be allowed into the primary search area, to avoid possible DNA contamination.

Kings Road, Beerwah, does not intersect the Bruce Highway, but it is only around 400 metres west of the highway, across the pine forests, as the crow flies. As the days progressed, Bruce and Denise chillingly realised they would have been driving up the highway from the Christmas party that fateful day and would have been less than half a kilometre from where Daniel had been taken to. The other end of Kings Road runs eastwards at right angles off Steve Irwin Way, home of the Australia Zoo, which is about ten kilometres away. Rogers's body, the man Bill Dooley had pleaded guilty to killing, had been found ten kilometres south of the zoo. Ten kilometres north of the zoo was where Bruce had been checking out Old Caloundra Road, following the map given to him by Grosskreutz and Eggy. They had been so close.

After running north-east through some neatly cultivated farmland, Kings Road takes a sharp right-hand turn through the pine plantation where it crosses a tiny, wooden bridge and, by now just a dirt track, snakes deeper into the forest before veering north again and suddenly arriving at the cleared area containing the farmhouse on the left and opposite, the large iron shed and with the old tobacco drying sheds behind it. The space in between the shed and the mango tree was where the demountable once stood. An old fibro house had also been there but had been removed. The rich, volcanic soil grows macadamia nuts. While none of the stories that Bruce and Denise had heard over the years ever mentioned a macadamia farm, many had mentioned pine trees and sheds or an old white house.

Between February and August, the harvest takes place, when pickers drive tractors to collect groundnuts, but when it is not harvest time, the place is usually deserted.

In December, when Daniel went missing, the only activity would have been sporadic visits from people to cut the grass, fertilise the soil and spray insecticide, readying the area for the following season of macadamia nuts.

Coochin Creek meanders behind Bassetts Road running almost parallel to Kings Road. It is here that a large body of water lies, created by past sand-mining endeavours, and it is here where Cowan, Fitzy and Ian had walked when Cowan was showing them where he had disposed of Daniel's remains. Leading off Kings Road, a dirt track skirts the boundary of the farmhouse leading to a clearing en route to the sand-mining site where Cowan told Fitzy and Ian he had parked his Pajero before disposing of Daniel's body. An abandoned excavator sits there. In the map Cowan had drawn for Arnold, he had mistakenly marked Roys Road which crosses the Bruce Highway further north than Kings Road.

* * *

From the roadblock, in front of the macadamia plantation, the bright-orange uniforms of SES volunteers were stark against the grey-green undergrowth. Police rode around in quadbikes. Two officers manned the perimeter of the search site, reprimanding anyone who stepped past the line drawn in the dirt. Dozens of vehicles, belonging to the Sunshine Coast District Tactical Crime Squad, the Sunshine Coast Water Police, scientific officers and SES volunteers, came and went throughout the day, choking the narrow dirt road. Helicopters droned overhead, and noisy generators on the ground powered satellite dishes.

Standing on top of the embankment, which led to the body of water, Condon pointed out an area to Bruce and Denise some 50 metres away through the forest. They looked through the dense growth of the trees, at the muddy swamp. Was this the final resting place of their son? Pine trees had naturally seeded and taken hold in the former sand quarry. To make matters worse, a steady drizzle fell. They watched, Denise straining for anything that might confirm Daniel was there, to feel his presence, but there was nothing other than the men and women in their orange boiler suits and navy-blue hats toiling in the distance, mostly on their hands and knees.

Hundreds of sandbags were trucked in to shore up the area. These were also used to dam off smaller areas of the lake, which was then pumped dry and manually searched. This primary search area was not much bigger than the size of a backyard swimming pool. Bruce and Denise felt the eeriness ooze from the place, in spite of it being a hive of activity. Ignoring the SES workers and police on the ground, they were paralysed with grief. Left alone for a while, they gathered their thoughts in private, saying a silent prayer and wondering all the time what might have happened to Daniel in this desolate place. Then they turned away from the embankment and slowly walked back to Condon's car. They were wearing their hallmark red T-shirts. In retrospect, it made them stand out like beacons. Media helicopters spotted them and even followed the unmarked car back to the Foundation office in Maroochydore, where they politely declined any attempt to be interviewed from the media that gathered outside.

Driving away from the site, Bruce had felt a curious sense of relief. He was glad they had come to see Daniel's final resting place. Denise, however, said later, 'You don't see anything, you don't feel anything, you just wonder, "Is this the spot?"' She found no closure at the scene. How could there ever be closure? Yet so many people would slip the word into conversation as though it were some kind of panacea for their pain.

Mid-morning, Kym Charlton, Executive Director of Queensland Police Service media, told the waiting media that the police were unable to provide any updates. But she said the number of people out searching for Daniel was likely to be 'scaled up' that day.

* * *

At the memorial spot under the overpass, more than one hundred bunches of flowers, mostly fresh, and almost as many cards of support were laid that morning. The Sunshine Coast community was again rallying behind the Morcombes. A copy of a Sunday newspaper with the news of the murder charge splashed across the front lay among the flowers. 'Daniel, don't worry, we'll find you and bring you home', one supporter had written, while another card simply said, 'Our thoughts are with you. RIP Daniel'.

As Bruce and Denise visited the site that day, Dean received news that the house he had bought only five minutes drive from Palmwoods had settled. It was a charming, three-bedroom, two-storey home with established trees and only a few neighbours. Life still went on.

When night fell that Monday evening, the temperature dropped. The SES packed up for the day, leaving television crews to perform live crosses from outside the police cordoned-off area.

* * *

On Tuesday 16 August, three days after the arrest, State Coroner Michael Barnes lifted the suppression order prohibiting the use of Cowan's name by the media. Submissions had been presented by media outlets requesting such a move. The Queensland Police Service and defence lawyers offered no comment either way, but Peter Boyce, acting on behalf of the family, said that there was a benefit in releasing his name as it could spark new information from other victims.

SES workers, still working in lines on their hands and knees, were methodically sifting through debris as well as using sophisticated equipment to separate mud from water. Part of their briefing, before they went to the site, was from a forensic pathologist, who showed them what they might be looking for. After so many years, it would be easy to miss an important find. Forensic experts at the site examined the mud collected by the searchers. A hydrologist had been consulted, and there had been discussion about draining the nearby dam.

Police remained silent on the questions of how the accused murderer had been apprehended and how they knew where to search. The only comment made by Assistant Commissioner Ross Barnett was that police did not want to prejudice any court proceedings. Barnett added, 'We will not walk away from that search until there is no avenue left and no hope left of us finding something. It is a tough task but one we're totally committed to, and we owe that to the family.'

On Wednesday, the search had extended to Coochin Creek, which was to form the third primary search area.

* * *

Bruce and Denise were in their lounge room at home when Mike Condon rang that afternoon. *The Australian Women's Weekly* had arrived to do a story on how they were coping. Denise had not been keen to do the story and was glad when they were interrupted by the phone ringing. But the purpose of the call was the last thing she expected.

At 3 pm, a shoe had been found partly submerged in mud by one of the SES workers at the original search site. Everyone had been primed for the search to run into months. What were the measurements of Daniel's shoes, Condon asked. Denise, her heart beating fast, raced to the garage, where she opened a plastic container to find Daniel's old school shoes that she'd kept. Bruce followed, grabbing a tape measure. Condon waited on the line. When they gave him the measurements, Condon replied, 'That size would be about right.'

Returning to the rear patio, where the journalists and photographer were still gathered, Bruce said, 'You'll have to leave. We've just had some distressing news.'

The photographer immediately began taking photos.

'I don't think that's appropriate,' Bruce said firmly.

The day after the unexpected discovery of the shoe, Denise and Bruce were supposed to meet up with some high-ranking government officials. When Denise woke up that morning, however, she felt sick and could not face a journey into the city. She rarely took time off, but the nightmare of the past few days and now increasing evidence that they were getting closer to finding Daniel meant she had no choice. Bruce went with Brett Winkler, to meet with Director General of the Department of Premier and Cabinet John Bradley, Police Commissioner Bob Atkinson and Director General of Education and Training Julie Grantham. Talk was productive and future meetings were diarised. A partnership which had been planned for weeks between the Queensland State Government and the Daniel Morcombe Foundation was gaining momentum. It was all part of the Morcombes' parallel lives.

PART FIVE

Daniel Comes Home

CHAPTER TWENTY-SEVEN

DANIEL IS FOUND

Above the guarded entrance to the search site for Daniel's remains was a small plastic owl. It belonged to the Sunshine Coast Tactical Crime Squad (TCS). It was found by one of the squad at the height of the aftermath of Cyclone Yasi, which had swept the North Queensland coast earlier in 2011, wreaking havoc. Most of the media and SES workers were unaware it was there. The owl made occasional television appearances, and only TCS members spotted it when it accompanied police on random breath-testing blitzes, outlaw motorcycle gang intercepts and drug searches on the high seas.

The search site presented all sorts of challenges. The legacy of previous sand-miners was a large depression in the sand that had filled with floodwater and rain and morphed into a dam. Floods had also changed the topography. Further south, there was a pond, which police had already begun draining in their hunt for clues. The search had initially concentrated on the place where Cowan had taken the undercover police officers down the embankment, not far from the pond.

Inspector Arthur Van Panhuis, a man with 30 years of forensic service, coordinated the crime scenes. There was an investigative crime manager and a search-and-rescue coordinator who liaised with police and SES workers. The crime scene was divided into three lots. The old macadamia plantation and disused tobacco drying sheds was Crime Scene 1; the old sand-mining area Crime Scene 2; and Coochin Creek, where Cowan had told police he had disposed of Daniel's clothes, Crime Scene 3. A forward forensic command post with vehicles and tents was set up on the flat land on top of the embankment where Cowan had parked his Pajero. The ground search was to continue for several weeks. Aerial photographs were taken and panoramic photographs compiled. Cadaver dogs were used and police divers brought in.

The day after Cowan's arrest, Van Panhuis had received information that the demountable, where Cowan had claimed he killed Daniel, had been bought and removed about 15 kilometres to the north to Mill Street, Landsborough, some years before. It had been re-plumbed and completely renovated. The wallpaper had been taken off the walls, and the carpet had been stripped out and buried near the large mango tree next to the road, adjacent to the old tobacco shed. Later, the carpet was to be excavated by the searchers.

The shoe had been found only four days into the search at 2.25 pm. Its top part, around the ankle, was only just visible to those on their hands and knees. Lodged in mud and covered in pine needles, it was lying in an area between a smaller body of water and the embankment to the north-west. It was photographed where it lay and then removed and photographed again before being packaged as evidence. Searchers had been told, during their briefing, that when an item was found the search would halt until photographs were taken. All items were to be given an electronic marker and label. Yellow ribbons would then be placed at the point where the object was found.

The day after the discovery of the shoe, Bruce penned a note to Peter Johns, Michael Barnes and Daniel Grice, thanking them and saying that he and Denise had recognised the importance of the inquest in finding new evidence and eliminating some of the POIs. Speaking on the discovery, Bruce said that, although the shoe had not officially been identified as Daniel's, he believed it could be a 'significant piece of evidence'. He told ABC News, 'It has the potential to be a bit of a game-breaker in terms of being some tangible evidence, which sadly this case has really lacked.

'We need evidence. We appreciate that's one thing this case has really struggled with. Evidence is going to be crucial and we'll just wait and see if the shoe may be the missing link.

'The shoe is significant but we'll wait for forensic tests and [the find] still hasn't changed anything ... we're still looking for Daniel. You don't have a funeral for a shoe.'

He said that the first phone call had signalled an arrest; the second had flagged a find at the alleged crime scene. 'It is only a matter of time until the next call comes. We're still waiting for a third phone call to identify that they've actually found Daniel's remains.' He described the phone calls that interrupted the family's 'perpetual waiting game' as being 'like a sledgehammer that gives you a mighty thump. You pick yourself up and there's another one. Of course, we're all waiting for the next sledgehammer and wonder if that will be today, tomorrow, in a month – or if it's ever going to come.

'People say that is welcome news, and it is, but at the same time we're crushed ... I don't know what the word is for "welcoming a beating".'

Thursday 18 August 2011 brought isolated showers and thunderstorms. Police dogs and divers joined the search. Earthmoving equipment arrived at the swampy bushland site to help with access by improving drainage to the area.

Friday marked day six of the search. Mark Porter, an engineering hydrologist from the University of the Sunshine

Coast, revealed that the waterways cordoned off for the search were prone to 'strong flows and sediment movement', and that the floods in January would have 'shifted a lot of sediment'. 'In the big events, you can expect the topography to change a bit,' he said. Extra divers were called in.

* * *

On 20 August, the Morcombe family boarded a plane for Melbourne to attend Kevin and Monique's joint 80th birthday celebrations. Bruce had sent emails to Mike Condon detailing their numbers and whereabouts. Speaking briefly to the media before they left, Bruce said, 'Really it's a matter of catching our breath and clearing our head and making sure we're fit and mentally capable of dealing with the things that may come up in the weeks ahead,' he said. 'We can't turn the phone off, because sadly we are still waiting for that phone call. But a change of scenery will be good.'

As Denise waited for the luggage once they touched down at Tullamarine Airport, Bruce went to get the hire car. She switched her phone off flight mode. There was a voice message from Mike Condon. A second shoe had been found. Bruce phoned Mike back from the car park before they even left the airport. Arriving at her parents' home in East Burwood, Denise tried to make the occasion happy, but everyone was unbearably sad. The shoe had been found slightly north of the first one at about ten that morning. After all these years, they were closer to finding Daniel than they had ever been.

Later that day, a trailer packed with filing cabinets arrived at the search site – a mark of how much information was unfolding. The area was patrolled around the clock. The search was picking up pace.

The following day, Sunday 21 August, the Morcombes attended the Glen Waverley RSL to meet Kevin and Monique's friends to celebrate their joint birthdays. Denise had a new mobile-phone number just for calls from the police. No one knew that number except Bob Atkinson and Mike Condon. It began to ring. She picked up the phone with a sense of dread. It was Bob Atkinson. A bone had been found not far from the second shoe, but they were not sure whether it was human. He would ring back as soon as he had confirmation.

The family gathering turned into a nightmare. Denise told Bruce. Smiling but saying nothing, not wanting to upset her parents' special day, Denise then motioned to Brad and Dean to go out to the back verandah, where they passed on the news. Later, Denise's brother Paul played a montage of photos for the party guests that included happy snaps of the family, with pictures of Daniel among them. It was unbearably tough. Kevin could sense that something was going on but Bruce and Denise were determined: their news could wait. Bruce, along with other family members, made a small speech praising Kevin and Monique as being 'terrific' human beings and role models. Watching the montage of family photos and vision of Daniel, Denise sat with tears streaming down her face.

Shortly afterwards, Bob Atkinson rang back confirming the bones were human and belonged to a young male. He told them he was about to inform the media. Their other phones began to ring shortly afterwards. Bruce had already rung Peter Boyce with the news. They did not tell Denise's parents until they returned to their house in East Burwood later that afternoon. Everyone then sat around numbly watching the television news. Bruce decided to fly home on Monday, leaving Denise and the boys to come back on their original flights on the Tuesday. That way, he could deal with the media and attend to anything else that was immediately required. It was another sleepless night for the Morcombes. They knew in their hearts that the bone belonged to Daniel.

* * *

That Monday at 8 am, a convoy of vehicles dropped off the searchers about 300 metres away from the primary crime-scene area to begin a walk along the banks of Coochin Creek. 'It's draining,' one of the 122 volunteers involved in the search told the media. But the finds buoyed their spirits as they took turns at working on their hands and knees, moving forwards inch by inch, wearing bright-orange overalls and gloves for protection. Police officers were already wading knee deep in mud.

Three bones were discovered near the second shoe. The first was closer to the water and further north again of the shoes. The second was almost level with the shoe and the water. As each bone was uncovered, it was plotted on a map. There was evidence of wild animals inhabiting the area: dingos, goannas and other native creatures. A fox lair on the northern side of the embankment was excavated, but no items of interest were found. A well was found on the site but a search again revealed nothing. The macadamia plantation was also searched on foot.

In between the gruelling searches, the nearby farm became the 'go-to zone' for the police and SES. In the shadow of the macadamia trees, they took coffee breaks between exhausting and mentally draining stints slogging through bush and swamp.

* * *

Rain continued to pour as the heavens opened. Bad weather meant a halt in the search for Daniel's remains. Police had released a statement saying conditions would be monitored to decide when the search could begin again. Meanwhile, police conducted round-the-clock security at the sites. Bruce called a media conference downstairs in the storage room at the Foundation office after returning from Melbourne.

He began the media conference by saying he wanted to give thanks from the family for all of the hard work the SES, police, the media and the public had put in throughout their long journey, which, he reminded them, was still not over. 'We've worked so hard to be with Daniel – to find him,' he told *Seven News*. 'Certainly not good news or celebration of any sort but maybe an indication it's the final chapter that we've been hanging on, waiting for, for a long, long time.'

Bruce confirmed that the forensic examination was expected to take weeks. He said it was hoped the tragedy of his son's disappearance would come to an end soon but that the family had no plans for a burial until it was proved the remains that were found were Daniel's. Describing the family's reaction to the phone call on Sunday about the first bone being found, Bruce said, 'We just want the job done properly, perfectly beyond question. We need definite proof. The significance of the bone find is not lost on the family, and we are aware that that primary site is definitely of interest to police. We are choked with emotion being the possibility that it is Daniel, and of course we are really hopeful that it is, which can bring to conclusion, you know, an extremely sad chapter in our family's life.' Bruce and Denise were not the slightest bit interested in Cowan at that time. They just wanted to find Daniel.

Bruce said that DNA would be extremely helpful in determining whether it was Daniel, as well as scientific tests for wear patterns on shoes. 'There are still many tests to be conducted to make sure beyond doubt that [the shoes and the bone] do belong to Daniel.' He said that he did not mind waiting for several weeks for confirmation.

Later that afternoon, Bruce received a phone call from Ross Hutton. In Coochin Creek, upstream from the primary search site, a belt and the remnants of underpants had been found. 'Would you have any matching clothing to compare sizes?' Hutton wanted to know. Bruce found some of Daniel's underpants in the plastic bags in boxes that Denise had carefully put away in the garage. He was glad he had made the decision to fly home early. He knew how upset Denise would be looking for Daniel's clothing she had stored.

Monday brought further news. Deputy Commissioner Ross Barnett also called a media conference to announce that the shoes that had been found in the muddy swamp were Globe shoes, the same brand that Daniel had been wearing. He would not comment on which bones had been found but said they would be sent away for testing, perhaps overseas, if required. However, further news on the bones and the shoes would take 'weeks', not 'days', to arrive, he warned. Barnett also stated that the searchers expected to find more at the site soon. 'Having found what we've found in relatively close proximity to each other, there's no reason why we shouldn't find further evidence,' he said, adding that the investigation of the material would be given 'the highest priority within Queensland Health and anywhere else that we need to take it if circumstances dictate'.

* * *

Bruce and Denise still had no idea how Daniel came to be in such an isolated spot, and proceedings against Cowan were months away. The story was left to their imaginations. Another piece of the puzzle they had waited so long to put together.

On Tuesday 23 August, Bruce arrived at Maroochydore Airport to pick up Denise and the boys, who were returning from Melbourne. He had bought four bunches of flowers in Coolum, as he had been told the family would be allowed to visit the search site. But this abruptly changed. Instead, Bruce drove the family to Beerwah Police Station, where they met Detective Superintendent Carless. As a matter of urgency, all four had blood samples taken for fresh DNA comparison. The nurse had difficulties getting blood from Denise. They had to use a baby's needle. Denise said she had been drained of everything, even giving blood. Then everyone had to make further addendum to their statements. After that, they were all fitted with blue, disposable, full-length forensic body overalls – a fact they found abhorrent – and accompanied to the car park with all but their faces covered. They decided not to take the flowers, as they had been told that they would not be allowed closer than 50 metres from where the remains suspected to be Daniel's had been found, due to potential cross-contamination.

Arriving near the search area, the whole family was on edge and unable to speak, the boys especially affected by the unexpected turn of events. They were handed surgical masks. The four of them approached the same elevated embankment that Bruce and Denise had visited a week earlier. It was the first time the boys had been there, and they were very moved and upset. Brad especially seemed in a state of shock as he confronted the reality of where his twin may have spent his last moments. All four of them clung together, supporting each other with hugs. After a few minutes, they turned and walked back to the car. The police drove them back to the Beerwah Police Station.

Whereas Bruce felt better for having known the bones and shoes had been found, Denise could not decide whether she would have been better off not knowing. One thing she did know, however, was that the discoveries of the past few weeks meant all hope had been extinguished. Even though the remains had not yet been officially declared by experts as being Daniel's, the family knew in their hearts that they had to be.

* * *

Wet weather forced the search to be suspended over several days, and it began again on Friday 26 August. After the discovery of so much evidence in the first few days, Bruce and Denise now began to feel that the elements were working against them. They had tentatively decided to plan a funeral for the eighth anniversary of Daniel's disappearance. Bruce said, 'The earliest possible date would appear to be the seventh [of December], but we have to wait for the complete search site to be examined, and that's not just the primary site. That's a date of extreme significance, but it might rain for six weeks in the next three months and suddenly [searchers] still have a task ahead that could roll into next year. We appreciate they're still searching for more evidence and we hope the bulk of his skeletal remains can be found.'

The search was scaled back because of the continuing bad weather. Finally, the decisive phone call was received on 28 August. Bob Atkinson phoned Denise with the news. The DNA tests had confirmed that the bones belonged to Daniel. Soon afterwards, Atkinson made the official announcement at police headquarters in Roma Street, declaring, 'It's a very sad answer, but it's the answer.' His words later echoed in many of the montages for the Dances for Daniel. That one sentence represented an end to so many years of speculation. Atkinson read a statement from the family saying that the news was extremely sad. 'The scientific confirmation is still enormously difficult to comprehend,' Bruce had written. 'It is that expected shock we had all been waiting for.' It was a dreadful day; family and friends visited or phoned. It was the first day they finally knew that Daniel was never coming home.

The following day was Bruce's birthday, but there were more important things to do. The media conference was again outside the Foundation office in Amaroo Street, Maroochydore. Denise spoke first: 'I feel that Daniel is your son as well and it's everyone's strength that's got us through the last seven and a half years, and you'll help us get through the rest of it.' Bruce said that each link in the chain, 'from the police, from the SES and a whole stack of ordinary

Australians that have chipped in, obviously the media, have all contributed to getting us where we are today'.

He added, 'Finding Daniel's remains is a monumental step in the family's life but also a monumental step in the investigation process, and we are quite traumatised by the findings but at the same time we are hoping it's the first step in the healing process and we can move forward from here and recover ...' He described it as a 'relief' to have forensic confirmation that the bones had been Daniel's. 'It's a place you don't want to be but perhaps we're entering the final chapter.' Later, he commented that birthdays no longer meant a lot. 'It's the eighth birthday that I've had without Daniel and eighth Father's Day I've had without Daniel.'

Denise pledged, 'We're going to bring him home. It will take a little while. We said we'd never give up and we've proved that we haven't.'

By the end of August, the Foundation's website was still inundated with traffic. It had peaked at 359,368 visitors on 13 August but was showing little sign of abating. The bandwidth had had to be frequently increased after numerous crashes. Sixty-nine per cent of the hits were from Australia. Amazingly, the rest were from around the world. And the emails were still pouring in. One was from Hetty Johnston, founder of Bravehearts Inc, the charity that fights for the rights and safety of children who have been sexually abused. Another was from Kate McCann:

> Dear Denise, Bruce, Dean and Bradley,
> We know there really are no words but just wanted to send all our love and solidarity. And very big hugs. Take care, we're right behind you.
> Kate, Gerry, Madeleine, Sean and Amelie xxxxx

* * *

As September finally dawned, it came with some welcome news after the trauma of August. On 1 September, Roger Lago, one of three businessmen who had bought the Big Pineapple, called to say he had space for the Foundation office. Lago was the facilitator of the $750,000 private reward for information on Daniel.

That same day, Bruce and Denise attended Parliament House to collect an award for Child Protection Week. The *Foundation Red* DVD had been voted the Best Educational Resource. After Bruce and Denise returned to their seats, Bob Atkinson, who was present, signalled that he would like a quiet word. Another bone had been found.

On 2 September, Bruce and Denise were taken by *60 Minutes* in a chopper to fly over the search site for a story segment entitled 'The Missing Years'. From the helicopter, Denise looked down on the rugged terrain beneath them. 'It's not a very nice place to be. I wish we could go down and help.' She said she still had not come to terms with this being Daniel's final resting place. 'It's not as though I can go and see him,' she said. Bruce added, 'It's a very lonely place and such a sad end.'

Bruce and Denise's wedding anniversary came around on 3 September. They were enjoying a morning coffee at home with *60 Minutes*' journalist Tara Brown who asked them what they were doing to celebrate. 'Filming with you,' Denise said straight back. Neither of them had even remembered, nor had they bought presents, their lives were so fraught.

Back in their house in Palmwoods, Tara asked whether it had got any easier with the passage of time. Denise replied, 'The last few weeks have been extremely difficult, firstly with the arrest and then some bones were found and they found out they were human bones. The week later, we found they do belong to Daniel. It's like a knife goes in your chest every single phone call ... People talk about bones and that's our son. It's not ... he belonged to us. He was a little human being and we get phone calls about bones. It's really hard.'

Tara then said, 'I want to cry looking at you.' She said she was sure she was speaking for a lot of Australia.

'We're just normal people,' Denise answered. 'We just want to get on with our life and walk up and down the street.' Bruce added, 'We don't want anyone to feel sorry for us. Pity is not on our agenda. Our mission is to make sure that kids in Australia are safe. The tragedy is that this doesn't need to occur again, so we can get that right.'

Brad and Dean appeared before the cameras, clearly uncomfortable. Dean showed his tattoo and the letters on his knuckles that spelt 'MEMORIES'. Asked whether Brad blamed himself, he said, 'Not entirely.'

When asked about Daniel's final moments and the time in between the first bus passing under the overpass and not stopping and the second bus arriving, Bruce added, 'We'd love to have those three minutes over again and change the whole slide.'

That evening, Bruce and Denise went on a river cruise, donated by Aquarius River Cruises, which allowed them to invite 60 friends, volunteers and family along with them to watch River Fire, a fireworks extravaganza on the Brisbane River in the heart of the city. It was a way of saying thank you for all the support, and was an enjoyable evening, in contrast to the angst around the search for Daniel's remains.

On Sunday 4 September, Bruce and Denise began a 4000-kilometre road trip, taking their child safety presentations to Queensland schools. At the launch, Queensland Premier Anna Bligh announced that Bruce and Denise would become Queensland's Child Safety Ambassadors. Bligh said that parents across Australia would be grateful that the Morcombes were using the profile of the terrible tragedy they had experienced to 'protect our children'. She announced that a program called the 'Daniel

Morcombe Child Safety Curriculum' would be created and implemented, to be made available to all Queensland schools.

Bob Atkinson was also there. In a repeat of the previous week, he patiently waited for the event to be finished and then told Bruce and Denise that more bones had been found.

* * *

By this stage of the search, around 850 SES workers had racked up a total of 5000 or so hours. It was Father's Day, 4 September. Putting on his uniform that morning, SES volunteer Pat McShane felt something was going to happen.

Searching for Daniel's remains was Pat McShane's first SES task. He explained to his children that day that he was giving his Father's Day 'to a man who needed it more'. When he got home, they would celebrate. As he was driven along Kings Road, he noticed the red balloons, red flags and red roses decorating all the houses. People waved as they drove past, and Pat felt greatly cheered.

At his first briefing at the SES field base, the workers were told that 'items of interest had been discovered yesterday afternoon', and that they were 'searching in a hot zone'. 'Be brave. It is likely some of you will discover something today. If you think you can't handle that, then now is the time to say so.' No one said a word. The SES workers headed towards the search area, around 300 metres away. Entering it felt surreal to McShane. There was blue-and-white-chequered police tape marking the path they were to walk on. It had been raining again and the sky was overcast. The dense scrub blocked out any light. The 39 SES workers walked in single file through the site, then began a long search line, shoulder to shoulder, on their knees. Each loosened the earth with a gardening tool, sifting through leaves and dirt down to a layer of gravelly sand to a depth of about 15 centimetres and a width of about 50 centimetres.

The search was painstakingly slow. Every bit of dirt was examined, and they covered around a metre an hour. Still, no one spoke.

Pat could hear the low hum of traffic on the Bruce Highway. Much of the time, he was thinking about Daniel. Police forensic staff had explained that bones might not be easily identifiable as they would be the same colour as the brown dirt. They were told to take particular notice of items with a porous surface texture, or white leaching of calcium on the sides.

Within minutes, ten metres to Pat's right, there were three separate discoveries. Then, after an hour, the person beside Pat unearthed two bone fragments, and, shortly after that, Pat unearthed a bone. A police forensic expert immediately came across. A few minutes later, Pat found another remnant and then another. After ten minutes, they marked the position where he had been searching and cordoned it off. Pat's hands were shaking. He was heartbroken. He knew instinctively it was both the saddest and the proudest moment in his life. His thoughts were firmly with Denise and Bruce.

Heading back to the base camp for morning tea, he stayed behind for counselling and to give a witness statement. Returning to the search, he was sent to the far end of the line, away from the discoveries.

Soon, a young man second to Pat's right made another discovery. Police asked that the man and the two searchers left and right of him stop searching and stand away. Pat continued searching. Loosening the earth with his trowel, he picked up three sticks about ten centimetres from the surface and examined each one carefully. One was not a stick. He knew what it was. On his knees, he held his find and said a little prayer for Denise and Daniel, the Hail Mary. That evening, on his way home, he rang his wife from the SES depot. He didn't have to say a word. His wife knew that something big had happened.

* * *

On Monday 5 September at Woombye State School – Bruce and Denise's first stop on their Queensland Child Safety tour north – the students and teachers had made a special effort to make them feel welcome. The presentation took about an hour. Outside, the media pack had arrived. The journalists had just discovered about the recent finds. Their very public crusade was big news, far beyond their expectations.

The journey was turning out to be more than just visiting schools and educating children on how to keep safe. On Wednesday 7 September at Rockhampton, the Morcombes met with Treasa Steinhardt, mother of nine-year-old Keyra, who was brutally killed by Leonard John Fraser on 22 April 1999. Bruce and Denise were then running late. The GPS in the car had sent them to the wrong side of Rockhampton when they were trying to find the school they were visiting, but they approached a taxi driver who said, 'Follow me.' In Mackay, they met with the Wallman family. Marilyn Wallman had gone missing 39 years ago. The family wanted to know how Bruce and Denise had managed to get an inquest for Daniel. Bruce offered to send them a copy of the letter he had sent to the Coroner when they returned home. In Bowen, too, they met with the parents of Rachel Antonio, who had disappeared as a 16-year-old in 1998. They also wanted to know how to get an inquest into their daughter's death.

All up the coast, as they continued on their way, the Morcombes were greeted by people wishing them well. Most of the motels would not accept payment for their accommodation. Cairns was the highlight, however, with around a thousand people there to greet them for the final day at a park in the Esplanade.

Senior Constable Bernadette Strow, one of their steadfast supporters in Townsville, had arranged to fly them home from Townsville at the end of the trip, and she and a friend drove their car and trailer back home. It had been an exhausting tour. They arrived home to find a new addition to the household: Bradley had bought Denise 'Rosie', a black and white kitten.

* * *

Since 4 September, there had been no further discoveries at the search site. On 3 October, Bruce wrote to Peter Boyce about a proposed meeting with Bob Atkinson and the Director of Public Prosecutions (DPP). They had still not heard about the outcome of the examination of the shoes, nor had they been told when the search would be called off. Most importantly, they both wanted to know when Daniel's bones would be released by the Coroner and lawyers for Cowan. They had begun to realise this might be yet another hurdle to tackle. Bruce had other questions too. Who would be called to give evidence at the committal hearing? Where would it be held and for how long would the committal and trial run? He also wanted Sandy Drummond's handwriting, using historic writing samples from 2005, to be compared with the handwriting on the letter sent to Jackway in jail. Drummond had now become a critical alibi for Cowan.

On 4 October, Dean's birthday came and went.

Finally, on 7 October, there was a media release from the Queensland Police Service that the search for Daniel's remains was complete. Denise, although upset, acknowledged it was the news they had been waiting for. She joined Bruce in Hobart, where they spoke to the girls at St Patrick's College in Launceston.

On 14 October, back on the Sunshine Coast, the Morcombes met up with Father Jan at the northbound Moby Vic's service station. He had been exchanging Christmas cards with Denise's parents each year. Occasionally, if he was in Maroochydore, he would call in to see Bruce and Denise, but he was busy in a new parish in Lutwyche, an inner-city suburb of Brisbane. Once, he had invited them to come to the school at his former parish to talk about child safety. Spiritually, however, he had stayed connected with them, often saying rosary prayers for Daniel and the rest of the family. He had kept Daniel's picture with the little candle attached from the memorial service.

Bruce and Denise wanted Father Jan to come with them to Daniel's resting place.

Now that the search was deemed over, Mike Condon had rung to say the family was finally allowed to go there. 'Wear long pants and good, closed-in shoes as it is overgrown and there could be snakes,' he advised. Condon met the Morcombes and Father Jan in the service station, and in one car they drove to Kings Road. Arriving at the site, they met another police officer, Brian Wilkins. Walking down the track, Bruce and Denise could appreciate all of the hard work that had gone into the search. Mounds of sand, three to four metres high, made it obvious. The trunks of the pine trees bore yellow-spray-paint markings, identifying the silt that had been removed due to flooding in the area over recent years. The marks showed the soil levels at the time of search compared with the levels in December 2003.

Chatting to the Morcombes about the enormity of the search, Condon turned, pointing to the base of a nearby tree. 'We believe that this is Daniel's final resting place just there.' Everyone looked at the tree, which looked like every other tree. It was closer to the lake. Coarse sand was underfoot and, like the rest of the search area, it was devoid of vegetation and leaf litter. The two police officers left the Morcombes and Father Jan alone. Denise had brought four red roses, separately wrapped in green paper and a red ribbon, a red candle, the prayer card from Daniel's first memorial service, with a Foundation badge pinned to it, and a sterling-silver necklace that said 'Mum/Daniel'. They tied some rosary beads at about eye height to the tree Condon had pointed out. Father Jan said a prayer, blessed the area and lit the red candle. It was devastating. Everyone was in tears. All they had to mark Daniel's final resting place was a tree, but Denise could feel Daniel's presence all around the area.

They returned to the car and were driven along a dirt track to a wooden bridge that crossed Coochin Creek, about one kilometre upstream from the search site. 'This,' Condon told them, 'is where Daniel's clothing had been found.' They were puzzled. Clothing upstream from Daniel's remains? Clearly, other than his shoes, he was naked when dumped in the pine trees. That bastard, they were all thinking.

Everyone returned to their cars at Moby Vic's and, after chatting with the police and Father Jan, the Morcombes said goodbye.

* * *

Five days later, Bruce and Denise, along with Peter Boyce, met with Bob Atkinson and Mike Condon at police headquarters in Roma Street. Later, Peter, Bruce and Denise were driven to the DPP headquarters to meet with Director of Public Prosecutions Tony Moynihan. He brought dismal news. Asked when they might receive their son's remains, Moynihan replied, 'Not until the trial is over and all of the appeals.' Bruce and Denise were shocked, both realising this could mean years. Peter Boyce also asked whether Bruce or Denise could attend the committal. 'No,' Moynihan said bluntly. That would not be possible.

They were rocked by this news. The family's needs were clearly not being considered. Trying to hide their feelings, they left the meeting personally crushed but had no time to feel sorry for themselves as they had a school to visit in their role as Child Safety Ambassadors. Their schedule, as usual, was hectic, but they were used to having to put on a brave face when emotionally it was difficult. A few days later, they were in Miles to attend a family-fun day organised by one of the local police. A young boy had emptied his moneybox to give to the Foundation. It was an action that touched Denise's heart.

The 28 October 2011 Day for Daniel was always going to be big. One million people around Australia showed their support. In Palmwoods, at 7 am, 2000 people took part in the annual walk. Anna Bligh, Bob Atkinson, and Kevin and Monique attended. Julia Gillard, then Prime Minister, sent a letter of support. There were 20 other walks taking place in different cities and towns around the nation. On 28 October, Nambour shopkeepers painted the town red: staff and shoppers wore red and most shop displays were red-themed. At 6.45 pm that evening, Bruce and Denise attended Siena Catholic College to present the Daniel Morcombe Award for the most outstanding Grade 10 student.

The road trip continued at this pace for the rest of October and into November. Denise's birthday came and went, and, as usual, the focus was elsewhere: on Daniel. On Thursday 3 November 2011, Bruce sent a reply email to the McCanns, who had been enquiring as to how they were going:

Dear Kate and Gerry,
Lovely to hear from you.

We have been quite overwhelmed since the arrest on 13 August. The media interest and public support but also everyone's thirst for information right around the country has been exhausting.

The weeks that followed – very difficult. Seemed like every 3–4 days searchers would find something. A shoe, another shoe, 3 bones, 2 more bones, underpants, shorts and belt. Sadly, the search was terminated about 2 weeks ago. Despite this major operation that is about all they found. The clothing is still being forensically tested but after seeing photos they are almost certainly Daniel's. The bones were confirmed by DNA as being Daniel.

More or less each of these finds resulted in quite intrusive media attention, often going 'live' around Australia.

So now we must sit and wait for the legal process to unfold. That will be around May 2012 for a committal hearing and at least another 12 months after that for a Trial – then appeals! Unfortunately, we have been firmly encouraged to go quiet on any aspect related to the trial. But the worst thing is that we have been denied any possibility of a funeral, probably until after the trial is complete. It all seems very unreasonable.

The police have allowed our family to visit the burial site now the search is finished. We dropped off a couple of special things, lit a candle and the family priest came with us to say a prayer. We could only wonder and shed a tear. Dean and Bradley were shaken by the finality of it all, as were we.

Denise's parents too have been hurt by this news. We were at their double 80th birthday celebration when we received the call about bones being found. We kept that a secret until their party was over.

How are you guys? Have you made any progress in finding Madeleine? I am not joking when I say that if you think of anything we can do to help then call. Not sure what that may be but we are there if needed.

All the best and stay strong.

Cheers

Bruce and Denise

On 4 November, Bruce and Denise attended Julie Elliott's wedding. She was marrying her new fiancé Darryl Mossop. The next day, they both flew to Melbourne for the city's Walk for Daniel. After the walk, they received a touching letter from Owen MacNamara, who had attended the event with his wife, Pip, who suffered from intracranial hypertension and had almost lost the ability to walk. Prior to the Walk for Daniel, she could walk no more than 200 metres, but on that day she walked the entire 4.8 kilometres pushing her wheelchair. 'So first I'd like to thank you as a parent for your work you are doing but also as a husband for the challenge you gave my wife.'

On 17 November, Bruce and Denise received one of their highest accolades yet. They were awarded joint winners as Queensland's 'Australian of the Year', which meant they would be put forward for the big award of Australian of the Year with the rest of the state winners. That night, Bruce and Denise attended GOMA, the Gallery of Modern Art in Southbank, Brisbane, and met the playwright David Williamson and other award nominees. On 18 November, they met the man who was to become the new Queensland premier – Campbell Newman – at a luncheon to launch John Connolly, the former Wallabies coach, as Liberal National Party candidate for the seat of Nicklin. While other VIPs, including former Prime Minister John Howard, received warm applause, the Morcombes were embarrassed to be given a standing ovation.

The eighth anniversary of Daniel's disappearance passed, with no prospect in sight of being able to hold his funeral. Christmas that year was spent at their Tasmanian retreat. Dean and Brad, Kevin and Monique also came. Even Rosie the cat joined them. She enjoyed sitting by the fire in the cooler climate of Tasmania. It had been one of the most eventful years since Daniel had disappeared.

CHAPTER TWENTY-EIGHT

THE BATTLE FOR DANIEL'S REMAINS

January 2012 brought sad news. On 8 January, Bruce's mother, Wendy, died aged 84 in Greenslopes Hospital after being at Regis Aged Care for eight years. Wendy had been living on her own since Bruce's father, Ted, had died in 1989. Wendy had always enjoyed travelling and the company of others. Once a keen gardener, she had visited Camellia Cottage several times and loved the place. Sometimes, there had been family lunches at Camellia Cottage, and once she came for Christmas lunch. However, Wendy always got anxious around mid-afternoon as she wanted to be back at the home by 5 pm. Often, Bruce's brothers or sister would come to pick her up to take her back to the nursing home in Salisbury, Brisbane.

After moving into the home, Wendy's short-term memory had steadily deteriorated. Whenever Daniel was mentioned, she would become upset. She loved all of the boys. Bruce had kept a cherished framed photograph of his mother with the boys. Just before Christmas, and before heading south, Bruce, Denise and the boys had been to visit

Wendy at the hospital. They knew her time was close. She could not speak, eat or drink. Her frail body was saying, 'No more.' Bruce had bent down to kiss her on the forehead. Even though she could hardly move, she rolled her eyes up to look at him. She did not blink. He knew in that moment that his mother knew this was the final goodbye. He had to leave the room as his eyes filled with tears. They all left knowing they would probably not see her again.

When the news came, however, so soon after Christmas, it was still hard to bear. Bruce, Denise and their cat, now a seasoned traveller, were in Tasmania so had to quickly change their flights to attend the funeral. But the plane from Hobart to Canberra, linking up with the one to Brisbane, was two hours late, so making their onward connection was unlikely. They were concerned they would miss the funeral. While sitting on the plane, a flight attendant approached Bruce and Denise to congratulate them on their work. Bruce was frustrated and annoyed at the seemingly hopeless situation and Denise explained to the attendant that they would probably miss Bruce's mother's funeral because of the delay. She spoke to the pilot, and Bruce and Denise were transferred from Canberra to Sydney, and then on to Brisbane. As always, they were touched by the kindness of strangers. They met Dean and Brad at Brisbane Airport, collected Rosie from the pet section at the airport and turned up in time for the funeral with Rosie in hand, who was kept in her pet travel box in the same room as the wake.

On 24 January, Denise and Bruce flew to Canberra for the Australian of the Year awards. The first evening, they had dinner in the gardens at Yarralumla, the residence of the then Governor General of Australia, Quentin Bryce, and they met her, as well as her husband, Michael, who told them he had attended one of the early searches for Daniel, being a long-time volunteer with the SES. The following day, they had morning tea at the Lodge and met Prime Minister Julia Gillard.

The Australian of the Year for 2012 was Australian actor Geoffrey Rush. Bruce and Denise felt a bit deflated, but they still thoroughly enjoyed the ceremony.

* * *

On 12 February, Bruce and Denise began visiting schools as far north as Ingham, inland to Charters Towers and back to suburban Brisbane. Ken Searles attended the Drive for Daniel golf day in their absence at the Carbrook Golf Course, organised by a group from the Queensland travel industry, who assisted the Foundation by raising $14,500.

The Morcombes were always answering emails while they were on the road. On 28 February, they received an email from Kate McCann:

> Dear Bruce and Denise,
> I want to ask 'how are you?' – that old question. I have
> no idea how it would feel to receive the news you did last
> year, nor how you are feeling months on but I'm sure the
> inevitable fall is much worse than you may have imagined.
> I truly hope that you're both doing ok. It's a slow process
> to a 'comfortable' place I suspect but as before, you will get
> there ... I have on several occasions and more so latterly,
> considered what I would prefer – to not know and live as
> we are with hope, all possibilities possible, or to know,
> even if this means bad news with no alternative, no more
> hope etc. In the early months and even years, I said 'to
> know' without doubt but over time, I did start wondering
> just how awful it would really feel to get the worst news
> imaginable. Having said all this, deep down and after
> much, much thought, I still feel it would be better to know.
> It's tiring trying to find out and the uncertainty never sits
> comfortably. For Sean and Amelie too, it would be better
> to know. I don't want their lives being hijacked with the

need to find out. Naturally, and with good reason, we still
hope that positive news awaits us. And who knows!
With love and good wishes to you and all the family.
Kate xx

That same day, they received an email from a journalist
saying Jackway would remain behind bars as an indefinite-
term prisoner. Meanwhile, they were catching a small
charter plane to Palm Island to speak with students with
predominantly Indigenous heritage, and then returning to
Townsville in one day. Many of the students there had not
heard about Daniel, as they had limited access to television,
radio and newspapers at home. But, when Bruce introduced
himself by opening with the stark truth that his son Daniel
had been murdered, they all sat up and listened.

The bright-red racing car with the Daniel Morcombe
Foundation logo all over it was launched on 1 March. Bruce
and Denise had received an email the day after Cowan was
arrested from a man who was building a new Holden VE
V8, which he wanted to brand with their organisation. They
attended the Townsville PCYC for the launch where they
discovered that most of the 200 people who turned up had a
connection with the car, from technical support to suppliers,
mechanics, panel beaters and spray painters.

Two days later Daniel's V8 car dazzled at the home
ground of the National Rugby League club the North
Queensland Cowboys. The Cowboys had invited the Daniel
Morcombe Foundation to be one of the first to participate in
their new 'Community Corner'. The car's bright-red bonnet
was up, exposing the new engine. Many onlookers stopped
to check it out. Daniel's face smiled down from the banner
behind the car.

Up in the corporate box, at the top of the grand stadium,
Bruce and Denise watched the game. The ball boys wore
bright red Daniel Morcombe Foundation T-shirts and caps

and were easily spotted on the large grass stadium. JT, Johnathan Thurston, the Cowboys' captain, was wearing special, red, Madison headgear, which he later signed and donated as a fundraiser in honour of Daniel. The community support was overwhelming for Bruce and Denise. They felt the Foundation's message was getting out there.

'Help Me', an iPhone 'app', was also launched in March, at Kangaroo Point. The app allowed children and adults to send off an SMS to two nominated 'safety' numbers as part of their Trusted Safety Network. Once activated, the text incorporated a GPS map, so the child's location could easily be identified. The app simply means 'Help' and could be used by teenagers or adults with medical conditions, or shiftworkers concerned about night travel. Speaking at the launch, Bruce said, 'If this was available for Daniel, we may have had a different outcome.' By August that year, the app would make 20,000 sales.

The Brisbane Women's Correctional Centre houses 258 prisoners and is the only reception, assessment and placement centre for women prisoners in southern Queensland. On 8 March, only days after returning home from up north, the Morcombes left home at 5.30 am to drive to the jail. Although Denise was the public speaker on this occasion, as it was International Women's Day, Bruce came with her for moral support. Some of the women had been rehearsing their 'hip hop' routine specifically for their welcome for several weeks. Addressing the women prisoners, Denise said, 'No matter what issues are in your life, forget about making excuses. Life is about getting up each day and making the most of what you have and being the best person you possibly can be.' Many of the women were in tears as she spoke. The women had done some fundraising and a cheque was presented to the Foundation. Some of the inmates wolf-whistled at Bruce as he left. 'The girls haven't seen men for a while,' he joked.

A complete contrast was the talk later that afternoon to the Australian Taxation Office in the Brisbane CBD. Denise couldn't help but compare the different audiences. One thing was certain – the Foundation was reaching across Australian society. Daniel's quiet presence was making large strides in helping others. For the rest of March, there were several other speaking engagements.

Bruce and Denise had a large canvas painting donated to them by Jason Swain, an international artist who lived in the US but had family ties in Caloundra. He had painted a montage of Daniel's happiest moments, including him standing at the bow of a rowing boat on Norfolk Island, doing his schoolwork and feeding a kangaroo at Australia Zoo. They loved it and it became the inspiration for the Foundation's new logo.

* * *

Only seven days before the Dance for Daniel on 31 March at the Caloundra RSL, Queenslanders went to the polls, voting in a new government for the Liberal National Party. For the first time, there was a waiting list for the dance, as tickets had sold out seven weeks beforehand. Band of Blue played again, and the singer/comedian Adam Scicluna performed. In spite of the new government only being announced the previous Friday, a letter was read out at the dance from the new premier, Campbell Newman, outlining his government's ongoing commitment to the soon-to-be-launched Daniel Morcombe Child Safety Curriculum. It was music to the Morcombe's ears.

* * *

There was still no indication of a committal date. The worst battle was brewing behind the scenes: a war waged on paper

Memorial under the overpass where Daniel was abducted, with flowers and tributes from the public and family. Pictured is the door on which Bruce wrote his appeal for help, 5 February 2004.

Bruce and Denise release balloons to commence a red day in Brisbane. This led to the 'Day for Daniel' held in Queensland State Parliament, 20 April 2004.

Above: Bradley and Denise atop Mount Wellington in Tasmania. This was their first vacation without Daniel, June 2004.

Daniel James Morcombe

Born 19.12.89 ~ Disappeared 7.12.03

Left: Prayer card with candle distributed at Daniel's memorial held at St Catherine of Siena, 7 December 2004.

Father Jan Bialasiewicz blessing a poinciana tree adjacent to
the abduction site in Woombye, planted in Daniel's memory,
7 December 2004. Each year in December it flowers red.

Bruce at the abduction site with a new sign appealing for
information, 7 December 2006.

Hamilton Island, Christmas 2005. Returning without Daniel.

Camellia cottage, the family home.

Above: Daniel Morcombe Foundation Committee. *Top*: Peter Boyce, Brett Winkler and Bruce. *Bottom*: Samantha Knight, Denise and Julie Elliott, 2006. Absent: Tim Ryan.

Left: Denise and Bruce at the Dance for Daniel held at Twin Waters resort, March 2008.

Julie and Denise at Mt Ossa, Tasmania, Easter Sunday 2008.

Photo Chris McCormack / APN

Dean Morcombe (centre) with his band Ablaze Withsin, 7 June 2008.

Students of St Mary Magdalen's Primary School in Chadstone, Victoria, show Denise class drawings as part of the Foundation's child safety campaign. This was the first school visited outside Queensland, 11 November 2008.

Bruce Long / Newspix

Bruce, Denise and Police Commissioner Bob Atkinson announcing the one million dollar reward at Queensland Police Headquarters, 1 December 2008.

Andrew Meares / Fairfax Syndication

Above: First International Missing Children's Day held by the Australian Federal Police. On the lawns of Parliament House in Canberra, Bruce and Denise release white balloons with photos of missing children from around the globe, including Daniel, 25 May 2009.

Right: Bruce with key material on various Persons of Interest outside Maroochydore Magistrate's Court at the start of the coronial inquest, 11 October 2010.

Megan Slade / Newspix

Bradley's 21st birthday surprise party. *Left to right*: Denise, Bradley, Dean and Bruce, 11 December 2010.

Dinner with the parents of missing toddler Madeleine McCann at the Dirty Duck, Stratford upon Avon, in the UK, June 2011. *Left to right*: Gerry McCann, Kate McCann, Denise and Bruce.

Bruce's birthday, the day after DNA results proved the remains found at Kings Road, Beerwah, belonged to Daniel, 29 August 2011.

The abandoned sand quarry in Beerwah at the very spot of Daniel's final resting place. The Morcombes say a prayer, 14 October 2011.

Over 2000 people attended the Walk for Daniel on the
Sunshine Coast, 29 October 2011.

Bruce and Denise are presented the award for joint Queensland
Australian of the Year by Premier Anna Bligh, November 2011.

Denise and Bruce with Kevin Rudd at Parliament House
in Canberra on their Day for Daniel in Federal Parliament,
October 2012.

'Big Red', the educational resource truck outside the Australian
Federal Police building in Canberra where a Day for Daniel
was held, 30 October 2012.

Harrison Saragossi / Fairfax Syndication

Police escort and motorcade driving from the funeral at St Catherine of Siena to Woombye Cemetery. People attending the funeral lined up outside the church grounds, watching the hearse depart, 7 December 2012.

Glenn Barnes / Newspix

Bradley, Dean and Daniel's friends carrying the coffin from the church.

Harrison Saragossi / Fairfax Syndication

Daniel's coffin in the hearse with SES volunteers behind, who searched tirelessly for Daniel, proudly wearing their orange overalls to the funeral.

Glenn Barnes / Newspix

At Daniel's funeral: Sienna, Dean, Denise, Bruce, Anna and Bradley.

Bruce and Denise receive the Order of Australia Medal at the Queensland Governor's residence in Brisbane, 17 September 2013.

The Walk for Daniel on the Sunshine Coast begins. Premier Campbell Newman, his wife Lisa, Bruce, Denise and others burst through the start banner, 25 October 2013.

The Morcombe family about to face the media after the guilty verdict, 13 March 2014.

Daniel's memorial at the abduction site a few days after the guilty verdict.

between Bruce and Denise, the Queensland Police Service and the Queensland legal system for Daniel's remains. At first, it did not spill into the public arena. Seventeen bones, five human bone fragments and several further bone fragments that could not be determined as human had been found at the site. Two of the bones had yielded DNA. DNA tests had been conducted in three laboratories: two in Australia and one in New Zealand.

When Bruce and Denise first heard that their son had been found in August, they had immediately thought that they could bring Daniel home and bury him. In the first weeks after Daniel was discovered, they began talking about it. Still in shock at the rapid chain of events, they had not even considered they could be refused such a simple human right.

It was up to the Coroner to decide whether to release bodies for cremation or burial, depending on whether the body was 'sufficiently identified' and it was no longer necessary to keep it to investigate the cause of death. Because the court case was pending, Daniel's remains were still subject to forensic testing. Bruce publicly questioned why, 'in this day and age', could testing not demonstrate beyond dispute the legal question of identification and demanded to know why the process took so long.

Knowing that they were powerless in the battle to bring Daniel home paralysed both of them. When they thought they were nearing the summit, it presented as yet another mountain to climb. They both also knew they had to reserve strength to confront the man who had been accused of killing their son. Bruce had only attended two of the 'mentions' in court. Denise had not attended any. Cowan had not been present at all of them and, if he was, he was on video link. While they had already 'eyeballed him' at the inquest, as Bruce put it, this time it would be different. Then, he had not been singled out.

On 11 April, Bruce wrote an email to Peter Boyce asking whether they should approach the new Queensland Attorney General, Jarrod Bleijie, to ask about releasing Daniel's remains. Boyce suggested, instead, that he would write to the DPP to see whether there had been any conclusions on the DNA sampling and whether they could give them a date when the tests might be completed. Meanwhile, Bruce and Denise continued their school visits, travelling to 15 schools in Hatton Vale, Toowoomba, Miles, Killarney and Goondiwindi. More than a fortnight later, the reply came from the DPP to Peter Boyce. Investigating police were still awaiting further DNA test results.

After the latest round of school visits, Bruce took advantage of his family's absence to act on something he had been thinking about since Christmas when Dean had given him a tattoo gift voucher. Denise was in Melbourne, Brad was working in the country and Dean was away. The striking tattoo that ran along the inside of his left arm was unmistakably the Glass House Mountains, with a dark sunset behind and the words 'Never Forget' in large, calligraphic handwriting across the picture. It was Daniel's final resting place.

* * *

By mid-year, there was still no news on the DNA on Daniel's remains. The next court mention for Cowan was set for 6 August. Bruce wrote an email again to Peter Boyce saying he did not want 'to make enemies with the DPP or damage Cowan's trial, but I cannot find another case where ten months after remains have been found they are not released to the family'. Again, he said he was happy to make a direct approach to the Queensland Attorney General and, if unsuccessful, would go to the media.

The launch of 'Big Red' in July complemented the Foundation's D-MAX ute. The Big Red truck had been planned for two years. Many businesses and people had given their skilled time or donated products. A smart television was mounted on the side of the truck. By logging on to the internet, Denise was able to display at the launch how the Daniel Morcombe Foundation Facebook page could educate people about safety aspects such as how to use privacy settings for social media. There was a ceremonial spray of 'champers' on Big Red's windscreen: she was ready for action immediately, heading north for duties.

On 14 July, it was Denise's niece's wedding. Ashlea was getting married to her fiancé, Shane. Returning to Queensland soon after the Melbourne wedding, they got behind the wheel of Big Red and drove to 12 schools in Gladstone, Rockhampton, Mackay, Bowen and then to the Gold Coast.

* * *

In the midst of the light they brought into their lives through the Foundation, the darkness still lurked. Since Cowan had been charged, many of the other POIs had slipped into oblivion. But, on 17 July, POI33 was charged with perjury after giving a 'disturbingly detailed account' of Daniel's death at the inquest. He had claimed that he was standing ten feet from Daniel when he was murdered. Bruce and Denise had learnt how to dismiss these 'horrid creatures', as Bruce had called them, from their minds.

It was getting on for a year after Cowan had been charged. Speaking to *The Courier-Mail*'s Kristen Shorten, Bruce said that, in spite of the arrest, people were still coming forward to claim the reward, saying it must have been their information that had led to the breakthrough. 'One [person] was after the million dollars but the window for that was only six months and it closed three years ago,' he said.

On 24 July, Cowan's legal team lodged a request with the Crown to cross-examine up to one hundred witnesses at the committal hearing. Meanwhile, Bruce and Denise were still on the public stage. On 25 July, they told Bond University students about the agony of not knowing whether the next phone call would be from police confirming their son had been brutally killed. The students were studying the impact of crime on victims.

When the Brisbane Magistrates' Court reconvened on 6 August for a 15-minute hearing, Cowan appeared via video link wearing a prison-issue tracksuit and with his long, bedraggled hair cropped short. Tim Meehan from Bosscher Lawyers filed an application to interview 51 of the witnesses after the DPP objected to the earlier request. Only 31 witnesses were approved. Meehan said, 'We're going to have to demonstrate to the magistrate that there are reasons why, in the interest of justice, we should be given an opportunity to cross-examine witnesses at the committal rather than wait until trial.' Committal hearings allowed the defence to test the evidence when the prosecution called its witnesses and the magistrate to decide whether, on the strength of the evidence, the accused person might be committed for trial. Meehan said that Cowan intended to apply for bail but would probably not do so until after the committal hearing.

Bruce used the preliminary hearing, which he attended with Brad, to issue a scathing attack via the media about the fact that the family were prevented from burying Daniel. Speaking outside the court, he said the family were 'sick of waiting for the release of his son's remains. The twenty-first of August is very close – that's when Daniel was found a year ago – and here we are still talking about it'. The family had been patient for long enough.

Responding to some of the media, the Coroner said he had not yet had an application for Daniel's remains from the family. Bruce and Denise immediately made a formal application through Peter Boyce, who wrote personally to Michael Barnes requesting a hearing, if necessary, for the application. Bruce filled in and signed the 'order for release of body for burial' form, noting down Daniel's death as 7 December 2003 and the place as 'Sunshine Coast'.

Two days later, Bruce emailed Peter Boyce asking if they could suggest a legislative change. 'I'm thinking that if we can help another family in the future at least that is a positive thing.' He suggested writing something along the lines of, 'Human remains must be returned to the family within a six-month period. All DNA testing must be completed within that time and independently checked at a second facility.'

* * *

On the anniversary of Cowan's arrest on Monday 13 August, Denise posted her favourite photo of Daniel on Facebook, the one of Daniel working at his schoolbooks, given to them by Graeme Hight, elbows on desk, his hair slightly tousled, the picture of innocence. She commented on the picture, 'Wanted to keep my favourite photo till we had a funeral but waiting is forever, this is a photo taken of Dan at school which we were given after the arrest that we hadn't seen until then.' More than 500,000 Facebook followers viewed the photo.

On the first anniversary of Daniel's remains being found, they used Facebook again to make another public statement: 'After 2790 days, our son's remains were unearthed in the Glass House Mountains exactly one year ago. However, we draw no comfort from that discovery because to us it feels like he has been abducted a second time. It is inhumane to treat Daniel's remains simply as evidence for a trial.' The note continued, 'Reasonable timeframes must be written into State law allowing the forgotten victim's family the right to say goodbye.'

Tributes on the Facebook page backed the family's call: 'Bring him home. You are such an inspirational family';

'Queensland is behind u all the way'; 'May Daniel be laid to rest with dignity soon'.

A few days later, they received a letter from someone whose son had been an old schoolfriend of Cowan's. Cowan, the woman said, had spent a lot of time at their house. She described him as a 'strange edgy kid with family problems' who, 'under his bright, polite exterior', was 'already showing signs of his troubled mind'. When she overheard him threatening to rape their 13-year-old daughter, Cowan had been banned from their house. He had often turned up in a car, she wrote, saying that it belonged to his brother, but she had always suspected it was stolen.

Bruce and Denise received other information on Cowan via a letter sent to Peter Boyce, from a teacher who had taught at the same school he had attended from 1983 to 1985, which was then named Marcellin College, at Enoggera – now Mt Maria – when he was in Grades 8 to 10. The teacher said he had been considered a bit 'weird' by the majority of students and told of an incident when he was caught 'flashing' to the primary school students next door. The former teacher also said that he believed Cowan had been taught by an infamous paedophile who had been at the school for a term and was later convicted of charges relating to indecently dealing with children.

* * *

On 21 August, the Morcombes were in Cairns to continue their 'Recognise, React and Report' tour. That same day, a government spokesman said Daniel's remains could be released to the family only after the defence team accepted the DNA test results or conducted its own tests. Meehan confirmed that the defence team would be conducting its own DNA tests. 'At this stage we're not in a position to provide any timeframes ... because we're consulting with our experts,' he said.

For Bruce and Denise, the news was a knife into their hearts. Bruce wrote to the State Coroner asking him to end the 'cruellest twist in a nightmare which began almost nine years ago'. He said the news was like a 'second abduction'. 'To have come so far and have what we thought was an opportunity to say goodbye late last year denied, denied, denied ...' he said. 'I want the police, the Coroner, the Director of Public Prosecutions or somebody to stand up and say that's not right. The system continues to violate Daniel even after his passing, but we will not let the next unfortunate family suffer as we have.'

Meanwhile, the Foundation channelled funds into worthwhile causes. Denise and Bruce met three children who were victims of a recent murder case. Their father had been charged with murdering their mother two months previously. The Foundation supported them with ballet and sports equipment, school uniforms and counselling.

The day after the appeal to allow Daniel's remains to be released, the Attorney General ruled out any legislative changes that would allow this to happen. Jarrod Bleijie said that, while he 'empathised' with the Morcombes and understood their frustration, he could not jeopardise an upcoming murder trial. 'I just make the point, though, that this is a murder trial. There are serious consequences and I do note the issue [they] have raised in terms of the release of the remains. In a murder trial, the general analysis is that if the defence wish to examine the DNA, then we run a real risk in terms of the prosecution if we release them.'

Mr Bleijie said he tended to avoid commenting on particular cases but offered his 'support to the Morcombes'. 'We have to let the courts run the way they're operating, under the law, at the moment,' he said.

* * *

News arrived on 4 September that Bob Atkinson was retiring, after 12 years of service, to be replaced by his deputy, Ian Stewart. As Queensland's new top cop, Stewart immediately warned he would be tough on internal discipline and on outlaw bikie gangs. The softly spoken Atkinson confessed that when he joined the force, his ambition had been 'to make a difference'. He had initially achieved fame for leading the successful investigation into the murder of schoolgirl Sian Kingi. As commissioner, he said, Daniel's case was one of the major investigations he had overseen. 'There were always two questions: where is Daniel and who is responsible? We've been able to answer the first one – Daniel's remains have been found – and the second one, a person has been charged and is before the courts.'

On the same day that Atkinson's retirement was announced, Bruce did an interview with *She* magazine about their relationship with Gerry and Kate McCann. 'They are truly lovely, wonderful people,' Bruce said. 'Like us, this just came out of nowhere for them. And like us, they have vowed to fight on for the truth. Unlike us, they still have no answers. And while they have always believed that Madeleine will be found alive, we've noticed a difference since Daniel's body was discovered. Every day that goes by, you know the chances drop again. But we will be there for them whatever the outcome may be – and we just hope for their sakes there is one. We're more than victims of circumstance and more than friends now. We're part of the family of survivors.'

On 5 September, the committal hearing date was finally set for 26 November. The case had been listed that day for mention before the Chief Magistrate, Brendan Butler. The defence requested that witnesses who had been hypnotised be called to give evidence at the committal hearing. The prosecutor – a quietly spoken, unflappable but determined man named Glen Cash – told the court that Michael Bosscher had given 'no significant reasons' why these witnesses should give evidence before a trial.

That same day, Bruce and Denise were launching the Daniel Morcombe Child Safety Curriculum at the Barcaldine State School in central west Queensland, with Education Minister John-Paul Langbroek. The curriculum, although not compulsory, was 'strongly recommended', Langbroek said. It provided teachers with resources and guidelines to integrate child-safety lessons into their classes and would first be taught to pupils in Prep, Grade 1 and Grade 2, before being rolled out for Grades 3 to 6 later in the year, and then Grades 7 to 9 in 2013. The program encouraged students to be aware of their surroundings, recognise warning signs, react by removing themselves from danger and report suspicious incidents to an adult. It also dealt with 'cybersafety'. Langbroek announced, 'This program will help teachers deliver valuable learning experiences, so that students can develop the skills needed to better manage their own safety.'

Speaking to the gathered students, Bruce said he wished he could have told his son to 'run' the day he disappeared. He and Denise said that the key to keeping safe were the three 'R's that underpinned the program: 'Recognise, React and Report dangerous or suspicious behaviour. If you Recognise danger, you React by running to a safe location.'

Talking directly to children and seeing their attentive faces was again a welcome diversion from the legal wrangling.

* * *

Behind the scenes, authorities were fighting over who had control of Daniel. Bruce and Denise received an email from Peter Boyce enclosing a letter from Michael Barnes. Barnes had sought submissions from the DPP, the Queensland Police Service and lawyers acting for Cowan as to whether or not he should grant the release of Daniel's remains to his family. The DPP had not made any submissions and Cowan's lawyers had advised they might be conducting further testing on the remains, depending on cross-examination of the DNA witnesses at the committal. The Queensland Police Service, however, had submitted that the Coroner had no control over the remains as they were 'seized under a crime scene warrant' under the *Police Powers and Responsibilities Act* and that, as criminal charges had been laid, the Coroner had no power to make any ruling on the application to have Daniel's remains returned. They quoted the 'crime scene warrant', which permitted police officers to take possession of 'a thing' at the crime scene.

Barnes's response to the Queensland Police Service's submission was that he did not believe 'human bodies or human remains are at law "things" and that, under the *Coroner's Act*, a Coroner still had control over the body'. Further, he wrote that the Queensland Police Service had not provided any explanation as to why the remaining bones could not be released to the family. He said the Queensland Police Service had made clear that if the Coroner did make the release order, the police would still not release the remains. Barnes said he wanted to defer what might happen to the remains until after the completion of the committal hearing. The letter was copied to the Queensland Police Service, the DPP and Tim Meehan.

That the man potentially responsible for Daniel's murder was being consulted about whether Daniel could be buried or not was particularly distressing to Bruce and Denise. But the most hurtful of all was that their son would be described as 'a thing', which made their blood boil. Daniel had clearly been violated already in his short life and now he was not even being treated as a human being in death.

As before, Bruce and Denise showed great determination to fight these dry words dreamt up by lawyers, which did not take people's lives into account. They had not come this far to stand by and disregard Daniel's right to be buried.

* * *

The Morcombes' fundraising and safety-awareness events carried on apace throughout September and October, including Townsville's inaugural Dance for Daniel, a tour of a PCYC and five schools in Far North Queensland, an emotionally charged talk at Brad and Daniel's old school, Mountain Creek State School, and a Day for Daniel at Parliament House in Canberra.

On 26 October, Kevin and Monique attended that year's Day for Daniel. The following day Bruce and Denise drove Big Red down to the Gold Coast for the Walk for Daniel and on to Coffs Harbour for the walk there. More than 600 attended.

That same day the Foundation offices moved into the Big Pineapple. There was much more space inside and even a boardroom for meetings and a separate office for Bruce and Denise. What's more, Big Red could be parked downstairs. They had a five-year handshake agreement from the owners, which meant, for the first time, they could concentrate on stability and growth of the Foundation. They could relax a little. On Denise's birthday, 3 November, Kevin and Monique, who had flown up for the Walk for Daniel from Melbourne, joined her for a birthday lunch at the Woombye pub.

Melbourne Cup Day on 6 November was the traditional time at the Sunshine Coast's Turf Club at the Corbould Park Racecourse with Peter Boyce. This time Kevin and Monique also attended. Monique was lucky enough to back a couple of winners.

While they were preoccupied with the Foundation, Bruce and Denise were well aware of the countdown for the committal hearing. The 26 November date fulfilled the promise that the proceedings would start before Christmas. On 7 November, they received a visit at their new Big Pineapple office from two detectives, Ross Hutton and

Steve Blanchfield. 'I'm afraid you won't be able to attend the committal hearing yourselves as you are potential witnesses at the trial,' Hutton said.

Bruce and Denise said they understood the recommendation but would be defying it. Privately, they had already decided they would be attending the committal and would only leave if ordered to by the magistrate. It was his call, not that of the police.

Peter Boyce had already given them advice on their legal rights. Michael Byrne QC, the deputy DPP, had advised that it was 'very undesirable' that Bruce and Denise attend the committal hearing and that the magistrate had the power to bar them from court. Boyce pointed out that the Morcombes had already attended the lengthy coronial inquest, which seriously undermined the argument that their evidence as potential witnesses at the trial might be tainted. Once again, they had to be prepared for a battle.

* * *

Ken King, the former police officer who, with his colleague, had spoken with Cowan less than two weeks after Daniel went missing, was now working in Federal Parliament. He had introduced himself to Bruce and Denise when they were in Canberra for the Day for Daniel. They had exchanged contact details and arranged a meeting.

After attending the Bidvest head office, a national foodservice business in Morningside in Brisbane on 8 November, Bruce and Denise left the city to meet with Ken King at his relative's house in a northern suburb of Brisbane. The hour-long meeting was spent with Bruce and Denise taking notes as King outlined his efforts to bring Cowan to the attention of the MIR and to get him further investigated. The Morcombes left feeling dumbfounded that the man who was now before the courts had been so easily within the grasp of the police all those years ago. What had gone wrong? Why had they waited so long to arrest him and why hadn't there been efforts to conduct search warrants? What happened to the results of the search of his Pajero? This was supposed to be Australia's biggest manhunt and the most resourced single case in Australia's history. How could things have gone so wrong?

Meanwhile, the battle with the Queensland Police Service and judicial system continued. Peter Boyce wrote to Bruce and Denise on 9 November, 'the question that needs to be answered is whether the Coroner is actually the person in control of Daniel's remains or whether the police are entitled to say that they are still in control'. Once again, the Morcombes and the Queensland Police Service were adversaries. Boyce also wrote to Michael Barnes requesting him to authorise a medical practitioner to issue a death certificate.

There were few people whom Bruce and Denise felt could understand the frustration they now faced over the lengthy delays in the judicial process. The McCanns at least understood the waiting game. Bruce had continued to let them know the ins and outs of their lives, and had outlined the moves to prevent him and Denise attending the court hearing, but the bigger concern, he wrote, was how long the authorities were holding onto Daniel's remains – until after a trial, and possibly even until the end of the appeal process, which was a further year away. Kate McCann responded quickly:

Dear Bruce and Denise,
I felt exasperated reading your email, both in relation
to how long the trial will take, or rather how far away it
still is, and also about not being able to have a funeral for
Daniel yet. You must feel like screaming! He's your son!!!!
So unfair. The Metropolitan Police are doing a great job,
are being meticulous and are managing to uncover a lot of

pertinent information – some of which is so relevant that we'd like it investigated NOW!

Gerry's working really hard – long days and the rest of the time is largely spent on his laptop!! I'm keeping busy with the campaign and helping the charity 'Missing People', as well as the usual unrelenting 'mummy' jobs. Sean and Amelie are doing really well and are great fun as always. Right, I better go and do the evening chores. I really hope you're all doing ok despite the frustrations of the process. Take care – and keep in touch.

With love,

Kate xx

* * *

On 19 November, it was the Walk for Daniel again in Melbourne. The following day, Denise flew back home while Bruce drove Big Red back to the Sunshine Coast. Three days later, Bruce was still on the road so Denise collected the 2012 Australian Crime and Violence Prevention Award for *Foundation Red*, their child-safety DVD. Amid the turmoil of their own lives, they were still making a huge positive impact on the lives of other children and families.

CHAPTER TWENTY-NINE

THE COMMITTAL BEGINS

The Brisbane Magistrates' Court was abuzz with media on Monday 26 November 2012, the first day of Brett Cowan's committal. To make the expected grieving process a little easier, Bruce and Denise booked a motel in the city just a few blocks away. That first morning, the family was apprehensive. They didn't know if they would be allowed in.

The courtroom was on the fifth floor. When the Morcombes arrived out of the lifts, there was no one else in the wide lobby, with its floor-to-ceiling windows at one end overlooking Roma Street parklands. This was the moment Denise had been dreading. Bruce was more accustomed to confronting the worst of humanity, as he described them to media. He was ready to keep fighting – for Daniel's sake, he needed to. They both were. This was the beginning of Daniel's day in court. Odds were that they would be thrown out, and that added more tension. Boyce had told them, if that was the case, he would make a formal approach to the magistrate presiding over the hearing for them to stay.

Apart from that, there was the continuing preoccupation about when they would be allowed to bury Daniel. The Thursday before the committal was due to begin, they had received a letter from Michael Barnes stating that they could apply for a death certificate from the Registry of Births, Deaths and Marriages. Barnes had added, 'The mechanism for release of Daniel's remains is, as you suggest, an order by me under section 26. I am hopeful that after the DNA evidence is heard at the committal proceedings, the defence and the prosecution will agree there is no longer any need to retain the remains. That would free the way for me to make a release order.'

After receiving the letter from the State Coroner, Bruce and Denise had travelled to Daniel's final resting place. It was an emotional trip as they made their way back down the dirt track that skirted the macadamia farmhouse, then picked their way down the embankment before entering the pine forest, where they felt the sandy soil underfoot. The forest was eerily silent. This time, they were alone. After walking around the mounds of earth left over from all of the searches that had taken place more than a year ago, they finally found the specific tree that Condon had shown them near the pond. Waterlilies could be seen on the pond surface through the trees.

'Hopefully soon we can lay you to rest,' Denise had whispered, tying a wooden cross to the tree.

They had held each other tight, the years of struggle and torment that threatened their existence culminating in this one moment. They had found Daniel. Too upset to speak, they walked silently back to the car, the sombre nature of their journey marking their determination that now, more than ever, they had to lay Daniel to rest.

Purely by chance, on the Sunday before the committal hearing, Bruce emailed an address from the council website for the Cemeteries Services team, asking whether it was possible to bury Daniel at the Woombye Cemetery, which was officially closed for burials. The journey to bring him home had begun in earnest.

* * *

Inside the courtroom, the media fidgeted. Bruce and Denise, Peter Boyce, the boys and other family members sat on the far side of the room from the dock where the accused would soon be brought up from the cells.

A few minutes after everyone was seated, the door next to the glass box suddenly opened. Between two Correctional Service officers, Cowan appeared, dressed in a grey suit that looked at least a size too big for him. His skin had a sickly hue and his cheeks looked weathered. His head hung forward, with his hair cut in a businessman's style, short at the sides. Bruce was struck by how different this man looked to when he had first seen him at the inquest. Here was the man accused of killing their son. Nothing could prepare them for that.

Avoiding eye contact with the public gallery, Cowan sought out his counsel and broke into a hangdog smile before being led into the box. Meehan immediately approached and the two became huddled in conversation. For the media, this was the moment many had believed would never happen. This time, the story would be focusing on what had happened to Daniel, not on the search to find him. A court artist sat as close as he could to Cowan, drawing on a large sketchpad with coloured crayons. No media outlets were allowed to publish or broadcast photographs of Cowan while court proceedings were underway as identification could be an issue in the trial. The only footage available for television news was the clip of a shadowy figure in a baseball cap being driven in by police to give evidence at the inquest the year before. The charges were read out.

By 9.13 am, Chief Magistrate Brendan Butler announced that the Morcombes would be allowed to stay for the proceedings. Bruce and Denise breathed deeply.

The first witness to enter the box was Inspector Arthur Van Panhuis, from North Coast Regional Command Forensics. As Van Panhuis spoke, describing the crime scenes where Daniel's remains had been found, images were flashed across the screen in the courtroom. The media and public gallery watched the screens intently. Cowan had been provided with a screen down in front of him inside the glass partitioned dock, which he watched with his head tilted down. Van Panhuis said that, when the first shoe had been located, about 20 metres away from where the police had been told to look, it had been covered in pine needles. He said that, when they found a bone that was thought to be human, it was 'quite some distance from where the shoe was'.

Bruce was impressed by Van Panhuis, who he felt was thorough and direct. This was the first time either of them had heard about how the shoes had been found. As they had both privately visited the search area only a few days previously, and had been several times, they felt more familiar with what flashed up in front of them as stills. To Bruce and Denise, it appeared that none of the defence team had ever visited the site, because they frequently seemed to give inaccurate descriptions. Detective Ross Hutton later also told them that the defence team had been given several invitations but had declined.

Bruce had been counting out the days of the search as the photos flashed up on the screen. As they approached Van Panhuis's descriptions of 20 August and the first discovery of a human bone, he turned to Denise. 'Would you prefer to leave?' he asked.

She shook her head. Then they discovered another fact they had not known. The first bone had been found on

20 August, the same day as the second shoe was uncovered. This was a complete surprise.

Since Daniel's disappearance, the landscape where his remains had been found had changed. Crime Scene 1 contained the demountable building, known as a 'donga', which had been relocated. A carpet from the dilapidated worker's hut and fittings and fixtures from the demountable had been removed and buried when the building was demolished, Van Panhuis said. It had been dug up by police and vacuumed, although he confirmed that the contents of the bag had not been examined. The public gallery all seemed puzzled. Why go through those motions and not test the contents? Crime Scene 2 was 150 metres away from Crime Scene 1. This area had been used for sand-mining operations in the late '90s. In those days, there were no trees, but, after the mining stopped, the vegetation had seeded naturally and grown back. During the flood times, silt had washed downstream and been deposited. It had meant searching in some places down to a depth close to a metre of sand, using heavy machines such as a bobcat and trench digger. Van Panhuis went through the rest of the discoveries, including further bone fragments and some clothing located on 20 August by the dive squad in Crime Scene 3 on the bed of Coochin Creek. Bruce and Denise had not been told of this find until 22 August.

At morning tea, an email arrived in Bruce's iPad's inbox. It was from Rob Luscombe, the Cemeteries Services manager from the council. He wrote that there were a small number of plots set aside for exceptional circumstances. Bruce and Denise's application to bury Daniel there would qualify for this. They were pleased at the news. They had somewhere to bring Daniel home to, but they still did not have Daniel's remains.

Peter Boyce told Bruce and Denise they were onto a winning streak. 'Being allowed to stay in court was your second,' Peter Boyce smiled over lunch. Bruce had raised an eyebrow. 'The first was the successful request for a coronial inquest,' Boyce continued.

After lunch, the focus of the evidence was on the DNA, and it was explained that mitochondrial testing for DNA was used because of the deterioration of the remains found at the site. In mitochondrial DNA the sequences were passed down from the maternal line. Although it could not be used to identify an individual, it could be 'used as an exclusion or inclusion tool'.

They were back in court at 9 am the next day. The defence team approached Cowan. A smile was never far from his face, but it had the sincerity of a typecast second-rate crook from a television cop show. Cowan looked like he lived the cliché. His stance immediately exuded an 'eager to please' demeanour. Cowan was not handcuffed, and he would often rub his hands together if he wasn't holding them clasped. His head would strain forward, always obsequious. Bruce noted that he was wearing the same clothes as the previous day and that he appeared more confident.

The first witness on day two of the committal hearing gave evidence via the video link from New Zealand. Catherine McGovern, from the Institute of Environmental Science and Research, confirmed that the DNA she had examined from one of the bones was from Daniel. It had been compared with DNA extracted from Daniel's toothbrush, and it was 540 times more likely to be Daniel Morcombe than anyone else in the Queensland population, she said.

Sergeant Donna Lee McGregor, a university lecturer in human anatomy on leave from the Queensland Police Service, told the court that among the bones had been rib fragments and recovered vertebrae. Working with a model of a skeleton the size of a child, she explained exactly which bones had been found at the site. As they were going through the details of the tibia bone, Denise got up and left the courtroom, clearly distressed. Both she and Bruce had been plagued with the thought that Cowan had put Daniel's body through the mulcher that he had picked up the day Daniel disappeared. It still haunted them, as one of those stories told to them by their imaginations that they had never been able to confirm or refute. They had watched Cowan, who was looking at the monitor beneath him, and Denise had thought he seemed fascinated with what was being displayed.

For Bruce, staying to hear all of the evidence was vital. As the evidence continued that day, he felt a huge sense of relief, especially as it was clear that the mulcher had been forensically tested for blood but that none had been found.

The next witness was Senior Constable Martin Heath, the police officer who had examined Cowan's white Pajero after it was recovered from Russell Island. He said that he knew police had examined it some years previously. This time, he had inspected the seatbelts and passenger grab handles, and had done a swab for DNA. The car had also been vacuumed, and nothing of 'evidentiary value' was found. Yes, they were eight years too late, Bruce thought to himself as he listened to the evidence. Then another thought occurred to him. As a towtruck driver, Cowan would have had easy access to carpets or seats, which he could have easily replaced in the Pajero.

Another witness, Michael Kelly, a wildlife expert, gave expert opinion as to why some of the bones had been scattered and why they were found where they were. Detective Ross Hutton had warned Bruce and Denise to expect such descriptions, which he knew would be distressing. Bruce listened to Kelly describe how animals would typically tear apart and consume a carcass. 'The bones that were found are consistent with the scattering of animal scavenging,' he said. 'They will detach it and take a piece away.' He said this would occur particularly when there was competition for a food source.

Bruce was glad Denise was not in court.

Addressing the swift gathering of the media at the end of day two of the committal, Bruce said, 'Let's not forget where we are and why we're here. All these years ago, Daniel was abducted. He was murdered. And that's the reason we're going through the legal process. Someone has done this and we need to find who it is and obviously they need to pay a price for it.'

Denise watched Cowan continually. It was his ghoulish behaviour that she despised and which upset her the most – his detachment from the proceedings, as though he were not the focus of the case and just an observer.

There was more evidence given about the DNA by Dabna Hartman, from the Victorian Institute of Forensic Medicine, who explained that the sample from the left femur found at the site matched both Bradley and Denise's DNA using mitochondrial DNA testing.

Professor Peter Ellis, regional senior forensic pathologist with the Queensland Health Forensic and Scientific Services, told the court that he had visited the site on four separate occasions. He had prepared a preliminary report, an autopsy report, and a statutory declaration and statement. On his first visit, there had been no bones recovered. On following visits, he had seen a bone partially exposed and still in the ground. On another occasion, he had seen bones inside a tent before they were dispatched to the mortuary. He told the court that his autopsy revealed that the bones appeared 'to have come from one person' and that their sizes were consistent with Daniel's age at the time of his disappearance. Taking into consideration the results of the DNA sampling, he had reported that the remains were Daniel Morcombe's. However, they could only tell him a 'limited amount of information' as to the cause of death.

The day finished before lunchtime with no time for any other witnesses to be called. The consistent confirmation that the DNA tests had proven the remains were Daniel's was a great relief for both Bruce and Denise.

That evening, the Morcombes received an email from Kristen Shorten from *The Courier-Mail*. Based on leaked documents, she had written a story to be published in two days time about the departmental tug of war going on about who held responsibility for Daniel's remains. She had reported that the Morcombes were 'absolutely gutted' by the stance being taken by the Queensland Police Service, who were treating their son's remains as 'a thing' in a crime scene.

* * *

As they walked up the familiar hill to the court on day four of the committal hearing, it was with a sense of trepidation. Back in court, nothing seemed to have changed. There was more DNA evidence, then a geophysicist, Michael Erpf, who explained how the distinctly layered soil at the site was made up of clay or sand. He said a computer model of the area had been developed for the Caloundra South Development Plan, which meant they had been able to look at flood velocities, depths and the volume of water that flowed historically through the site, as well as looking at the amount of sediment that might have occurred.

Shortly after the court reconvened at 11 am, Michael Bosscher abruptly got to his feet. 'Your Honour, if I might have a moment. Our client has signed a consent order saying he has no interest in further testing, your Honour, so will not require the remains to be held any longer, thank you.'

The DPP and Queensland Police Service appeared to have been taken by surprise. Crown Prosecutor Glen Cash asked for a short adjournment to inform investigating officers of the defence's decision. 'I just want to be immediately able to convey that to them,' he said. 'I'd say there would be a desire to move rather rapidly ... allow them to put things in place.'

Butler nodded and the next witness was called. Bruce and Denise inwardly gasped. They were, as Peter Boyce predicted, on a winning streak. This was win number three.

Denise Lincoln was the first public witness of the day. She said she had been at a service station at Yabulu on 3 January 2005 when she had seen a boy who looked like Daniel who was with an older man. She claimed that the man had forced the boy into the toilets after she addressed him as Daniel. A number of other witnesses gave evidence of having seen Daniel on various dates after 7 December 2003, including a man who said he had seen him the following day at a block of units in Toowong and that a neighbour of his had joked that Daniel's body had been in his car.

During the lunchbreak outside the court, with a bevy of journalists eager for a new lead, Bruce addressed the television cameras. 'Daniel's remains were discovered 467 days ago,' he said. 'He has not been in the family's unit for 3280 days. On anyone's perception, both of those are long numbers. We treat this as no joy, but it is a step in the process to getting Daniel's remains released to the family and, once they are released, obviously we can make plans for a funeral from there.'

Back in court, Arthur Whitworth, a witness who had driven under the overpass the day Daniel went missing, testified that he had been returning from a camping trip with his son and was driving from Nambour to Maroochydore when he saw 'an oldish' blue car parked on the southbound side of the road about six metres from the overpass. A boy with a red shirt had been standing only a metre away from the car. A man, of medium build and height, had been leaning against the front passenger door of the car, and he and the boy were facing each other about a metre apart. The back passenger door of the car was open.

* * *

506

Within two hours of leaving the courtroom that morning, Peter Boyce rang with the news that the Coroner would release the remains as soon as possible, possibly even that afternoon.

As the afternoon wore on and each witness appeared, Cowan would look sharply at the door, appraising their entrance as they came into the court. Keith Lipke, a barber from Nambour, told the court that, while driving past the Kiel Mountain Road overpass on the way to Maroochydore the day Daniel disappeared, he had seen an old blue car. While the car was alongside his vehicle, he had seen a 'tarp' moving on the back seat. He described the car as a 'squarish, older-looking model' and a four-door sedan. 'It went behind our vehicle. I seen the driver turn around – say something to the back seat ... he appeared to be annoyed.' He said they had continued driving and that he had then seen the same car closer to Maroochydore, and there was another person in the passenger side. He had said to his wife, 'That looks like the same car.' The car, he said, took off 'like a rocket' and weaved in and out of traffic, heading towards Maroochydore. Cross-examined by Meehan, Lipke said that, the moment the driver had seen him looking in the car, it had 'triggered a response', and that was when the car had begun weaving in and out of the traffic.

Various other witnesses gave evidence of seeing a blue car and two men under the overpass. One witness described one of the men as unkempt, and one woman said that the sketch in the paper had looked like the man she had seen.

* * *

No one expected what would happen next. At 4 pm, after court had finished for the day, Michael Barnes, the State Coroner, released a media statement saying that Daniel's remains were now available for release to the family. The news was out. *The Courier-Mail*'s unpublished story was now old news. A public airing of the inhumane treatment of the Morcombes was no longer required. Bruce and Denise had been given what should be everyone's right – the opportunity to bury their loved ones – but they both felt curiously flat. Their family motto was to always 'be prepared'. The event that had preoccupied them for so many years was now suddenly a reality.

They had planned a trip to Europe on 12 December, to travel from Amsterdam to Budapest on a luxury river cruise ship, knowing from past experience that they would be utterly exhausted after the court hearing. They could not imagine flying overseas without burying Daniel and leaving him instead in a mortuary. So, back at the hotel, they began making calls about options for a funeral. In between, they fielded interviews following a media frenzy. Bruce told journalists that the move was a 'huge milestone' and the family hoped to lay Daniel to rest in the next seven to ten days. He said the family was having a meeting to work through possible funeral arrangements and what they could achieve in that time frame. 'It's been an amazing couple of hours really. We never started today thinking we'd be in this position at the close of the day.'

Friday of the next week would mark the ninth anniversary since Daniel had gone missing. Unbelievably, fate was, for once, on their side. In a week of steady 'wins', the doors were opening.

* * *

Graeme Hight was at his school's annual graduation dinner that evening when he got the phone call from Denise. Daniel's remains had been released; could she and Bruce meet with him the next day? She was hoping the funeral could be held at St Catherine's Catholic Church at Siena College, the

508

venue that had marked the occasions of the early memorial services, when they had no idea what had happened to Daniel. Would it be possible, Denise wanted to know, to have the funeral the following Friday, the anniversary of when Daniel disappeared?

Hight thought quickly. There would be no kids at school that day, as the last day of school was that Thursday – another win. It was a traditional pupil-free day for the staff. Without even asking the staff, his reply to Denise was immediately, 'Yes.' Hight had always known, somehow, that one day there would be a funeral and that it would be a very special occasion. He had even been thinking, if that day ever came, children from Daniel's school could make a contribution – perhaps singing some songs.

Hight had to brief the staff that the traditional lunch would no longer be happening the following Friday. 'We are going to do this,' he told them as soon as he was able. His news was greeted with joy. He knew he had made the right decision. Word went out. Catholic schools on the coast delivered canapés. Ovens were turned on and multiple plates of homemade food were prepared later in the week. The common catchcry from everyone was 'I want to be a part of this'.

Denise invited Father Jan to attend and he agreed immediately.

* * *

Still in town that evening, Bruce and Denise were joined by Scott and Shelly. That night, Bruce could not sleep, so he got dressed and walked down to the botanical gardens and sat for a couple of hours looking at the Brisbane River. He was remembering as he watched the ebb and flow of the tide that Denise, Dean, Brad and Daniel had gathered there many years ago to watch the fireworks that marked the close of the Riverfire Festival each year. How they had all watched in wonder as the city exploded with thousands of fireworks attached to the multiple bridges linking the CBD and the inner-city suburbs of Southbank and West End. It was a memory from another life.

CHAPTER THIRTY

DANIEL COMES HOME

Friday 30 November marked day five of the committal hearing, but Bruce and Denise's minds were elsewhere. The proceedings had become an anticlimax as they went through the motion of listening to witnesses giving evidence. The DNA had been conceded by the defence. There was no dispute that the bones that had been found were Daniel's.

Denise had selected a photograph of Daniel for the front of the memorial-service program. It was the picture that Daniel had never seen, the school photograph that Graeme Hight had given them the week after Cowan's arrest. Daniel had a look of such innocence that it pierced Denise's heart every time she saw it. His pen in hand, he was doing his schoolwork, oblivious to the danger into which he was about to stumble.

Denise's forte was organising large events. It was her attention to detail that always helped the Foundation's events to run smoothly: that and her ability to delegate. Now, the most important occasion of all had to be arranged in a few days while the court proceedings were still going on. At morning tea and lunch intervals, she fretted about the details, busy on her iPad emailing people and sorting through what music would be played, the invitations, the kind of ceremony, planning for the day she always feared would one day come.

That morning, Bruce had sent an email to Rob Luscombe, in charge of the Woombye Cemetery, to let him know that Daniel's remains would be released that day. The undertakers were scheduled to collect Daniel's remains at 11 am from the Brisbane city mortuary, returning them to the Sunshine Coast. Luscombe replied to the email, agreeing to meet them at the Woombye Cemetery at 3.30 pm to choose a plot.

Witnesses came and went inside the court in a blur. Mid-morning, Bruce and Denise went down to the car park at the basement of the hotel. They waved goodbye to Brad and his girlfriend Anna, who had been attending the court case, and then made their way up to the Sunshine Coast.

The phone rang as they headed north. It was Ross Hutton. He was ringing to say that there was a small portion of Daniel's bones at a laboratory in Adelaide that had been held in case there was a need for further testing. Unfortunately, Hutton said this might not be available for Daniel's burial because of the short notice. He suggested options, including sending the remains to Queensland Health for disposal, but Bruce was firm. 'We don't have a lot of Daniel, but what was found must be kept together. Please have it sent to the funeral director next week for Daniel's burial.' Hutton apologised, saying that the way 'the defence dropped this on us' had meant they hadn't prepared for the sudden change.

The first stop back on the Sunshine Coast was Siena Catholic College, to discuss the service and begin arrangements to manage the large crowd that was anticipated. Police would clearly need to be involved. Inside the empty church, they met with Father Joe Duffy and began making plans for the day. Then they visited Dean Gregson from the funeral directors. As they discussed the kind of coffin they wanted and which colour – they decided on white – they both felt their hearts would break. The finality of the moment had caught up with them.

* * *

The Woombye Cemetery on the Woombye-Palmwoods Road is on the same road that Daniel walked that fateful day. Established in 1889, the cemetery has a dedicated war memorial as 24 soldiers, one airman and one Canadian soldier are buried there. The headstones, which include those of early Palmwoods settlers, run all the way up a grassy hill. As the crow flies, the cemetery is no more than 1500 metres from where Daniel was last seen and only 400 metres from his old family home. Bruce and Denise always travelled past there when they were joining the Nambour Connection Road. Each year, the participants in the Walk for Daniel would walk past. Now, they would finally be able to acknowledge the boy who had captured everyone's hearts and who had now been found.

Shortly after 3 pm that Friday afternoon, Bruce and Denise drove into the avenue of giant camphor laurel trees inside the entrance, trying to comprehend that the following Friday they would be gathered there for Daniel's burial. As soon as they got out of the car, the peacefulness of the place seeped through them – a small, well-kept country cemetery. They had made the right choice.

It was meant to be, they thought, as one after another plans clicked into place. That afternoon, the date for the funeral was set; the plot was chosen; the media was informed. Channel Seven was to film the service and share footage with the other television stations. Kay McGrath and her editor, Marc Wright, were adding a professional touch to a montage of photos. Bruce had chosen 'Bring Him Home' from *Les Misérables* to play as the photos screened. Kay had also sent a few songs as options for the end of the service as people were leaving, and Denise had chosen Elton John's 'Daniel' sung by Tori Amos.

Graeme Hight asked if students Bridget and Genevieve O'Brien could sing the haunting Leonard Cohen song 'Hallelujah', as requested by Denise. Later, the girls recorded a version, which was presented to Bruce and Denise.

When asked about the date of the funeral on one of the television news channels that night, Denise said, 'It's sort of like fate. I don't know. We always hoped we could have it on 7 December.' Since the butterfly had landed on Daniel's Hibiscus the previous August after Cowan had been arrested, she had felt it was a sign that there was a new direction after all these years in their fight to find Daniel.

On *Seven News*, anchorwoman and Foundation patron Kay McGrath urged people to make a donation for the Daniel Morcombe Foundation. 'The Morcombes want people to wear red. They want the day to be a celebration of Daniel's young life,' she said. Bruce was also interviewed, saying, 'We don't want a sad day. We like to think because of his life, the Foundation has grown and with enormous support we have seen the good work that the Foundation does in the community. Daniel's life has made a difference to other kids.' Many of the news outlets ran with the expectation that around a thousand people or more would be attending the funeral.

* * *

On the weekend, the Morcombes continued with funeral-service arrangements, deciding on the prayers they wanted and making a final list of songs and photos. Denise had managed to track down some of Daniel's old friends – Tom Palmer, Scott Balkin, Matt and Josh Hannah – through Facebook. They had all agreed to be pallbearers. Many of her family from Melbourne had replied, saying that they would be attending the funeral. Bruce tried to do ordinary things to keep his mind off how much was happening and how much had to be done. He helped Brad move his barbecue and fridge to his new rental property.

On Sunday, Bruce and Denise had lunch with the mining magnate Clive Palmer and his wife, Anna, at the Palmer Coolum Resort near Coolum Beach, 20 kilometres north of Maroochydore. Palmer had committed to donate $10,000 to the Daniel Morcombe Foundation and wanted to know more about its work. With all of the developments over the past week, they had been debating whether to go, but it proved to be a healthy distraction. The aim was to raise funds for the Foundation, which always gladdened their hearts. For the rest of the day, Bruce penned his eulogy and also helped Dean with some starting points for his. Denise spent hours working on the service.

Brad, like Denise, had chosen not to speak, and he wanted to keep his role to a minimum.

* * *

On Sunday night, the Morcombes drove down to Brisbane knowing this would be the last time they would make this journey until after Christmas when the court reconvened. The two weeks initially set aside for the committal before Christmas would clearly not be needed. As Bruce put it, they were 'flying through the witnesses'. After Christmas, they would finish hearing the evidence. For the second week in court, they were joined by Brad and Bruce's older brother, Perry, along with Perry's wife, Joan.

Cowan entered the court, still dressed in the same pale, grey-green suit. Throughout the proceedings, he would sit in his customary position, hands clasped in front of him, head bowed. Occasionally, he would turn swiftly and eyeball a member of the media. The tactic was quite unexpected. His return stare was clearly meant to make gazers uncomfortable, as he would single a particular person out. After so many years of imagining the person or people responsible for Daniel's death, and having burnt a mannequin that they thought looked uncannily like the man before them, Bruce and Denise stared at him across the courtroom. This was the man accused of killing their son.

The first evidence that morning was from Ralph Dowling, from the Queensland Herbarium, who compared the vegetation at two site locations. He viewed aerial photography of the search site and some shots of the same site that had been taken in the 1990s. He said he did not think the vegetation and ground coverage would have been markedly different in 2003 compared with 2011 but that the trees back then would have been shorter. The 2011 floods would have had little or no effect on the southern section of the site but in the northern area, where Daniel's remains were found, a layer of sandy material would have been deposited on top.

Other witnesses included Terry Theuerkauf, who was on the bus that went past Daniel. His sister, Fiona, had given evidence the previous week. Abby North, who had provided one of the COMFITs to police, followed. She was only 13 years old when she was on the bus that passed Daniel but her sketch had been chosen as one of the original three released to the media. All witnesses were cross-examined, after a preamble from the prosecutor Glen Cash, who asked them their full name and went through cursory details of their statements. Some of them had been called by the defence through the prosecution.

Judith McIntyre was convinced she had been the last person to see Daniel alive. She told the court she had been hypnotised by a psychologist as part of the investigation. She said she first spoke to police on 17 March 2004. She had seen a 'pumpkin-coloured car' parked just in front of the bridge on the exit lane. She saw a man trying to get what she thought was his child into the car but, as she had pulled alongside, she heard him shout at the child to get in and the child had replied, 'You can't make me. I'm not gonna.' The boy, she said, had started to run but the man tried to grab him. She said there was a white van on the other side of the road and a blue car, and she had seen a car similar to a white Pajero with a black funnel north of the overpass, across the road from the motel. She had thought it was broken down or abandoned, as there was no reason to park there.

The following witness, Gregory Roberts, had also seen a white van and blue car on the Nambour side of the overpass.

Throughout the proceedings, Cowan still rarely changed his posture, sitting slouched forward, his hands clasped. Occasionally, he pressed his two forefingers together in a prayer-like position.

Mid-afternoon, Bruce, Denise and Brad drove to Wilston in the northern suburbs of Brisbane, near Lutwyche, as they had been invited into Father Jan's presbytery opposite St Columba's Church to discuss Friday's service. They sat around his long, wooden table in the dining room to plan the religious part of the service. Father Jan explained the ritual of the Requiem Mass that Denise had requested. 'This is the format, this is a structure. And you've got to fill in these spaces with your personal messages.' He agreed with both Bruce and Denise that he did not like the word 'closure'. He could see that Denise was still close to God. They discussed laying a white cloth called 'the pall' on the coffin, then the gifts, and when to take them off again.

As they drove away, Bruce and Denise were overwhelmed by how many people wanted to contribute to make Friday special for them and Daniel.

* * *

Tuesday 4 December culminated in another early finish in court – around 11 am. As Bruce sat listening to the evidence that seemed to have no consistency to it, he became increasingly convinced that Cowan had no defence. Would Cowan plead guilty, he wondered?

Several more witnesses gave evidence of what they had seen happening under the overpass the day Daniel disappeared. One witness, Belinda Russell, described being overtaken by a blue sedan after driving under the overpass travelling towards Maroochydore. She estimated it was between 12.30 and 1 pm. The sedan had cut closely in front of the car she was in, and it was apparent 'there was a lot of action in the back seat'. The car was 'violently jumping' from side to side. She said there was a man in the back seat who seemed to be sitting high up. He was apparently 'sitting on top of something' and his head was 'close to the roof of the car'. She said he was 'actively punching down' into the seat and down into the cabin of the car. She said the movements were 'continual and it was violent and it was fast'. She said she saw 'arms and a light-coloured sneaker come up' in a defensive action as though someone was trying to kick away the person 'punching down'. She described the other person in the car as having 'very short hair' and a thin build. The driver did not seem disturbed and did not turn around. She had looked for her phone in the car and then looked for a pen. She found a pen but it didn't work. She imprinted the number onto a shopping list, but at the end of the day she had thrown the piece of paper away.

As Bruce sat watching, he thought that the continual mention of a 'blue car' would confuse the media. Ross Hutton had warned that the defence would try to 'muddy the waters'. But Bruce was also shocked. There was a lot more detail that was coming out about the police investigation. Photoboards did not appear to have been shown to any witnesses until at least 2009, and then only to a few people and mostly those with Jackway's image, rarely Cowan's. Now, they were asking people to remember what they saw all those years ago. It seemed ridiculous to Bruce. With his knowledge of the inquest behind him, he wondered what might have happened if the key POIs had been included in a thorough review in 2004. He was convinced more than ever that from the beginning the investigation lacked a formal plan and, importantly, a mandatory review system. Cowan had been right under their noses less than two weeks after Daniel went missing, and now they officially knew that Ken King's urge for further action appeared to have been ignored.

* * *

At 11 am on the Tuesday, the Morcombes returned to the Sunshine Coast. They spoke with Tracey McAsey and Brett from the Foundation committee, who were keen to assist with planning for the funeral. Denise was working with the media to ensure the day would not be like 'a circus' but would instead command the respect that Daniel deserved. It was definitely not a Foundation event, they had both decided. It was their son's funeral. While they had been busy in Brisbane, Dean Gregson from the funeral parlour had organised flowers for the coffin and for the family to wear: red roses for family members and pallbearers. Tracey from the Foundation committee stepped up to offer to help with the invitations, the car parking and the ushers. They gave her a list of family and dignitaries. Robin Sherwell was organising the wake at Palmwoods Bowls Club.

As Friday approached, Denise kept a firm hand on the direction of the media stories. There were pre-records for some shows, such as the *A Current Affair* interview with Tracy Grimshaw. When Denise discovered that the *Sunshine Coast Daily* was about to print all of the details for the funeral in Thursday's newspaper, she immediately called Mark

Furler. An apology was quickly forthcoming, and the story did not appear.

By late morning, Kevin and Monique, Denise's brother Damien and his wife, Kerry, and Denise's brother Paul arrived. Bruce and Denise drove to Maroochydore Airport to meet them. They had lunch together. Kevin and Monique were visibly distressed. Tomorrow was the day they had never wanted to face, even though they wanted to lay Daniel to rest.

At 4.30 pm, Bruce and Denise visited the funeral home in Nambour. They took several items with them: the Christmas presents Daniel had never opened, his Grade 9 report card, which arrived after he went missing, and the school photograph he had never seen. They were to be displayed on the coffin the following day. Inside the chapel, during their private time with Daniel, Bruce and Denise sat looking at the white coffin. It was the size for a 13-year-old, just what they had wanted. Bruce felt strangely peaceful in such a unique space and time. It had taken nine years of torture to find their son, and here he was. Both of them began to cry. Then they stared at the coffin again, sometimes touching the attached decorative cross on the buffed white surface. They both felt much better for the visit, the calmness continuing through to the evening.

* * *

The skies were grey on 7 December 2012, the morning of the funeral. Bruce and Denise had woken early and were biding their time to drive down to Siena Catholic College. It was raining that morning, a fine drizzle. Denise was not surprised. It always rained when something important was happening for Daniel. Clouds covered the Glass House Mountains.

From 7.30 am, there was a growing buzz of activity at St Catherine's, as preparations were made for the more than

1500 people expected to mark the important occasion. The school had arranged the printing of the mass book, liaised with police, organised the guard of honour and taken care of the seating, as well as making sure the choir knew the order of the service. There was room for 400 people inside the church and around 1000 outside.

That morning, SES workers, police and the community were already turning up. Red ribbons were tied to the pillars at the entrance to the school. One mourner, who arrived early, had driven up from the Gold Coast. She said she had a nephew who looked like Daniel and she did the walks every year. 'I decided to take the day off work and here I am.'

Outside the church, a large screen was erected, with rows of white plastic chairs in front of it under pavilion tents.

Police Commissioner Ian Stewart told the media that the day had been a long time coming. 'It's wonderful to see so many people arriving here to provide support to the Morcombe family while they go through a very significant part of the grieving process. I know that all Queenslanders join with me in grieving with the Morcombe family.'

Students from Siena Catholic College also spoke to the media. One boy said Daniel 'has been a big part of Siena and, as a community, we've come to support this event'.

Father Joe Duffy said the Morcombes were looking for an opportunity to grieve but they were also keen to keep the focus on the fight for justice. Graeme Hight told the media he knew of former classmates of Daniel's who were coming back for the funeral.

As the morning moved on, the lines of white chairs were filled with rows and rows of grey uniforms and white panama hats from Siena Catholic College. The SES workers were a flank of orange and navy-blue hats. A roar from motorbikes filled the air as leather-clad bikers parked their bikes among the cars. Everyone was there for Daniel.

* * *

Finally, at about 10.40 am, the Morcombes left their home in Palmwoods and got into their maroon ute, driving past the cemetery where they would be returning later that morning. Denise had chosen to wear a necklace bearing a stone given to her by some SES volunteers, who had picked it up from the creek near where Daniel was found. When they arrived at the church, the Foundation committee members were ushering guests to their seats. As Denise walked down to the front row, her eyes were immediately drawn to the white coffin covered with red roses in the middle of the room. It felt surreal.

The priests sat on the elevated altar. Bruce was beside her. Dean and Bradley were there with their respective girlfriends. Denise sat next to Dean, and Bradley sat on the other side of Bruce. Nearly everyone they knew and who had been connected to Daniel or the case in any way was in attendance, along with prominent figures such as former Prime Minister Kevin Rudd and Queensland Senator Clair Moore. As she watched the coffin, Denise was glad that she had visited the funeral home the previous day to have some private time with Daniel. As the music started – the music they had chosen – she felt an unbearable sadness. The entire morning felt like a dream from which she could not wake up.

Addressing the packed church, Bruce said, 'What is truly ironic about all the recognition, support, help and publicity his search has attracted is that he was such a quiet kid. He was not an attention seeker, but because of his sparkling eyes and beaming smile he is someone that everybody took into their hearts.'

Looking calm and unruffled, taking charge as always, Bruce then set the tone for the morning: 'Please do not be sad. Appreciate [that] the evil act which took Daniel happened a long time ago. Today's about ... embracing his return to family and being reflective of what might have been. The way forward is to feel blessed that we have known him. He may no longer be with us, but Daniel's legacy lives on. The Daniel Morcombe Foundation is committed to doing all it can to make sure this never happens again by educating children on ways of keeping safe and supporting young victims of crime. Our children and grandchildren are safer because of Daniel.'

Bruce paid tribute to the police service, SES volunteers, media outlets, government and business leaders, Crime Stoppers, the Queensland Homicide Victims' Support Group, Daniel's former schools, parishioners and the broader community 'for never forgetting Daniel'.

While Bruce was reading his eulogy, Dean's girlfriend, Sienna, looped her arm through Denise's.

Dean in his eulogy remembered his younger brother, saying lasagne was his favourite food and adding, 'you don't stand between him and a birthday cake'. He continued, 'Daniel was my riding buddy. We would encourage each other to go that bit harder, higher and faster. He was tough. I remember him taking a fall one afternoon trying to attempt a big jump on his new bike. Over the handlebars he went. Smack into the ground – with the bike just missing him. He refused to show pain. That was what made Daniel so special.'

Those who were Catholics took part in the Requiem Mass. Brad hugged his mother close and kissed her on the cheek, as people lined up for the communion. Father Jan told mourners, 'We thank God for strength and for hope that this journey is finished.'

The two O'Brien sisters began to sing 'Hallelujah', their sweet voices filling the large space inside the church. Then, the montage of photographs played to the *Les Misérables* song 'Bring Him Home'. The innocent shots of Daniel's youth suddenly switched to a series of upsetting images: SES workers searching the bush; a diver surfacing from a dam; milk cartons with Daniel's face on it; posters being stuck on telegraph poles; Siena kids marching over the hill and hugging each other. Then, abruptly, a newspaper with a front-page headline: 'Murder Charge'. There was more footage of the search, then footage of the Daniel Morcombe Foundation trailer and schoolkids raising their hands and shouting 'No!' – the response Bruce and Denise had taught them to stay safe. Then, red balloons were released and a recording of former Police Commissioner Bob Atkinson was played: 'It's the answer. It's a very sad answer, but it's the answer.'

The mass had lasted 90 minutes. Denise and Bruce knew it was nearly time to say a final goodbye to Daniel. The last song Denise had chosen began to play. It was a signal for the pallbearers to pick up the small white coffin and to start walking out of the church. A guard of honour led the procession under the covered walkway to the road. Mourners and school students lined each side of it. The procession was led by a young boy carrying a crucifix. Several paces behind the guard of honour were the pallbearers, carrying Daniel in the white coffin. Scott Balkin and Matt Hannah were at the front, Tom Palmer and Josh Hannah were in the middle, and Dean and Bradley at the end. Slowly, they approached the white hearse. Red ribbons had been tied around its side mirrors.

* * *

The drive to the Woombye Cemetery in the Foundation ute seemed to take forever for Denise, who sat in the passenger seat next to the driver, while Bruce, Brad and Anna sat in the backseat. Dean and Sienna had gone in their own car. This time, they were not driving across Australia to spread Daniel's legacy but travelling only a handful of kilometres to bring him home. Only family and the pallbearers had been invited to the gravesite. Father Jan and Father Joe Duffy arrived. Daniel was taken from the hearse in the white coffin with the gold handles. Slowly and carefully, it was lowered into the grave by Dean, Bradley, Damien and Scott.

Father Jan then said some prayers. Bruce, Denise, Brad and Dean, and the family and the pallbearers, each removed the red rose from their lapel and placed it onto the coffin.

After the church service, the 1500-plus mourners congregated to complete a truly remarkable day inside the Casuarina Hall. Bruce, Denise and the rest of the family and close friends left the cemetery to meet up with other invited guests just two kilometres down the road at the Palmwoods Bowls Club for a quiet drink. Everyone was talking about the service and how very special it was. Dean, Bradley, Denise and Bruce were emotionally spent, but they rode the wave of support from the seemingly endless number of people who had pulled together to make it so memorable, and all in honour of a young boy called Daniel.

On 12 December, only five days after they had buried Daniel, Bruce and Denise left Brisbane Airport bound for Amsterdam. They were to stay there for five nights before boarding the Scenic Tours river cruiseship *Scenic Crystal*, for the two-week trip down the Rhine and the Danube to Budapest. Glen Moroney, the owner of Scenic Tours, had personally offered the trip as a gift, having known Bruce's brother, Perry, as an independent travel agent. They would then fly from Budapest to London and on to Cornwall for a week before heading home.

On the plane, they looked at each other, feeling similar emotions. 'It's over,' Bruce thought. Denise felt they had finally done what they had set out to do: bring Daniel home.

PART SIX

The Trial

CHAPTER THIRTY-ONE

PRE-TRIAL HEARING

Leaving as the sun rose on 4 February 2013 Bruce and Denise drove past Daniel's resting place at Woombye Cemetery. 'We will see justice done for you, Daniel,' Bruce said, nodding to the hillside of headstones. Daniel was now back home but the fight for justice was not yet over.

After crossing the Kiel Mountain Road overpass, they were driving past that other significant location: the memorial to Daniel. It was not a place they liked to visit but it was where the community could come and pay their respects. On the way down the Bruce Highway, they passed yet another signpost that marked their long, hard journey: 'Coochin Creek', an unremarkable, small sign missed by most passing motorists. The bridge they had driven over all those years ago on their way back from the work Christmas party when they were a happy family with three boys building an energetic future. How could they have known that only 400 metres as the crow flies their son had been so close and in mortal danger? This coming December would mark the tenth anniversary of Daniel's disappearance.

The usual media contingent, if fewer in numbers, awaited their arrival outside the Brisbane Magistrates' Court as the committal hearing against Cowan was set to resume.

The first witness in Court 20 was Sandy Drummond. Drummond said she still had no clear recollection of what she was doing on 7 December 2003 but confirmed she was friendly with Brett Cowan and that he would buy marijuana from her. She had told the police her grandson's birthday was on 8 December and that she had gone to a birthday party for him at McDonald's that year but couldn't remember which weekend in December they had the party. Usually on Sundays, she said, she went to the Beerwah RSL, where her daughter worked and held the raffles.

She said she had told the police about that when they first spoke to her.

After Drummond's evidence, Brendan Butler asked everyone to leave. The public gallery was closed so he could hear evidence from six of the undercover police officers involved in Cowan's arrest. The ruling to close the court had a non-publication order, so no media could report on proceedings.

Later that day, Bruce received a call from Ross Hutton: 'They've only got Mike Condon to go, so you probably should go down in the morning.'

The following day, the Morcombes waited with the media outside court for Condon to finish his evidence. Hutton, Glen Cash and the senior public prosecutor, Michael Byrne QC, then met up with them inside one of the glass interview booths immediately outside the courtroom to go through the evidence that would be upcoming once open court resumed.

'Look, it's likely they'll be going through Cowan's confession,' Byrne said quietly. 'This means they will be going into how Daniel was killed, how he went in Cowan's car with him, how Cowan dumped his body and ...'

'What else?' asked Bruce.

'How he crushed Daniel's bones with a shovel.'

Denise said nothing. Her face crumpled.

Outside in the court vestibule, Lyn from Queensland Homicide Victims' Support Group sat with Denise. Both Bruce and Denise were shocked. They looked at the closed door of the courtroom. Soon, they would have to go in there and hear what Byrne had forewarned. But they got up as they always did, prepared to do battle. This would be the first time it had ever been outlined how Cowan had been caught and what he had told police.

Cowan looked more gaunt than usual. He was dishevelled, almost as though he had just got out of bed. His hair had grown since December and he had smoothed it back behind his ears. He fell to his habitual way of watching the door as people arrived late into the courtroom. The first witness in the reconvened court, now open to the public, was Detective Steve Blanchfield from the Homicide Investigation Unit, one of the principal investigating officers and one of the men who had arrested Cowan. Blanchfield confirmed he had been responsible for 11 staff at the MIR. On 9 August 2011, he confirmed he had had a conversation with an undercover police officer and had watched a recording that they had made.

None of the media had been given details of the covert operation. Glen Cash went through the evidence with Blanchfield asking whether this was his understanding of events. Bruce looked at Cowan and was sure he was smirking. He had seen him with the same expression the day before. The cocky bastard, Bruce thought, grinding his teeth.

Cowan, Blanchfield said, had gone to Kings Road, Beerwah, on the Sunshine Coast on 13 August 2011 with two undercover police officers. A transcript had been prepared of the conversation he had with the police. Blanchfield then relayed that conversation to the court, the media frantically typing into their iPads and notebooks. After so long with no answer as to Daniel's fate, this police officer's words dramatically changed the landscape.

Tim Meehan was on his feet questioning Blanchfield. For Bruce and Denise, their prior warning had helped, but the idea that Cowan had used a shovel to smash their son's bones was haunting. What made it worse was that Bruce and Denise could well imagine Daniel saying, 'Oh no.' The small phrase reverberated over and over, and they knew it would haunt them forever.

Asked about how police came to question Drummond, Blanchfield explained that she had been provided as an alibi by Cowan during the Family Court hearing in September 2006, after he sought to have access to his children. Bruce was staring directly at Cowan. Unusually, he found the accused man's eyes met his. Bruce stared back at him smiling, as though to say, 'You are done.' Cowan looked away without emotion. Bruce felt satisfied, however.

* * *

The following day, Bruce and Denise drove to the Foundation office at the Big Pineapple. Bruce felt particularly flat. He was struggling to get motivated. It was difficult to see past the next day's expected news that Cowan would be committed for trial.

Early on 7 February, the Morcombes, Brad and Anna, a Correctional Services officer and one court watcher were the only people in court apart from Cowan. At exactly 9 am, the media came in as a group. Detective Blanchfield was back in the stand. He confirmed, when questioned by Meehan, that Cowan had changed his name by deed poll to Shaddo N-Unyah Hunter. Meehan questioned Blanchfield about photoboards.

After Blanchfield's cross-examination, Hutton was back in the stand. He went through evidence about the demountable that was in Kings Road near the site where Daniel was found.

When the evidence concluded at 9.31 am, the court was packed. Michael Bosscher got to his feet, agreeing that the prosecution had a 'prima facie case' to commit for trial in all of the charges and that the threshold test had been met. The media began typing furiously.

The Chief Magistrate looked up at the court, his face serious. 'I must determine whether there is sufficient evidence to charge. It's not my role to make findings in fact. That's for the jury. Test is whether the jury "could". I'm not assessing the guilt of the accused – merely that there is sufficient evidence to place him on trial.' As Butler went on, Bruce and Denise's eyes never left his face. 'The defendant had admitted he abducted, assaulted and then disposed of Daniel's body,' Butler said. 'It will be for a jury to determine whether these admissions were made and they were true and reliable. I'm of the opinion that the evidence is sufficient to put the defendant on trial as charged.'

Cowan stood, his hands folded, facing the Chief Magistrate. Butler read out the charges. Cowan blinked a few times but otherwise did not flinch. Butler asked Cowan whether he wanted to say anything. He advised Cowan he was not obliged to answer any plea, nor did he need to say anything. Cowan responded, 'No, sir.'

Butler then committed Cowan to a trial date notified by the DPP and ordered that he be remanded in custody. Bosscher advised the court that there would be no application for bail. By 9.43 am, the hearing was over. The news everyone expected to hear was broadcast to the nation.

* * *

With the committal hearing behind them and little belief the trial would be held that year, Bruce and Denise concentrated on speaking engagements and other Foundation activities. By the end of January, their personal assistant, Alice, had resigned and Robin Sherwell had stepped into the role. They had also sponsored a counsellor to be engaged under Bravehearts Inc, the organisation set up to educate, empower and protect kids from sexual assault. After 16 years, Bravehearts Inc was one of the groups that had successfully managed to lobby the Federal Government into having a Royal Commission into Institutional Responses to Child Sexual Abuse, and Bob Atkinson had been appointed one of the commissioners. The Foundation had already joined Bravehearts Inc in public events promoting a safer world for children, and there had been a clear need for a counsellor, who was to work one day a week at the Foundation's offices at the Big Pineapple and four days a week at Bravehearts Inc's Strathpine office. The counsellor aimed to see 15 children a week across both locations.

Linking arms with like-minded charities to minimise duplication and costs was on the Foundation's agenda. In recognition of the support over the past 12 months, Bravehearts Inc presented Dean, representing the Daniel Morcombe Foundation, with their highest annual 'ThankShoe Award'.

The line-up of a national tour of schools on top of the Queensland schools commitment left them little time for anything throughout February, March and April except packing and unpacking, and preparing for the next public event. There was no time for socialising. Denise began to wonder what they had let themselves in for, committing to so many public events after the exhausting legal proceedings.

One evening in late April, Bruce suspected something was afoot. Brad had dropped in, as he often did, but had begun asking questions.

'How old were you when you married Mum?'

Denise had fossicked through and found the photos of her and Bruce on their special day, when they had been so full of happy expectations for their lives together.

Brad arrived around again a week later. This time, he brought a small box and a dazzling diamond ring, proud to show it to his mum and dad. One of Anna's girlfriends had helped him choose it, he explained. Bruce and Denise were moved by his decision. He had been going out with Anna for four years. Now, he was making an adult commitment to the relationship. Brad had formally asked her father, Michael, for permission.

The next day, Dean and Brad went skydiving. Sienna, Dean's girlfriend, had given Dean a gift voucher for Christmas, and Dean had asked Brad to join him. Bruce and Denise were there to watch the boys land. They were both wearing their Daniel Morcombe Foundation red T-shirts. Anna was there too, with her mum, Marg. Everyone who was gathered there knew about the engagement ring and was convinced Brad would pop the question as soon as he landed on terra firma. They were all watching Anna, who was oblivious to what was going on. But nothing happened. Brad, the quiet one in the family, was keeping things to himself as usual.

The following Sunday, 28 April, Brad took Anna to the Mary Cairncross Scenic Reserve, off Mountain View Road near Maleny in the Sunshine Coast hinterlands. Brad pulled out the ring some way along the path and proposed. They were standing next to the same tree where they had first kissed, he reminded the beaming Anna after she had replied, 'Yes.'

By 29 April, the makeover of the children's waiting room at the Caloundra Child Safety Service Centre, sponsored by the Daniel Morcombe Foundation, was finished. On 2 May, Bruce and Denise attended King George Square in the Brisbane CBD for their now annual appearance at the Queensland Homicide Awareness Day with the Foundation trailer. At their next school engagement, on 7 May, ten local schools turned up at Stanthorpe, a town near the New South Wales border, 223 kilometres from Brisbane. Balloons were released and there were cakes for those who attended.

While Bruce and Denise were driving from Warwick, on the New England Highway, the phone rang in the truck and Denise pressed the speaker. It was the Queensland Governor's Office. Bruce and Denise were being considered to receive an Order of Australia Medal (OAM). Would they like to accept the award and, if so, could they please complete some forms and send them in? It was a complete surprise. Whoever nominated them never came forward.

* * *

Sunday 12 May 2013 was Denise's tenth Mother's Day without Daniel. On each of the previous nine years, Bruce, Dean and Brad had tried their hardest to make the day special. Bruce always cooked lunch and either Dean or Brad, or both, would take Denise for a drive in the morning, and they would have morning tea. When they lived in Camellia Cottage, it was a custom on Mother's Day to prune the hundred rose bushes that lined the driveway. This year, however, marked the first in which Denise was able to go and visit Daniel in the Woombye Cemetery. She had bought a colourful array of flowers the day before, spending some time making her selection.

Bruce and Dean drove Denise to the cemetery, where they stayed for about ten minutes. Even though Daniel's headstone had not yet arrived, Denise felt relief that, for the first time, she could be with Daniel on that special day. They returned home and then Bradley called in and joined them for lunch.

That afternoon, Denise was looking at her photos of the three boys on her iPad. She uploaded one onto the official Foundation Facebook page of Daniel and Bradley when they were only a few months old, asleep on Denise's chest. Denise was also half-asleep, sitting up on the couch. Nearly a million people viewed the photo in the first few hours. Her boy had reached the hearts of so many people. She was touched by the thought, and by the thought of all mothers out there who were celebrating the love of their children.

Even then, the thought of the impending trial was never far away. On 15 May, Peter Boyce challenged the Crown to present an indictment that year. Media reports criticised Attorney General Jarrod Bleijie's assurance that there were enough prosecutors within the Department of Public Prosecutions to deal with the cases that were before it. Boyce asked, 'If the court has availability and the defence are ready, why can't a trial commence?' Boyce said he was following up comments by the Chief Justice of the Supreme Court, who was on the record saying that, if the DPP had more resources, Daniel's case could be heard in 2013.

After Daniel's remains had been found, Bruce and Denise had amended the Foundation's objectives, replacing 'Continue the search for Daniel' with 'Support the families of missing persons, particularly where it involves children'. On 27 May, they went to Canberra to attend the International Missing Children's Day, as part of their increased focus on this issue. On 8 June, on the Queen's Birthday weekend, Brad and Anna celebrated their engagement with barefoot bowls under lights at the Palmwoods Bowls Club. Two days later, Bruce and Denise were recognised in the Official Queen's Birthday Honours list, each receiving an OAM. The medal would not be presented until later in the year.

Back on home turf, briefly, in July, 'Morky' the mascot was launched. The Foundation committee had been talking about a mascot for some time. Bruce had become intrigued by the idea of having a mascot figure made out of latex rubber. A company was commissioned to create it. Morky, so the Foundation newsletter joked, was born 'weighing in at 25 kilos and 2-metres tall' – a giant, red T-shirt with large, white gloves for hands.

Bruce and Denise were happy with the result. The oversized gloves had safety messages written on them. On his back were the Foundation's three key words from the Daniel Morcombe Child Safety Curriculum: 'Recognise, React and Report'. Morky became the centrepiece of many new child-safety projects and also attended some school presentations with Bruce and Denise. That same month, the Morcombes attended the launch of Missing Persons Week in Adelaide, with the AFP.

* * *

The African red granite on Daniel's headstone had been chosen by Denise for its colour. There were three photographs of Daniel on the headstone: one of him standing at the bow of a rowing boat beached on Norfolk Island, from Christmas 1999; the second a school shot and the third a headshot of him in the backyard enjoying life – all on a background of red. Denise posted a photo of the headstone on the official Facebook page. Bruce said that he and Denise selected photographs that 'encapsulate Daniel's enigmatic smile'. 'We wanted to incorporate a photo that sort of captured his eyes and his unique smile that people have held close to their hearts.'

Knowing now that Daniel had a headstone in place, Bruce and Denise embarked on a national road trip around Australia. If they had thought they had a punishing schedule in the previous years, 2013 marked the most challenging yet. The trip started at Queensland Parliament House after receiving a Child Protection Week Award for Day for Daniel. They covered 30 schools across the country, attending many media events, meeting the education ministers in Victoria, Tasmania, South Australia, Western Australia and the Northern Territory. These meetings were to promote the Day for Daniel event nationwide, as well as to discuss the Daniel Morcombe Child Safety Curriculum, now fully launched and available throughout all of the Queensland secondary schools. Bruce and Denise would meet with the New South Wales education minister in early 2014.

On 17 September, they flew back to Brisbane to collect their OAMs at the Queensland Governor's residence. The award was presented by Governor Penelope Wensley. It was a prestigious affair and a great honour. Dean and Sienna, Brad and Anna, Kevin and Monique, and Perry and Joan all joined them as guests at the OAM ceremony.

After 55 days on the road, Bruce and Denise returned home finally on Sunday 20 October, dropping into the Brisbane Botanical Gardens to help launch Children's Week. They were absolutely exhausted and looking forward to sleeping in their own beds and cooking their own dinners, after too many meals from room service and takeaway outlets. But they fully agreed it had all been worth it.

Only four days after they returned from their national trip it was the 'Day for Daniel'. The Walk for Daniel on the Sunshine Coast that year had 1100 walkers. Premier Campbell Newman and his wife Lisa turned up, as did Mal Brough, the MP representing the Prime Minister, Attorney General Jarrod Bleijie, and Counsellor Jenny McKay who was instrumental in the first Walk for Daniel, as well as the Foundation patron Kay McGrath.

Straight after attending the Walk on the Sunshine Coast, Bruce and Denise had to race home and change from their red T-shirts and casual attire into business clothes to attend another launch. The University of the Sunshine Coast in Sippy Downs, next door to Siena Catholic College, was launching 'Orbit' after a four-year partnership between the university, the Queensland Police Service, Telstra and the Daniel Morcombe Foundation. Orbit is a free interactive game on the web designed for children aged eight to ten. Harking back to Bruce and Denise's fond memories of Daniel and Brad in Grade 1, it is set in a spaceship. The game teaches children about body ownership and the importance of developing a trusted network of adults.

* * *

One date on the annual calendar that Bruce and Denise were determined not to miss was Wednesday 6 November, the first day of the pre-trial hearing when evidence was being presented. Justice Atkinson and the legal teams had begun the pre-trial hearing the previous day in order for her to make rulings. 'The reason why we're having directions is because this is a complex criminal trial ... I have an application from the defendant which deals with the exclusion of evidence – certain evidence and, of course, that evidence will have to be aired and discussed and a ruling will have to be made.' She said any publication of rulings on the admissibility of the evidence could be damaging, particularly for the defendant and his ability to get a fair trial. The date clashed with a meeting arranged with the federal education minister Christopher Pyne in Canberra. They were in a dilemma: to go to the pre-trial hearing or to go to Canberra? Bruce wanted to go to court. He had promised Daniel all those years ago on 9 December 2003 at the chapel with Father Jan that he would see justice done. Denise, too, was going to cancel the visit to Canberra, but in the end she decided she would represent the Daniel Morcombe Foundation and she arranged for Robin Sherwell to go with her.

Arriving at the Queen Elizabeth II Law Court building, next door to the Brisbane Magistrates' Court, where the committal had been held, Bruce noted the security staff seemed even more alert than usual. Later, he learnt that there were court proceedings underway involving bikies.

On the fifth floor, he found Court 11, the same courtroom that was earmarked for the trial. Ross Hutton and Steve Blanchfield showed them the family quiet room provided by

Justice Roslyn Atkinson, the judge who was to preside over the trial. Michael Byrne QC, the Crown prosecutor, came to tell them that a video would be shown to the court. It was Cowan's confession to the undercover police officer in Western Australia. He was letting them know so they could decide whether or not to watch it. Bruce decided almost right away that he would. Everyone else agreed. Bruce, Dean, Bradley and Anna walked into court. At 9.50 am, they took their reserved seats, on the back row on the right, facing the judge. Joan, Bruce's sister-in-law, joined them soon after 10 am.

Justice Atkinson was once a hearing commissioner for the Human Rights and Equal Opportunities Commission and had been a Supreme Court judge since 1998. Bruce soon learnt she was a woman of swift decisions who, in his opinion, seemed fair and precise. Within 30 minutes, a non-publication order was issued until after the trial was over. Keeping the court hearing open to the public while restricting publication, however, adhered to the principles of open justice, she said.

Various witnesses appeared during the morning, starting with Detective Senior Sergeant John Hutchinson, the head of the Undercover Unit from Western Australia Police, at 11 am. Sergeant Hutchinson asked if officers within his unit could be referred to by numbers rather than names, so their identities would be concealed. Justice Atkinson expressed concern that anyone lying in court or committing contempt of court could avoid this charge if they had not given the oath using their names. She told Hutchinson to write the names and corresponding numbers on paper and place them in a sealed envelope to be handed to her associate.

As Assistant Commissioner Mike Condon entered the courtroom at 12.26 pm to give evidence, the huge sunshade blinds behind the judge closed. That was nothing to do with Mr Condon, Justice Atkinson quipped; the blinds were automatic. Condon told the court that initially there was to be an undercover operation on Cowan for two weeks. Condon was asked about several POIs, including Dooley, Meyer and Smythe. He also gave evidence about the POIs Jackway and Cowan. Condon said he had ordered a cold-case review of Cowan in December 2010. He said that he had learned of an undercover technique which had been initially developed in Canada, and that Cowan was someone they could 'test' the technique on. This was the first time Bruce had heard of this. Later, under cross-examination by Edwards, Condon said he estimated that the undercover operation would have cost less than $100,000. He said it had taken four and a half months and included 36 police officers, including those undercover. He said there were 25 different scenarios to engage Cowan to join the so-called 'crime syndicate', which was made up of undercover police. The scenarios had involved prostitutes, gun-running, drugs, false passports, diamonds, stolen cigarettes and a corrupt cop.

Condon confirmed the initial stages of the operation when Cowan had been cultivated. He said it was important that the police involved in the covert operation worked within the Police Powers and Responsibility Act in Queensland. Condon also said he was informed after Cowan gave evidence at the inquest that the counsel assisting the Coroner wanted to recall Cowan. He said several scenarios were played out, all to convince him of the legitimacy of the 'crime syndicate' that included being introduced to a crime boss who could pay to have anything 'fixed'. Cowan had provided a video confession on 9 August 2011, and an arrest had been made on 13 August 2011. Condon was asked questions about why Cowan's alibis weren't checked more thoroughly and about Ken King's evidence. He was re-examined by Byrne about Jackway. Condon still maintained that the timeline of Jackway's movements made him an unlikely accused and that police had exhausted the enquiries. At 3.30 pm, Condon was stood down.

Detective Howard Hickey then gave evidence. Hickey confirmed that there did not appear to be any record in the transcript of Cowan's 2006 interview with police that Cowan had been cautioned. Hickey was followed by Covert Officer 508 from the Western Australia Police. Officer 508 went through several of the gun and drug scenarios which had been planned for Cowan. He confirmed the guns used in the various scenarios were real and that Cowan had wiped fingerprints from guns.

By 4.45 pm, the evidence was finished. Bruce was gobsmacked by the whole concept of the operation and the stories they had heard about how the police had caught Cowan. That night when Denise arrived back from Canberra with Robin Sherwell she was excited that Pyne had asked the Daniel Morcombe Foundation to supply him with information he could send to all federal members of parliament to educate them on the merits of the Daniel Morcombe Child Safety Curriculum and Day for Daniel. Daniel's story could go national and help keep kids safe country-wide.

She couldn't believe her ears when Bruce told her of the covert operation. It was an incredible operation to attempt, and Bruce was astounded by the level of detail and effort. They were eager to find out more as the trial unfolded, and to shake hands with the covert police officers and thank them once the trial was over.

The Morcombes started early the following morning, ready for the second day of evidence at the pre-trial hearing. Dean and Brad joined their parents. In court, Detective Sergeant Grant Linwood, who had been attached to the Homicide Investigation Unit, gave evidence. He had been engaged to work with Detective Senior Constable Emma Mcindoe on the review of Cowan. The prime motivation for the change of heart for police, he said, was that Cowan's alibi had been 'unconvincing'.

Again, Bruce could not help wondering why it had taken police eight years to work this out.

Ken King, the former Queensland Police Service senior constable, took the stand at 12.10 pm. He confirmed he had left the police service in 2008 and that he had been the first to interview Cowan. He said he had recorded the meeting but had been told that the recording had been lost. He said it was his belief that Cowan was a strong suspect and he had written this on his job log. He had also made a separate report with these concerns clearly noted, as well as personally addressing the MIR group. After driving the route Cowan had taken, King had also been concerned about Cowan's alibi, because of the time where his whereabouts were unknown. Detective Dennis Martyn, now serving with the Homicide Investigation Unit, told the court that he had also noted a 45-minute hole in the timeline.

Detective Sergeant Mark Wright told the court he had also spoken to Cowan, on 23 December 2003, and he and Detective Senior Sergeant Tracey Barnes had interviewed him again in 2005. Wright had also been present at the 2006 interview with Cowan after the information about Sandy Drummond surfaced from Cowan's Family Court proceedings. Justice Atkinson asked later why Cowan had not received a legal warning before the 2006 interview. Wright replied that the interview had just been to firm up Cowan's movements.

Justice Atkinson pointed out that nevertheless opportunities had been presented to Cowan to make admissions during that interview and that Wright had agreed inducements had been made to Cowan.

'Why didn't you think of giving him a warning then?' she asked.

'Well, he … he wasn't … he wasn't in the frame as far as I was concerned, as … for the disappearance of Daniel Morcombe. We'd had many other people similar to him that we were looking at.'

The decision not to warn Cowan about his legal rights meant that the 2006 interview was not able to be played to jurors in the trial.

After lunch, Officer 452 got into the witness box and told the court that 'Paul Fitzsimmons' or 'Fitzy' were his covert names. He said he had first met Cowan on 4 May at a shopping centre in the eastern suburbs of Perth with the undercover Queensland Police officer, 'Joe Emery', who had started cultivating Cowan on the plane. They had met with Cowan again on 16 May 2011. All meetings had been recorded.

'Arnold' was then called to give evidence. As his evidence was led, it was difficult for the Morcombes to see any video played in the courtroom because of the position of the screen. As they had been forewarned that Cowan's video confession would be played, Bruce and Brad decided to move seats to the other side of the court, which was also the public gallery, to get ready to watch Cowan's video confession. The move meant sitting quite close to Cowan. The video of the 9 August meeting at the Hyatt Regency in Perth inside the Swan River Room was played. At first, there were technical difficulties, but when the video started again Cowan suddenly entered the frame.

He began talking of his past offences, how he abducted Daniel and what he did with his body. Bruce, Denise and the two boys were disgusted by what they had heard. Cowan, as usual, sat again in the dock like a statue. Little was said as the court began to empty and proceedings finished for the day.

Driving back home, Bruce could not help himself. Turning to the rest of the family, he said, 'Cowan should get 25 years for murdering Daniel and another 25 for being so stupid to tell someone he had known for less than ten minutes how he did it. Granted, he was set up for three months first.'

The following day, Friday 8 November, Brad told his parents he did not want to listen to any more evidence and returned to work. Dean, Denise and Bruce drove to court, leaving early. They sat in court listening and watching more of the covert operation. The vision and audio were surprisingly clear they thought. When Cowan described how he had gone back to get rid of the body a week or more later and only found a piece of bone, Bruce and Denise steeled themselves for the upcoming details they had been warned about. When Detective Senior Sergeant Blanchfield gave evidence, he confirmed, after looking at the map drawn by Cowan in the Swan River Room, that his drawing resembled Kings Road.

* * *

The following Monday, 11 November, Bruce and Denise left for court early. They felt the boys' absence. Dean had also returned to work. Brad would usually be sitting in the back seat of the ute reading *The Courier-Mail*. Dean would predictably have his headphones on, listening to his heavy-metal music.

The entrance to the court was noticeably quiet without the media contingent because of the media ban court order, but it had the benefit of them being able to come and go without the usual attention. Denise noticed straightaway that the prosecutor, Glen Cash, was wearing a red tie.

Peter Johns, who had assisted the Coroner, Michael Barnes, was the first to give evidence. He said he had wanted to recall Cowan straight after his evidence at the inquest following the new material that had come out about his alibis. The fact that Cowan had also admitted in the witness box that he had smoked cannabis that day was also discussed. Justice Atkinson asked whether Cowan had been tested for drugs, and Johns said he had not been. Johns also said that, on 12 April 2011, he had received a letter from Peter Boyce saying that the Morcombes also wanted Cowan recalled. Johns said he had not been told about the undercover operation but that he had thought it might be going on. On 3 June 2011, he said, there had been a meeting between Michael Barnes and Michael Condon at Roma Street. Johns had been asked to wait outside. Barnes had then been asked to delay a summons against Cowan because of the police investigation. Johns said he had been working closely with Detective Grant Linwood. Edwards requested that Daniel Grice, the coordinator of the State Coroner investigation team from the Coroner's office should also be called. Grice confirmed that the Coroner had signed the summons on 29 July 2011 for Cowan to return to give evidence on 26 October at the resumption of the inquest.

At 12.35 pm, Brett Peter Cowan took the stand. He was wearing a blue suit jacket, grey pants that seemed too short, dark cream and green shirt, and a green tie. His glasses, to Denise, seemed too big. Justice Atkinson, her right hand under her chin, stared at the man in front of her. Cowan bumbled his way through, giving unconvincing answers to questions, Denise thought. Justice Atkinson called for a lunch adjournment as she was always precise: 1 pm to 2.30 pm each day.

After the court resumed, Cowan said he was using his original name now as he was in the process of changing it back. Questioned for some time by Michael Byrne QC, he conceded finally, when aspects of his evidence were shown to him, that he was 'an accomplished liar'. 'You're prepared to be in these court proceedings to suit your own means. What do you say to that?' Byrne asked him.

'I'd have to say yes,' Cowan replied.

The next day, 12 November, he was again on the stand, confirming that Arnold, 'Mr Big', had said he would have his previous convictions wiped. Cowan said he had wanted to have the stigma wiped as well, so he could see his children.

By 11 am, Cowan had completed his evidence, but not before Justice Atkinson remarked for the record that she had observed Cowan smiling during proceedings. 'For the benefit of the bar table, I've been able to observe Mr Cowan during proceedings and there did appear to be times when he was smiling. I haven't made any comment about it. I mention it now so that it's on the record.' Justice Atkinson noted this was particularly when the interview with Arnold was being played.

'You are a person, Mr Cowan, I suggest, who tells lies to authority figures to suit your own needs,' Byrne said.

'Not all the time.'

'I suggest the reason you've told deliberate lies here is because you wish to portray yourself in the best light in order for your applications to succeed. Do you agree with that or not?'

'I don't understand ...'

'You deliberately lied to give yourself the best chance in this hearing is what I'm suggesting?'

There was a lengthy pause.

'Yes.'

'For the record,' Byrne said quickly. 'There was a pause of about eight seconds before he answered.'

Denise was also struck at how relaxed Cowan appeared and that he seemed to be 'acting' dumb, yet he clearly knew how to lie. She also thought he had the longest fingers she had ever seen and she, too, had noted his habit of clasping his fingers together with his first two fingers pointing forwards. But all she could think about were those long fingers around his victim's throat. Court was adjourned to attend to procedural matters. No further witnesses of interest were expected.

* * *

On 18 November, Bruce and Denise drove to Brisbane and had a meeting with a film-production company to discuss a revised version of the Foundation's child-safety DVD to be produced the following year. They continued on to the

Gold Coast, where they spoke to two more schools the following day and also met with the employees working on the Light Rail project in Southport to receive a donation for the Foundation. Detective Steve Blanchfield had phoned around lunchtime to inform Bruce that Cowan's father was unexpectedly called and was going on the stand that day. Bruce and Denise rushed back to the court in Brisbane but were too late to see him give his evidence.

On 20 November, they did a film shoot with *A Current Affair* for the Foundation, then finally they visited the last school for the year, Kawana State College, on the Sunshine Coast, to talk to Grade 8 students. This was followed by a trip to Brisbane to thank the staff at the Commission for Children for their fundraising efforts for Day for Daniel.

Five days later, Bruce and Denise flew to their sanctuary in southern Tasmania. Even though they had to make several return trips, including a hasty flight home to celebrate Christmas, they relished this opportunity to get away.

The tenth anniversary of Daniel's disappearance was spent in Tasmania in the peace of the eucalypts and the view from their home overlooking the D'Entrecasteaux Channel. That same day, they received news that former sergeant Laurie Davison had died of cancer.

On 12 December, they received the welcome news that Justice Atkinson had ruled that Cowan's covertly recorded confession was admissible at trial. It was another nail in his coffin, they both felt. The wheels of justice were slowly rolling towards a conclusion.

CHAPTER THIRTY-TWO

THE TRIAL BEGINS

On the Saturday of the Australia Day long weekend in 2014, the Morcombe family held a reunion at the 170-acre cattle-country property just outside of Warwick owned by Bruce's sister, Lindy, and her husband, Andrew Colebrook. There were drinks and a family barbecue. Everyone stayed the night.

After leaving on the Sunday, Bruce and Denise drove to Suttons Beach in Redcliffe, north of Brisbane, for Australia Day celebrations. On Sunday, as Australia Day ambassadors, they delivered a speech at 2 pm. At 3 pm, they were judges at the mud-crab race. It was lots of fun, and the event attracted many people. They spent the Tuesday on Foundation work, followed by a committee meeting in the evening. Dean had joined the executive board. The committee worked on planning numerous events and school visits for the year ahead.

The next day, Dean, Denise and Bruce met with Peter Boyce at his offices in Nambour for legal advice on the upcoming trial. In spite of the distractions, it loomed large. On 30 January, they attended the Maroochydore Police

Station to collect subpoenas for the whole family. Detective Ross Hutton advised that all four of them were expected to give evidence at the trial, which had been set to begin on 10 February.

* * *

Just before Christmas, Bruce and Denise had made the decision to leave their Palmwoods home. Various doors were closing, finally, after so many years. They had laid Daniel to rest, and what they hoped would be the last of the court proceedings was coming to an end. The decision to move on seemed right. They had found a block of land with ocean views that was a 15-minute drive to the Foundation's office. The new home would not have the bittersweet memories of their Palmwoods homes, steeped as they were in the past. No longer would they be driving past so many landmarks that, for the past decade, had contained their life. But their new home was still not too far away from Daniel. At least they could continue to visit him.

Their Palmwoods property sold quickly. In just over a month, they had signed the contract, with settlement on 28 February. Two weeks into the trial, they would be looking for rental accommodation while their new house was being built. The timing wasn't the best. As always, however, Bruce believed that you ran with whatever ball was delivered.

On Wednesday 5 February, they met with Michael Byrne QC at the DPP offices. Byrne was heading the Crown case and was friendly and informative. He had a calmness about him, an old-school worthiness that they found reassuring. He seemed to genuinely care about their role in the upcoming trial and the kinds of challenges it presented. He ran through the court procedure, sensing that their anxiety was building.

'Dean and Brad won't be required to give evidence,' he informed them. 'Just you two.' This pleased everyone.

* * *

The following Friday afternoon, they began packing up the house. By this stage, they had ceased questioning why so many things in their life happened at once. On Monday, the sale of the Palmwoods house had gone through unconditionally. They had signed up on a rental home that same day. On Sunday, they had a family barbecue and then returned to the packing. That evening, they headed to Brisbane. They turned left off George Street, opposite the building that would be the focus of their following weeks, into a small lane called Tank Street, which headed towards the river.

Their apartment this time was on the 22nd floor. The court was one block away – a five-minute walk. But for now it was the nerve-racking start to the new week and once again confronting their son's alleged killer in a trial set down to last six weeks.

* * *

On 10 February 2014, at 10.24 am, a courtroom on the fourth floor of the Queen Elizabeth II Law Court was especially convened for the empanelment of the jury in the case of *R. v. Cowan*. Three charges were read out against Brett Peter Cowan, aka Shaddo N-Unyah Hunter: one count of the murder of Daniel Morcombe; one count of indecent treatment of a child under 16; and one count of interfering with a corpse. Cowan pleaded not guilty to all three counts.

The empanelling of the jury began, with six men and six women eventually being selected. Justice Roslyn Atkinson listened to objections from both the defence and the Crown, as well as any from the jurors themselves as to why they could not undertake jury duty. Three more, who sat through the whole trial, were nominated in reserve in case any of the 12 jurors became sick or had to absent themselves from the trial.

Glen Cash was one of the two trial prosecutors for the DPP. He began outlining a list of witnesses he would call. The judge asked the jury to listen carefully in case they recognised any of the names. Among the lengthy list of witnesses read out – including police officers, eyewitnesses, and Bruce and Denise Morcombe – was Douglas Brian Jackway. He was listed as 'living in Brisbane' without the jail address being given and also listed as having 'no occupation'.

Justice Atkinson reminded the jury that the events surrounding the alleged abduction and murder of Daniel had 'received a great deal of publicity', and that they were not to take into consideration anything they had heard or read about the trial through the news media or social media. They were also not to bring to the court any personal reasons that 'may cause you to wonder whether you can be completely impartial in this case'. It was the first of many warnings she would issue throughout the hearing about their duty to only decide on the facts of the case that were placed before them.

Court 11 on the fifth floor had been selected for the trial. Behind the judge, through a large glass window, loomed inner-city skyscrapers of all shapes and sizes, including a residential block where people continued their everyday lives on their balconies as the fate of those before the courts played out across the street. Occasionally, as the trial progressed, the shadow of an ibis, the archetypal Brisbane bird that frequents its many parks, would flit across the buildings.

On the right side of the bar table, facing the judge, Michael Byrne QC, deputy director of the DPP, and Glen Cash sat next to each other with their legal assistant. On the other side of the bar table, representing Cowan, was Angus Edwards, who had joined the bar in 2009 after working as principal Crown prosecutor at the DPP. Tim Meehan assisted, and Michael Bosscher came and went. Behind Meehan was a female clerk.

Cowan sat in the middle of the dock that held six seats and which was located behind the bar towards the rear of the court facing the judge. A specially designed thick glass screen was immediately behind him, separating him from the first row of the public gallery. He had his back to members of the public. He was so close that those in the front row could almost touch him. At his feet were the customary flat-screen monitors so he could see any displayed evidence. In front of him were several microphones. Two Corrective Services officers were seated on either side of him about two metres away. From where the Morcombes sat in specially reserved seats for them and their family members on the right-hand side of the public gallery facing the judge, they could see Cowan in profile.

The fifteen jurors took the seats they were to occupy for the entire trial, at the opposite side of the court to the witness box and on the right-hand side of the judge. There were two youthful-looking men, several middle-aged women, a large man with a ready grin, an Asian woman and several more elderly men. An overflow court had been provided, given the anticipated interest from the public, as well as a media room, which could only be accessed via a keycode. Both rooms were video linked to the trial room.

Addressing the jury for the first time, Justice Atkinson reminded them that any accused person was 'presumed to be innocent and that it was up to the prosecution to satisfy the jury "beyond reasonable doubt" that the accused person was guilty of any charge. This was common law. Their task was to decide the facts of the case'. Justice Atkinson decided that the Crown's opening address would be adjourned until the following day. The court would start at 10 am each day and have lunch from 1 pm to 2.30 pm. Fridays would be free for legal argument if necessary, she told them, and for planning for the days ahead.

On 11 February, shortly after 10 am on a cloudless day in Brisbane, Michael Byrne QC opened the case for the Crown.

Police, he told the jury, had found 17 bones that belonged to Daniel Morcombe in an area in the Glass House Mountains. Later, he outlined the items of clothing Daniel had been wearing that had been found at the site. He told the jury that Cowan had 'provided a complete confession' to the three charges. He explained that the jury would be shown aerial photographs of the abduction scene so that they would be able to see the various points described by witnesses. He went through witnesses previously listed, explaining the evidence that they would be questioned about. He alerted the jury to the fact that the defence would be attempting to convince the jury that a blue car was involved in the abduction of Daniel to create doubt in their minds. The Crown case was that the crimes against Daniel had 'nothing to do with the blue car'. Although Douglas Jackway was to be called to give evidence, Byrne said that the Crown case was that he also had 'nothing' to do with the case. Byrne outlined the covert investigation, describing it as 'a highly sophisticated, elaborate and effective undercover police operation'. Concluding, Byrne said that the Crown case 'substantially rested on the confessions that Cowan had made, particularly to "Arnold" and "Fitzy", between 9 August and 11 August of 2011'. He advised the jury they had firstly to be satisfied that Cowan's confessions were actually made and that they were truthful.

'Our case is there'll be little doubt as to the first matter because it's recorded ... We will point to a number of features to suggest that the confessions are honest and accurate and hence reliable ... They are supported ... in important ways, most notably by the fact that the clothing and skeletal remains were located ... and they were located where he said they were.' Byrne pointed out that the jury was not obliged to find everything in Cowan's confession to be true. He said if the jury was not satisfied that Cowan had murdered Daniel, it was able to consider that he was guilty of manslaughter. By 12.27 pm, the Crown had finished its opening address.

When Angus Edwards, the curly-haired, bespectacled youthful counsel got to his feet, it was obvious right away that his style would be different. More accustomed to prosecuting criminals than defending them, his was a more informal approach and more prone to the dramatic. He began: 'Who dunnit, ladies and gentlemen? Who committed these horrendous crimes? Who abducted and killed Daniel Morcombe? The prosecution will attempt to prove that it was Brett Cowan, and there is no dispute in this trial that he confessed, no dispute that he took some undercover police, people he didn't know were police officers – took them to about 60 metres away from where some bones were later found and to a creek where some remnants of clothing were found. But does that mean he did it? You see, Brett Cowan was driving a white four-wheel drive that day, but what you will hear from a number of eyewitnesses in this trial is that the car they saw was a blue sedan, and I ask you to pay particular attention to that body of evidence. Police were told again and again about this vehicle and its connection with the Kiel Mountain Road overpass and the abduction of Daniel Morcombe. It was one thread that was repeated so often that it became, as you will hear, a major focus of this investigation, the investigation into who abducted and killed Daniel Morcombe.'

Police, he told the jury, had focused so much on the blue car that a 'blue car room' had been set up with photos of various models of older vehicles. This was to allow those witnesses who had identified a blue car to point to the make of car. He said witnesses had also seen a blue car driving away that day close to the abduction scene with 'violence being done inside the car'. 'Though it is the fact that the Crown case is that there was a blue car under that overpass and they say that it's a completely innocent blue car that had nothing to do with this, no one has come forward and said, "Well, that was my car. I had nothing to do with the disappearance of Daniel Morcombe."'

Edwards told the jury that Douglas Jackway had only got out of jail two weeks before Daniel was abducted after serving a jail sentence for the abduction and rape of another boy some years earlier, and that he had also admitted to breaking down near the abduction site the day after Daniel was abducted. 'You see, at the end of the trial, I would invite you to conclude that Mr Cowan's confession was a false confession, not a true one. Now, you might wonder to yourself why someone would falsely confess to a crime like this? Well, I'm sure it won't surprise you to hear that people have been known to falsely confess to high-profile murders, and this case is no different. Several people have made false confessions. Other areas have been searched off the back of false confessions. So don't think that people can't falsely confess to a crime.

'But it will be a matter for you whether or not you think Brett Cowan had a motive to make a false confession to this crime. And, in that regard, I'd ask that you pay particular attention to his conversations with the undercover police officers, who he thought were part of a criminal gang, a national crime syndicate from which he was about to make $100,000 in a big job coming up. But because he was being subpoenaed to give evidence at an inquest, they told him unless they could make the whole thing go away, he would be dropped like a hot potato. Not only that, but you'll hear about his concerns that he speaks about that because Sandra Drummond could not recall whether he went to her house on the day of Daniel Morcombe's disappearance – that he didn't have an alibi – and again, you will hear the undercover police officers say that they can provide him an alibi. Then you'll hear – despite his repeated denials of involvement – you'll hear that the undercover police, the gang, made it clear that unless they could sort this all out for him that he'd be dropped out of the gang. Of course, that would have meant no $100,000, no alibi. And it's only after that that he confessed. Not only did he confess, but you'll hear the police, the keenness of the police – the undercover police, I should say – to find some corroboration of Mr Cowan's confession. So you'll hear them asking questions about things that might have supported that he was telling the truth when he said he had abducted and killed Daniel Morcombe.'

Edwards said that the defence did not dispute many of the facts of the case, including the alleged abduction site and the fact that the recovered bones and clothes belonged to him. 'You see, while there is not a lot that is in dispute, the key issue in all of this is whether you think Cowan was telling the truth when he confessed or was not telling the truth when he confessed – whether he was making it up. And that, ladies and gentlemen, that will be the central issue in this trial.

'How did he know where the bones and clothes were unless he killed Daniel Morcombe? Have the Crown proved that the only way he could have known where the bones and the clothes were is if he was the killer? Or is there some other explanation that someone else abducted and killed Daniel Morcombe in a blue sedan and that Brett Cowan somehow came to know in the eight years following the abduction those locations?'

By just after 12.45 pm, a little over an hour after he began, Edwards had finished. The formal admissions made by Cowan were tendered. Bruce and Denise were not present, because they were witnesses.

They were called up first. Bruce was very nervous. He went through the movements of the boys the morning Daniel went missing. He identified a photograph the Crown showed him of Daniel wearing his red Billabong T-shirt at the Archerfield Airfield on Father's Day 2003 and agreed that the red T-shirt had never been found. He also identified other photographs of Daniel wearing the shoes while patting a kangaroo, and of the shorts he had on the day he disappeared.

'He wasn't in the habit of speaking to strangers …?' Byrne asked Bruce.

'He wasn't in the habit of initiating conversation. No.'

'… And certainly, if a conversation was initiated … he'd have as little to do with the stranger as he could?'

'I believe so, yes.'

'Certainly he wasn't the sort of boy who would go into a car with a stranger?'

'I don't believe so.'

When Denise was called, she explained how she had grown concerned when Daniel had not come home. She said she went through all of Daniel's clothing and told the court that she had provided the police with many items belonging to him, including a shoebox and toothbrushes. Edwards said he had no questions in cross-examination. It was a great relief for both Bruce and Denise that this step was out of the way.

Inspector Arthur Van Panhuis, who had previously given evidence at the committal, went through the designated crime scenes as he had previously. He described how, on 14 August 2011, he had visited an address in Landsborough, a town in the Glass House Mountains, where the demountable had been taken from Kings Road and totally renovated. His evidence continued until the end of the afternoon, and he was still in the stand the following day.

Van Panhuis said the first discovery of the right shoe was made at 2.25 pm on 17 August, north-west of the smaller body of water and the embankment. The second shoe had been located three days later. Shortly after that, the first bone had been found. All of the discoveries had been plotted on a map and given a letter and number to identify them. He said the searchers had used metal detectors and cadaver dogs, as well as special sieving equipment. They had bought gardening implements especially for the search.

Several DNA experts went through similar evidence as had come up at the committal, establishing through the various tests that the remains belonged to Daniel. Professor Peter Ellis, the forensic pathologist from the Queensland Health Forensic and Scientific Services, told the court that he represented the Coroner and his role had been to look at the cause of death. He said he had done 7500 autopsies and had been involved in excavations of mass graves. He had attended the search site four times. Dr Ellis said that, in a young adolescent male, the bones would still have been growing, so their ends were softer and more prone to degeneration or being attacked by predatory animals. He went through the various bones that were found.

When Edwards got up to cross-examine him, instead of focusing on the bones, he questioned Dr Ellis about strangulation and how long it would take to lose consciousness and cause irreversible brain damage. Denise had left the courtroom at this stage. It was all too distressing. Dr Ellis said that, if the airway was compressed, you could lose consciousness quite quickly, perhaps in 10 to 20 seconds, and cause irreversible brain damage some two or three minutes after that, as it would take around that long for the flow of oxygenated blood to the brain to cease, causing permanent brain damage. Edwards also asked him what would cause a 'cracking' noise in the neck, which Cowan said he had allegedly heard when he strangled Daniel. Dr Ellis said he could only think that it might be the cervical spine breaking, but 'I can't think why it should'. He agreed that it might be a 'possibility'. He said it would have to involve a particular movement 'of the head or neck in relation to the body'.

Rocco Venturiello told the court that he owned the property at Lot 1, 510 Kings Road, Glass House Mountains that had been a sand mine from the early '80s, when his family first bought the property, to the early 2000s. He said his family had also owned the lot that now included the macadamia farm, which they had sold in the mid-'80s. Drew Gowen, the owner of the macadamia farm, said the demountable building had been put there for the farmers but had been later sold and moved to Landsborough. He was asked to identify a photograph of the demountable, which was shown to the court. It looked similar to a caravan but without the wheels and with a verandah attached. It was positioned between an electricity pole, a worker's cottage and the mango tree. Brian Russ from Landsborough later confirmed he had bought the demountable.

The rest of the evidence that day concentrated on a large number of SES workers, who detailed how they had found each of Daniel's bones, identifying them by number.

* * *

On the fifth day of the trial, a podiatrist confirmed that the shoes found at the Glass House Mountains showed similar wear in the treads to other shoes worn by Daniel. A field botanist compared the vegetation across the years that Daniel had been missing, and a zoologist who had worked with dingos and dingo hybrids said he had visited the site in September and that, over the years, he had seen a hundred 'wild dogs' captured in the Maroochydore/Nambour/Caboolture area. He said the dogs sometimes hunted live prey but more often scavenged carcasses using creek ways as corridors to get around. Various other expert witnesses gave evidence relating to Daniel's clothing – the Bonds underpants and blue shorts he had been wearing, and the Globe Occy shoes. It was confirmed that only two pairs in Daniel's shoe size had been sold that summer from stores on the Sunshine Coast. Denise had been amazed that Daniel had kept the box.

Just before lunch, the first of the eyewitnesses began their evidence, beginning with Jessiah Cocks, who had noticed the white four-wheel drive on the northbound side of the Nambour Connection Road parked 50–150 metres from the overpass opposite Caravan World. He said he had also noticed a boy on his haunches on the embankment and had seen at least two buses at the Woombye turn-off, one of which appeared to have broken down.

Several eyewitnesses from the bus gave evidence of seeing only a man and a boy under the overpass. The witnesses included Abby North, now a young woman of 23 with her hair up in a bun, who said what she most remembered about the man she saw under the overpass was his 'gaunt face and prominent eyebrows'.

It seemed from the many eyewitness accounts that none of them had been shown photoboards until June 2009 and much later, in 2011.

Some witnesses spoke of the blue car, such as Keith Lipke. He retold his story of seeing a blue, four-door sedan pull up close to his car somewhere near the Big Pineapple and described seeing something moving in the back seat under a tarpaulin.

Barry Kelsey, grey-haired, bearded and dressed conservatively, was one of the few to say he had seen three, not two, buses stopped at the Woombye turn-off. When he saw the boy, he said he had been 'walking a tightrope on a stick or line on the ground' and, as he drew level with him, he had seen a man with lean build, darkish hair with some growth like a goatee, and a thin face standing under the overpass. The boy seemed to be talking to himself, and it was not until he saw the man that Kelsey later wondered if he had been talking to him. Asked whether he had seen any cars, he said he had seen a dark-coloured older sedan once he had driven past the overpass, where there was a nursery on a service road, which he later marked as Shires Road on the map. The touch-screen technology in the courtroom allowed witnesses to point to the computer screen in front of them and it would light up as a dot on the screens throughout the courtroom making it easier for the jury to identify what was being discussed. Kelsey said that the sketch obtained from Abby North looked similar to the man he had seen. It was Kelsey's sketch, drawn by Sergeant John Garner, that bore the best resemblance to the effigy Bruce and Denise had burnt.

The trial was draining for both Bruce and Denise. But the committal and pre-trial were worse because they'd been hearing the distressing facts for the first time. The trial was moving along at a fast pace.

* * *

On day eight of the trial, 19 February, there was a discussion before the jury entered between the judge and the lawyers about Jackway's impending evidence. Edwards had called Jackway to give evidence in court, but the judge had decided his evidence should be relayed by video, which would be transmitted from the prison where he was still incarcerated, in case he became volatile. Justice Atkinson reminded Edwards that, although the defence's case was to point the finger at Jackway as a potential person who committed the crime, the latter's 'appearance might be difficult for his client' and that he would probably exhibit a great deal of 'hostility' towards Cowan.

The jury was then called. Later that morning, several more motorists appeared to give evidence. At 11.17, after the jury had left for morning tea, Justice Atkinson addressed both the defence and Crown, saying that 'it might be a mystery to the jury' because witnesses were being called but no questions were being asked by the Crown. When the jury returned, she pointed out to them that the Crown had a duty to be fair and therefore some of the witnesses had more relevance to the defence than the prosecution. The defence had, in fact, asked the Crown to call them.

Sunbus driver Ross Edmonds was the first to give evidence after morning tea, stating that he had signalled to

Daniel as he drove past that there was another bus coming. As he left, he gave Denise a small sideways glance, then looked back down at his feet. Katherine Bird, one of the bus passengers, gave evidence immediately afterwards, saying that she had stood up in the middle of the bus to ask the driver to stop to pick up the boy. She relayed that the driver had said she would be thrown off the bus unless she sat down.

Kevin Fitzgerald – a skinny man with a small ponytail and bushy moustache – gave evidence that he had been living at Sandy Drummond's address for some time. He said that Brett Cowan would sometimes drop in to 'score marijuana' and usually bought between $25 and $30 in foil. He could not recall whether he went to the RSL that day or not, or whether Cowan came to the house. In cross-examination by Edwards, he acknowledged he had had a 'few knocks to the head' and that he had smoked cannabis himself for many years.

He confirmed that, if Cowan had shown him a mulcher that day, it would have stuck in his mind as he would often spend five or six weeks fixing a mower.

Belinda Russell followed on from Kevin Fitzgerald and repeated her evidence, saying she had been behind the Sunbus as she approached the overpass and had seen a boy hail the bus and that a blue car had suddenly cut in front of her at the Maroochydore roundabout and there appeared to be a violent altercation in the back seat.

Frank and Hazel Davis confirmed that Cowan had come to pick up the mulcher from their Nambour home on 7 December 2003. Their evidence corresponded with the times they had provided previously.

Thursday 20 February marked the end of the second week of evidence. Sandy Drummond was among the first witnesses to be called. She said her daughter ran the 'Crazy Kerry' raffles. She agreed that she always put her membership card into the pokie machine before playing and she would never have lent it to anyone. She could not specifically recall whether she had gone to the RSL that day but said it had been a common Sunday activity.

When Toni Lutherborrow gave evidence, she burst into tears as she described how she had seen a man in the front of a blue-grey car 'punching into something with his right hand ... hitting down with a fist like a hammer'. She said she had been driving down Eudlo Road and was turning right into Chevallum Road when a white ute had headed towards her, followed by the blue-grey car.

All the while, Cowan barely moved. Occasionally, he leant forward in his customary position.

When Ken King entered the witness box, he displayed all the confidence of a former police officer. His deep, baritone voice rang out through the courtroom. He said that he understood the recording of his interview with Cowan on 21 December 2003 had not been found but that he had made written notes, compiled at the first opportunity after the interview and he referred to the notes, when permitted, as he gave his evidence.

The photo King had taken that day of Cowan flashed on the screens across the courtroom. Cowan's blue eyes looked warily at the camera. His hair was short and his face slightly stubbled. The time showing on the photo was 1.36 pm. Photos were then displayed of Cowan's tattoos on his upper left and right arms. King had noted that Cowan had no tattoos on his legs or elsewhere.

King then described how he and Martin had measured the duration of the drive from Cowan's house on Alf's Pinch Road to the overpass, and then on to Perwillowen Road, where Cowan had got the mulcher, and that it had taken 23 minutes to get to the overpass and a further seven minutes to get to Frank Davis's house. He said that, while at Cowan's property, he had taken photos of his Pajero, including from beneath the vehicle. There was no discussion about King's strong belief that he and Martyn had got their man. Courtrooms were not the place for conjecture.

Cowan's ex-wife, Tracey Lee Moncrieff, had returned to her maiden name. A plump woman with dark, brown hair cut in a semi-bob, she spoke quietly to a packed courtroom, avoiding eye contact with Cowan, who watched impassively from the dock. She described how she had first met him through his uncle and aunt, Keith and Jenny Philbrook, who were pastors at the Christian Outreach Centre, and that she and Cowan had married in September 1999, separated in June 2004 and divorced in 2008.

Byrne asked her to speak up, as her voice was so soft he was concerned the jury would not hear her. He also asked her to slow down.

She confirmed that, when they had first met, Cowan had attended church every Sunday. They had two children: now aged eleven and nine. She said that when they were married Cowan had worked on and off welding windmills for Hitweld Windmills, as well as working for Suncoast Sandblasting for Trevor Davis.

She went through the events of the day Daniel disappeared and how she had attended church with the baby while Cowan had stayed at home. She said he had left 'around one-ish', after lunch. Later that afternoon, she had heard the mulcher outside. She did not see him arrive and had first heard the machinery running at around 2.40 or 3 pm, she thought, but she had not consciously looked at her watch. Cowan had stayed out in the garden.

Asked whether she knew Sandy Drummond or Kevin Fitzgerald, she said Drummond's name was familiar and she thought she was the lady who lived up the road, and she knew Fitzgerald 'just a little'. She said she had visited occasionally with Cowan but mostly 'stayed in the car' as she 'didn't like the place'.

Asked about Cowan's physical appearance and the length of his hair, she said it was 'sometimes short and shaved and then he grew it', and that he went a few months in between haircuts. Sometimes, he would grow it down to his shoulders before he would cut it again. She said he had a goatee but never a full beard, and he had two silver earrings – one hoop and one stud on the left ear – and tattoos on both arms from before they got married: a skull and a gun and marijuana on one arm and a scroll and skull on the other. She assumed his hair would have been short in December 2003 as he did not like having it long when he was sandblasting, but if he was not working he would grow it. Later, she agreed that Cowan had a habit of resting with his foot against the wall like a stork. She also agreed, in cross-examination, that she had not given a formal statement to police until 1 May 2005.

The jury was shown a family photo that she had given police of Cowan swinging their elder son. Asked when the photo was taken, she said it 'could have been October/November', as their son looked about three or four months old. This surmisation was to become a focus of the summing up for both the defence and prosecution. How old was the baby in the photograph where Cowan clearly had short hair? If he had only been a few weeks old and the photo was taken in September, that would have given Cowan three months to grow his hair by December 7 when Daniel disappeared. Another photo of Tracey and Cowan with Peter, taken at Redland Bay on Boxing Day 2003, flashed onto the screens. Cowan had short-cropped hair, was wearing a red, floral, short-sleeve shirt, and looked tanned and relaxed. The court had already seen that Cowan's hair was short when King and Martin turned up almost two weeks after Daniel disappeared but had he cut it after he was told police would be calling on him?

It was these happy, innocuous photos that were flashed across the media that day for a public eager to see the man who had finally been charged with Daniel's murder. Anchored in a family snap, in a bright floral shirt, Cowan managed to look civilised, an unlikely image of a man who would commit such a heinous crime. That image was to change after the trial finished.

The witness following Tracey Moncrieff painted a different picture, describing for the court how Cowan had taken her to the demountable one night while four-wheel driving, the place he later confessed to police he had killed Daniel. She confirmed she was now 24 years old and lived in Ipswich. She told the court she had first met Cowan when she was 18 in 2008 in a share house in Durack, an outer suburb of Brisbane about 15 kilometres from Brisbane's CBD. Cowan had also just become a tenant there and they had started a relationship two months after they moved into the share house. They had lived in a caravan park on Bribie Island and in 2009 she had a son to him born in December 2009. She said they had a red Daihatsu Rocky four-wheel drive and that Cowan had taken her four-wheel driving at night and in the daytime. She had been to Beerwah with him on several occasions and he had driven on a back road through forestry to a macadamia farm with demountable buildings that 'seemed away from everywhere' and was 'secluded'. She said one of these trips was after midnight and they had stopped out the front of one of the demountables. A big tree had been there and it was overgrown and unkempt. She said inside the demountable it looked 'like a really old building that someone had moved there and left and appeared nobody was living in it'. She said it was dusty, with old car parts and shelves and she said they had spent five to ten minutes there, and that it was the same in the other building, but even more broken. There were no steps leading up to the back door. There was a broken toilet and broken headlights from cars and buckets, rusty bolts and dust everywhere. There was a storage shed near where the buildings were which was overgrown with vines and this shed was a much bigger building and was padlocked. They had spent one to two hours there before returning to the caravan park.

Asked whether she had ever returned there, she said that she had, with Detectives Hutton and Macindoe on 19 August 2011, and that the demountables were no longer there and that the grass had been cut with a slasher. She agreed that, in April 2010, Cowan had left and moved to Perth. As she left the witness stand and walked past Cowan in the dock she began crying. A dark-haired woman stood up from the public gallery and put her arm around her.

CHAPTER THIRTY-THREE

EVIDENCE AND LEGAL ARGUMENTS

The third week of the trial began on Monday 24 February, with further eyewitnesses being called. One such was Kaylene Densley, who gave evidence that she had passed under the overpass at around 1.45 pm on the day Daniel disappeared and had noticed a dark, blue, boxy car on the side of the road. A man and a boy, who were both kicking the ground with their heads down, had been standing in front of the car, and there was a man standing at the back. She said the man at the back of the car was heavy set, with grey or white hair and a red nose, and had looked up at her as though he did not want her to see him. A white van had been parked further up the road on the opposite side to where the blue car was, she said.

Detective Sergeant Nicole Tysoe said she had examined Cowan's Pajero on 24 December 2003. She was told to look for any blood, in the days before police routinely collected trace DNA from people touching or brushing up against things. She had not detected any blood in the car. She said the Pajero had grass and dirt on the floor and lots of items inside, including a baby seat and rubbish, a pram, fishing gear, paperwork, golf balls, bags, raincoats and tools. She had found rope in the back. She said she had taken 'tape lifts', which were A4-size sheets of adhesive, from the passenger seat, the driver's seat, the rear bench seat and the cargo area. These had been sent to Queensland Health, who at that time conducted such tests, whereas today the Queensland Police carried them out.

She said they were stored and not examined until 2011 when 'someone else looked at them'. Bruce was rocked by the news they'd never been tested. They suspected a stuff-up and it seemed to be the case.

Gary Gersbach, one of two licensed monitoring operators in Queensland for pokie machines, confirmed that a card in Kevin Fitzgerald's name was removed from one of the pokie machines at the Beerwah RSL at 2.20 pm on 7 December 2003, after 13 plays on the machine. Also, a card in Sandy Drummond's name had been removed at 2.22 pm after recording 70 plays.

On 25 February, the opening discussion centred on Jackway. Justice Atkinson commented, 'This is the trial of Brett Cowan, not the trial of Douglas Jackway, and it's because of the relevance to the fact in issue with regard to Brett Cowan that the questioning will be allowed.' She added, however, that she did not want the trial 'derailed'.

Two lawyers from Legal Aid Queensland, barrister C. L. Morgan and solicitor Mr Heilbronn representing Douglas Jackway, joined the other barristers in a bench behind the main players. Bruce and Denise had moved to the other side of the courtroom, directly behind Cowan, to be able to see Jackway give evidence on the video monitor. Julie Elliott and Robin Sherwell had both attended court as well that day, to support Bruce and Denise. A nervous anticipation hummed through the courtroom. The public gallery had no seats available. There had been much discussion about how

Jackway might be physically restrained if he had appeared in the courtroom, how the videolink might have a time delay and how what he might say could cause the trial to be aborted if he made prejudicial claims against Cowan. When he finally did appear on the video screen, it was something of an anticlimax. Dwarfed by a large prison door with a shiny window behind him reflecting the video screen, he was sitting at a desk and dressed in prison green. Outside the room where he spoke into the microphone for the videolink, muffled sounds of prison officers and other prisoners could be heard.

After eliciting a response to his name, Cash asked him whether he was on the Sunshine Coast on 7 December 2003.

'No, I was not.'

'Did you abduct Daniel Morcombe?' Cash asked him.

'No, I did not.'

'Were you in any way involved in the abduction of Daniel Morcombe?'

'Beg you pardon. I didn't catch that ... you blanked out.'

The screen froze for about four seconds.

After they reconnected and Cash had finished, Edwards got to his feet and began his questions. There was a moment of tension when the screen froze again, leaving Jackway mid-sentence, his face suspended. 'F—ing hell, mate,' Jackway swore.

Justice Atkinson suggested that the technology was seriously undermining the value of his evidence and that Edwards must be able to cross-examine properly. Cowan, meanwhile, remained in his immobile position, seemingly unperturbed by the appearance of someone who would clearly be hostile at being forced to give evidence at his trial and who was being implicated as being responsible for the crimes for which he had been charged. They disconnected the video. Justice Atkinson said that Jackway had to give his evidence 'in such a way that the jury could evaluate it properly'. In the kerfuffle that followed the jury being stood down, she questioned whether Jackway's legal representatives had anything to say.

Morgan said that she and her solicitor were 'not aware of any reason why Mr Jackway couldn't be here in person. There's certainly not an objection on his part, as we understand it, but it's a matter for the Crown'.

'Well, it was more a concern of the court that he might – any outburst that he might engage in would be less able to be controlled,' Justice Atkinson replied.

When Jackway's video connection was reconnected after a short adjournment, it was completely silent in the courtroom. In what seemed to be a trial within a trial, Jackway's previous convictions were canvassed by Angus Edwards, who took a no-nonsense approach, seemingly unruffled by Jackway's volatility. He began with his offences in Gympie on 25 October 1994, and went through all of Jackway's subsequent criminal activity, in disturbing detail.

Edwards continued through Jackway's history. 'I suggest you didn't do the sexual offender's course.'

'No, I didn't do that.'

'… And that's a program specifically designed for people who've committed sexual offences. True?'

'Yes, yes.'

'You were aware of some psychological and psychiatric material which was tendered at your sentence?'

'Yeah, I think so. I can't really recall.'

'As at 30.10.95 you showed no desire to change your behaviour?'

'No, not really.'

Jackway admitted he had assaulted another prisoner and twice destroyed a television set.

Edwards then asked him whether, when he was at Moreton Correctional B Prison, he knew another prisoner called Les McLean.

'Not that I recall.'

'He was taking drugs to go through a sex change. Does that ring a bell?'

'No.'

'He also went by the names of Billy Joe McLean, Bobby Jo McLean, Melissa McNicholl, Jessica de Lorna,' Edwards said. 'Do any of these names ring a bell?'

'No. That's – no, not now anyway.'

'You were released from prison on 7 November 2003?'

'Yep.'

'And it's true that, prior to your release, you had told an inmate you would abduct, rape and kill a child, and bury the child in an area where the child would not be found?'

'No.'

'Upon your release, did you seek counselling or psychological assistance?'

'I seen a psychologist at Goodna Centrelink.'

'Did you go back to consuming lots of alcohol?'

'Not really. I was drinking ...'

'Did you go back to taking drugs?'

'... I was smoking pot at the time, yes, but not heavily. It was occasional.'

'You were drinking heavily?'

'No, I wasn't drinking heavily.'

Edwards took him through aspects of his life after he was released: his relationship with Danielle Richardson and association with Paul Carrington. 'Now, you knew that Carrington had a history for sexual offending, didn't you?'

'No, I ... no, I did not.'

He agreed he had met Carrington at the Woodford Correctional Centre. He then went through how he had befriended Stephen Park, who was in Grade 9 at school. Edwards put to Jackway that he had not revealed the truth to Park about his previous convictions but had told him that his jail time was for armed robbery. Jackway denied this.

After going through the car chase with police and ascertaining that Jackway was driving a blue Commodore at the time, Edwards asked him what his movements were on the day Daniel disappeared. Occasionally, Jackway would arc up and swear at Edwards.

'Now, as at December 2003, would it be a fair description of you to say you were about 180 centimetres tall?'

'I wouldn't have a clue.'

'Right. Fair complexion?'

'What do you mean? I'm white.'

'Tanned?'

'No, I'm not tanned. I'm white … I'm white. I'm not an Aboriginal.'

He denied he had started dyeing his hair after 7 December 2003 and agreed he had a tattoo on his left calf.

'And I suggest you said you stayed at Carrington's house drinking and left about 4.30 or 5?'

'I was drinking at Paul's that afternoon, yes.'

'I suggest you said you got there at 10.30 or 11.'

'No. I never stated that I stayed there all day. So you're calling me a bloody liar?' Jackway peered towards the camera, his face looming large.

'It's not true to say you were at Carrington's place having left your place at 10.30 or 11?'

The questioning continued as Edwards went through Jackway's various accounts of his whereabouts on the day Daniel disappeared.

Asking about the mattress he had taken from Park's mother's house, Edwards said, 'That didn't happen on Tuesday … that's what you're saying?'

'I can't recall what day it was. Are your ears painted on, mate? F— me.'

Throughout his evidence, the Morcombe family focused on Jackway. Their stares never left the video screen.

When Edwards pressed on for more details about his visit to Park's mother, Jackway erupted again. 'Are you going to keep asking me the same question a hundred times?'

'... I suggest you became edgy and aggressive with Scanlan ...'

'I'm out of this. You can do me for contempt of court. I'm refusing to answer your questions. You're calling me a blatant liar ... Like I'm the one sitting on trial.'

'Mr Cowan is on trial,' Justice Atkinson intervened.

'I do understand it. I'm not being called a blatant liar by some stupid lawyer.'

Justice Atkinson announced that she intended breaking for lunch and the court would resume in the afternoon: '... but you must answer questions,' she admonished Jackway. 'Unless you claim privilege.'

'And what happens if I don't?'

'Well, Mr Jackway ...'

'What happens if I refuse to answer questions? What happens if I don't? What are you going to do? You can't do a single thing ...' Jackway spat out, showing his clear disregard for the judiciary and the law.

After lunch, Jackway's interrogation continued, with an occasional hum on the line and the muffled conversations of the guards. Mostly, he looked down at the microphone, avoiding eye contact. Edwards went through more details of what Jackway claimed to have been doing the day Daniel disappeared. He tendered a photo of Jackway's blue Commodore as an exhibit. He also went through Jackway's admissions that his car had broken down opposite the Big Pineapple on the Monday after Daniel disappeared.

Jackway confirmed that he had gone back into custody on 23 January 2004, having been convicted of committing rape some time between 1990 and 1994.

When questioned later, Jackway agreed he knew another prisoner, Trevor Bettiens, and that he had been charged with assaulting him. He denied that he had ever spoken to him about Daniel Morcombe, that he had called Daniel 'Christmas Cake' and that he had been laughing with Bettiens about the Morcombes 'starting something up to help people with their grief'.

'And I suggest you said to Mr Bettiens, "Daniel was in the forest …"'

'I just told you I never spoke to the guy.'

'And I suggest you said to him, "He is no one's Christmas cake no more." Do you accept that …?'

'No. I've never stated that …'

He agreed he had been interviewed by Detectives Emma Macindoe and Steve Blanchfield on 27 May 2009 at the Rockhampton Police Station. Edwards took him through the version he had given the detectives.

Edwards returned to Jackway's conviction for rape. 'Mr Jackway, do you still deny you raped [the victim]?'

'Yes I do, actually.'

'You deny you abducted Daniel Morcombe?'

'Yes. I had nothing to do with the Daniel Morcombe case.'

By 3.50 pm, Jackway's evidence was finished. The Crown had no re-examination. Jackway was excused from further attendance at the trial. Bruce felt Cowan was done. If their only defence was that it had to be Jackway and there was no evidence that put Jackway on the Sunshine Coast on 7 December, then Cowan was done. The drama of the day had passed, the public gallery began to thin out.

* * *

On 26 February, the court began with legal argument and a discussion about the jury's visit to the site where Daniel's remains had been found. Justice Atkinson made it clear she did not want members of the public or the media present, including filming the events from the air.

Detective Constable Ross Hutton gave evidence and confirmed that Jackway had been the first POI in the case and was the subject of a lengthy report and review process. The detective went through various surveillance photographs that had been taken of Jackway in early 2004. Hutton confirmed that he was present at Cowan's arrest and said that, after Cowan had made a call to a woman, a man called Les McLean had called on Cowan's phone.

Then followed several eyewitnesses. They had seen either white vans or a blue car under the overpass.

When Les McLean was called, Edwards requested a five-minute break as he said he had not been able to speak with him. A sickly thin man with gold-rimmed glasses and his greying hair in a ponytail, his clothes seemed to hang off him. He took his oath on the Bible. Cash asked him his name and to confirm where he lived, and then he sat down.

McLean agreed, after questioning by Edwards, that he had a multiple-personality disorder. Cowan's eyebrows arched slightly as McLean gave evidence. A photograph of Jackway was shown to him. McLean agreed he had been asked by the prosecution whether he knew that person, and he said it might have been someone he knew from being in jail in 1996 or 1997 called 'Rat'. He agreed that he had only seen this person one other time, when he had been in the same room with him and the man had taken heroin. He could not remember what year that was. He agreed that he knew Cowan and said Cowan had been with Tracey when he used to visit him, denying Cowan had been with Leticha at that time. He said Cowan had instead been living in Bli Bli with his aunt. He also denied he had gone with Cowan to a sand-mining site, saying he did not know anything about such a site. He also said that he knew nothing about a demountable, nor had he gone with Cowan to one. He said that, when he knew Cowan, he had been making windmills. He agreed that, while Cowan had been living in Western Australia, he had rung him 'a couple of times'.

He said he did remember Cowan coming to him and telling him he had been interviewed about Daniel Morcombe.

'And you told him that you had been told something about the disappearance of Daniel Morcombe, didn't you?'

'No.'

There was some legal argument before Edwards continued with the same line of questioning. 'I suggest to you that you told him that someone else had told you where Daniel Morcombe's bones could be located.'

'Never.'

'And I suggest to you that you told him that it was at this place near this demountable building at the sand-mining site.'

'Never.'

'And I suggest to you that you went into some more detail and told him that it was down the gully near the sand-mining site and described to him where you'd been told the bones were?'

'Never.'

'And you asked him what he was going to do with the information you'd given him?'

'Never.'

McLean said that Cowan had called him the morning he was arrested and that he did not recall trying to ring him several times. He also denied telling Cowan that he shouldn't tell anyone about the information because he was scared of being beaten up.

Straight after McLean's evidence, the first of the undercover police officers appeared in the witness box. 'Joseph Emery' was a Queensland undercover officer and said he had got involved in the operation in March 2011. He went through how he had befriended Cowan over some period of time, beginning on the plane journey back to Perth in April 2011. 'Fitzy' followed Emery, and 'Arnold' came after him. Edwards cross-examined each one, asking about the intention behind what he described as 'the ruse'.

When he got to Arnold, after lengthy evidence from both Joe and Fitzy, he asked him, 'You were the Big Boss?'

'Yes.'

'Cowan ... believed he was trying to get into the organisation ...'

'Yes.'

'And part of the operation was to dangle the carrot of big jobs and big money ... and promises to buy an alibi if necessary.'

'I mentioned that, yes.'

'And the threat that he would be dropped like a hot potato if it couldn't be sorted out?'

'That's right.'

'It was designed to gain an admission?'

'It was designed to obtain the truth from him.'

'Well, I suggest to you it was designed to get a confession from him?'

'If that was the truth, yes.'

* * *

Monday 3 March marked the fourth week of the trial. The court heard seven hours of secret recordings of Cowan at various locations: talking to Arnold in the Swan River Room, in the lift with Fitzy, on the way to Albany for jobs, and in the car in Brisbane and the Sunshine Coast with Fitzy and Ian. The matter-of-fact tone of the discussion as Cowan described how he had killed their son stung Denise and Bruce to the core. The days of listening to the condensed covert transcripts were taking their toll. Even members of the public gallery and the media looked drained.

The following day, the jury visited the Kiel Mountain Road overpass, as well as the site where Daniel's remains had been found. On 5 March, after everyone returned to court the next day without the jury present, there was almost an hour of legal argument. Bruce and Denise arrived in court to the beginning of an abrupt change of pace. The defence was making an application for a mistrial following a note from someone being left under the overpass implicating Cowan as the murderer. At 10.40 am, the jury was brought back in and directed by Justice Atkinson.

'While you were at the scene under the overpass, you saw, as I warned you would, memorials to Daniel Morcombe and no doubt you would have found that very moving. Remember, your task on the trial is to be objective and to have regard only to the evidence led in court. What you saw at various locations, including under the overpass, was not evidence but merely so you could see the locations to understand better the evidence that has been given in court.

'After you left the overpass, my attention was drawn to a note given by some stranger giving his opinion as to the defendant's guilt, and I tell you in the strongest possible terms to ignore it. Dismiss it from your consideration and have regard only for the evidence led in the trial. As I said to you at the beginning of the trial, you should not be influenced by the opinions of anyone: friends, strangers, media, anyone at all. You are the sole objective judges of the fact.'

The jury was dismissed again, and the court returned to legal argument.

After lunch, Detective Ross Hutton was back in the witness stand, in spite of being dismissed from giving further evidence in the trial. This time, his evidence was *voir dire*, meaning it was given without the jury present and therefore could not be reported, but the public and media could still be in court. Hutton said he had been sent to the overpass on 3 March that week in his capacity as liaison officer between the court and police after being made aware that the jury would be visiting the following day. When he inspected the memorial site, he said he had not seen a note, but he had taken a photo of the memorial on his mobile phone and upon blowing up the photo, it was clear that the note had been there between two bunches of red flowers. It had a business card attached, he said. Detective Hutton had printed the photo during the lunch adjournment and it was shown on the screens.

Two police officers from Maroochydore CIB then gave evidence that they had been near the overpass on the day the jurors visited with instructions to be watchful for any media or members of the public recording the visit but they had not inspected the site nor noticed any note. Michael Byrne QC argued that the incident was 'miscommunication', which should not have occurred, but no more than that. Edwards countered that there was 'negligence' involved and that the incident had been 'highly prejudicial' to his client.

'It would have taken one police officer to make a cursory check because it was immediately apparent [that the note was there]. Trained detectives with 18–30 years' service could not see what was plainly there,' he said.

Justice Atkinson ruled that it was her view 'that no reasonable person could form the view that the jury is biased against the defendant because of any note that they read in the circumstances of the directions given by me to them'.

The Morcombes collectively breathed a huge sigh of relief. For some hours, it had looked like all of the hard work and the days of sitting in court were to be of no avail.

* * *

On 6 March, following further evidence from Fitzy, Detective Senior Sergeant Steve Blanchfield from the Homicide Investigation Unit gave evidence. He was the last witness for the Crown. He told the court he had been involved in the case since the outset. In March 2011, he had been appointed Operations Investigations leader and coordinator of the investigation. He had also attended Lot 1, at Kings Road, for Cowan's arrest, with Detectives Farlow and Hutton, and he confirmed that Cowan had his rights read to him when he was arrested at 11.15 am. Little was said about Cowan's reaction to the abrupt change of events.

Asked by Byrne what had happened after they arrived back with Cowan at Roma Street, Blanchfield repeated earlier evidence to the committal about Cowan resting with his left leg up against the wall. Later, Byrne asked Blanchfield whether he had checked a satellite photograph taken of 510 Kings Road on July 2010. Blanchfield agreed that a demountable building had been on the property then but did not show on a satellite photograph taken in May 2011.

Under cross-examination by Edwards, Blanchfield said that he had been involved in other aspects of the investigation, including interviewing Jackway on 27 May with Detective Emma Mcindoe. Edwards took him through more versions of Jackway's movements the day Daniel disappeared. Blanchfield agreed with Edwards that there had been false confessions made by other people, including Bill Dooley and a person who became POI32, which had led to other areas being searched. He agreed there had been no connection uncovered between Cowan and Jackway, POI32 or Dooley.

Under re-examination by Byrne, Blanchfield confirmed that POI32 had been charged with perjury by the Crime and Misconduct Commission after giving false evidence at the coronial inquest into Daniel's death.

By 11.11 am, the case for the prosecution was closed.

* * *

After the morning-tea adjournment at 11.40 am, Justice Atkinson addressed Cowan, who was asked to stand in the dock to answer the question of whether he intended calling or giving evidence.

Edwards said he had been instructed to speak on his client's behalf, and that he would be neither giving nor calling evidence. The jury was sent home, ready for addresses to start on Monday.

For the Morcombes, this was nearly the finish line. They had heard all they needed to hear. It would all be over next week. They were tired.

CHAPTER THIRTY-FOUR

THE DAY OF RECKONING

Sunday was a sleepless night for Bruce and Denise. On Monday 10 March 2014, Byrne's address to the jury was concise and deliberate. He began by pointing out that Cowan's decision not to give evidence at the trial, while his right, had practical consequences, meaning that the Crown had to make the first address and could not address the jury after the defence gave its address. He said that all the evidence in the trial given by Cowan had been unsworn, in that it could not be contested as he had not got in the witness box. He reminded the jury that Cowan had said in his 2005 interview that he wouldn't have told police even if he had killed Daniel, plus he had denied he had done it to the police officers King and Martyn. Byrne suggested that the jury should discard these denials as 'unreliable'. 'He's more likely to tell the truth to "false friends" than people he knows are police officers,' Byrne said. He said there was 'no evidence' to explain how Cowan came to know where the bones and clothing were. 'It means there is no evidence to contradict what we will submit to you is the naturally arising inference, that is, he knew where these things were because he is the one who killed Daniel Morcombe and put them there.'

He suggested the jury should look at the dates on which the various witnesses who had driven under the overpass that day gave their statements, as well as other factors to test reliability. 'We are asking you to draw some rational, logical and reasonable inferences from the known facts.'

There were four topics to his address, he explained: that the jury accept that the human remains and clothing belonged to Daniel; that he would make observations about how to approach the evidence given by motorists at the Kiel Mountain Road overpass; that he would address them on Cowan's confessional evidence; and, lastly, that he would make submissions on how all of those things would tie into the guilt of the defendant on each of the three charges.

Firstly, he said, there was evidence that the 17 bones belonged to Daniel and that the clothing found at the Kings Road site belonged to him.

He reminded them that all of the people on the bus had seen one man and a boy at the overpass, and that none of them had seen a car, 'be it blue, white or crimson'. He said many witnesses had been trying to help and had made sinister connotations but not deliberately. He then went through various witnesses, pointing out the strengths and weaknesses of their testimony. He said there probably was a white van in the area and that it may have broken down.

'We don't deny that there was a man or even possibly men in the area of these cars when they were seen, and we accept that at some stage, on the whole of the evidence, it's quite possible that this man or men spoke to Daniel. What we say is it's speculative to say that any of these vehicles or people actually had anything to do with Daniel's disappearance.'

After particularising the witnesses' evidence, the Crown came to Barry Kelsey, relaying the description he gave of the man he saw under the overpass. Asking that the exhibit be shown of the sketch prepared from Kelsey's evidence, he said it was a 'remarkable likeness' to Cowan.

He said that no one had identified Jackway as the man seen at the overpass, and it was speculation to say he was there on 7 December 2003. He pointed out that reciting Jackway's criminal history made him a 'cheap target' as the man responsible for Daniel's death. He also suggested that the body of evidence referring to Jackway was 'nothing but a red herring'.

He went through the evidence about Cowan's physical appearance and suggested that Tracey Moncrieff may have got the photographs mixed up, based on her guesses about the age of the baby which would have potentially meant Cowan's hair could have been longer at the time Daniel disappeared.

He asked them to consider the confessions made by Cowan suggesting that it was not something that would be done lightly: 'Something of that magnitude is likely to be true by its very nature'. He drew the jury's attention to the video footage with Arnold, pointing out how relaxed and relieved Cowan had looked when he had finished his confession. Cowan had been continually reminded that honesty was vital to be a member of the gang, and when he took Fitzy and Ian to the location of Daniel's remains, he had known he was at the wrong bridge.

He told the jury: 'Ultimately we say the confessions are reliable … we say that they are so compelling that they'll overcome any lingering doubts you may have in respect of the evidence.'

In conclusion, Byrne urged the jury to be rational not speculative. 'We ask you to return verdicts of guilty on all three counts.'

* * *

When Edwards got to his feet at 3.30 pm after a short adjournment, he began by summing up the case for the prosecution.

'Unless the Crown has disproved two important possibilities to you, then you will find Brett Cowan not guilty.

'Unless they have proved there is no possibility that a blue sedan was involved in the abduction and killing of Daniel Morcombe, you will find Brett Cowan not guilty. It is for the prosecution to disprove those two possibilities, because it's only in disproving those two possibilities that they prove Brett Cowan's guilt – prove it beyond a reasonable doubt. They attempt to do so by asserting that you will accept Brett Cowan's confession as the truth.'

Edwards said there was 'no room in this trial for both Cowan and Jackway. There is no room in this trial for both Mr Cowan and a blue sedan. Brett Cowan has no connection to Jackway, and he has no connection to a blue sedan.' He said unless the Crown proved that a blue sedan or Jackway had nothing to do with Daniel's case, the jury must find Cowan not guilty.

He said a third issue was that others had made detailed confessions to Daniel's murder but these had not been played to the jury.

'You know very well there is no forensic evidence – no fingerprints, no DNA, no hairs, no tyre marks, no shoeprints, or any other forensic evidence – linking Brett Cowan to the abduction of Daniel Morcombe. And you know very well that every detail of Brett Cowan's confession was out in the public arena, except for the location of the bones and the clothes ...'

Edwards, too, pointed out Cowan's appearance in December 2003, suggesting if there was a single photo of Cowan with shoulder-length hair at that time, the jury would have seen it.

On the subject of Cowan having a motive to make a false confession, Edwards said, 'Brett Cowan stood to make hundreds of thousands of dollars a year – millions of dollars over the course of his connection with the gang.' He said that Arnold had offered to buy Cowan an alibi. He said Arnold had not told the jury how concerned Brett Cowan was about the cross-examination of him at the inquest over two days or that Brett Cowan was scared. He had nothing before the gang got its claws into him.'

He went through further details of his motivation: 'What the prosecution wants you to do is to say, "Well, I've heard enough. There's a detailed confession backed up by bones and clothes. That's enough for me." Forget the compelling case against Jackway. Forget the compelling evidence of a blue sedan's involvement. Forget the obvious alternative ways that Mr Cowan could've heard about the locations of the bones and the clothes, and the obvious and powerful incentives for Brett Cowan to make up a false confession. Just ignore all of that and convict Mr Cowan.' He said they had to decide on Cowan's guilt 'beyond reasonable doubt'.

He warned the jury that there was a lot of pressure to convict Cowan: '... to bring an end to this tragic episode in the lives of the Morcombes and in the State of Queensland. You would not be doing anyone any favours by closing this chapter in convicting the wrong man. The fool, Brett Cowan, who played his part just a little too well, who thought he could use what someone had told him to make himself millions of dollars ...

'... You might not be sure what happened, who did it or what the circumstances were. You may have a terrible bad feeling about the whole thing, but you could still not find Mr Cowan guilty, unless it is proved beyond a reasonable doubt. This isn't a popularity contest. You mightn't like the way that Mr Cowan spoke. You mightn't like the terrible things that he said he had done. You mightn't like the appalling nature of his confession. But still, unless you are satisfied beyond a reasonable doubt that he committed these offences, you would find him not guilty.'

Edwards reminded the jury that the Crown had called Jackway a 'cheap target'. 'They suggest that I'm picking a cheap target. I didn't pick him. The police did. He wasn't a cheap target for them. They investigated Douglas Jackway. They investigated the blue car. Until Cowan's admission, Jackway was under suspicion by the police, as was a blue car.'

Edwards then went through much of the evidence about Jackway. 'Now, as far as the blue car goes, you would expect witnesses to have variances in their memories. A brief moment driving down the road and seeing something happen by the side of the road. So you would expect that there will be variances, sensible variances between people when they're trying to describe what they saw.

'What they all agree on: it is an older model. Many of them said "1980s model", which is what Jackway's car was. Blue, square, boxy-shaped sedan parked in the area of the Kiel Mountain Road overpass between about 1 and 2.30 on the day of Daniel Morcombe's disappearance. But can I say nobody refers to seeing a blue sedan parked near the Kiel Mountain Road overpass after Daniel Morcombe's disappearance … You might think that it was the same car. They were all describing the same car that went around and around, stalking Daniel Morcombe.'

Edwards asked that another exhibit be shown. Edwards pointed out how easy it would have been for the blue car or white van to cross from one side of Nambour Connection Road to the other using the overpass.

He also suggested: 'You may very well think the reason the descriptions of the people are so varied is because there was more than one person involved.

'That explains, you might think, why people saw the blue car in different positions: because it wasn't always in the same position. It was stalking Daniel Morcombe, stopping the first time on the Nambour-bound side of the road to watch him and then coming back around to the Maroochydore-bound side and, as you know, Daniel Morcombe wasn't very talkative with strangers, certainly not the sort of boy who would go with a stranger to his car. So you might think that blue car was doing circles and watching him. Whoever was in there was watching him, perhaps leaving one person behind underneath the Kiel Mountain Road overpass to watch him while they came around between the two buses for the last time, grabbed him, pulled him into the car and sped off to do goodness knows what.'

He then went through many of the witnesses in detail, highlighting the involvement of the blue car and how their timings or evidence matched the theory that Daniel had been abducted in the car. 'But even on the Crown case, Brett Cowan is a liar, whether it be his repeated denials of involvement or his confession. One way or the other, he's a liar. But can you really reject the possibility beyond reasonable doubt that Mr Cowan made this story up? The police were able to pretend they were gangsters, be convincing that they were gangsters. He was able to pretend that he abducted, molested and killed Daniel Morcombe. He used the details, you might think, that he'd seen in the media and from what he'd been told to flesh out his lies and try and create a convincing story. Well, why would he make such a story up? You know the reasons.

'What the gang offered him was not just money but a chance to be part of something, part of a national brotherhood of criminals making millions of dollars. How very, very tempting. Powerful inducements to make up a false story. He was a day away from hitting the big time. They told him the big job was going to happen tomorrow.

'They wouldn't accept his repeated denials. He denied it and denied it, but that wasn't accepted. They were about to cut him loose and all he had to do to make millions of dollars was tell a lie – a convincing lie. And he had all the details, you might think. And it was all out in the world. All the details were all out in the world, except for one piece of information, you might think, he was told.

He said Cowan had made several mistakes in his confession to police, such as saying he had taken Daniel to Roys Road, not Kings Road. 'Daniel Morcombe's father says, "Daniel is just not the sort of boy to get into a car or even talk to a stranger." So do you not think that a scenario is much more likely that these men in a blue sedan stalked and abducted – dragged, pulled Daniel Morcombe to the car than the story that Brett Cowan told?

'But perhaps the biggest and most obvious mistakes are the shoes. I mean, he got the location of the bones wrong. He was close. Do you really believe that ten days later, he'd go out there and there'd be nothing left? On his version, ten days later, there's a decomposing human body 50 metres away and he can't find the bones on his version. He takes them to the wrong spot because he doesn't know where in that area the bones were. He just knows the area. Now, bodies and bones don't float upstream, and they're found upstream. The Crown says, "Well, the dogs must've dragged the body up there." But you know from the expert … that dogs don't do that.'

Edwards went on to suggest that the jury might draw inferences from the evidence about Les McLean.

'The fact that, on the day of his arrest, McLean tried repeatedly to telephone Mr Cowan, and Mr Cowan asked to speak to him, but was prevented from doing that by the police. They turned his phone off. Does that not all lead you to one rational, logical conclusion: that Jackway, together with others, abducted and killed Daniel Morcombe. That, on heroin, he told McLean about it, and McLean told Mr Cowan, and Mr Cowan made up a story. Is that not supported by the fact that, in 2006, there was information in jail about the location of the bones and the clothes at the creek near Beerwah.'

He went on: 'Unless you can say beyond reasonable doubt that Jackway had nothing to do with it, that a blue sedan had nothing to do with it, that the only explanation for Mr Cowan's knowledge is that he's the killer, then you must find Mr Cowan not guilty of all charges. Thank you, your Honour.'

* * *

At 2.33 pm on Tuesday 11 March, Justice Atkinson began her summing up.

'The structure of the summing up I'll give you is as follows. First of all, I will address you on how to approach your function of assessing the evidence. The second matter I'll cover will be the elements of the offences and any relevant defences in the context of the allegations against Mr Cowan, focusing on the principal issues in the case. Thirdly, I will give you a summary of the relevant evidence, and then I'll give you a summary of the submissions made by the prosecution and the defence, and, finally, I'll give you a question trail that sets out the matters you have to consider in a logical order.'

She told them she had prepared a PowerPoint presentation to help them.

'My task has been to ensure that the trial is conducted according to law, and, as part of that, I will direct you on the law that applies. You must accept the law from me and apply all directions I give you on matters of law. You are to determine the facts of the case based on the evidence that's been placed before you in the courtroom. That involves deciding what evidence you accept.

'You then apply the law, as I'll explain it to you, to the facts as you find them to be and in that way arrive at your verdict. I may comment on the evidence if I think it will assist you in considering the facts, but, while you're bound by my directions as to the law, you're not obliged to accept any comment I make on the evidence. You should ignore any comment I make on the facts, unless it coincides with your own independent view. You are the sole judges of the facts.'

As an example of how juries might make an inference from the facts, she gave the following anecdote: 'Say you went home on a Friday afternoon and you thought, "Will I do the mowing this afternoon or can I wait till the morning? It doesn't look like it's going to rain. It should be fine to leave it to the morning." Or you thought, "Will I hang out the washing tonight? It doesn't look like rain. It should be fine. I'll hang out the washing tonight." When you got up in the morning – you've been asleep all night, you got up in the morning, the clothes you'd hung out were absolutely sodden and the grass was covered with water. There were puddles around. It had obviously rained during the night. You hadn't seen it rain, you hadn't heard it rain, but you could safely conclude, you could infer from the facts that it had rained during the night. That's the ordinary process of drawing inference from facts. But, of course, you can only draw reasonable inferences and your inferences must be based on the facts you find proved by the evidence. There must be a logical and rational connection between the facts you find and your deductions and conclusions. You are not to indulge in intuition or guessing.'

She went through the elements of the offences with which Cowan had been charged, reminding them that it was not up to Cowan to prove anything. It was up to the prosecution to satisfy them of his guilt. She then went through a summary of the relevant evidence. When referring to Les McLean's evidence, she said that, even though Mr Edwards had suggested McLean had gone with Cowan to a sand-mining site, there was no evidence of this as McLean had refuted it, and that McLean had adamantly denied telling Cowan where Daniel's bones were buried.

At 4.30 pm, when Justice Atkinson was partway through her summary of the undercover evidence, the jury retired for the day.

* * *

Wednesday 12 March was clearly going to be the day the jury retired to consider its verdict. All that remained was for Justice Atkinson to finish her summing up. She continued to go through a summary of the evidence, remarking that Jackway was a 'vile individual' but 'there's nothing in the evidence that puts him on the Sunshine Coast on 7 December 2003'.

She went through a summary of the summing up from both the prosecution and the defence. Then she turned to the elements of the different offences, outlining the various paths the jury might take in deciding on guilt or innocence in each charge.

'When you return after having reached your verdicts, my associate will ask, "Have you agreed upon a verdict?" You will all then say "Yes" to show that you have.'

The jury retired at 12.15 pm. The three jurors who had been placed on reserve were dismissed.

Now that the jury had retired, Cowan was more relaxed, sitting with his right leg across his left, but as the legal argument continued, Cowan began to look more agitated, less robotic, as though it had just dawned on him that this was the day of reckoning.

At 1.30 that afternoon, Bruce and Denise had retired to their apartment. There was a charged sense of tension as they gathered with family members, leafing through newspapers. Bruce felt agitated and short on conversation, avoiding discussion of how long the jury might go out for. Denise changed into a black dress, and joked she was 'mourning for Cowan'. She had the red jacket at the ready in case the phone rang. Detective Steve Blanchfield had promised he would call as soon as he heard from the judge's associate. Michael Byrne QC, who had been briefing them daily on upcoming witnesses and what to expect, had already advised them the previous week to have their victim-impact statements ready. These would be used when Cowan was sentenced if there was a guilty verdict.

As the afternoon wore on, Bruce announced to everyone that he was convinced they would have a verdict by 4 pm, but 4 pm ticked by and Blanchfield's call had not come through. Someone turned on the television. A newsflash came up. The jury had been sent home. There would be no verdict today. Shortly afterwards, Bruce and Denise got the call confirming it. As he said goodbye to the family, Bruce looked deflated. 'The worst is the waiting,' he said as he hugged them goodbye. Denise and Brad went and bought some dinner.

They talked quietly among themselves that night, reflecting on all that had happened. After the covert police officers had completed their evidence and were preparing to return home, the Morcombes were able to grab a moment with each of the men who had done so much to bring their son home. In a private interview room at the court, Bruce and Denise spoke with Joe Emery, Jeff, Ian, Fitzy and Arnold. The officers were at pains that Bruce and Denise should know that the way they referred to Daniel while undercover was not representative of who they are. 'You were on a mission, and we can't thank you enough for that,' Bruce said. It was an emotional exchange of thanks, with handshakes and hugs. The warmth and respect on both sides was palpable. Bradley also spoke with Arnold privately.

Bruce and Denise had a surprise for these remarkable officers, who they regarded as heroes. They presented them with 'Morky', the Foundation's mascot, specially engraved, to keep at their headquarters and inspire future operations.

After going to bed, Bruce and Denise slept a sleep of exhaustion. Knowing that they were so close to the moment in their lives for which they had longed for more than ten years was impossible to bear. Neither of them would consider that the verdict might be not guilty.

Thursday 13 March was another bright, sunny day. In the parkland in front of the court, the major television stations had erected marquees. Live-broadcast vans were parked on the footpath and around the back of the building, with huge antennae ready to transmit the news nationally. Several stations were doing a continuous live broadcast, filming various people who had been involved in the case outside the court, filling in time while waiting for the all-important verdict. Bruce and Denise had been up early and had decided to stay in their apartment. At 8.10 am, Bruce, dressed in shirt and tie, stood alone, looking out at the view from one of the bedroom windows, quietly rehearsing his victim-impact statement.

Denise was doing the same in the other room. Sitting in the court day after day had emotionally drained her, no matter how hard she had tried to prepare for the marathon of the trial. She had been particularly affected by Cowan's jovial interaction with his defence team, wondering how they could represent such a person. Every time Cowan's lawyer cross-examined witnesses on their sighting of a blue car, she had felt like screaming, convinced it was irrelevant.

But worse had been watching Cowan's face during the broadcast of the audiotapes and the confession, and the way he had sat there like a statue, unresponsive. Listening to his voice on the tapes and hearing him laugh after he had confessed to Daniel's murder, saying he was glad he had got it off his chest, was greatly distressing. She had felt physically sick when he had described how he'd gone 'chop chop chop chop' on Daniel's skull with a shovel after returning to cover up any trace of his body. Watching Fitzy mime the actions of the shovel and what he had said while on the police video when they revisited the crime scene had been even worse. As she listened to Cowan describe the final hour of Daniel's life, she was more and more convinced that Daniel would not have sat in Cowan's car outside the demountable in Kings Road while Cowan went in to 'talk to his wife'. He must have thought something was wrong. Somehow, he had been tricked into going with Cowan. She knew that, as soon as they had turned onto the Bruce Highway instead of going straight ahead to Maroochydore, Daniel must have known he was in trouble.

After Bruce had finished his rehearsal, he sat on his own on the balcony, alone with his thoughts. He cast a solitary figure looking out at the Brisbane skyline. He hoped this was Daniel's triumphant day in court. The day when justice would be done. After ten years and three months, it had been a journey that he and Denise had never foreseen when Daniel first went missing. They had somehow survived the agony of those first few days, the heartache of waiting all those years, the false alarms, the hideous stories about his fate, but most of all they had had to adapt to having their son snatched from their family.

Bruce was remembering the satisfaction he got when, on 3 March, someone had turned up in the public gallery, the only apparent visitor Cowan had during the many weeks of the trial. Bruce had intentionally positioned himself in between this person and Cowan at the break so they did not get a chance to talk to each other. Denise had laughed when Bruce told her. Bruce also ran through the facts of the case, imagining how the jury might view the evidence. He was convinced that the blue car had not been involved in the abduction of Daniel. There may have been more than one blue car. What was that about? Drugs, he believed, and

Daniel happened to be there when drug deals were going down. That was why the owner of the blue car had not come forward. The defence had run a very negative strategy. Attempting to link Jackway to the case had backfired, as there was no credible link between Jackway and Cowan. He thought the judge in her summing up had been a master of poise and impartiality in identifying every witness's evidence.

The morning dragged on. At 10 am, the family joined them again for what they hoped were the final hours. Lunchtime arrived as a welcome distraction. Some of them headed downstairs to get some air and buy some lunch. While everyone began heading for the lifts, Bruce and Denise stayed in the apartment. Suddenly, Bruce's mobile began buzzing with text messages.

Back in Court 11, the bailiff had told the media who had gathered in the public gallery that a verdict had been reached. 'We have a decision on Mr Cowan,' he said. Those quiet seven words announced what everyone was waiting for. He told those gathered that he was contacting the judge to see if the court would reconvene before lunch.

Back in the apartment, Bruce rang Detective Blanchfield. Not yet, he was told. More texts arrived from those inside the court. 'Get ready,' Bruce said to Denise. 'We're going to be recalled.'

Two minutes later, Blanchfield rang. Within minutes, Bruce, Denise, Dean and Bradley were in the lift and heading down 22 storeys into the street below. Outside, a gaggle of cameras and reporters had gathered. Heading towards the Queen Elizabeth II Law Courts, they walked past the marquees, followed by running cameramen and microphones. This was the moment everyone was waiting for. The news was about to hit the streets. They went up in the lift to the fifth floor for the last time, walking to Court 11.

Inside, the court was packed. The media's eyes were on the Morcombes as they arrived at 1.08 pm. Denise wore black pants and a red jacket, Bruce was in his black suit, red shirt and black tie, and Brad and Dean wore red ties. By 1.10 pm, Cowan was also seated in the dock. The 12 remaining jurors filed into the court, this time all standing in the front row. The buzz of anticipation was palpable. At 1.11 pm, Justice Atkinson entered the court. Everyone bowed, before the bailiff invited them to be seated.

The judge's associate stood up and addressed the jury. 'Have you agreed upon your verdicts?'

'We have.'

'Do you find the accused, Brett Peter Cowan, or Shaddo N-Unyah Hunter, guilty or not guilty of murder?'

'Guilty.'

Denise whispered, 'Yes, yes, yes.'

Sobs and a sharp intake of breath greeted that one word. Tears streamed down Brad's cheeks. Bruce clutched Denise's hand and tears sprang to their eyes. He turned to the rest of the family in the rows behind and shook their hands. Dean stared ahead, his eyes wet. Guilty verdicts for the other two counts followed. Bruce then turned to Denise, Dean and Brad. 'Turn around and face the family,' he said. 'Give your back to Cowan and his defence team.'

Justice Atkinson addressed the standing jury members. 'You brought an end to this terrible case,' she said. 'You considered all the evidence. You considered all the verdicts carefully. You have been a truly magnificent jury and I thank you very much for what you have done.'

The Morcombes did not even see Cowan led away.

CHAPTER THIRTY-FIVE

DANIEL'S LEGACY

As everyone filed from the court, dazed, Bruce and Denise elected to stay in the precinct when Justice Atkinson adjourned for lunch, ready to hear the sentencing submissions that afternoon. Denise could not even think of eating. Family members huddled around them. There were congratulations from the media, the prosecution and members of the public who had been in the gallery.

The Morcombes shook hands with the prosecution team, and gave them a red Foundation tie and silk scarf. 'Next time you have an important case, please wear these with pride.' They seemed quite moved.

They had also given the key police officers a Foundation tie and badge each. After the verdict, they walked outside wearing those ties. Denise was extremely touched.

When the court reconvened at 2.30 pm, eight jurors returned and quietly took up the positions that had been occupied by police in the back row of the public gallery. Michael Byrne QC told the court that Cowan had already spent 943 days in custody and that he had 'prior convictions both numerous and on occasions highly relevant'. It was then that Cowan's previous convictions were finally revealed: how, aged 18, Cowan had coerced a seven-year-old boy into a toilet in a park and had sexually assaulted him. He had been on probation at the time of the offence and had been sentenced to two years in prison. As well as more minor crimes such as housebreaking, stealing and false pretences, the court heard about the case in Darwin. The sordid details were read out by Byrne, who described how the six-year-old boy had trusted Cowan as he knew him when he took him to an abandoned site with wrecked cars and assaulted him. The seriously injured child had managed to escape and staggered into a service station dazed and confused. His injuries had been so bad people had thought he had been run over by a car.

After Cowan's previous convictions were read by the Crown, the Morcombes were invited up to give their victim-impact statements. Never before had the family exposed themselves in this way, even after facing the media hundreds of times.

Bruce read from his notes but also calmly looked across at Cowan. He had waited so long for this moment. He wanted Cowan to hear it. During his delivery, the now convicted man avoided his stare, looking instead at the empty seats vacated by the jury.

'Over ten years ago, you made a choice that ripped our family apart.

'Your decision to pull over and abduct Daniel for your own evil pleasure ultimately caused a level of personal pain to each of us that at times made it hard to go on.

'Over the years, we may have faced the media with determined self-control on the outside, but on many occasions, particularly in those first few months, I was physically ill each morning with the unbearable images of what may have happened to our son Daniel.

'Even today, I am haunted by thoughts of how long he was actually held captive and what unspeakable things you did to him in those sheds at the end of Kings Road, Beerwah. Why was he really dumped without clothes? Why was his belt loose and not still looped through his pants? It makes me nauseous thinking about your total lack of respect of a child's life. Listening to you describe, and watching a smirk grow on your face, how you threw Daniel's lifeless body down the embankment and a week later you returned and crushed his skull with a shovel! "Chop, chop, chop, chop, chop," you coldly explained in an emotionless, matter-of-fact way.

'We now have to live out our days with the unimaginable image of wild dogs devouring our much-loved son's remains.

'Daniel did not deserve that. He was a great kid and would not hurt a fly.

'You have robbed him of 70 years of life.

'Our family's sleepless first night without Daniel on 7 December 2003 haunts me even today. That feeling of helplessness and unimaginable pain never leaves you. The next day, I recall picking up Dean after work on the afternoon of Monday 8 December and he asked me, "Have they found Daniel?" These are four small words that torture me even today; because I had to answer "No". I listen to Denise's broken sleep punctuated by frequent nightmares. And looking into the face of my young twin boy who has lost his soulmate are raw visions often relived which have had a profound effect on how I function.

'Nothing about my life today resembles how we enjoyed life as a family before that day. Our friends from 2003 are different for we are no longer the same people. We can be short tempered and have a streak of bitterness and carry anger caused by your deliberate, selfish actions. We were forced to move away from our unique garden paradise and much-loved family home. We were running a successful small business and were forced to sell it. We could not return to regular employment because we were constantly distracted with disturbing thoughts. We were forced to sell all our hard-earned investments just to survive. But survive we did, because you made a monumental mistake that day.

'You picked on the wrong family. Our collective determination to find Daniel and expose a child killer was always going to win.

'Perhaps the greatest impact your heinous crime has had on me is being witness to the impact it has had upon the people that I love. You have caused immeasurable mental stress and anxiety to not only me but Daniel's mother, Denise, Daniel's twin, Bradley, and Daniel's brother Dean.

'I have also witnessed the impact your cold, calculating actions have caused to extended family. Daniel's grandparents have had years of healthy living trimmed from their life. Daniel's uncles and aunts and cousins, plus his mates from school, have all been severely impacted by what you did.

'I often wonder about the other victims who are left in your wake. That too causes me moments of great sadness.

'Your own children are of course victims of your crimes. I wonder about them. In a strange twist of fate, we established the Daniel Morcombe Foundation to educate children about personal safety and also to help young victims of crime.

'I have sat watching you in the same courtroom for close to 40 days covering the coronial inquest, the committal hearing, the pre-trial hearing and here at your trial. Throughout this time, you have been completely devoid of any remorse for what you did to Daniel. Your deliberate actions are now recorded for all to see. It is the most brazen of crimes, which has shocked a nation.

'Sitting in the same room as you revolts me. How you sit there day after day almost frozen in the one position is chilling.

'You have been convicted as a repeat sex offender, leaving a trail of damaged souls for three decades. Predators like you cannot be rehabilitated.

'A cunning plan by police and your greed has brought you undone.

'You have been exposed as an opportunistic, perverted, cold-blooded, child-killing paedophile.

'Central to the facts are not "Who done it" but "You done it".

'May Daniel's soul rest in peace!'

The public gallery immediately burst into spontaneous applause. The courtroom was overwhelmed with emotion, and this provided a release.

As Bruce was reading out his statement, Denise recognised she was not in a fit emotional state to carry out the task and she signalled as much. Instead, Michael Byrne read out hers.

'The first second after Daniel was born eight weeks premature, I knew he was special. His big eyes stared at me and we bonded immediately.

'Nobody will ever know the love I felt for Daniel. At 4 pm, Sunday 7 December 2003, while getting Daniel's clothes off of the line, I knew something was wrong. Daniel wasn't due to return to the bus stop until 5.30 but for some unknown reason I was anxious. Hence, I went to see if he was there at 4.30.

'I don't know what it was but I knew when Bruce returned home soon after 5.30 from the bus stop without him, I knew I would never see him again.

'I made a vow to Daniel I would find out where he is and that justice will be done. For years, I haven't slept for more than three hours at a time. I have lived and breathed each day to find the answers.

'I have bad nightmares every couple of weeks, screaming at night, "No, no, I won't go with you." I see my son lying by himself in that dark, eerie bushland, being destroyed by wild animals. You, Mr Cowan, left him there. You have no respect for a human life. He was an innocent boy starting to grow up and learning about life. He was gentle. He loved animals and wanted to be a vet. He would never hurt a soul. He was scared of the dark and often slept on the floor next to me. Mr Cowan, only you know how petrified he was as you drove down Kings Road with him, but I can only imagine. Mr Cowan, only you know Daniel's last look in his eyes as you choked him to death, but I can only imagine.

'My life is not the same as ten years ago: a different house, a different job, different friends.

'My family has also been destroyed. Not only has your deliberate, calculated actions affected me, Bruce, Dean and Bradley, but it has destroyed my parents, my brothers and extended family. Gone are happy family functions we all enjoyed. You took that away from us. We all know one person is not there, and we will never recover from that.

'Mr Cowan, I saw you smiling with your son and former wife in a photo taken on Boxing Day 2003. You had a smirk like nothing happened, a happy family snap. Meanwhile, my family was living in hell, searching for our son, who you knew was dead. I hope you live a life of loneliness and are unloved for your entire life. I hope you are never released, as you have no remorse for any of your past horrific crimes against innocent children.

'This day hasn't brought closure but the streets are safer without you walking them and looking for your next target to destroy.

'Your mistake was that you picked on Daniel to release your animalistic sexual needs. You are a perverted soul and didn't realise that his mother would never give up searching for answers and how much I loved him. He was and still is a part of me. That was your mistake, you evil, evil, un-human thing.

'I hope your jail time is difficult and you're never released. For me, I have a purpose. As thanks to all who have searched for Daniel I wish to explain his tragic story. I will continue my work with the Daniel Morcombe Foundation, teaching children to be aware of people like you. By doing this, I hope there will never be another child who goes through what Daniel did from a sexual freak like you.

'I have accepted I will never see Daniel again, and I have no control on what your sentence is, but if there is a God and He knows the love a mother has for her son, you will pay for your actions. You will pay big.'

Dean's delivery displayed a great sense of maturity from a young man of 26. He was calm and deliberate, but the words he spoke were deeply felt. He told Cowan that what he had done had impacted hundreds of people. 'You have robbed me of a life.' And he said they would never be a 'normal family ever again'.

'Right from the start, when Daniel didn't come home … while working, I broke down – having to give a police statement and police being there. At Daniel and Brad's 14th birthday – how crushed everyone was, especially Bradley – trying to celebrate an enjoyable day … and Christmas that year. The years that followed, seeing my grandparents going downhill – the pain putting such pressure on my parents … Not finding a body – and wearing a full forensic suit, gloves and mask to visit where you left Daniel. I'm glad you have been exposed.'

Michael Byrne read Brad's statement.

'It's ten and a half years since you robbed me of my twin brother. In December 2003, we had just finished Grade 9. We shared hobbies and interests and a bond that was special, a bond only twins can experience. Twelve days after you abducted and murdered my brother, it was our fourteenth birthday. Teenage birthdays are supposed to be something you look forward to. This was not a day of fun. It was torture. Another week would pass and that was Christmas

Day. Daniel and I had a trip booked to visit my grandparents. I ended up flying on my own. Milestone celebrations were never celebrated like they should have been.

'The first day of returning to school was tough. I struggled with all the attention. I could never be that boy in the background again. It caused me to not return after Grade 11. I have become very withdrawn. I wanted to go to uni and had plans of becoming a pilot. I am not the person I could have been. Daniel can never join me for a beer or join me as a best man at my wedding.

'Cowan, you have hurt me in ways you cannot imagine ...'

After the statements were read, there were submissions from both the defence and the prosecution about the length of the sentence.

Edwards had little to say. He said that Justice Atkinson should take into account that his client had been diagnosed with emphysema on 1 March 2011 and that he had children.

Addressing the Morcombe family, Justice Atkinson commented, 'There's nothing to assuage the hurt you've felt, each of you individually and as a family, but your strength and the way in which you've conducted yourselves has been one of the main factors that's brought us to the outcome we have today.

'The police – your determination to bring this investigation to conclusion and to ensure there was evidence that Cowan could properly be convicted is to be commended. It sends a message not just to Cowan, but to anyone who conducts a terrible crime and thinks they are smart enough to get away with it that you won't, and you will use whatever you have available to make sure that person is brought to trial.

'To the jury who are still here ... There are many other people who are not here. The covert police officers are not here, unless I can't see them if they are. They are truly amazing, the officer who played the crime boss particularly, and the men known as Paul Fitzsimmons and Joseph Emery. They were required to perform their role week in, week out, day and month out. They did and they performed it extremely well. We all owe them a great deal of gratitude in the way they conducted themselves.

'We've seen from the witnesses the trauma that was inflicted on the whole community about these events. The SES volunteers are heartwarming – from all walks of life – members of the community who do the most horrible and dirty of tasks. Physically horrible yet mentally and spiritually horrible. They did it so well that they were able to uncover remains for the Morcombes to be able to bury their son and also to show that these crimes had been committed and corroborate the confession made by Cowan.

'It has been a long haul. For the defence team, this is a difficult job, defending someone who the community has a right to hate ... with the gravest offences that have been committed.'

The bailiff then gave the familiar direction: 'All rise.'

Outside the court, some of the jurors who had been sitting in the back row approached Bruce and Denise with a hug and a handshake. Bruce and Denise thanked them. Several said they had been so relieved the verdict had been guilty after hearing Cowan's previous convictions. This was confirmation, they said, that they had got it right.

Downstairs, on the ground floor, Bruce, Denise, Brad and Dean and the extended family left the elevator to cross the large, shiny floor towards the exit. Bruce straightened his jacket, his face getting ready to confront the largest media contingent either of them had ever seen. Denise's expression had changed. There was more confidence, the stress and fear now replaced with something else. It was apparent in the way she strode forth.

Bruce, however, seemed more hesitant, as though the emotional toll of the morning's proceedings had eventually caught up with him. Their roles were momentarily reversed. Together, they walked towards the phalanx of cameras. Reporters surged towards them, two ordinary parents and their two sons, caught for the last time in a media frenzy.

This was the day when they had done Daniel proud. He had had his day in court, and justice had finally been done. Daniel was not forgotten. He was walking with all of them that day. As Bruce and Denise took their final steps towards the cameras, they were thinking, the children of Australia are safer because Daniel's tragic story has touched a nation.